THE OXFORD HISTORY OF THE BRITISH EMPIRE

COMPANION SERIES

Wm. Roger Louis, CBE, D.Litt., FBA

*Kerr Professor of English History and Culture, University of Texas, Austin
and Honorary Fellow of St Antony's College, Oxford*

EDITOR-IN-CHIEF

❧

Gender and Empire

❧

Philippa Levine

Professor of History, University of Southern California

EDITOR

OXFORD
UNIVERSITY PRESS

OXFORD

UNIVERSITY PRESS

Great Clarendon Street, Oxford OX2 6DP

Oxford University Press is a department of the University of Oxford.
It furthers the University's objective of excellence in research, scholarship,
and education by publishing worldwide in

Oxford New York

Auckland Bangkok Buenos Aires Cape Town Chennai
Dar es Salaam Delhi Hong Kong Istanbul Karachi Kolkata
Kuala Lumpur Madrid Melbourne Mexico City Mumbai Nairobi
São Paulo Shanghai Taipei Tokyo Toronto

Oxford is a registered trade mark of Oxford University Press
in the UK and in certain other countries

Published in the United States
by Oxford University Press Inc., New York

British Library Cataloguing in Publication Data

Data available

Library of Congress Cataloging in Publication Data

Data available

Typeset by SPI Publisher Services, Pondicherry, India
Printed in Great Britain
on acid-free paper by
Antony Rowe Ltd.,
Chippenham, Wiltshire

ISBN 978-0-19-924951-0 (Hbk.)   978-0-19-924950-3 (Pbk.)

1 3 5 7 9 10 8 6 4 2

FOREWORD

The purpose of the five volumes of the Oxford History of the British Empire was to provide a comprehensive survey of the Empire from its beginning to end, to explore the meaning of British imperialism for the ruled as well as the rulers, and to study the significance of the British Empire as a theme in world history. The volumes in the Companion Series carry forward this purpose. They pursue themes that could not be covered adequately in the main series while incorporating recent research and providing fresh interpretations of significant topics.

Wm. Roger Louis

PREFACE

In the past three or four decades or so, a new attention to issues of gender and gender role has transformed historical scholarship, not merely adding women to an already rich historical tapestry, but also suggesting exciting new ways to think about the field. This new attention to how the social and sexual roles assigned both to men and to women has, in the past two decades or so, also had a significant impact on the writing of British imperial history. Such work has looked not only at the role of women within the Empire, but has also been keenly interested in exploring why the Empire was so dominantly male an environment for so long.

In one register, historians have begun to examine specifically the effects of Empire and of colonial conquest and development on indigenous and migrant women. Even a cursory glance at colonial labour markets will show that colonized women worked in jobs that, in Britain, would not have been open to them. In India, and elsewhere in the colonies, women worked in the building trade and in heavy manual labour as well as in areas more traditionally associated with female work: domestic service, agriculture, sex work, and other service jobs. Just as was the case for the working women of Britain, they also shouldered the bulk of childcare and personal domestic labour in their own households, but while they shared many such strains and stresses with white working-class women in the metropole, they were also often subject to greater control than their British counterparts as imperial social reform began to characterize colonial rule from the middle of the nineteenth century. Historians investigating the lives of colonial women thus look simultaneously at the impact of colonization and at customs and laws that predate colonialism, investigating how the former has shaped and changed the latter, and how this might have affected the lives of women.

With a focus more upon the West and its effects on Empire, historians have also demonstrated how central Western women were to imperial development, despite their traditional absence from its historical record. Alongside the intrepid women explorers and travellers who cast off traditional female roles and recognized in Empire the possibility of adventure unattainable at home, an increasing percentage of the white imperial population, especially from the mid-nineteenth century, was female. British women came to work in the colonies as doctors and nurses, as barmaids and servants, as farmworkers and in a host of other industries and employments. Many came as single women, hoping that the female job market in the colonies would be wider, better, and more lucrative than that which they could access at home. Women came, too, as wives of farmers and farm labourers, of businessmen and soldiers and civil servants, and salesmen and scholars. How different were their lives from those they might have led had they stayed at home? What effects did colonial living, temporary or permanent, have on how women understood their role and place in society?

Such questions, often central to the new scholarship on gender and Empire, suggest also that explicit connections between domestic policy and the politics of Empire form a fruitful area of enquiry. It is all too easy to see home as 'here' and Empire as 'out there', when in reality the connections between Britain and its Empire were close and critical. Whether one looks at economic ties, wartime alliances, or migration policies, the connections are palpable. Scholars of gender have pushed that idea a logical step further, examining, for example, how women fighting for a political voice in Britain self-consciously fashioned a rhetoric about their superiority to, and protection of, their 'lesser' colonial sisters. Such studies have neatly demonstrated the interconnections between 'home' and Empire not just at the material level of policy but also in the circulation and exchange of ideas.

The scholarship on gender and Empire is not, however, exclusively concerned with the position and role of women. In examining the roles ascribed to people as a result of gender, in highlighting both the similarities and differences between expectations about male and female behaviour, in being sensitive to the ways in which language and ideas reflect or challenge dominant social roles, historians of gender are also well positioned to wonder why the Empire has for so long been represented as a virtually exclusive masculine preserve. Even now, popular representations of Empire tend to focus on men and on traditionally male pursuits. New scholarship has shown unequivocally that the story of Empire is a far more complex one, and that the image of masculinity so intimately associated with imperialism is itself a topic worth investigating.

Gender, then, connotes more than simply the 'returning' of women to stories of Empire and expansion, and all of these issues are among the questions taken up in this volume. The intent of these chapters is to offer readers interested by the *OHBE* project a more inclusive interpretation of the significance of Empire and of the importance of gender, studying the experiences of men as well as women and exploring how the different roles ascribed to men and women affected the course of imperial history over a period of some three centuries.

In any new field, and perhaps more especially where scholars draw self-consciously on other disciplines, a new and specialized vocabulary is bound to develop, and while that vocabulary quickly becomes recognizable in a professional environment, there will always be some words that the general reader will find unfamiliar. For the most part these words are clear from their context, and we have tried in this volume to be consistent in their usage. Still, it may be worthwhile to define here several terms that have only recently acquired widespread currency, and which the general reader may not yet have encountered in the context of historical writing.

The etymology of the word *homosocial* would suggest that it refers to social activities or relationships amongst similar persons. For feminist and gender scholarship, its meaning is more precise and extremely valuable, connoting communities or societies not only composed solely of men, but exhibiting or endorsing behaviours or characteristics more readily associated – certainly historically—with men. Thus the rough and ready frontier societies of the settler colonies were not merely peopled in their early days almost exclusively by men, but were also characterized by hard drinking, lawlessness, and a disregard for polite social norms.

The verb *translate* is used in these pages as a tool for investigating how cultures understood one another, how certain practices, customs or ideas as well as words did or did not 'translate' across cultural as well as linguistic boundaries. It is, of course, a literary term, and one which offers a far nore nuanced picture than would the verb *understand*. For while a 'mistranslation' is also often a misunderstanding, it is less about confusion than about incommensurability, the non-equivalence of ideas or customs in different parts of the world. The concept of 'translation', with its emphasis on correspondence, clearly offers a deeper mode of investigation.

While 'translation' is a term historians have borrowed from literature, *companionate marriage* is a term indelibly associated with the work of a historian: the early modern historian of marriage and family, Lawrence Stone. The term is used to distinguish between marriages in which women were a commodity and an investment to their husbands and those – dubbed companionate – in which affection and companionship were key components. A companionate marriage was not necessarily a marriage of equals, but it did assume companionship as a significant factor in a couple's nuptials, regarding matrimony rather than purely as a business arrangement.

Some of these new terms are more well known than others; all of them fulfil helpful functions which allow historians a certain leeway or shorthand in expressing sometimes complex and often innovative ideas. In this volume our belief is that the introduction of new and exciting concepts via this terminology will help readers grasp the significances and nuances of considering gender and empire in the same breath and will, at the same time, help move forward the purpose of the *Oxford History of the British Empire* in new directions and new areas of study.

The editor would like to thank the following for their generous financial support of the contributor's conference: the College of Letters, Arts and Sciences at the University of Southern California; Doheny Library at the University of Southern California; the History department at the University of Southern California; the University of Southern California's Center for International Studies; the Ahmanson Foundation; the University of Texas; and St. Antony's College, Oxford. For support of her own work, she would also like to extend profound thanks to the Rockefeller Foundation for permitting her to spend a glorious month at their Bellagio Center. Without the help, efforts, and advice of Tyson Gaskill, Wm. Roger Louis, Roy Ritchie, and Laura Sjoberg, this volume would surely be the less rich.

Philippa Levine

CONTENTS

LIST OF CONTRIBUTORS

ALISON BASHFORD (PhD., Sydney) is Senior Lecturer in History at the University of Sydney. Her books include *Imperial Hygiene* (2003) and *Purity and Pollution: Gender, Embodiment and Victorian Medicine* (1998).

ANTOINETTE BURTON (PhD., Chicago) is Professor of History at the University of Illinois Urbana-Champaign. Her most recent book is *Dwelling in the Archive: Women Writing House, Home and History in Late Colonial India* (2003).

BARBARA BUSH (PhD., Sheffield) is Senior Lecturer in History at Sheffield Hallam University, and author of *Slave Women in Caribbean Society, 1650–1838* (1990) and *Imperialism, Race and Resistance: Africa and Britain, 1919–1945* (1999).

URVASHI BUTALIA (MA, Delhi; University of London) is co-founder of Kali Books in New Delhi, and author of *The Other Side of Silence: Voices from the Partition of India* (1998).

PATRICIA GRIMSHAW (PhD., Melbourne) is Max Crawford Professor of History at the University of Melbourne, Australia. Her most recent publications are the co-edited *Letters from Aboriginal Women of Victoria, 1867 to 1926* (2002), and the co-authored *Equal Subjects, Unequal Citizens: Indigenous Rights in British Settler Colonies, 1830 to 1910* (2003).

CATHERINE HALL (D. Litt., East London) is Professor of Modern British Social and Cultural History, University College London and author, most recently, of *Civilising Subjects: Metropole and Colony in the English Imagination 1830–1867* (2002).

A. JAMES HAMMERTON (PhD., British Columbia) is Reader in History at La Trobe University, and co-author, with Alistair Thomson, of *Ten Pound Poms — The Invisible Migrants: A Life History of Postwar British Emigration to Australia* (forthcoming, 2004).

JOCK MCCULLOCH (PhD., Monash) is Reader in International Development at Royal Melbourne Institute of Technology University. His most recent book is *Asbestos Blues: Labour, Capital, Physicans and the State in South Africa* (2002).

PHILIPPA LEVINE (D. Phil., Oxford) is Professor of History at the University of Southern California and author of *Prostitution, Race, and Politics: Policing Venereal Disease in the British Empire* (2003).

FIONA PAISLEY (PhD., La Trobe) is lecturer in History at Griffith University, and author of *Loving Protection? Australian Feminism and Aboriginal Women's Rights, 1919–1939* (2000).

MRINALINI SINHA (PhD., State University of New York at Stony Brook) is Associate Professor of History and Women's Studies at The Pennsylvania State University, and author of *Colonial Masculinity: The 'manly Englishman' and the 'effeminate Bengali' in the Late Nineteenth Century* (1995).

KATHLEEN WILSON (PhD., Yale) is Professor of History at the State University of New York at Stony Brook. Her most recent book is *The Island Race: Englishness, Empire and Gender in the Eighteenth Century* (2003).

1

Introduction: Why Gender and Empire?

PHILIPPA LEVINE

The British Empire always seems a very masculine enterprise, a series of far-flung sites, dominated by white men dressed stiffly in sporting and hunting clothes, or ornate official regalia. The Empire was, in many ways, a deeply masculine space of this sort, but acknowledging that reality tells only a fraction of the story. Such a depiction obscures both colonized populations (who in most places out-numbered the colonizing), and the growing numbers of colonizing women who also lived and worked in colonial settings. To think about gender and empire, however, is not only to re-populate the stage with a more diverse cast of historical protagonists but to explore social processes and power using sexual difference as a key but by no means unique analytic.

Studying gender means, of course, far more than acknowledging the actions and presence of women, and more, too, than merely arguing that the British Empire was run by men and in ways that they claimed were universal, but which materially differentiated on grounds of sex as well as other kinds of social divisions. The premise of this volume goes deeper, arguing that in addition to these factors in understanding the Empire, the very idea as well as the building of empires themselves cannot be understood without employing a gendered perspective. In an earlier volume in the Oxford History of the British Empire series (vol. IV), Rosalind O'Hanlon reminds us that 'men too are gendered as are the public political arenas which some of them dominate'.[1] To that end, we cannot, for example, understand why particular policies or laws were enacted, or why Empire developed as it did and in the areas it did, without seeing at work the hand of gender: why men were politically dominant; what role women were supposed to play and

[1] Rosalind O'Hanlon, 'Gender in the British Empire', in Judith M. Brown and Wm. Roger Louis, eds., *The Oxford History of the British Empire. IV. The Twentieth Century* (Oxford, 1999), p. 396.

what roles they actually claimed for themselves; how decisions, major and minor, affected the lives of everyone touched by, responsible for, and on the receiving end of colonial doings. In the chapters that follow, a distinguished group of feminist historians vividly demonstrate the critical ways in which the construction, practice, and experience of Empire for both colonizer and colonized was always and everywhere gendered, that is to say, influenced in every way by people's understanding of sexual difference and its effects, and by the roles of men and women in the world.

To see gender as central to our understanding of the complicated processes at work in British colonialism is not, however, to claim that gender is universally recognizable as the same or as having the same effects and influences in all places or at all times. On the contrary, one of the lessons of feminist history has been about the dangers of too readily assuming that group identifications always work: that all men, for example, opposed greater female participation in the public sphere or liked to play sports, that all Britons supported colonial expansion, or that all colonized peoples found colonial rule an encumbrance. Such generalizations are invariably inaccurate, yet historical writing is often surprisingly full of claims that come close to stating such bald fictions. The relevant point here is that in invoking gender as a significant historical consideration by no means pre-supposes that experiences of colonial practice were common to all women or all men. Instead, what this analytical tool signifies is 'the multiple and contradictory meanings attached to sexual difference', and how these multi-plicities shaped and influenced the way people lived their daily lives and how they thought about the world around them.[2]

Equally important in emphasizing the rejection of universalist explan-ations is the view, apparent in all the chapters which follow, that an under-standing of gender does not stand alone or somehow 'above' other factors, such as class and race, also at work. In particular, the emphasis on inequal-ities, which gendered interpretations necessarily highlight, reminds us that other important divisions also structure colonialism. Differences in material wealth and social status, hierarchies based on race and skin colour, and other such divisions are also always at work in social relations. Gender in short is always central to the ways in which social relations have been navigated, built, and secured as well as challenged and resisted. The contributors to this volume stress what Susan Thorne has called an 'inchoate interdependence'

---

[2] Joan Wallach Scott, *Gender and the Politics of History* (New York, 1988), p. 25.

between gender and those other social categories that shape and influence peoples' lives and the power structures in which they are located.[3]

Whether we focus on gender, race, or class or—more commonly—a combination of these factors, as historians we must maintain a sensitivity to change. Attitudes to political representation among and for colonial subjects have undergone significant change, for example, during the period of Empire, changes that make sense only if we understand them in the light of these critical categories of difference. When the American colonists declared their independence from Britain, a move enshrined above all in the principle of political representation, the prevailing ideas about gender and race served to exclude from these new rights Native Americans, forcibly imported and enslaved Africans, and all women. All of these groups were prevented from exercising the franchise that was at the heart of the new American constitution. Some hundred years later and continents away, the governor of Hong Kong, Sir John Pope Hennessy, championed the cause of political representation for the numerically dominant Chinese population of the colony. His focus—quite radical for the period—was none the less limited to the educated, Westernized, and always male merchant elites, ignoring the majority, the labouring population, who literally built the colony. Gender and class thus shaped his quite radical and controversial insistence that the Chinese deserved a voice in colonial governance. In both instances, then, the idea of extending political rights was moulded by prevailing ideas about gender and about race, about the relative participation of men and women, of subjects and citizens, but in every case shaped by local circumstance and context. While both these examples demonstrate that considerations around various forms of difference (social, economic, sexual, racial) were always at work, they also reveal that these considerations did not operate everywhere in the same way. Hennessey's arguments could not have swayed the British community in Hong Kong or indeed in Britain in the 1850s, just as the vision of the founding fathers required later amendment, as values and ideas about the organization of difference changed in the years after the Constitution was written.

Amendments to the American Constitution guaranteeing voting rights to former slaves and to women are historical markers of change which should caution us against employing universalizing and totalizing historical inter-

---

[3] Susan Thorne, *Congregational Missions and the Making of an Imperial Culture in Nineteenth-Century England* (Stanford, Calif., 1999), p. 92.

pretations. As America changed, alterations to its basic political organization were deemed necessary. The same was so in colonial contexts where discussions about the political representation of the colonized became increasingly common in the twentieth century, but again, not everywhere. India's contributions, both military and economic, to the First World War made some concession to Indian nationalist demands unavoidable. In Hong Kong, by contrast, despite the changes ushered in by Hennessy in the nineteenth century, governance remained wholly unrepresentative, with officials appointed rather than elected, until 1985. Clearly different instances of how race and gender (probably the two most significant factors affecting electoral rights, as property ownership waned as a qualifier) operated shaped decisions about voting rights in these varied locations. India, Hong Kong, the United States all at some stage faced these issues but the outcome, the attitudes, the arguments in each were contingent upon time and location, invariably producing different results and different struggles.

The relationship between gender and Empire also offers us the opportunity to re-imagine some of the traditional periodizations which have shaped historical writings. Astute readers will appreciate the difficulties faced most especially by Kathleen Wilson, Catherine Hall, and Barbara Bush in this collection. Their contributions provide overviews of a century's worth of colonial experience rather than a single topical theme. No clear breaks separate these three centuries; indeed, Barbara Bush argues that those characteristics we most often identify as typifying the twentieth century—an increased emphasis on Western-style democracy foremost among them—date from the period after the First World War, after almost one-fifth of the century had passed. Yet many of the changes of the post–1918 years can equally be traced back to earlier periods, complicating any simple and neat definition of what constitutes the characteristics of any particular century. As Kathleen Wilson points out, eighteenth-century thinkers prided themselves, not least because of the existence of a British Empire, on what they saw as their own modernity. Rather than seeing Bush and Wilson as disparate in their views of when modernity 'occurred', adopting a perspective grounded in a gendered methodology allows us to appreciate the historical-ness of such seeming contradiction. Periodization—often neatly packaged as the 'Victorian age', the 'post-war years', 'high imperialism', and so forth—is a useful convenience on the one hand, but a misleading and often rigid problem, on the other. Since gendered analyses encourage us to reject totalizing interpretations in favour of contingent ones sensitive to context, they also necessarily question the idea that there are recognizable foundational or originary moments, 'ends of', and 'last gasps' in history. Urvashi Butalia's chapter on partition and decolonization in India movingly demonstrates the long term effects and consequences that imperialism and colonial decision-making continued to exert on the lives of millions of people, and on the stability of the region, long after British withdrawal from the area. Mrinalini Sinha, likewise, shows how nationalist responses to colonial rule resonated in post-colonial settings long after the formal end of Empire. Both invite us to appreciate how a gendered perspective reformulates traditional temporalities, allowing us to see familiar stories in a new light.

In such a context, neither a 'beginning' nor an 'ending' date for a collection of this nature seemed feasible. How might we persuasively date the beginning of British imperialism? Was Elizabethan exploration the precursor or the start of Empire? Were the religious refugees of the seventeenth century, who sought a new life on the east coast of North America, pioneers or colonizers? As for the end of Empire, Hong Kong was decolonized only in 1997, Rhodesia was transformed into Zimbabwe less than two decades earlier, and Britain still retains a handful of Dependent Territories even now. Is Empire at an end? In light of such difficulties, this volume makes no claims as to the origins or ends of Empire. None the less, it follows the convention of other volumes in the OHBE series, focusing on Empire from the eighteenth century, despite recognizing the limitations that govern chapters that conjure an eighteenth, a nineteenth, or a twentieth century. Why, then, do we include chapters which appear to impose arbitrary datelines around centuries? In a word, to effect coverage. Considerations of gender affect every historical arena from daily life to high politics, from religion to sexuality, from enslavement to rebellion, from soldiers to field workers. To give readers a flavour of what considerations gender makes possible, three 'overview' chapters are included alongside nine thematic essays. We do not claim to offer a comprehensive account, but a combination of overview and theme which allows a host of common ideas and topics to emerge.

Some readers may find the instabilities and uncertainties written into this approach unsettling. We prefer to see gender, however, not as a fixed concept offering us the 'truth' about the history of the British Empire, but more excitingly, as an opportunity to explore historical ideas and options. For feminist historians, gender opens up a web of questions which allow one to think not just descriptively about Empire (how, who, where) but about why it came about and what made the particular sets of relations that might be identified as characteristic of the British Empire possible. It is this idea of 'contingency', exploring the *why* of Empire as one among a series of possibilities, that most defines the following essays.

Focusing predominantly on the meaning and effect of sexual difference, the chapters gathered in this book offer a variety of topics and approaches, all aimed at investigating why it is so critical to yoke together the terms 'gender' and 'empire'. For if, indeed, Empire was as avowedly a masculinist environment as it is so often portrayed, then what difference did that make to men and to women, to the subjugated and to the ruler? Did the very fact of domination itself reflect, echo, or partake of the kinds of power relations at work in sexual difference, in the relations between men and women?

As many of the authors in this volume point out, it was not uncommon for colonized peoples to be seen by imperialists as weak and unmasculine because they were colonized, an opinion that already assumed that male weakness and lack of masculinity were central to the process of becoming a colony. Many images of colonized men stressed their apparent unmanliness, sometimes hinting that homosexual preference further sapped their masculine potential. In yet other imagery, the colonized man was imagined as a sexual predator unable to control his physical desires and dangerous to women. In turn, all of these representations palpably affected ideas about women. As a number of the authors, Kathleen Wilson and Catherine Hall in particular, point out, a society's treatment of women was frequently held up as evidence of its degree of civilization, with 'rude' societies cruel to their womenfolk and 'advanced' ones respectful of them. Such representations were themselves what we might call masculinist, for they assumed that a critical function of society was to *care* for and protect women, an idea which logically secured that women would be defined by men and compared against male behaviours. Whether cosseted or brutalized, women in such thinking (and it was commonplace British thinking in the period of Empire) were, like children, a group apart from men and a group to be defined and managed by men. As Dipesh Chakrabarty notes, European imperialism reduced the idea of the human 'to the figure of the settler-colonial white man'.[4] It was the white settler who was the brave, heroic figure of nineteenth-century imperial rhetoric, and it was his needs and prerogatives which frequently shaped the contours of imperial policy.

[4] Dipesh Chakrabarty, *Provincializing Europe. Postcolonial Thought and Historical Difference* (Princeton, 2000), p. 5.

This imperial vision was gendered in a host of ways. The focus on a group of pioneer men taming wild terrain into productivity and profitability put the spotlight on physically courageous and industrious men, posing an ideal white male figure. That emphasis celebrated a very particular vision of white maleness as physical, responsible, productive, and hard-working. These were qualities denied to women and to the colonized. Over and over, imperial rhetoric dwelled on the laziness or unproductivity of 'natives' in colonized lands from the neighbouring Irish to First Nations people in Australia and Canada. Likewise, women's femininity was seen to derive in large part from their lack of physical prowess, their delicacy, and nervousness. This vision of masculinity as that which could transform unproductive spaces profitably was simply not on offer to women or to the colonized. Gender, then, was more than descriptive; it became a hierarchical ordering of quality, skill, and usefulness.

It is in such ideas that we can also see most vividly the critical reasons why gender cannot, as an interpretive tool, be wholly separated from considerations of other social relations. For this rather formulaic assumption that women's place in society stood as an index of civilization also carried significant racial overtones. It was whites of European descent who knew how to 'treat' women. The 'savage' societies which isolated women, or sold them, or used them as pack horses mapped remarkably closely and certainly not coincidentally, on to non-white colonial peoples: the Chinese in South-East Asia, Australian and Canadian aboriginal peoples, Africans, and Indians. That the position of women in white societies at this juncture was perhaps less than ideal for women was not an issue; it was 'primitives' who apparently failed to respect proper womanhood and not the British.

Of course, the British vision of what constituted proper womanhood not only guaranteed that its Empire would look as masculine as it mostly did, but it also made other societies' arrangements seem improper. The British found equally faulty societies—such as some communities in north India and in Chinese-populated areas—where they saw women, as they understood it, caged and isolated and those, such as in some Pacific Islands, where women displayed what the British regarded as excessive independence. The behaviour, the demeanour, and the position of women thus became a fulcrum by which the British measured and judged those they colonized. Women became an index and a measure less of themselves than of men and of societies.

Once again, change over time had a critical effect in these arenas, for while in the eighteenth century domesticity was not yet a revered commodity, by the middle of the nineteenth century its ordering function in the metropole had far-reaching consequences. By the 1850s, the image of colonizing as a rough-and-ready frontier practice was beginning to give way to an insistent demand for white settler areas to look more like Britain, and in particular more like a domesticated Britain of both natural and familial order. The hard-drinking licentiousness of frontier living, careless of the niceties of proper relations, was an increasing spectre for respectable Britain. And alongside a propensity for planting trees and flowers that would remind them of the British Isles, settlers increasingly bowed to the prescriptions of metropolitan domestic conformity. As A. James Hammerton shows in his contribution to this collection, peopling such colonies with greater numbers of women became a desirable social policy intended to domesticate, to Anglicize, and to mollify some of the excesses of masculine societies at the frontier. Migration as it became a mass phenomenon was increasingly closely tied to ideas around 'home', the ultimate motif of domesticity and by the mid-nineteenth century, also of respectability. 'Making a new home', became the colonial task given to women, whether planting roses in the withering Indian sun to emulate an English cottage, or braving the winters of the Canadian prairie in log cabins.

While domesticity has been represented as the province of women, if not always correctly, the public sphere has often been dealt with in historical work as if it were a naturally male environment. While it might be cogently argued that men have in the past dominated the conduct of politics and business to a significant extent, such a picture neither tells a complete story nor proves that such a division is necessary or natural. In her chapter on gender in the historical archive itself, Antoinette Burton recounts the experiences of scholars engaged in studies of colonialism and asks what effects gender may have had on how they are viewed in such environments, how they approach the materials, and whether gender has played a role in the choice of materials that are preserved in the first place.

Patricia Grimshaw and Fiona Paisley take up the theme of domesticity in a different way. Grimshaw looks at missionary work in Australia, while Paisley considers the growing science of child-rearing and its racialized expectations in her chapter. Their work in these fields also vividly demonstrates how a feminist perspective has helped to make central to historical investigation stories such as the removal of Aboriginal children from their natal families.

This is an issue to which both authors allude as central to the narrative of Australian history and yet one regarded as worth studying only in recent years by mainstream Australian historians.

Another recurring issue in these chapter is the incidence of violence, and how it, too, is shaped by gender. Alongside the violence involved in forcibly removing Aboriginal children from their parents in Australia and elsewhere, many of the contributions in this volume also focus on events and incidents of violence coloured by gendered considerations, from the incidence of slavery to the violence of decolonization. Urvashi Butalia details the particular forms of violence—rape, abduction, forcible reversion to former lives—experienced by women in the years after the partition in 1947 of the Indian Empire into Hindu India and Muslim Pakistan. Partition itself was an act of violence and in more than symbolic ways. It uprooted families and friendships, setting off a terrifying range of violent reactions, and in the case of the experience of abducted women, violence at the physical, the emotional, the legal, and the political level. Yet it has been a long-standing historical assumption that the British Empire, relatively speaking, was a less violent colonizing force than some of its rivals. This is the theme upon which Jock McCulloch focuses his attention, turning from the more usual question of sexual violence against women to a broader exploration of the ways in which other forms of violence are also shaped by gender. McCulloch takes issue with the idea of the British version of Empire as a kinder, gentler Empire, inviting our attention to the gendered violence that always circulated around the employment, management, and control of indigenous labour in the colonies. His discussion of the ways in which violence moved indoors, into the private sphere where it was not only invisible but where the state was reluctant to intervene, is a sophisticated example of how a gendered perspective—in this case one focused on the divide between public and private spheres—might reshape our considerations of well-rehearsed and well-researched themes in innovative fashion. This perspective allows McCulloch to see the violence wrought by white women on black men, and the equally gendered consequences of women's actions, a theme rarely touched upon in studies of colonial violence.

McCulloch's attention to themes of gendered violence other than that of sexual violence is certainly unusual, but this volume in no way ignores the centrality of sexuality to a full appreciation of the gendered nature of Empire. While Philippa Levine's chapter deals specifically with a variety of sexual issues of critical concern in the shaping of imperial policy, Alison Bashford, writing on medical practice in the Empire, also sees a central role for sexuality. Both these chapters suggest the many ways in which governance can and should be viewed through more than merely the traditional lens of 'high politics'. Sexual preference and practice and reproductive imperatives were issues which aroused fear and anxiety on the part of governments, both metropolitan and colonial. They became the focal point of considerable political debate and policy, and the policies in these arenas were often carried out by and represented as medical in intent. As a key element in the growing reverence with which science, seen as neutral and above politics, was treated in the nineteenth and twentieth centuries especially, medicine effected changes and practices which often helped intensify gendered and racial distinction. The paucity of women practitioners in the Empire bolstered the idea of medicine, and especially colonial medicine, as a properly male field of endeavour. As Alison Bashford's discussion of the variolation–vaccination controversy demonstrates, however, the reasons which lay behind preferences for particular medical techniques (or indeed personnel) were often less about efficacy and efficiency, let alone 'good' science, than about views of the world shaped by gender and race.

Medicine, of course, was by no means the only Western commodity shipped to the colonies by imperial rule. In her chapter on nationalism and resistance to colonialism, Mrinalini Sinha demonstrates the many ways in which women were, despite the rhetoric of modernity which invariably accompanied the rise of nationalist sentiment, cast aside or used as symbolic representatives of a culture in nationalist struggles against colonial rule. Women's bodies, she argues, often became the site where nationalist sentiment could find an outlet, even while women's voices were excluded from the debates which decided what nationalist struggles should look like. Such an argument finds echoes in Kathleen Wilson's discussion of slavery, where women's reproductive value often worked to efface, rather than drive home, the realities of hardship and suffering that female slaves endured.

Representations of women—as mothers, as guardians of value, culture, religion, as the property of men, as frail creatures or scheming witches—drew heavily upon the ideals that dominated British imperial culture, and in which divisions were drawn between metropole and Empire, work and home, business and pleasure, public and private. The idea of 'home' as the natural sphere of woman was a critical one, though its ability to describe the lives of most women was severely limited. None the less this idealized vision of woman guarding the hearth was palpably at work in how Empire was depicted. Patricia Grimshaw demonstrates how Christianized Aboriginal women were taught homecraft to better equip them for the life of the Western housewife, while Jock McCulloch spells out the sometimes harsh consequences for women who adopted 'male' roles. A. James Hammerton shows how migration fed on and idealized visions of home in its attempts to distinguish male from female migrant experience. Catherine Hall conjures for us missionary disappointment when freed Caribbean slaves found life-styles which did not conform to the binary world of home and workplace which the missionaries worked so hard to import to the West Indies and elsewhere.

Clearly, these themes, findings, and ideas all constitute both significant issues for historical investigation and comment, and a major departure from more traditional avenues of historical enquiry. Central to the argument of all the essays presented here, and indeed to how we understand the relationship between gender and Empire, is an emphatic insistence that studies of gender issues cannot be relegated to a sub-branch, a supplement, of historical enquiry. They are not 'additions' or secondary knowledges subordinate to some more important set of considerations. Rather these are questions and issues which are central to any historical enquiry because they deal with issues and contests and influences that are always at stake, always also challenged, and always present. Whether our attention is drawn to the all-male corridors of Whitehall in the nineteenth century where notions of a highly masculinized public space influenced the policies which colonies experienced, to the lives of migrant women moving from colony to colony in search of work and always haunted by attitudes that saw them, because they were women, as potentially promiscuous or as necessary home-makers in a rough environment, ideas about gender influenced, moulded, and shaped the attitudes alike of ordinary people and of power brokers and policy-makers. Moreover, in turning our attention to issues such as those discussed in the succeeding chapters of this volume, we gain not only new insights and fresh perspectives on gender roles, but perhaps also come to appreciate whole new modes of understanding the world. In refusing to see gender as supplemental or additional but rather as always integral and always at work, there lies also the suggestion that previous histories, neglectful of these processes and issues, may themselves need challenging or updating.

In 1992 Billie Melman commented in an influential study of women and colonialism that women had been relegated 'to the periphery of imperialist culture and the tradition of "empire" '.[5] A decade on, that is no longer the case, as more and more exciting and sophisticated work—the best of which is represented in this volume—re-shapes our vision of, and ideas about, Empire. While the Empire may still seem a very stuffy and masculine environment (in some respects at least), that apparent stuffiness and masculinity are themselves now under scrutiny from a gendered perspective. They no longer adequately describe a world that is or was; instead they are themselves considered not just worthy of, but necessitating, scrutiny.

[5] Billie Melman, *Women's Orients. English Women and the Middle East, 1718–1918. Sexuality, Religion and Work* (Ann Arbor, 1992), p. 1.

Select Bibliography

ANTOINETTE BURTON, *Burdens of History: British Feminists, Indian Women, and Imperial Culture 1865–1915* (Chapel Hill, NC, 1994).
—— 'Thinking Beyond the Boundaries: Empire, Feminism and the Domains of History', *Social History*, XXVI (2001), pp. 60–71.
HELEN CALLAWAY, *Gender, Culture and Empire. European Women in Colonial Nigeria* (Urbana, Ill., 1987).
INDIRA CHOWDHURY, *The Frail Hero and Virile History. Gender and the Politics of Culture in Colonial Bengal* (Delhi, 1998).
VEENA DAS, 'Gender Studies, Cross-Cultural Comparison and the Colonial Organization of Knowledge', *Berkshire Review*, XXI (1986), pp. 58–79.
ANNA DAVIN, 'Imperialism and Motherhood', *History Workshop Journal*, 9 (1978), pp. 9–65.
INDERPAL GREWAL, *Home and Harem: Nation, Gender, Empire, and the Cultures of Travel* (Durham, NC, 1996).
FRANCES GOUDA, 'The Gendered Rhetoric of Colonialism and Anti-Colonialism in Twentieth-Century Indonesia', *Indonesia*, LV (1993), 1–22.
CATHERINE HALL, *Civilising Subjects. Metropole and Colony in the English Imagination, 1830–1867* (Chicago, 2002).
CLAUDIA KNAPMAN. *White Women in Fiji, 1835–1930. The Ruin of Empire?* (Sydney, 1986).
REINA LEWIS, *Gendering Orientalism. Race, Femininity and Representation* (London, 1996).
JOANNA LIDDLE and RAMA JOSHI, 'Gender and Imperialism in British India', *South Asia Research*, V (1985), pp. 147–65.
BILLIE MELMAN, *Women's Orients. English Women and the Middle East, 1718–1918. Sexuality, Religion and Work* (Ann Arbor, 1992).

CLARE MIDGLEY, ed., *Gender and Imperialism* (Manchester, 1998).

CHANDRA TALPADE MOHANTY, 'Under Western Eyes: Feminist Scholarship and Colonial Discourses', in *Third World Women and the Politics of Feminism*, ed. Chandra Talpade Mohanty and others (Bloomington, Ind., 1991), pp. 51–80

FELICITY NUSSBAUM, *Torrid Zones. Maternity, Sexuality, and Empire in Eighteenth-Century English Narratives* (Baltimore, 1995).

ROSALIND O' HANLON, 'Gender in the British Empire' in Judith M. Brown and William Roger Louis, eds., *The Oxford History of the British Empire. IV. The Twentieth Century* (Oxford, 1999).

KALPANA RAM and MARGARET JOLLY, eds, *Maternities and Modernities. Colonial and Postcolonial Experiences in Asia and the Pacific* (Cambridge, 1998).

KUM KUM SANGARI and SUDESH VAID, *Recasting Women: Essays in Colonial History* (Delhi, 1993).

MRINALINI SINHA, *Colonial Masculinity. The 'Manly Englishman' and the 'Effeminate Bengali' in the Late Nineteenth Century* (Manchester, 1995).

MARGARET STROBEL, *European Women and the Second British Empire* (Bloomington, Ind., 1991).

2

Empire, Gender, and Modernity in the Eighteenth Century

KATHLEEN WILSON

What role did gender play in motivating, maintaining, and challenging the eighteenth-century British Empire? Recent scholarship has just begun to address that question. Spurred by a growing interest in questions of identity and cultural difference, historians of eighteenth-century Britain are beginning to bring the histories of the British nation and the British Empire together and in relation to each other. The importance of gender as a relation of power has been one of the most prominent themes of this new work: the constitutive roles played by gender in nation-making, consumption, and colonization, the gendered rhetoric of imperial projects and aspirations, the gendered nature of slave regimes and anti-slavery movements, and the varied roles men and women played in British expansion. Our knowledge about the meanings and realities of imperial power and the politics of everyday life under the first three Georges (1714–1820) is consequently under revision.

This chapter will examine the centrality of gender to British dominion and British modernity and to the categories of difference that Empire claimed to have 'discovered', vindicated, and sustained. Before turning to that project, however, some clarification of our central terms is in order. Gender is not a synonym for women; neither is it a 'fact' of the past (or present) awaiting discovery. Historians have argued that gender was both a relation of power and a way of signifying relationships of power that produced and orchestrated the changing meanings of sexual difference in time, shaping social institutions, privileges, expectations, and experience.[1] Gender was also a means of marking the body for cultural ends in eighteenth-century Europe where vision was held to be an increasingly important way of ascertaining reality. As such,

---

[1] Joan Wallach Scott, *Gender and the Politics of History* (New York, 1996); M. Roper and J. Tosh, eds., *Manful Assertions: Masculinities in Britain since 1800* (London, 1991).

gender was a source and a marker of identity for British people in metropolitan and colonial settings, and like other national, ethnic, and familial
identities, was always in process. Bound to a historical-social order and both
consolidated and challenged through the practices of everyday life,
gender was cross-cut with other identifications and was neither natural nor
inevitable, but was ascribed, challenged, adopted, and even forced to give way.[2]
Given recent emphasis on the role of eighteenth-century nation and empire-
building in disrupting traditional understandings of difference, the changing
modes and meanings of gender may lie at the forefront of the century's
transformations. Tracking the relations between gender and Empire also
requires a revision of the model of metropole–to–colony diffusion traditionally used by historians, for such attention makes clear that the most decisive
breaks with established practices and attitudes occurred in the novel and
culturally hybrid environments of colonial frontiers, correspondingly reshaping the understanding of difference at the supposed 'centre'. Gender, in other
words, was a mode of power through which metropolitan and colonial
modernities were mutually constituted, construing the categories and experience of sexual, national, and racial difference within Britain and without.

Empire also requires clarification, and not only because the mercantilist
British Empire of the eighteenth century was a different creature from its
Victorian and Edwardian successors. It is also because 'empire' has come to be
used by many scholars as a shorthand to describe the entire set of global,
national, and local processes set in motion by European 'discovery' and
settlement from the sixteenth century onwards, dramatically conflating dis-
junctive historical practices, intentions, and outcomes. The British 'Empire of
the Seas'—of factories, forts, and maritime colonies—was founded on two
essentially contradictory visions and sets of principles: on 'liberty' (that
religious, political, and economic freedom guaranteed to Protestant settlers
of European descent by the transplantation of British political and legal
culture to the colonies) and on coercion (through the exertion of metropolitan power aimed at controlling or profiting from the colonists, indigenous
peoples, and the enslaved, via Navigation Acts, expropriation of land and
labour, British legislative supremacy, and plantation slavery).[3] Because of

---

[2] Kathleen Wilson, *The Island Race: Englishness, Empire and Gender in the Eighteenth Century*
(London, 2003), pp. 1–4, and references there.

[3] Jack P. Greene, 'Empire and Identity from the Glorious Revolution to the American
Revolution', in P. J. Marshall, ed. *Oxford History of the British Empire*, (hereafter *OHBE*), II,
The Eighteenth Century (Oxford, 1998), pp. 208–30.

these complexities, the eighteenth-century Empire was also a crucible of eighteenth-century modernity: a generator for ideas about gender, nationality, and difference that affected metropolitan culture and categories of knowledge in both profound and quotidian ways. These patterns of cultural exchange continued after the loss of the American colonies and the extension of a more rationalized and authoritarian Empire in the East and South Pacific, continuing to shape British imperial visions and national debates about gender and social relations 'at home' into the next century.

Although its various sites had divergent and changing relations to the metropole over the century, the Empire and the wars that threatened, maintained, and extended it over the century created a *network* that, although imperfect, was also remarkably efficient in allowing people, gossip, connections, ideas, and identities to travel and be transformed. In these complex historical settings, gender identities, ascribed or adopted, were situational and commodified, not natural or inevitable. They served most importantly to mark who was protected by British 'rights and liberties' and who was not. Further, British people confronted other cultures and gender systems which were not structured by the binaries and complementarities familiar to Europeans and which used alternative markers of social relation and difference. Colonial institutions none the less strove to regulate the sexual, conjugal, and domestic life of all those within their purview. The struggles and exchanges produced by these cultural and political encounters influenced contemporary meanings of 'men' and 'women,' Britishness and Englishness, and 'home' and 'abroad' across a wider imperium.

Eighteenth-century British understanding of gender was intricately linked to the formulation and dissemination of other categories of difference produced by Enlightenment initiatives that proliferated across broad social terrains, largely in consequence of British colonial contacts and expansion. For example, categories such as nation, race, rank, geography, and religion, as well as degrees of civility, politeness, and 'stage' of civilization, were mulled over by British intellectuals and ordinary people in an effort to bring order to the marvellous cultural, linguistic, and physical multiplicity of the modern world. 'Nation' provided perhaps the most important category of difference of the period, combining older biblical and juridical concepts of a people located in fixed spatial and cultural terrain with emergent concepts of a political and territorial entity worthy of allegiance. Britons' vigorous explorations of self and world confirmed that various nations had different moral, social, and intellectual characteristics, yet also produced a more precarious sense of national self.[4] 'Nation' thus provided a way of imagining community that tied people together less by physical characteristics (although these were significant) than by customs, descent, and 'blood', that mysterious, if 'common substance passed on through heterosexual relations and birth'.[5]

Ideologies of nation brought gender and sexual practice, as sources and symbols of a common inheritance, to the forefront of social and political theories. Gender, however, became at the same time a topic of controversy. In contrast to the sixteenth and seventeenth centuries, when gender was understood to be the stable marker of a cosmic and largely inscrutable divine order, it emerged in the eighteenth century as both 'natural'—the product of the universal and discernible (if still divine) laws of human nature and society, akin to other phenomena in natural science—and acquired, moulded by environment and custom. Georgian debates over 'the sex', and the respective roles of men and women in national life, consequently turned on gender's status as a social or natural category and the body's role as anchor of social roles and identities. These debates dominated public and private discussion, saturated the new arenas of polite culture in British and colonial towns, and spawned new forms of literary and visual representation.[6]

Gender attributes were equally at play in the cultural and political project of state and empire-building and in the concern with the national identity it produced. The British 'fiscal-military state'—so called because of its expanding abilities to wage war and levy taxes under the rubric of the consent of the people—conjoined big and small investors to produce far-flung networks of power and kinship with a global reach. As a result, many Scots, Protestant Irish, Americans, Africans, Asians, and Amerindians (men and women) began to identify with a culture 'both distinctly British and distinctly imperial'.[7] Britain's continuing struggles with the Bourbon

---

[4] Wilson, *Island Race*, pp. 6–16; Kate Teltscher, *India Inscribed: European and British Writing on India, 1600–1800* (New Delhi, 1995), p. 62.

[5] Tessie Liu, 'Teaching the Differences Among Women from a Historical Perspective: Rethinking Race and Gender as Social Categories', *Women's Studies International Forum*, XIV (1991), pp. 270–71.

[6] Kathleen Wilson, *The Sense of the People: Politics, Culture and Imperialism in England 1715–1785* (Cambridge, 1995), chap. 1; James Walvin, *Fruits of Empire: Exotic Produce and British Taste, 1660–1800* (London, 1997); David Shields, *Civil Tongues and Polite Letters in British America* (Chapel Hill, NC, 1997).

[7] Eric Hindraker, 'The "Four Indian Kings" and the Imaginative Construction of the British Empire', *William and Mary Quarterly* (hereafter *WMQ*), Third Series, LIII (1996), p. 504; John Brewer, *The Sinews of Power: War, Money and the English State* (London, 1987).

monarchs for supremacy drew colonists as well as domestic populations into the 'demands and meanings of Britishness' while also underlining for all the importance for national prosperity and glory of British colonies in the New and Old Worlds.[8] War and the political opposition generated by the Whig state also reinforced in the minds of metropolitan and colonial subjects an idealized notion of the national character as comprised of the 'manly' qualities necessary for military triumph and successful colonization: independence, fortitude, courage, daring, resourcefulness, and paternalistic duty. This conceptualization of British dominion abroad was first aggressively retailed to a wider public during the War of Jenkin's Ear (1738–41), and continued to have purchase for decades thereafter.[9]

Civic humanists and other critics of the burgeoning consumer society were quick to point out the iniquitous domestic effects of Empire and commerce, generating webs of patronage, credit, and dependence as well as inessential commodities that allowed the forces of luxury and moral turpitude to flourish.[10] Women were emblematic and symptomatic of such corruption, by virtue of their proclivity for excessive consumption and their capacity to seduce men from their civic obligations. They were accordingly urged to give up their 'natural' inclinations towards 'effeminizing' luxuries to promote the stoicism and love of country within the home that produced a manly fighting force at the front.[11] 'Effeminacy' was a complex notion that appeared in a range of discourses. Designating, according to Johnson's *Dictionary*, both the 'admission of the qualities of a woman' and 'addiction to women,'[12] effeminacy demarcated a failed English masculinity and a compromised masculine authority, signalled by the excessive consumption of goods and sex or the disorder threatened by prostitutes, sodomites, and fops. As the discourses of civic humanism were transformed by merchants and other owners of moveable, rather than landed, property, however, the venal world of commerce, once represented as driven by 'effeminate' and dependent forces, became a space of manly fortitude where discipline, nerve, and foresight were required to triumph over the volatility of markets. This generative and acquisitive version of independ-

---

[8] Linda Colley, *Britons: Forging the Nation* (New Haven, 1992), p. 281.

[9] Wilson, *Sense of the People*, pp. 140–65; David Armitage, *The Ideological Origins of the British Empire* (Cambridge, 2000), pp. 180–98.

[10] John Pocock, *Virtue, Commerce and History* (Cambridge, 1992).

[11] Wilson, *Island Race*, chap. 3.

[12] Michèle Cohen, *Fashioning Masculinity* (London, 1999), p. 7.

ence and masculinity was best set off by its frequent comparison to an allegedly effeminate and dependent aristocracy.[13]

The troubling link between Empire and 'effeminacy' none the less continued to surface for the rest of the century. During the early years of the War of the Austrian Succession (1741–48) and the Seven Years War (1756–63), defeats to France, a French-funded Jacobite rebellion and French encroachments on the American colonies fomented a pervasive sense of crisis. Opposition spokespeople and village shopkeepers alike blamed the 'effeminacy' of the nation's Frenchified aristocratic leadership for having produced a weak and enervated fighting force that threatened to relinquish to France Britain's 'Empire of the Seas'. In the wake of the Peace of Paris (1763), the defensive, polyphonic, and demographic dimensions of an extended Empire—now understood to be an Empire of conquest—soon posed urgent problems, raising doubts about the capacity of dominions to shore up manliness and virtue in the domestic polity. Playwrights, pamphleteers, and parliamentarians pilloried British colonies as a source of 'luxury, effeminacy and tyranny' that corroded national mores and wreaked havoc with the gender order, with West Indian planters and East Indian nabobs coming in for special censure. The American war, represented in stridently gendered images of familial dysfunction, sexual excess, and effeminate aristocratic languor, further undermined Britons' confidence in its empire of virtue, as did the anti-slavery movement.[14] The rehabilitation of political and military leaders following that war—through resplendent new costumes and the embrace of ethical, liberal, and religious reform—thus strove to restore confidence in social and political hierarchies, from the monarch down.[15] In the meantime, the discourses of effeminacy privileged the claims of the white, trading, and commercial classes to political status while excluding a range of 'effeminate' others who threatened their supposedly distinctive goals: women, Frenchmen, aristocrats, non-white colonial subjects, the foppish, the irrational, the dependent, and the timid.

Women still had key conceptual, ideological, and practical roles to play in the projects of nation-and empire-building. Women's bodies served as

---

[13] Carroll Smith-Rosenberg, 'Domesticating "Virtue": Coquettes and Revolutionaries in Young America', in Elaine Scarry, ed., *Literature and the Body* (Baltimore, 1988); Toby Dietz, 'Shipwrecked, or Masculinity Imperiled', *Journal of American History*, LXXXI (1994), pp. 51–80.

[14] Wilson, *Sense of the People*, chap. 5; Stephen Conway, *The British Isles and the War for American Independence* (Oxford, 2001), pp. 89–90.

[15] Colley, *Britons*, pp. 195–236.

symbols of national virtue and martial potency for much of the century, as the growing ubiquity of the pale-skinned figure of Britannia in prints and paintings revealed.[16] Real-life women's superior capacities for civility, refinement, and sensibility could also be put to work on behalf of the common good, even as tastes for luxuries meant that they had to be well-regulated and kept from unnatural exercises of authority. However, views of women's power and influence were changing. In the 1770s, women's role in Empire and patriotism was represented as more beneficial if less direct than previously, as their domestic virtue was promoted as a source of moral authority in the broader imperial polity.[17] Two ideological developments linked to Empire were crucial here: the rise of the cult of sensibility, and the dissemination of Enlightenment social theory, or the 'natural history' of man.

'Sensibility' emerged as the hallmark of 'modern' and polished nations across the Anglophone Empire, the bedrock of an ethical system in which the moral qualities of compassion, sympathy, and benevolence guided men and women in their negotiations with modern commercial society. Women were central to sensibility's foundation, for it was best developed in the bosom of the family where the 'natural affections' and the 'habitual sympathies' required were taught and internalized.[18] In the 1780s and 1790s, and especially as war with Revolutionary France intensified, evangelicalism gave the cult of sensibility an even higher moral purpose, exhorting men and women to join in a reformation of manners, at home and abroad, to save heathen souls and advance Britain's imperial, commercial, and moral ascendancy in the world.[19]

The 'natural history of man', one of the primary modes through which eighteenth-century thinkers rehearsed and understood their modernity, was integral to ideas about sensibility. Scottish intellectuals, natural historians, and social scientists culled traveller's accounts, colonial histories, and exploration narratives for the evidence that would enable them to plot the progress of humanity through time and space, from its earliest 'savage' state (found most frequently in the torrid zones of the southern hemisphere) to its most

[16] Alan Bewell, 'Constructed Places, Constructed Peoples: Charting the Improvement of the Female Body in the Pacific', *Eighteenth Century Life*, XVIII (1994), pp. 37–54.

[17] Harriet Guest, *Small Change: Women, Learning, Patriotism* (Chicago, 2001); Wilson, *Island Race*, pp. 21–25.

[18] G. Barker-Benfield, *The Culture of Sensibility* (Chicago, 1993); Susan Kingsley Kent, *Gender and Power in Britain, 1660–1990* (London, 1999), pp. 67–71; Shields, *Civil Tongues*, pp. 99–139.

[19] Susan Thorne, *Congregational Missions and the Making of an Imperial Culture in Nineteenth-century England* (Stanford, Calif., 1999), pp. 23–88.

advanced and polished 'commercial' state (typical of the temperate northern zone). What is most remarkable for our purposes is that gender and Empire were at the centre of this story of progress. Each stage of development was marked by specific gender relations, running from the treatment of women as drudges and packhorses in the first, to the respect and esteem accorded to women in the last. These histories thus drove home the point that the order imposed by the British example of bifurcated gender roles and restraint of sexuality were central to civilization's advance. Hence Adam Ferguson, William Robertson, John Millar, William Falconer, and David Hume may have quarrelled over how climate acted on nerves, but all agreed that the status of women marked civilization and progress. 'That women are indebted to the refinements of polished manners for a happy change in their state, is a point which can admit of no doubt', William Robertson asserted; 'To despise and to degrade the female sex, is the characteristic of the savage state in every part of the globe.'[20] European and especially British women were believed to have attained the highest levels of physical, mental, and moral refinement and chastity, a view widely disseminated by such popular writers as William Alexander and Hannah More.[21]

These constructions of female capacity and nature played innovative parts in articulating contending relationships between Britain and the colonies. In the late 1780s, the much vaunted moral influence of English women saturated colonial reform initiatives such as anti-slavery. Deploying the language of sensibility, British women brought their supposed feminine compassion and sympathy to bear on the sexual exploitation of black women and the break-up of families slavery enjoined.[22] Their methods and the connection they claimed with women across the Empire through the language of universal womanhood enlarged their role in political life; but it also produced images of enslaved Africans as victimized, passive, and silent, immoral savages who needed enlightened British women to lift them to freedom. Embracing the idea that English women represented the highest level of civilization, they felt entitled to dominate other women of the Empire, to serve as 'teachers of

[20] William Robertson, *The History of America*, 4 vols. (London 1777), II, p. 98; Adam Ferguson, *An Essay on Civil Society* (London, 1766), pp. 146–47; 201.
[21] William Alexander, *The History of Women, from the Earliest Antiquity to the Present Time*, 2 vols. [1779; London, 1782]; Hannah More, *Essay on Various Subjects* [1777; London, 4th edn., 1785].
[22] Clare Midgley, *Women Against Slavery: The British Campaigns, 1780–1870* (London 1992); Charlotte Sussman, *Consuming Anxieties: Consumer Protest, Gender and British Slavery 1713–1833* (Stanford, Calif., 2000).

nations' and manners to the less well-positioned. Those who failed to exhibit these qualities—which, by the 1780s and 1790s, included working-class women within Britain, as well as colonized and enslaved women—were denigrated as savage or depraved, redeemable only by acquiescing in the division of labour and standards of domesticity set for them by their betters.[23]

Sensibility and belief in the modernity of the British nation also helped reshape notions of manliness and of Empire. The 'man of feeling' with a capacity for sensibility and sentiment generated new requirements for imperial leaders. General Amherst and even Lord Clive had briefly joined General Wolfe in popular representation as examples of military men who were also noble men of Empire, revealed in their sympathies for vanquished foes and indigenous peoples alike.[24] The Pacific voyages of Captain Cook (1768–79) set new standards in enlightened exploration, and Cook himself became the exemplar of this new imperial masculinity, combining expertise, humanitarianism, and compassion in equal measure. By the time of Warren Hastings' impeachment (1788), Empire could no longer be imagined as an extension of Britain, but a place where disorder, dependency, excess, and savagery required a disciplined, authoritative, but compassionate masculine English subject to rule. Men such as Lord Cornwallis, Governor-General of India from 1786 to 1793, who placed tax-gathering and law in British India on an English basis, demonstrated the requisite firm, civilized, but restrained authority for governing in dangerous times and climes. Governor Colonel Arthur Phillip of New South Wales (1788–92), who subjected convicts to a strict and arduous regime of hard work, moral reform, and religious instruction, similarly regenerated the depraved sensibilities of his charges and turned them towards progress and improvement. Such exemplars, along with the awful spectacle of revolution across the Channel, encouraged Thomas Malthus, by century's end, to bring the knowledge and theories forged by Empire 'home': turning the precepts of stadial theory (development by stages) on the domestic population, he predicted that savages and the European poor, conjoined in their inability to control their sexual urges, were doomed to reproduce beyond the food supply. Only the European and especially English middle classes were able to exercise the 'moral restraint' necessary to liberate reason from the forces of instinct and

---

[23] Deborah Valenze, *The First Industrial Woman* (London, 1998).

[24] Miles Ogborn, *Spaces of Modernity: London's Geographies 1680–1780* (London, 1998), pp. 144–46.

avert apocalypse.[25] In all of these ways and more, Empire provided a proving ground of national character and an emblem of the superior nature of gender and class-specific forms of English authority, coding and recoding metropolitan categories of being and becoming.

The definitions and practices of gender roles and relations within Britain and the vaunted purposes of Empire were certainly carried by British settlers, traders, missionaries, and adventurers to colonial environments, but in the act of crossing—oceans, territories, cultures—these meanings and practices acquired new uses. Colonial encounters generated a 'gender frontier', where 'two or more culturally specific systems of knowledge about gender and nature' met and confronted one another, forcing the invention of new identities and social practices.[26] Of course, the contradictions and ambiguities within gender categories meant that they could never confront themselves or each other as fully realized entities. Moreover, colonization brought together populations with discrepant perspectives and intentions and grossly unequal power. And the confrontation of rival gender systems presented, to historians as well as to historical actors, the problem of translation, 'a practice producing difference [and similarity] out of incommensurability', that directly impinged upon the success or failure of colonial projects.[27] The *instability* of gender and national identities is thus brought into relief in colonial settings, as desire and recognition as well as disavowal shaped the categories of difference that Empire was believed to discover, vindicate, and sustain. All of these unsettling processes of constructing and maintaining difference, both creative and violent, were evident in English relations with indigenes and in the plantation colonies of the Atlantic.

As shown above, ideals about gender-differentiated roles and status were the key to British assessments of the stage of civilization of indigenous societies and to the type of treatment meted out to recalcitrant local people. This had long shaped English relations with Celtic peoples within the British Isles. In Scotland, the commercial and property reforms instituted by the British government following the Jacobite uprising of 1745 targeted Highland

[25] Thomas Malthus, *An Essay on the Principle of Population*, ed. Patricia James (Cambridge, 1989), I, pp. 1–3; 21; 47.

[26] Kathleen Brown, *Good Wives, Nasty Wenches and Anxious Patriarchs: Gender, Race, and Power in Colonial Virginia* (Chapel Hill, NC, 1996), pp. 33; 45.

[27] Meaghan Morris, 'Forward', to Naoki Sakai, *Translation and Subjectivity* (Minnesota, 1996), p. xiii.

clan culture which was said to subordinate women 'barbarically' (despite the greater freedoms allowed them in Scottish law and custom).[28] Centuries of English domination of Ireland was continually legitimated by the allegedly backward character of native Irish gender relations: the women were 'brazen' and lascivious, partial to strong drink, and wielded too much power over their husbands; Irish men were lazy, tyrannical, and lacking proper ties to property (indicated by their serial use of common lands for pasturage). Early modern English writers asserted that the Irish were non-Europeans, descended from the Scythians, and sharing customs with the Tartars. The so-called 'Celtic fringe' thereby provided models of 'primitive' peoples who both required and benefitted from English civility and rule.[29]

In eighteenth-century America, intercultural and sexual exchange between English colonists and Native Americans, and wars with France coaxed British settlers, fur traders, missionaries, and soldiers, from Canada to Carolina, to scrutinize Native American societies in order to gauge their progress, if any, from 'savagery' to civility (defined as their willingness to cooperate with the British).[30] Gender and sexual relations were deemed of particular importance, as English emissaries sought to find some evidence of a household order from which they could extrapolate or coax stable political relations. Male authority, however, seemed conspicuous in Indian communities by its lack.[31] The women's sexual 'libertinism', the effortlessness with which they gave birth (that infallible indicator of savagery the world over, in British eyes) and the ease with which heterosexual partnerships were made and dissolved underscored the problem of masculine deficiency and debased femininity. 'To cuckold her Husband is so little a [crime] that no notice is

---

[28] R. A. Houston, 'Women in the Economy and Society of Scotland 1500–1800', in Houston and I. D. Whyte, ed., *Scottish Society* (Cambridge, 1989), pp. 119–47; Leah Leneman, *Alienated Affections: The Scottish Experience of Divorce and Separation* (Edinburgh, 1998).

[29] David Dickson, 'No Scythians Here: Women and Marriage in Seventeenth-Century Ireland', in Margaret MacCurtain and Mary O'Dowd, eds., *Women in Early Modern Ireland* (Edinburgh, 1991), p. 224; Nicholas Canny, 'The Ideology of English Colonization,' *WMQ*, Third Series, XXX (1973), pp. 575–98.

[30] Michael Zuckerman, 'Identity in British America: Unease in Eden,' in Nicholas Canny and Anthony Pagden, eds., *Colonial Identity in the Atlantic World 1500–1800* (Princeton, 1987), pp. 153–57; Nancy Shoemaker, ed., *Negotiators of Change: Historical Perspectives on Native American Women* (Chicago, 1995); Richard Godbeer, 'Eroticizing the Middle Ground: Anglo-Indian Sexual Relations along the Eighteenth-century Frontier', in Martha Hodes, ed., *Sex, Love, Race: Crossing Boundaries in North American History* (New York, 1999), pp. 91–106.

[31] Richard White, 'What Chigabe Knew', *WMQ*, Third Series, LII (1995), pp. 152–53.

taken of it ... Their Maids do not keep that Name ... they lie with whom they please before marriage', noted John Oldmixon disapprovingly.[32]

Yet although colonial governments passed laws to outlaw mixed-race marriages in the early eighteenth century and colonists proclaimed Indian–English intermarriage would be 'reckoned a horrid crime with us', the attractions of Indian culture, and of Indian mates, remained potent in fact and fiction.[33] British captives taken by Indians in war, including women, not infrequently began to prefer life with the Indians.[34] Indian women continued to act as culture brokers; marriage and sexual relations with them provided colonists with 'sleeping dictionaries', as well as access to gossip circulating through nearby or rival settlements and across plantations, and produced transculturated 'ethnic districts' of mixed-blood (African, European, and American) offspring.[35] By the time of the Revolution, intermarriage and the adoption by Native Americans of selective regulatory aspects of Anglo-dissenting culture had made indigeneity a matter of English law, and Indian gender and legal systems matters of 'custom'.[36] The failures of translation, in other words, wreaked a particular type of cultural and epistemic violence.

As this account intimates, what most animated British observers was Indians' apparently anarchical domestic life, which was (mis)translated as an index of social disorder. Historians of British America are in substantial agreement on this point: 'patriarchy', in the form of the supreme authority of the white, predominantly property-holding male heads of household, was the building block and organizing principle of British–American societies, and the household was the main unit of social order and indigenous reclamation. The power of the male heads of households in law and practice from New England to Carolina owed much to colonization and to the novel forms

[32] Colin G. Calloway, *New Worlds for All: Indians, Europeans and the Remaking of Early America* (Baltimore, 1997); David Milobar, 'Aboriginal Peoples and the British Press, 1720–1763', in Stephen Taylor and others, eds., *Hanoverian Britain and Empire* (Woodbridge, 1998), p. 76; John Oldmixon, *The British Empire in America*, 2 vols. (London, 1708), I, p. 279.

[33] John Bartram, quoted in Zuckerman, 'Unease in Eden', p. 146; Henry Timberlake, *Memoirs* (London, 1765), pp. 89–90.

[34] Rebecca Blevins Faery, *Cartographies of Desire: Captivity, Race and Sex in the Shaping of the American Nation* (Norman, Okl., 1999); Linda Colley, *Captives: Britain, Empire and the World 1600–1850* (London, 2002), pp. 186–97.

[35] Calloway, *New Worlds for All*, pp. 178–79.

[36] Ann Marie Plane, 'Legitimacies, Indian Identities and the Law', in M. J. Daunton and Rick Halpern, eds., *Empire and Others* (London, 1999), p. 232.

of servitude and slavery it generated.[37] It was also a response to the relative weakness of the regulatory apparatus of Church and State in societies where whites could be a minority. Claiming the right to 'dispatch wives, children and slaves', the patriarch's will was expressed and enforced by the whip. 'Like one of the patriarchs, I have my flocks and my herds, my bond-men, and bond-women, and every soart [sic] of trade amongst my own servants, so that I live in a kind of independance [sic] on every one, but Providence', wrote the notorious sexual profligate and successful planter William Byrd in 1726.[38] A great deal of the work of male authority took its most potent form in the regulation of sexual behaviour of household and family members, which was enforced or extended by colonial law. Female sexual access was a jealously guarded and valuable commodity. Laws against interracial unions, legal limitations on the freedoms of free blacks, and prosecution of white women for bearing mixed-race children (while being indifferent to those fathered by white men with enslaved or native women) meant masters intervened in the most intimate of connections. When combined with measures to establish legal standing for definitions of 'race', as occurred in Virginia and Maryland, legal constructions of patriarchal privilege and female honour provided 'assurance that white female domesticity and sexuality would remain the preserve of white men'.[39] The gender power of patriarchy reinforced that of colonialism, as the appropriation of land, labour, and sexual entitlements went hand in hand.

Men and women's experience of colonization was shaped by their positions within these various hierarchies. In the early years of settlement, many British people emigrated to the New World as family members or as indentured or forced labourers. Impoverished Irish women were recruited by promises of money or new clothes, or impressed into emigration to relieve the 'vagrant' problem; in either case, once in the New World, they suffered the highest number of miscarriages and birth deaths in the hemisphere, in an unsavoury anticipation of the fate of African women.[40] On the mainland,

[37] John Demos, *A Little Commonwealth: Family Life in Plymouth Colony* (Oxford, 2000); Carole Shammas, 'Anglo-American Household Government in Comparative Perspective', *WMQ*, Third Series, LII (1995), pp. 104–44; Mary Beth Norton, *Founding Mothers and Fathers: Gendered Power and the Forming of American Society* (New York, 1996).

[38] William Byrd, quoted in Brown, *Good Wives*, p. 265; Philip D. Morgan, *Slave Counterpoint: Black Culture in the Eighteenth-Century Chesapeake and Low Country* (Chapel Hill, NC, 1998), pp. 274–75.

[39] Brown, *Good Wives*, pp. 195–97; 203.

[40] Jerrold Casway, 'Irish Women Overseas', in *Women in Early Modern Ireland*, pp. 126–27.

frontier conditions undermined traditional distinctions between men's and women's work, ranging them both in a variety of intensive agricultural and domestic employment. Female indentured servants were liable to sexual abuse or harassment by masters or their sons; men had difficulties finding partners, which delayed their progress to the vaunted position of head of household. As high rates of natural reproduction in the mainland colonies balanced sex ratios, and enslaved labour increased, the demand for female indentured servants' productive and sexual labour slackened. Women who were not servants were largely excluded from the skilled trades, while law and custom limited the social significance of women's work, subordinating them to fathers, husbands, and masters as 'good wives' and 'helpmeets'.[41] Outside marriage, women's increased freedoms in law, medicine, and employment declined over the eighteenth century.[42] The 'gender frontier' on the colonial front of America closed down rather than opened up opportunities for many, especially the poorest for whom the promise of good marriages and social betterment was cruelly belied.

As the harsh conditions of frontier settlement gave way to greater prosperity and diversification, British women were enjoined to bring their special moral qualities to bear on the arts of colonization and to administer the social, rather than legal and political, practices that maintained the boundaries of nationality and entitlement. The requirements of 'politeness' in the colonies ensured the adaptive reproduction of English culture and stock far from home. However, strategies of social engineering (of which 'patriarchy' was certainly one) collided with individual motivation and condition to produce unexpected results. British women arrived in the western Atlantic colonies and eastern trading outposts (in Africa, India, and Sumatra) from all over the British Isles and in all conditions: not only as forced and indentured labourers, but also as soldiers, sailors, and officers' wives, nurses, sutlers, merchants, prostitutes, the partners or daughters of religious pilgrims, slavers, planters, and officials, and as slave-traders and explorers themselves.[43] Where the men greatly outnumbered them, as in the Caribbean

[41] David Eltis, *The Rise of African Slavery in the Americas* (Cambridge, 2000), pp. 100–02; Lisa Norling, *Captain Ahab Had a Wife: New England Women and the Whalefishery, 1720–1870* (Chapel Hill, NC, 2000), pp. 48–49.

[42] Cornelia Hughes Dayton, *Women before the Bar: Gender, Law and Society in Connecticut 1639–1789* (Chapel Hill, NC, 1995); Elaine Forman Crane, *Ebb Tide in New England: Women, Seaports and Social Change, 1630–1800* (Boston, 1998).

[43] For which, see Wilson, *Island Race*, chap. 3; Eltis, *Rise of African Slavery*, 92n; Lillian Ashcraft-Eason, ' "She Voluntarily Hath Come": A Gambian Woman Trader in Colonial

or New South Wales, British women from fairly petty backgrounds could aspire to good marriages; widows, as women of property, were highly desirable. 'Widowarchy' prevailed in other Atlantic colonies too, from Virginia to St Helena, where the regulation of marriage as a means of transmission of property was of critical import.[44] Even the penal colony of New South Wales afforded social mobility. Esther Abrahams, a Jewish convict transported for stealing lace, became the mistress and then wife of a future Governor of the colony, serving as a beacon of hope to other convict women.[45] Within the socially conservative domain of family life, aspirations for the colonial gender order did not survive acts of cultural transplantation and translation unchanged.

As a cultural system and a social performance of gender power, patriarchy was most put to the test in the crucible of the Atlantic plantation, where the clash between and integration of rival gender and social systems were intensified by slavery's brutalities. In these fraught settings, the relationship of white male authority to other forms and strategies of power and to other 'patriarchies', was never fully established, but had to be enacted and put at risk in the politics and practices of everyday life. Slavery, of course, was not unique to the Atlantic world. As coerced labour based on putative kinlessness, slavery existed across Africa and Asia as well as in parts of the Russian empire, and Europeans captured by hostile princes on both continents had been forced to work as slaves.[46] However, the chattel slavery controlled by Europeans in the New World was among the most vicious and dehumanizing variants. In British America the vast majority of slaves were of African descent.[47] Their experiences were diverse, but most worked on the sugar, tobacco, and rice plantations of the Caribbean, Chesapeake, and the North American Lowcountry. Men outnumbered women two to one in slave importations until the 1760s, although the rates of reproduction in the mainland colonies produced a rough parity between the sexes by the middle

Georgia in the Eighteenth Century', in Paul Lovejoy, ed., *Identity in the Shadow of Slavery* (London, 2000); Deirdre Coleman, ed., *Maiden Voyages and Infant Colonies: Two Women's Travel Narratives of the 1790s* (Leicester, 1999).

[44] Brown, *Good Wives*, pp. 253, 257.

[45] Suzanne D. Rutland, *At the Edge of the Diaspora: Two Centuries of Jewish Settlement in Australia* (Sydney, 1997), p. 11.

[46] Claire C. Robertson and Martin A. Klein, *Women and Slavery in Africa* (Madison, 1983); Martin A. Klein, ed., *Breaking the Chains: Slavery, Bondage and Emancipation in Modern Africa and Asia* (Madison, 1993).

[47] Morgan, *Slave Counterpoint*, pp. 479–81.

decades of the century. Plantation labour affronted the customary gender systems of West Africa in many ways, not least by employing men in agricultural labour, routinely considered 'women's work'. Women were put out to work in field gangs. This was one of the most remarked-upon features of plantation life, removing white women of all ranks entirely from planta-tion field labour, and enabling enslaved men to vie for skilled and supervis-ory jobs. Plantation slavery not only transgressed West African gender occupations (and West African patterns of bondage, where slaves were predominantly women and more highly valued than men); it also reversed the custom of male lineage typical of British law. For in order to ensure a future supply of slaves, all children at birth took their legal status from their mother. This meant that white women, white men, and black men, free or slave, could, at least theoretically, produce free children; but enslaved mothers could only produce more slaves.

Slavery was thus first and foremost a system of gender and racial power: black women were made responsible, materially and symbolically, for the reproduction of plantation slavery.[48] The black woman's body and its in-ternal character had long been objects of intense scrutiny. Stereotyped images of African women as 'masculine', unfeminine, and monstrous had circulated in European culture since the sixteenth century; old and new images got a fresh lease on life with the popularity of voyagers' accounts in the eighteenth century. Depictions of West Africans and the so-called 'Hot-tentots' of South Africa appeared in English narratives as perfect examples of the way in which 'each Nation has retained certain Lineaments or Features' as 'infallible signs of their Dispositions'. African women were 'masculine', reported explorers and traders after seeing heavily armed Dahomey women warriors guarding a fortress, and witnessing their crucial agricultural and manufacturing labour. The men and women's depraved and lascivious sexual appetites were shown by their 'preference' for polygyny as well as by the size and shape of genitalia and even the means of copulation 'from behind, the Woman lying on one side ... scarce differing in this point from the Bruits' [sic] as one 'eyewitness' account from the Cape of Good Hope put it.[49] This was the European strategy of using gender and sexuality 'to convey an emergent notion of racialized difference' and so define themselves as 'religiously, culturally, and phenotypically superior' to the peoples they

---

[48] Hilary McD. Beckles, *Centering Women: Gender Discourses in Caribbean Slavery* (Kingston, 1999), pp. 2–22.

[49] Awnsham and John Churchill, *Collection of Voyages* (London, 1704), pp. 835–36; 838.

confronted or imported to the frontiers of Empire.[50] In the 1700s these tropes of difference were reorganized and formalized through the taxonomies of natural history and the rigours of plantation life. All observers agreed that in terms of civility, morality, capacity for progress, and the treatment of women, Africans lagged far behind Europeans, existing in a prior historical time of savagery that only slavery itself could modernize. These prejudices were imported along with the enslaved, allowing planters to re-imagine their 'paternalism' as a beneficial force not only for themselves but also for their slaves: slavery 'reclaimed' Africans 'from a savage, intractable' state, gave them 'equal access to the civil Magistrate', improved the treatment of their women, and so became part of the civilizing process itself.[51]

Needless to say, the enslaved carried with them their own values and practices, radically different from those of their European captors. Wrenched from extended kinship networks, Africans had to be inventive and pragmatic in forming social and family connections, and engage in their own processes of translation to make sense of their new circumstances within a hostile white culture. Some newly arrived families developed a 'fictive kinship' with their shipmates, looking after each other's children as if they were their own. On the mainland, the growing balance of men and women meant they could form lasting monogamous connections—provided one of them was not traded or sold—and maintain kin over a region of several plantations.[52] In virtually all cases about which historians can learn, kinship, 'real' (in terms of ethnic origin or blood ties) or fictive (through voluntary affiliation), provided the basis of the enslaved's most important social networks, and slave women were central to the constitution and mobilization of such networks.

Not surprisingly, then, enslaved women's bodies were sites of acute struggle between the contending hierarchies of authority that sought to claim a stake in the property of slavery. Slave-owners across the European, African, and Mogul empires used enslaved women for sex and companionship. In British America white masters and overseers alike forced themselves on slave women at will; sexual duties were considered part and parcel of an

[50] Jennifer Morgan, ' "Some Could Suckle over their Shoulder:" Male Travelers, Female Bodies and the Gendering of Racial Ideology 1500–1770', *WMQ*, Third Series, LIV (1997), pp. 167–92.

[51] *Gentleman's Magazine*, V (1735), p. 91; Edward Long, *The History of Jamaica*, 4 vols. (London, 1774), I, p. 271.

[52] Philip D. Morgan, 'The Black Experience in the British Empire', in Marshall, ed., *OHBE, II*, p. 474; James Walvin, *Black Ivory: Slavery in the British Empire* (London, 2001, 2nd edn.), pp. 174; 176–7.

enslaved woman's work, and the master's claims trumped those of any other men. Enslaved women's exploitation caused them trauma and suffering, and aroused the hostility and occasionally violence of enslaved men: although impossible to calculate precisely, 'there was a deep and sullen hatred for what happened to the women'.[53] Yet despite the impossibility of truly 'consensual' intercourse between master and slave, deep attachments sometimes formed. The notorious overseer Thomas Thistlewood, whose diary (1750–86) records forced sexual relations with thousands of black and coloured women on Vineyard Pen and Egypt plantation in Jamaica, took his favourite lover, Phibbah, as his 'slave wife', but she had sometimes to stay at home to attend her master, rather than spend nights with her 'husband', to the distress of them both.[54] Even taking Thistlewood's account with a grain of salt, the concept of the 'slave wife' is significant; designating the enslaved woman who shared sleeping quarters with her white lover without implying any monogamous obligation on his part, it bestowed a legitimacy upon the male ownership of enslaved women's bodies, implied a degree of mutual esteem and affection contrary to ideas about human property, and exposed the commodification of female sexuality upon which legitimate marriages were based. Indeed, enslaved men, stripped of almost all other masculine privileges, were allowed to retain in some circumstances the 'right' to chastise or beat women with whom they maintained connections or families.

White male perpetrators justified their conduct by imagining black women as sexually voracious, adept at the arts of pleasure, and incapable of fidelity, or by arguing that slave wives were a transcultural product, based on the mix of an alleged African polygyny and Christian culture with its ideals of monogamous couplings. In fact, while masters depended on their enslaved mistresses for gossip about slave relations and potential conspiracies, their 'wives' frequently used their positions to gain advantages for themselves and their children, or to seek retaliation for ill-treatment through domestic sabotage. Mulatto women, in particular, used their colour and attractiveness to ensure a favourable place within the hierarchies of plantation life; in the West Indies they almost never worked in the fields, but were

---

[53] Quoted in Walvin, *Black Ivory*, p. 172; Elizabeth A. Eldrede and Fred Morton, eds., *Slavery in South Africa: Captive Labor on the Dutch Frontier* (Boulder, Colo., 1994).

[54] Trevor Burnard, 'The Sexual Life of an Eighteenth Century Jamaican Slave Overseer', in Merrill Smith, ed., *Sex and Slavery in Early America* (New York, 1998), p. 176; Douglas Hall, *In Miserable Slavery: Thomas Thistlewood in Jamaica 1750–86* (London, 1989).

favoured servants in the household. Enslaved women of all hues could exploit their sexual or emotional intimacies to acquire property or establish themselves in trade and freedom. By the time of Thistlewood's death, Phibbah had secured the freedom of their son, John, and her own future manumission, as well as a small estate and two slaves of her own. Significantly, despite their clear emotional involvement, Phibbah and Thistlewood never married. As Bryan Edwards remarked, '(so degrading is the melancholy state of slavery) [that] no man who has the least respect for himself will think of marrying a female slave'. Neither, he concluded, 'is it within the reach of Human Authority to restrain the Appetites of Nature': hence sexual liaisons between white men and black women (although not, apparently, of black men and white women), and their product, mulatto children, would continue to be inevitable.[55]

Colonial law still attempted to circumscribe the rights of such offspring to shore up distinctions on the basis of national origin, caste, and class. Sumptuary legislation, lineage laws to determine when mixed-race people were allowed to call themselves 'English' ('free from all taint of the Negroe race') and so claim English rights and liberties, and, as in Jamaica, restrictions on the amount of property a planter could leave to his mulatto children in order to reduce the numbers of free coloureds who could become slave-owners themselves, were passed and refined over the century.[56] Yet the enslaved and the freed stayed one step ahead of efforts to legislate on juridical subjects, by continually inventing new practices to circumvent the intent of the law, adopting styles of dress, modes of economic entrepreneurship, and social relations that demonstrated their status as individuals with taste and resources of their own.

The enslaved's resistance to the masters' power extended from maroonage, or slave rebellion, to lethargy, entrepreneurship, and personal style. One of their more potent weapons was reproductive refusal. The demographic crisis inflicted by high mortality and low birth rates among the enslaved in the West Indies was for decades blamed on the black women themselves, whose supposedly lascivious or magical practices rendered them infertile, or who spirited away to Africa their newborns. There is limited evidence that enslaved women took measures to avoid producing more slaves, or passed such know-

---

[55] Bryan Edwards, John Carter Brown Library, Brown University, Providence, Rhode Island, Edwards MS, f. 17v.

[56] Winthrop Jordan, *White Over Black: American Attitudes toward the Negro 1550–1812* (Chapel Hill, NC, 1966), p. 176; Long, *History*, I, pp. 332–33.

ledge on to their daughters.[57] By exerting rights and power over their own persons and fates, enslaved men and women made perfectly clear that they were not property but human beings. Their success ultimately led planters to adopt pro-natalist policies to encourage reproduction. Beginning in the 1770s, slaves were encouraged to form Christian-style marriages, pregnant slaves were given reduced work loads, and financial payments for successful live births to enslaved mothers and enslaved midwives became commonplace. In 1809 Jamaica and the Leewards passed legislation exempting female slaves with 'six children living' from hard labour, and their owners from taxation on them.[58] As a result, the Leeward Islands joined Barbados in having a female majority in the slave population by the end of the century. These policies also had an important impact on gender representations and identities. As we have seen, the African woman's 'unfeminine' nature—masculine, muscular, aggressive, and strong, devoid of feminine tenderness and graciousness—had been seen as suiting her to the civilizing processes of slavery. As anti-slavery agitators began to emphasize the idea of 'woman' as the softer sex, to interpellate slave women as 'mothers', and thus to criticize the system of gender dominance that perverted this 'natural' role, slave-owners felt called upon to respond with examples of happily productive and reproductive slave women with access to prenatal and postnatal care. Thus, some two hundred years before feminists and eugenicists advocated maternalist policies in Europe, the contradictions of slavery had forged their invention at the colonial frontier. More immediately, owners and abolitionists, black men and white, began to make claims for and about the enslaved woman's body and reproductive potential to mobilize its powers for their own ends.

Within the theatres of power and debasement in plantation societies, white women played crucial but complicated roles. As economic agents and mistresses of slave-based households, they could appropriate the 'paternalism' of the masters with a vengeance. Recent work has stressed white women's agency in reproducing plantocratic values. Certainly many who left records displayed repugnance towards the institution of slavery and compassion for the slaves. Elizabeth Fenwick of Bridgetown, who ran a school for privileged white children, was distressed by the plight of slaves. Yet when her female slaves flouted her authority, lied and stole, and otherwise caused her

[57] Barbara Bush, *Slave Women in Caribbean Society 1650–1838* (London, 1990).

[58] Barbara Bush, 'Hard Labor: Women, Childbirth, and Resistance in British Caribbean Slave Societies', in David Barry Gaspar and Darlene Clark Hine, eds., *More than Chattel: Black Women and Slavery in the Americas* (Bloomington, Ind., 1996), pp. 198–99.

'endless trouble and vexation', she sold them and purchased male slaves.[59] Most mistresses brooked no insubordination, meting out physical punishment for the slightest perceived offences; the cruel white mistress became a notorious sign of the degrading effects of slavery on masters and enslaved alike.[60] Such behaviour may have been a retaliation for the low esteem in which they were held by their men. Although socially and symbolically superior by law and custom, white Creole women were considered pallid imitations of 'real' English ladies: gauche, indolent, extravagant, and prone to display the 'vulgar manners' of their black servants. Neither politeness nor gentility, it seems, could survive transplantation intact. The young ladies wanted 'that indispensable requisite of complete beauty, the glow of youthful vermilion,' Bryan Edwards opined, 'which heightens the graces of the English fair'.[61] The high rate of concubinage was thus blamed on white women's cultural and physical insufficiencies. On the other hand, white, black, and mulatto women organized slave brothels that serviced urban populations of slaves, merchants, planters, sailors, and soldiers, and so availed themselves of the formidable power of slaveowners over their property. The complexities and symbolic politics of the systems of power entangling gender, sex, class, and race in plantation societies meant that the categories of 'white' and 'black', 'men' and 'women', and 'slave' and 'free' were continually at risk, undercut by the performances of difference that all groups enacted in the tasks of everyday life and the commodification of freedom itself.

The violent interplay of cultures and peoples from Africa, Europe, and America in the British Atlantic generated exploitative social and gender relations that cast their shadow over British settlements and outposts in the rest of the world, from the slave coast of West Africa to the Pacific. In garrisons, forts, and factories, the use of enslaved and indigenous women's bodies, the regulation of sexuality and lineage, and the demarcation of gender roles and privileges constituted in no small part the substance of imperial power and dominion. The eighteenth-century history of colonial efforts to regulate quotidian intimate relations, and its link to the consolidation of a racialized dynamics of rule in British dominions, is just beginning

[59] Beckles, *Centering Women*, pp. 168–69.

[60] Mary Prince, *The History of Mary Prince: A West Indian Slave, Related by Herself* ed. Moira Ferguson (London, 1987), pp. 56–57.

[61] Bryan Edwards, *A History Civil and Commercial of the British Colonies in the West Indies*, 2 vols. (Dublin, 1793), I, pp. 127–28.

to receive serious attention.[62] Yet the 'gender frontier' remained the first line of offence of British imperial power.

The East India Company, as a representative (albeit a contested one) of British metropolitan authority, proved itself particularly vigilant in adjudicating social and sexual contact among the intermix of African, Indian, Asian, and European inhabitants in its domains. The supervisory and discretionary role of the masters in the Atlantic was taken on by the Company, sometimes at the behest of residents themselves. On the island of St Helena, for example, a strategic supply station and aspiring planter colony, the records of the Governor and Council are crowded with the grievances of planters and traders, both men and women, whose dependents and slaves were 'debauched' or harassed by neighbours, other slaves, or the sailors and soldiers who crowded into the taverns and halls of St James. In these disputes, the Council invariably supported the patriarchal rights of men, including the enslaved, over those of their subordinates.[63] At the East India Company's factory at Fort Marlborough in west Sumatra, the regulation of sexual and gender relations provided an index of moral and fair-minded British guardianship. Joseph Collet, Deputy-Governor from 1712 to 1716, targeted men and women, Malay, European, and Eurasian, for improvement. He made no connection with a local woman and discouraged the making of such alliances among his subordinates, which he held to be contrary to the proper exercise of the paternal and political responsibilities vested in him. Malay men were 'addicted to Women', Collet observed disapprovingly, likening women to other colonial products, such as sugar and tobacco, that enticed men into an enervating cycle of dependency and passion. The women were little better, he wrote to his sister-in-law in London. Native women were bestial, masculine, highly sexed, and oppressed by their men; the handful of British women were derisive imitations of their English counterparts, or, worse yet, the scabrous camp followers of the army.[64] The failed femininity of all these women signified and legitimated Collet's masculine direction and governance in

[62] For the nineteenth century, see chap. by Catherine Hall. See also Ann Laura Stoler, *Carnal Knowledge and Imperial Power: Race and the Intimate in Colonial Rule* (Berkeley, 2002). For the eighteenth century, see Indrani Chatterjee, *Gender, Slavery and Law in Colonial India* (Delhi, 1999); and Durba Ghosh, Colonial Companions: Bibis, Begums and Cancubines of the British in North India, 1760–1840 (Ph.D. Diss. University of California at Berkeley, 2000).

[63] Dispatches from St. Helena, 1731–40. unfol,. British Library, Oriental and India Office Collections (hereafter BL, OIOC), G/32/120.

[64] Collet to T. and J. Hollis, 24 Sept. 1712; BL OIOC, Eur[opean] MS 1153/2, f. 77; Collett to Ann Bedwell, 10 Oct, 1715, BL OIOC, Eur. MS. 1153/1, ff. 170–71.

the East Indies, and provided the proving ground for the 'honour' and 'sense' on which he staked his reputation.

Collet's self-denial would be an anomaly in the East Indies in the later eighteenth century. In British settlements in Madras and Calcutta, the absence of white women had led officers and servants of the East India Company to make 'connections' with local women. These 'connections' were less romantic than contemporaries or some historians have suggested. Unlike America, which had been conceptualized as a 'virgin land' free to be taken and shaped at will, India was recognized as an ancient if barbaric nation, and imagined as Oriental exoticism incarnate, conjured through images of the 'female mystery' of the *zenana* and the veil, the 'Oriental despotism' of polygamy, child marriage or *suttee* (widow immolation), and the 'effeminacy and resignation of spirit' of Hindu men.[65] In this setting, romance and marriage among high-ranking Company officials and Indian noblewomen, such as that of orientalist James Kirkpatrick, Resident at the Hyderabad Court, and Khair-un-Nissa, added to the mystique. Having and maintaining 'bibis', as they were called, was widespread among Company officials and servants. George Bogle, Secretary to the Company in the 1770s at Calcutta, maintained an alternative family of Indian mistress and children, which he kept secret from his relations 'at home', as did surveyor Richard Blechynden. In the latter's case, his 'wife' (a paid servant) and their children were 'betrayed' to his English relatives through the gossip and correspondence networks created by Company employees.[66] British and native conjugal relations would be discouraged and even prohibited by Cornwallis and Wellesley, in order to maintain the boundaries between British and native and to keep people of colour from becoming a significant factor in local politics, as they had in the West Indies and the Cape. But the practice of maintaining native mistresses and slave concubines continued into the nineteenth century, even if the strategies of managing them changed.[67]

[65] Robert Orme, *Government and People of Indostan* (London, 1753), Book IV, pp. 38–44; Thomas R. Metcalf, *Ideologies of the Raj* (Cambridge, 1995), pp. 8–9; 92–93.

[66] C. A. Bayly, *Empire and Information* (Cambridge, 1996), pp. 92–94; Kate Teltscher, 'Writing Home and Crossing Boundaries,' in Kathleen Wilson, ed., *A New Imperial History: Culture and Identity in Britain and the Empire 1660–1840* (Cambridge, 2004); Peter Robb, *Clash of Cultures? An Englishman in Calcutta in the 1790s* (London, 1998), pp. 40–43.

[67] See Chatterjee, *Gender, Slavery and Law*; Sudipta Sen, 'Colonial Aversions and Domestic Desires: Blood, Race, Sex and the Decline of Intimacy in Early British India', *South Asia*, XXIV (2001), pp. 36–37; P. J. Marshall, 'The Whites of British India, 1780–1830: A Failed Colonial Society?' *International History Review*, XII (1990), pp. 26–44.

The British effort to understand, convert, or exert mastery over 'despotic' Muslim and 'degenerate Hindoo' society also enabled the exploitation of indigenous power structures. The *burains* or 'old ladies' and midwives of the women's quarters as well as royal mistresses were initially used as spies and informants by Indian and British intelligence alike, crucial components in the 'information order' that allowed the British to consolidate their power on the subcontinent.[68] Poor women's continued willingness to attach themselves or their daughters to British soldiers and Company servants, on the other hand, was evidence of native women's degradation. In fact, Company officials tacitly encouraged British men to exploit indigenous female slavery to encourage assimilation, and to discourage 'unnatural' attachments between men. Local women, many of whom had been impressed by indigenous middlemen into joining the regimental bazaars or itinerant provisioning units that followed the army, were hired out by the day or night. Native women who 'married' a soldier or Company servant through a secret ceremony were left behind when the man returned 'home', as were their children. By an order of 1783, only children with two parents of European birth could be removed to England.[69] Following West Indian models and contrary to indigenous custom, the Company's administration of the British rule of law adjudicated the maternal descent of slavery and nationality. Hence although, as in Sumatra and Cape Colony, a conjugal connection to a British man could give native women limited agency in positioning themselves or their children for social advance if the father claimed them, the price was the extinction of maternal lineage.[70] The military orphanages established for such 'half-caste' children in the late eighteenth century were organized to maintain English distinctions of class and national belonging, while amplifying the resources of the Company. The Upper Orphanage, for officer's children, provided future unconvenanted servants of the Company, and Lower Orphan School pupils were educated as bandsmen for the military corps. Girls were trained as domestic servants for the households of officers and magistrates of the Company, or even selected while still children to be 'wives'.[71] This traffic in women and children

[68] Bayly, *Empire and Information*, pp. 19–20; 63; 69–71; 91–92.

[69] Indrani Chatterjee, 'Colouring Subalternity: Slaves, Concubines and Social Orphans in Early Colonial India', *Subaltern Studies*, X (1999), pp. 49–97, 85. The remainder of this paragraph is based on Chatterjee's ground-breaking essay.

[70] E.g., Robert Shell, 'The Tower of Babel: The Slave Trade and Creolisation at the Cape 1652–1834', in *Slavery in South Africa*, pp. 30–34.

[71] Chatterjee, 'Colouring Subalternity', pp. 89–90.

undergirded British wealth and power in India, while allowing the East India Company to maintain the boundaries between 'home' and 'abroad' by keeping the less savoury aspects of Empire hidden from metropolitan view.

From the 1770s onwards, East India merchantmen were carrying increasing numbers of married, betrothed, or marriageable women to the male servants of the Company on the subcontinent, perhaps in a move to stabilize the Company's transition from a trading to a political, fiscal, and territorial power. English women changed the tenor of Anglo-Indian life, presiding over the rituals and social performances of cultural affiliation, with the result that, for the moment, they had greater freedom to engage in public and social life than they would in the next century. In Calcutta, newly arrived visitors were greeted with an 'astonishing spectacle' of 'Asiatic splendour, combined with European taste exhibited around you on every side', as Eliza Fay exclaimed, 'under the forms of flowing drapery, stately palanquins, elegant carriages, innumerable servants, and all the pomp and circumstance of luxurious ease, and unbounded wealth'.[72] Here British women maintained hectic schedules of balls, concerts, plays, races, visits, and elaborate masquerades. The *Calcutta Gazette* liked to boast about 'our numerous beauties, who charm the eye and enthrall the ear', and declared them central to 'the rapid progress we are daily making in all those polite and refined entertainments, which have so strong a tendency to humanize the mind, and render life pleasing and agreeable'.[73]

Obviously a multi-directional cultural traffic resulted from British colonial experience in India. The social life of Anglo-Indian women in this period none the less demonstrated to the English themselves the fact of English cultural difference and modernity amid a traditional and barbaric society, and the inviolability of the settlers' tie to the 'mother country'. British women's presence certainly did not create pernicious racialized categories of national belonging among inhabitants.[74] But white, Christian, and properly married or chaperoned British ladies did give visible embodiment to the demarcations of national and lineage politics and the personal and political boundaries of rule. Their presence also offered an implicit critique of the arranged marriages of

---

[72] Eliza Fay, *Original Letters from India*, ed. E. M. Forster (New York, 1925), p. 170; 161.

[73] *Calcutta Gazette*, 21 Oct. 1784, BL OIOC, Eur. MS. A172.

[74] Cf. Perceval Spear, *The Nabobs: English Social Life in Eighteenth-Century India* (New York, 1983); E. M. Collingham, *Imperial Bodies: The Physical Experience of the Raj, c. 1800–1947* (London, 2001).

Indian society and the miscegenated alliances and cultural practices of Company officers and servants. As elsewhere in the Empire, British women held a social and symbolic position that defined appropriate relations of power and subordination and clarified who was entitled to claim the 'rights and privileges' of British people and who was not.

In settings where European women were absent, such as the South Pacific prior to the late 1780s, gender and sexual practices provided crucial but mutable markers of identity, difference, and dispossession for British men and Oceanic men and women alike. Indeed, the South Seas was a place where the 'sexual interface of the colonial encounter' generated endless fascination, both at the time and in generations to come.[75] The voyages of Captain Cook and the founding of New South Wales offer some intriguing examples of the centrality of gender to the conditions of possibility envisaged by British imperial power.

Captain Cook's celebrated explorations of the South Pacific which, among their many achievements, accurately mapped as well as 'discovered' Pacific island groups and surveyed the east coast of the unexplored continent of Australia, were stridently gendered as well as intensely nationalistic.[76] Twinning the sensibility of enlightened masculinity with the benevolent and humanitarian goals of 'discovery', the voyages sought to bring indigenous peoples 'within the pale of the offices of humanity... to relieve the wants of their imperfect state of society', and so evince British modernity and achievement.[77] The distinguished naturalists and artists on board (including Joseph Banks and Daniel Solander on the first voyage, Johann Reinhold Forster, his son, George, and William Hodges on the second, and John Webber on the third) as well as Cook and his crew were well-armed with Enlightenment social theory to gauge the 'stage' of material and civil progress of each new society encountered. Central, of course, to this taxonomic effort was the assessment of the place of women. 'It is the practice of all uncivilized nations to deny their women the common privileges of humans beings', George Forster noted. 'The ideas of finding happiness and comfort in the bosom of a companion only arise with a higher degree of culture.' Indeed, women, their physical and moral attributes, and social status, were more enthusiastically studied than in any previous colonial encounter. Through male

[75] Stoler, *Carnal Knowledge*, p. 43
[76] See Wilson, *Island Race*, chaps. 2 and 5, for an extended discussion of the voyages.
[77] Andrew Kippis, *The Life of Captain James Cook* (Basel, 1788), p. 371.

connoisseurship and observation, the details of Pacific island women's position were made vital to the Forsters' influential distinction between the two 'races' in the South Pacific and their divergently moving cultures and to the incorporation of South Sea peoples into History.[78]

Tahitian women, for example, had quickly become legendary for their beauty and their supposed proclivities for 'free love'. The overtly erotic dances performed by young Tahitian women, the polygamous sexual antics among the *arioi*, the élite group of performers and religious chiefs associated with the war god, Oro; and the more exogamous sexual trysts of their non-élite sisters with British tars, as they were were known, or sailors sparked fantasies in English, as in French, minds about the lack of guilt in the 'state of nature'. Tahitian society, however, was set apart by the Forsters for the high esteem and good treatment meted out to its women. Although their greater nonchalance towards matters of the flesh—alternately explained as a product of class (for example of aristocratic luxury or lower-class depravity), simplicity, or tropical excess—showed they had some way to go, Tahitian women were still taken quite literally to embody their society's progress.[79] In Johann Forster's account, their bodies were made to bear the signs of both their primitiveness and its transmutation to a higher stage: their tattooed buttocks, well-shaped breasts, and delicate demeanours, along with their 'wonderful quickness of parts and sensibility, a sweetness of temper, and a desire to please ... contribute to captivate the hearts' and soften the manners of their men, and so move their society towards civilization.[80] Among less advanced peoples, such as the Maoris (considered to be the most degenerate examples of the 'first' race) and the New Caledonians and Tannese (exemplars of the 'second' race), women were not only less attractive but also wretchedly treated by their husbands and offspring; nevertheless, their bodily and mental difference could still contribute towards the improvement of their men's intellectual faculties.[81] Women's appearance, behaviour, duties, and status thus provided evidence both of racial difference—understood by Forster to mean a line of descent that interacted with language, climate, and

---

[78] George Forster, *Voyage Round the World During the Years 1772–1775* (London, 1777), II, p. 324; Johann Reinhold Forster, *Observations made on a Voyage around the World* (London, 1778), pp. 421–22.

[79] James Cook in J. C. Beaglehole, ed., *Journals of Captain Cook*, 3 vols. (Cambridge, 1955–1965), I, pp. 127–28; II, pp. 238–39; G. Forster, *Voyage*, I, pp. 327–29; II, pp. 83–84, 132–34.

[80] Forster, *Observations*, p. 422.

[81] Ibid., pp. 419–20; 278–79; 419–20.

social practice to produce distinctive national cultures—and of women's 'universal' character as the agents of progress.[82]

Yet this apparently successful incorporation of South Pacific women into the 'history of man' masked the less salubrious aspects of the gender frontier of 'discovery': the venereal disease spread by British tars, the production of part-European children, the disruption of indigenous social and ecological systems, and destabilization of dynastic regimes. Further, 'gender' itself proved an extremely unstable marker of identity. Mistranslation and confusion abounded, and misdirected efforts marred attempts at contact and commerce, sexual and otherwise. British sailors were, of course, delighted that the favours of Tahitian beauties could be won by bits of ribbon or mirror. What appeared to them to be the 'libertinism' of Tahitian women, however, was in the women's eyes, a traffic in men that allowed them to exploit the arrival of boatloads of strangers for their own advantage. In the face of a Polynesian cosmogony, obscure to the voyagers, that linked sexuality with access to divine power and social advancement, British explorers complained of excessive female force: 'they would almost use violence to force you into their Embrace regardless whether we gave them any thing or not.'[83] Alternately, the explorers valiantly struggled to turn confusing encounters into facts that could be used in social theories of progress. John Marra, gunner's mate on the *Resolution*'s second voyage, theorized on the basis of his experience that Society Islanders were 'an effeminate race, intoxicated with pleasure, and enfeebled by indulgence'. Cook himself ventured a universal law on female chastity when, on the third voyage, contrary to expectations, the women of Van Diemen's Land (Tasmania) refused the tars' advances:

I believe it has generally been found amongst uncivilized people that where the Women are easy of access, the Men are the first who offer them to strangers, and where this is not the case they are not easily come at, neither large presents nor privacy will induce them to violate the laws of chastity or custom.[84]

Such misunderstandings of gender and sexual practice occurred on both sides. The Polynesians had their own doubts about the virility of their

---

[82] Harriet Guest, 'Looking at Women', in Nicholas Thomas and others, eds., *J. R. Forster, Observations Made on a Voyage Round the World* (Honolulu, 1996), pp. xli–liv.

[83] Samwell in Beaglehole, ed., *Journals of Captain Cook*, III, pp. 1085; 1159; Henry Homes, *Sketches in the History of Man*, 4 vols. (Edinburgh, 1778), II, pp. 80–81.

[84] [John Marra], *Journal of the Resolution's Voyage* (London, 1775), p. 54; Beaglehole, ed., *Journals of Captain Cook*, III, p. 56.

visitors, regarding the homosociality of the British explorers' sloop as suspect and even derisive. Sailors or officers who, like Cook, refused the embraces of island women became the object of taunts by locals. Conversely, at several places (Tahiti, New Zealand, Tanna, and Australia among them) the natives believed the manly British sailors to be women. This misapprehension led the British who were approached by native men to regard the natives as 'sodomites' and thus exhibiting the most depraved and the most aristocratic of sensibilities. In late eighteenth-century Britain such 'effeminacy' was under scientific scrutiny as a symptom of a moral weakness that 'pervert[ed] those appetites which nature has bestowed for the most beneficial purposes'.[85] The supposed exhibition of 'degenerated' and failed masculinity not only influenced future political judgements about colonization, but animated British missionaries, who eschewed Enlightenment niceties, to condemn the 'heathen' practices and 'depraved' sensibilities of South Pacific peoples as a whole. Within a year of their arrival in 1796, London Missionary Society members reported back to eager audiences in Britain on the human sacrifice, infanticide, polygamy, transvestism, uncontrolled sexuality, and total absence of revealed religion of indigenous Pacific society. Their missionary ethnography demonstrated not only the continued importance of gender and sexual practice to the motivations and targets of colonization, but also that the most absolutist definitions of difference were generated by religious rather than secular discourse.[86]

The effort to understand the *terra incognita* of the Pacific, as elsewhere, forced everyone involved to 'cross over', to some extent, into another culture, and envisage becoming different kinds of national and sexual subjects. This was self-consciously the case in the penal colony of New South Wales in 1788, where an insular British colony of convicts, guardians, and soldiers were deposited on the edge of a vast continent only partially charted by Cook and inhabited, in British eyes, by a 'savage' and strangely incurious people. Governor Phillip wanted the colony to be a model of enlightened reform, efficiency, and reclamation, where slavery was prohibited, humane and mutually beneficial relations with native peoples established, and convict men redeemed by hard work and, eventually, freedom as labourers, artisans, and even landholders. In fact, familiar patterns of coercion, subordination,

---

[85] Henry Home, Lord Kames, *Sketches of the History of Man* (London, 1778), I, p. 400–01; II, pp. 90–91; John Millar, *The Origin of the Distinction of Ranks* (Edinburgh, 4th edn., 1806), pp. 100–05; 180; 191, first quotation at p. 102.

[86] Wilson, *Island Race*, pp. 80–84.

and multi-directional cultural traffic quickly established themselves in relations between men, men and women, and British and Aboriginals. The initial
shortage of white women led to 'gross indecencies' that led Phillip to want to
make sodomy a capital crime. Women felons were soon sent out by the
boatload, a situation described by contemporaries as a 'floating brothel'.
Phillip had hoped arriving women could be ranked according to 'degree of
virtue', with some prepared for marriage and others, 'the most abandoned',
encouraged to live as prostitutes.[87] In the event, men and women, British and
Aboriginal, made unconventional arrangements that crossed the spectrum
from rape to marriage to concubinage. Many British men came to prefer
their Aboriginal mistresses, who they found to be 'soft and feminine', and
British women would escape their 'husbands' for better prospects, sometimes with other women. The customary and casual violence undergirding
officially sanctioned relationships was revealed by Governor King's
(1800–06) policy of allowing newly arrived convict women to be 'selected
and applied for' by 'industrious' settlers, 'with whom they either marry or
cohabit' despite the will or desire of the women themselves.[88] Aboriginal
women, too, were abducted as sexual partners by British men, leading to
intensifying violence between black and white on the frontier. Missionaries,
who began arriving in New South Wales in the 1810s, decried Aboriginal
women as 'bond-slaves of Satan', mistranslating the complex gender and
lineage systems in which female-exchange played an important diplomatic
role. The consequent depiction of Aboriginal women as oppressed by cruel
menfolk, and of the absence of recognizable households through which
Aboriginals could be redeemed, gave rise to the practice of collecting children in the effort to attract their kin to the missions.[89] The cultural and
topographical mappings of Pacific exploration and colonization that
changed the world thus also suggested that late Enlightenment ideas of
sexual difference and 'natural' and self-evident gender roles could be disrupted, rather than confirmed, by the 'arts of discovery' as by the practices of
everyday life.

[87] Alan Atkinson, *The Europeans in Australia: A History* (Oxford, 1997), pp. 129–30.

[88] Tim Flannery, ed., *Watkin Tench 1788* (Melbourne, 1996), p. 55; Joy Damousi, *Depraved and Disorderly: Female Convicts, Sexuality and Gender in Colonial Australia* (Cambridge, 1997); Michael Flynn, *The Second Fleet: Britain's Grim Convict Armada of 1790* (Sydney, 2001), pp. 99–100.

[89] Annette Hamilton, 'Bond-Slaves of Satan: Aboriginal Women and the Missionary Di-
lemma,' in Margaret Jolly and Martha Macintyre, eds., *Family and Gender in the Pacific: Domestic Contradictions and the Colonial Impact* (Cambridge, 1989), pp. 236–58; 252.

This survey of gender, Empire, and modernity in the eighteenth century has demonstrated that gender functioned in symbolic and material ways to consolidate and maintain British dominion in transoceanic settings. The distinctions between colonizers and colonized, British and 'natives', black and white, free and unfree all relied on mobilizing gender difference to demonstrate and sustain the historical and cultural distance between British and indigenous or enslaved people. Such efforts were uneven and sometimes unsuccessful. The 'rule of law' in British colonies across the globe, however, had at its heart distinctions of nation, lineage, and gender that were deemed indispensable to imperial projects and to the maintenance of the supposed gulfs between 'home' and 'abroad'. Women's productive, reproductive, and symbolic bodies were central to these projects. Moving through the Empire armed with essentializing ideas about 'national characters' and 'stages' of civilization, British explorers, traders, and colonists saw in indigenous and enslaved women evidence of cultural inferiority and backwardness, but they also felt desire for them.[90] The racialized versions of sexual difference forged in colonies, with their complex entanglements of recognition, desire, and disavowal, would be brought back to Britain in the guise of the degraded sexualities of subaltern women at 'home'. As the outmoded languages of women's overriding lust were projected on to native and enslaved peoples and creole colonials, femininity and womanhood were defined in terms that distinguished not just British women from savages, but British middle-class women from working women: in both cases, capacity for labour, sexual proclivities and lusts, and fecundity become the markers through which proper femininity and its variants were signified. The innovative discourses and practices of gender and national differentiation—of English women's sexual delicacy and of indigenous, enslaved, and subaltern women's debased femininities—thus travelled across the networks of Empire to shape domestic gender ideologies and provide the materials for the language of class in the nineteenth century. The 'basis for a new order of sex and gender' that Thomas Laqueur has identified as emerging 'in or about the late eighteenth century' had in fact already been formulated through the practices and ideologies of colonization and slavery, which bequeathed it to metropolitan modernity as 'a critical issue of political theory and practice'.[91]

[90] Morgan, 'Some could Suckle', p. 191.

[91] Thomas Laqueur, *Making Sex: Body and Gender from the Greeks to Freud* (Cambridge, Mass., 1990), pp. 4–5.

Select Bibliography

HILARY MCD. BECKLES, *Centering Women: Gender Discourses in Caribbean Slave Society* (Kingston, 1999).

KATHLEEN M. BROWN, *Good Wives, Nasty Wenches and Anxious Patriarchs: Gender, Race and Power in Colonial Virginia* (Chapel Hill, NC, 1996).

BARBARA BUSH, *Slave Women in Caribbean Society 1650–1838* (London, 1990)

INDRANI CHATTERJEE, *Gender, Slavery and Law in Colonial India* (London and New Delhi, 1999).

JOY DAMOUSI, *Depraved and Disorderly: Female Convicts, Sexuality and Gender in Colonial Australia* (Cambridge, 1997).

MARTIN DAUNTON and RICK HALPERN, eds., *Empire and Others: British Encounters with Indigenous Peoples, 1600–1850* (Philadelphia, 1999).

DURBA GHOSH, *Colonial Companions: Sexual Transgression, Racial Mixing and Gendered Order in Early Colonial India, 1760–1840* (Forthcoming).

MARGARET JOLLY and MARTHA MACINTYRE, eds., *Family and Gender in the Pacific: Domestic Contradictions and the Colonial Impact* (Cambridge, 1989).

ANN MARIE PLANE, *Colonial Intimacies: Indian Marriage in Early New England* (Ithaca, NY, 2000).

KATHLEEN WILSON, *The Island Race: Englishness, Empire and Gender in the Eighteenth Century* (London, 2003).

—— ed., *A New Imperial History: Culture, Identity, Modernity, 1660–1840* (Cambridge, 2003).

3

Of Gender and Empire: Reflections on the Nineteenth Century

CATHERINE HALL

In 1861 Herman Merivale concluded the new edition of his popular *Lectures on Colonization and Colonies*. Merivale had occupied a senior position in the Colonial Office since 1848 and was in a good position to reflect on Britain and Empire. 'The sense of national honour', he argued, 'pride of blood, tenacious spirit of self-defence, the sympathies of kindred communities, the instincts of a dominant race, the vague but generous desire to spread our civilization and our religion over the world', it was all this which made the British an imperial people. National honour was at stake in ruling the ever-expanding Empire, and ensuring Britain's position as a Great Power. Britons were hardy in their self-defence, when faced with the might of any enemy. Anglo-Saxons were proud of their blood, and of the racial instincts which marked them out as a people who would conquer and propagate, in the name of their superior civilization and their Protestant religion. Their 'kindred communities' were the white Britons who had settled across the globe. 'The alliance of blood, and language, and religion', Merivale argued, 'bids fair to subsist as long as human society endures'.[1] It was the bonds of blood which made a race, and the notion of civilization—the culture of that race—which together tied gender irrevocably to empire.

Civilization, for men and women like Merivale, was a term which described their own society, an industrial capitalist society, divided by class, united in its nationhood, its Protestantism, and its white ethnicity, with a gender order built on the notion of separate spheres for men and women. An

Thanks to Philippa Levine and Ann Whitehead, and audiences from the Department of Anthropology at University College London, the Faculty Seminar of the Centre for the Study of Social Transformation at the University of Michigan at Ann Arbor, and the Department of History at the University of Sussex for comments on earlier drafts of this chapter.

[1] Herman Merivale, *Lectures on Colonization and Colonies* (London, 1861), p. 675.

imperial people had not only to reproduce themselves but to seed themselves in their colonies, making new Britons across the globe. If men's imperial work was to 'discover', to explore, to conquer, and dispossess others, women's was to reproduce the race, to bear children, maintain their men, and make families and households. In that sense, the work of Empire was gendered work. This was part of British commonsense. Blood tied white Anglo-Saxons one to another, race spoke to the characteristics of that hardy and determined people, it was civilization which offered the others both within and without, the poor and dispossessed of both nation and Empire, the possibility of being Britons, whether subjects or citizens. Other peoples, other races, could be British subjects, they might even learn to be like Britons, to be civilized, but civilization required a particular gender order, and it was part of the work of Empire to teach it.

Merivale re-published his *Lectures*, first delivered in 1839, in 1861. In the late 1830s he shared the optimism characteristic of liberal thinkers at that time. Britain had led the world and abolished slavery, Europe's destiny lay in conquest and domination, but native peoples would either die out or be brought to civilization. The areas of new white settlement offered hopes of an Empire, part of which would be built on principles of internal self-government and commercial freedom. The greatest days of Britain's Empire, to be compared with that of Greece and Rome, were ahead. By mid-century, however, Merivale's mood was somewhat different. Disillusionment with the conduct of freed slaves both in the Caribbean and Africa, and fears about Maori aggression in New Zealand, combined with terror provoked by the 'Indian Mutiny' of 1857 when Britain reacted to the challenge mounted to white supremacy in India. Fears emanating from settlers in the colonies were articulated in new ideas about the nature of racial difference and fostered a less benign view of Empire, one which informed the 'scramble for Africa' and the popular imperialism of the 1880s and 1890s.

The nineteenth century was a period of expansion for the British Empire. The late eighteenth century had been a time of trouble, with the loss of the American colonies, serious worries about the nature of British rule in India, and problems both in the Caribbean and Ireland. By 1815, however, there had been a strong recovery in territorial as well as administrative and military terms. In 1820, after the Napoleonic Wars, 26 per cent of the world's population lived on soil defined as British. The area under East India Company rule in India had grown hugely since 1756, and conquest had brought significant new lands. The colonial state was exercising its power more effectively and experimenting with forms of aristocratic military government.[2] There was a massive expansion of European interference with non-European societies, and 'the forging of wholly new forms of dependency worldwide', particularly with the shift from slavery to indenture and other forms of forced labour.[3] Imperial expansion, both formal and informal, was intimately connected to Britain's growing economic dominance as the most advanced of industrial capitalist societies. By the late nineteenth century, there was a growing recognition that this pre-eminent position could no longer be assumed, and that the rivalry of Germany and the United States threatened Britain's global position. Still, between 1815–1914 the European balance of power was not, for the most part, disrupted.

The growing claims of Britons in the new areas of white settlement produced fierce conflicts with indigenous peoples and forms of resistance across the Empire. By the mid-1860s it seemed that Indians, Afro-Jamaicans, Xhosa, Maori, and Khoisan had all been defeated, and Aboriginal populations decimated by disease, famine, and violence. The power of settlers had been recognized in forms of responsible government, and the dependence of 'native' peoples in forms of direct rule. The explicit distinctions between those white British subjects of Empire who claimed, as Lord Mansfield had put it, 'that every Englishman carries with him English liberties into any unoccupied country in which he may settle', and those brown and black British subjects who were ruled as dependent peoples became more marked over the century.[4] White Britons in Australia, New Zealand, the Cape, and Canada negotiated their ambivalent position as both colonizer and colonized, both not quite British, and not quite metropolitan. Yet it was they who were the colonizers in the territories they claimed, the front line in the expropriation of land and labour. For red, brown, and black subjects of Empire, colonial rule meant the 'rule of colonial difference', the rule that distinguished the colonizers from the colonized, and this was predicated on the power of the metropole over its subject peoples.[5] A harsh logic of racial difference formed the prelude to the partition of Africa in the late nineteenth

---

[2] C. A. Bayly, *Imperial Meridian. The British Empire and the World 1780–1830* (London, 1989), pp. 3, 8–9.

[3] C. A. Bayly, 'The British and Indigenous Peoples, 1768–1860: Power, Perception and Identity', in Martin Daunton and Rick Halpern, eds., *Empire and Others. British Encounters with Indigenous Peoples 1600–1850* (London, 1999), p. 27.

[4] Mansfield is quoted in Merivale, *Lectures*, p. 638.

[5] Partha Chatterjee, *The Nation and its Fragments: Colonial and Post-Colonial Histories* (Princeton, 1993), p. 10.

century, the high noon of popular imperialism in Britain itself, and the emergence of nationalist and anti-colonial movements.

How was the 'rule of colonial difference' established in this period of expansion and consolidation? How did white male colonists, traders, settlers, or colonial officials, or white missionary wives or teachers separate themselves from 'native' populations and construct 'grammars of difference' which would legitimate their right to possess the land and rule over others?[6] One of the critical carriers of that difference became their white skin. As brown and black skin, particular hair types and bone structures, came to signify inferiority, so whiteness became a signifier of power. This was always a relational phenomenon: whiteness carried with it particular privileges from which those with brown or black skins were excluded. And whiteness had its own hierarchies: poor whites across the Empire, sometimes Irish, provide the clearest examples of those who were in danger of not being quite white enough. Creole whites, the plantocracy of the West Indies, for example, were seen as not properly white, not properly British. White skin in itself was not always enough to secure full belonging whether to the nation or the Empire. Furthermore, whiteness was always unstable. Intersecting as it did with other axes of differentiation, whether of caste, class, gender, age, religion, or sexuality, whiteness was 'co-constructed' in relations of inequality.[7] Whiteness was the sign of dominance, not of subordination. It posed as a non-racial category, yet was produced 'from the cauldron of racial thinking', its normative presence marked by its differentiated others.[8] The characteristics of whiteness were rarely explicitly delineated. They provided the absent presence; the norm against which the inadequacies of other races were defined.

Who was white? This was a supposedly straightforward issue but was often not so. Given the privileges and power that whiteness carried in the colonial

---

[6] The 'grammar of difference' is a concept employed by Frederick Cooper and Ann Laura Stoler, 'Between Metropole and Colony. Rethinking a research agenda', in Cooper and Stoler, eds., *Tensions of Empire. Colonial Cultures in a Bourgeois World* (Berkeley, 1997), pp. 1–56. On the centrality of difference to the writing of imperial histories, see Catherine Hall, 'Thinking the Postcolonial, Thinking the Empire', in Hall, ed., *Cultures of Empire. A Reader. Colonizers in Britain and the Empire in the Nineteenth and the Twentieth Centuries* (Manchester, 2000), pp. 16–20.

[7] Ruth Frankenberg, *The Social Construction of Whiteness: White Women, Race Matters* (London, 1993), p. 237.

[8] Gail Lewis, 'Racialising Culture is Ordinary', in Elizabeth de Silva and Tony Bennett, eds., *Contemporary Culture and Everyday Life* (Durham, 2004).

world, questions of racial mixing and sexual control were crucial to the maintenance of imperial authority. Those of mixed race could challenge the distinction between colonizer and colonized and act as sources of subversion, threats to white prestige. The production of the distinction between those who were colonists and those who were colonized was always a matter of 'mutual constitution': making self, making others. Furthermore, colonial discourses were always gendered, articulating men and women as having different characteristics and mapping hierarchies of racial difference on to those of gender difference, and vice versa. Gender-specific sexual sanctions and prohibitions were ways of marking power and prescribing the boundaries of race.[9] In making despised or desired others, the colonizers made themselves; in demarcating black masculinity they enunciated white masculinity, in demarcating brown femininity, they elevated white femininity. Colonial discourses were critical to this process of mutual constitution. These were particular ways of talking about, representing, and behaving towards colonial peoples and their cultures, for the term 'discourse' refers to practices as well as textual representations, whether verbal or visual. From the moment of first encounter, the British struggled to explain and codify the men and women on the various sites of their expanding Empire with their different skin colours and sexual and bodily practices, their religions, languages, and cultures. They mapped hierarchies from Anglo-Saxon to Aboriginal, from African to Pacific Islanders, hierarchies which were never stable, for race, like gender, is a matter of social construction. There were no essential meanings of blackness and whiteness, of masculinity or femininity, only discursive practices which articulated and organized particular sets of relations through the workings of knowledge and power. The characteristics associated with different races shifted, as, for example, the sexually degraded enslaved African woman of the abolitionist imagination became the freed and domesticated wife and mother, or the 'docile and loyal sepoy' of the pre-1857 British imagination, became the 'treacherous nigger' of the Mutiny.

James Mill in his *History of British India*, first published in 1818, articulated in ways which were to be constantly repeated, the lessons which he had learned from Scottish Enlightenment thinkers as to women's position as an indicator of social advancement.[10] 'Nothing can exceed', he suggested, 'the habitual contempt which the Hindus entertain for their women ... They are

[9] Ann Laura Stoler, *Carnal Knowledge and Imperial Power. Race and the Intimate in Colonial Rule* (Berkeley, 2002).
[10] See chap. by Kathleen Wilson.

held, accordingly, in extreme degradation.' 'Among rude people', he continued, 'the women are generally degraded; among civilized people they are exalted.' As societies advanced, 'the condition of the weaker sex is gradually improved, till they associate on equal terms with the men, and occupy the place of voluntary and useful coadjutors'.[11] Such ideas, linking 'progress' to women's 'improvement' and forms of companionate marriage, have had a powerful life since the eighteenth century. Civilization in Mill's day meant a set of 'proper' relations between men and women. Thus in particular colonial discourses, the Indian woman was constructed as a degraded victim of her barbaric society, the Bengali man as effeminate and incapable of caring for his own dependants, the freed African man in the Caribbean as industrious and independent. The standards by which the masculine and feminine characteristics of other peoples were defined and judged were those of the one 'truly civilized' society, Britain. And Britain celebrated, in theory at least, the family as the keystone of that civilization, with its manly, independent, male heads of households, dignified by their labour and operating in the world of work and politics, and its feminine, dependent, wives and mothers, confined to the sphere of home.[12] This superior form of family, with its elevated yet inferior female, was critical to the British legitimation of colonial rule.

Empire was about the political, military, economic, and cultural exploitation and domination of the British over subject peoples. Britain's colonial projects were always in relation to those of other empires, as French, Dutch, or German planters, or slave-holders, or traders intersected, whether in the Caribbean, Africa, or South-East Asia. In this chapter, however, the focus is on the specificities of the British Empire, mapping it as a field of gender relations. Metropolitan discourses claimed power across nation and Empire, and the emphasis here is on the ways in which Britons tried to shape their own lives, and those of subject peoples, in varied sites of Empire. The practices of colonial rule were different from those of the metropole. Working-class Britons were not thought to be the same as Aboriginal or African peoples, even though a similar language might sometimes be used to describe them. Each site of Empire had its own history, its own set of economic and social relations, its own peoples, its own patterns of gender

---

[11] James Mill, *The History of British India*, 2 vols. (1818; New York, 1968), pp. 309–10.

[12] Leonore Davidoff and Catherine Hall, *Family Fortunes. Men and Women of the English Middle Class, 1780–1850* (1987; London, 2002). See the introduction to the new edition for an assessment of the current thinking on 'separate spheres'.

relations, even though a common language of race was employed to map those peoples.

Colonial rule meant interventions in varied indigenous institutions and practices, the forms of politics and civil society. It depended in part on directives from the metropole, but always translated by particular people, whether colonial officials, the military, or settlers. The contexts were always different, the forms of contention and resistance specific. There was no single colonial project, rather there were multiple colonial projects, often in tension with each other, those of missionaries, or sugar planters, or social reformers, or imperial governments, each constructing multiple subject positions. The practices of building settler societies in Australia or New Zealand, or operating a system of slavery or indentured labour in the Caribbean, or constructing colonial rule as legitimate in India, all depended in part on particular ideas of the family, of sexuality and reproduction, of manliness and femininity. In looking at the construction of the 'Hindoo woman', the creation of the mission family, and the demarcation of whiteness, both in settler societies and in India, this chapter aims to illuminate, through specific instances, something of the complex web of gender relations across the Empire. Much recent scholarship has emphasized the instability and fragility of colonial rule. Focusing instead on the multiple attempts to reconfigure gender relations in different locations recalls the power of the nineteenth-century metropole.

In this section the focus is on the set of related colonial discourses which constructed India as a degraded place in need of civilization, and which utilized the figure of the Indian woman, and particularly the Hindu woman, as the index of Indian society's desperate need for help. The idea that the British were saving Indian women from the barbarities of their archaic world, and that this was a necessary precondition for modernizing India, became a critical tool in the legitimation, whether amongst colonial officials, missionaries, or social reformers, whether utilitarian or evangelical, of their country's right to rule. This was a colonial discourse: a justification of conquest and domination, and a way of representing Indian women which assumed their inferiority to European women.

From the 1780s, when the British were set to become the real rulers of India, the practice of *suttee*, (widow-burning) became an issue. By the early nineteenth century, it had become a cause for concern in Britain too and was seen as symbolizing the degradation not only of Indian womanhood, but of Indian society more generally. The colonial state was primarily interested in the extraction and appropriation of revenues, commodities, and labour rather than in deliberately reconfiguring social relations. As a number of scholars have suggested, however, shifts in social, economic, and ideological relations associated with British rule resulted in a reconstellation of 'the mutually consolidating systems of caste, class and patriarchy'.[13] In the interplay between colonial officials and the emerging middle class, for example, indigenous male power over women and children was undermined in some respects, reaffirmed in others. The construction of the 'Hindoo' woman provides one example of this process, both in colonial and indigenous discourse. The focus here, however, is on the impact of colonial discourse.

In the late eighteenth and early nineteenth century, British scholars attempting to make sense of India adopted the notion that there were distinct and fixed communities of Hindus and Muslims with established sets of beliefs and particular characteristics. Muslim men were defined as violent, despotic, and masculine, Hindu men as passive, indolent, and effeminate, easily conquered whether by Mughal Emperors or the British. The effeminacy of Hindu men, especially Bengalis, brought with it the degradation of Hindu women. Debates over *suttee*, a predominantly upper-caste Hindu practice, had started in the 1780s. Its prohibition by the British in 1829 was greeted as an indication, both by officialdom and Indian social reformers, that the process of emancipation had begun. The official British position on matters of religious practice amongst their subject peoples in India was one of toleration. In reality, however, the ascendance of liberal reforming perspectives towards India from the late 1820s meant there was intervention in matters that were seen as particularly undermining to British notions of civilization.

The degradation of Hindu women was symbolized for the British by their seclusion and a life of idleness associated with over-sexualized bodies. By rescuing them, the British could both reinforce their own masculinity and legitimate their rule.[14] Widow-burning was a potent symbol of what was wrong with India. Importantly, however, the British justified intervention by reference to indigenous doctrine. Some Hindus claimed the practice to be the duty of a virtuous wife. By burning on the funeral pyre with her husband, both would enjoy 'heavenly pleasures'. Other Hindu pundits, however,

---

[13] Lata Mani, *Contentious Traditions. The Debate on Sati in Colonial India* (Berkeley, 1998), p. 5.

[14] Thomas R. Metcalf, *Ideologies of the Raj. New Cambridge History of India*, Vol. III. 4 (Cambridge, 1994), p. 94.

disputed that there was scriptural authority for the practice. Colonial officials, whether they were for or against prohibition, shared the view that religion was central to the indigenous population, that 'natives' were submissive to its dictates, and that *suttee* had a religious basis. Furthermore, they stressed that the widow was a victim, either of barbaric Hindu men forcing her to accompany her husband to the pyre, or, if it was an apparently voluntary act, of her subjection to the appalling dictates of religion. Widows were victims who must be saved by the civilizing power of the colonial state.

In 1813 parliamentary debate on the renewal of the charter of the East India Company provided an opportunity to raise the issue of *suttee* in the metropole. William Wilberforce, a prominent evangelical and key spokesman in the campaign against the slave trade, stressed the degradation of indigenous society representing the evils of Hindoostan as 'family, fireside evils', paying particular attention to the treatment of women.[15] It was Britain's Christian responsibility, in India as in the West Indies, to ensure that its rule brought with it moral improvements. Missionaries active in India used *suttee* to demonstrate the appalling condition of Indian women and the necessity, therefore, of evangelical work. India was represented as a place of timeless superstition, where sacrifice and self-abuse were all too prevalent. By the 1820s missionary and evangelical audiences in Britain were familiar with the terrifying effects of Hindu idolatry on Indian character. The Hindu widow was seen as the victim of her family, her community, and her religion which was characterized by the British as superstitious, ritually processing around the pyre and burning women alive. The widow was represented as without agency: in need of others who were prepared to save her. The petitions and public meetings of the 1820s did succeed in putting pressure on the Government. Combined with the actions of reformers in India, who had taken up the question, this pressure resulted in a prohibition in 1829.

The degraded 'Hindoo' woman surfaced again and again in nineteenth-century colonial discourses. Issues of child marriage, the treatment of widows, the segregation of women, and polygamy, all provided opportunities to compare the victimized status of Indian women with the freedom of British women. 'The daughters of India are unwelcomed at their birth', as one writer

[15] Clare Midgley, 'From Supporting Missions to Petitioning Parliament: British Women and the Evangelical Campaign against *Sati* in India, 1813–30', in Kathryn Gleadle and Sarah Richardson, eds., *Women in British Politics, 1760–1860. The Power of the Petticoat* (Basingstoke, 2000), p. 75.

put it in 1880, 'untaught in childhood, enslaved when married, accursed as widows, and unlamented at their death.'[16] It was these signs of cruelty and depravity which made British intervention necessary and legitimized colonial rule. Action took varied forms from missionary work to social reform initiatives, sometimes supported by British feminists. For the colonial state, the incapacity of Indian men to care properly for their women was a sign of their incapacity to rule themselves. Both weak men and abjected women needed to be regulated. It was up to the British to introduce systems of law and social reform which would 'improve' the indigenous population. While the particular foci of concern shifted across the decades, persistent stereotypes emerged.[17] Hindu men were seen as engaging in unnatural practices, while the women were characterized as passive and over-sexed. Both stereotypes were part of a system of symbolic constitution, 'of inferior "others" *and* the enlightened self of Europe.'[18]

This process of symbolic cultural constitution was Empire-wide as can be seen in the context of imperial labour. The figure of the degraded Indian woman was central to the debates over indenture from the 1830s to the early twentieth century. This time she was a poor labouring woman, alongside Indian men who, on this occasion, were constructed both as victims and as perpetrators of archaic Hindu practices. After the abolition of slavery, fully operative in 1838, West Indian planters were anxious to ensure uninterrupted sugar production on their estates. They were reluctant to pay decent wages and, not surprisingly, freed men and women were unwilling to remain on the plantations. Drawing on the experience of Mauritius, planters began to investigate the possibilities of winning British government support for the importation of Indian indentured labour to the Caribbean. John Gladstone, father of future Liberal Prime Minister, William Ewart Gladstone, used his extensive contacts across the Empire to develop a plan for indentured labourers on his sugar estates in Guiana. Labourers from the hills to the north of Calcutta were said to be, 'very docile and easily managed, and

[16] Quoted in Jane Haggis, ' "Good Wives and Mothers" or "Dedicated Workers"? Contradictions of Sisterhood in the "Mission of Sisterhood", Travancore, South India', in Kalpana Ram and Margaret Jolly, eds., *Maternities and Modernities. Colonial and Postcolonial Experiences in Asia and the Pacific* (Cambridge, 1998), pp. 85–86.

[17] Mrinalini Sinha, *Colonial Masculinity. The 'Manly Englishman' and the 'Effeminate Bengali' in the Late Nineteenth Century* (Manchester, 1995).

[18] Himani Bannerji, 'Age of Consent and Hegemonic Social Reform', in Clare Midgley, ed., *Gender and Imperialism* (Manchester, 1998) p. 38.

appear to have no local ties, nor any objection to leave their country'.[19] Gladstone's plan was the prelude for the transportation of over one million Indians to parts of Africa, Mauritius, South-East Asia, the Pacific, and the West Indies. This was a new system of unfree labour, operating across the Empire, utilizing accumulated 'knowledges' about the character of Indians and the experience of planters and governors in different sites of Empire.

In the wake of the first attempts to use indentured labour in the 1830s, abolitionists, horrified by what they saw as an attempt to reinstitute slavery under another name, organized opposition. As with the debate over the prohibition of *suttee*, both sides assumed Indian degradation and the need for indigenous peoples to be rescued and improved. The planters focused on the kindness they were doing in offering 'natives' the opportunities for stable work, the possibilities of accumulating money, and the access they would have to civilizing processes. British subjects, argued many, should have the right to carry their manual labour to the most productive market. Planters claimed that life would be much better in the West Indies than in India. Poverty-stricken landless labourers could not be 'men'. They were emasculated by their dependence. Migration, it was argued, meant improvement. Productive labour brought full masculinity with it. Those who 'went to Mauritius monkeys', it was claimed, 'returned to India men'.[20] The opponents of indenture represented Indian workers as vulnerable to abuse by ruthless recruiting agents and employers. They were starving, desperate, and abandoned men and women, wretched creatures, who should be protected by the imperial government. The conditions of indentured labour were all too reminiscent of slavery and required similar action. The numbers of men were grossly out of proportion to women (for the planters assumed that men would make better plantation workers than women), family life was violated, and women exposed to the dangers of sexual abuse both by masters and their rapacious fellow-workers. Indian men were likely to be castigated for their lust and immorality but at the same time their supposed docility. These effeminate men were supposed to act as an example to African workers in the Caribbean or in Natal, inciting them to compete. This marked the beginning of tensions between communities, tensions

---

[19] Cited in Madhavi Kale, *Fragments of Empire. Capital, Slavery, and Indian Indentured Labor Migration in the British Caribbean* (Philadelphia, 1998), p. 16.

[20] Cited in Kale, *Fragments of Empire*, p. 82.

which have had a powerful life right into the twenty-first century. While each site of Empire had its own specificities, each was locked into an imperial division of labour.

What of the women? Planters did not regard Indian women as capable agricultural workers and would have preferred a male labour force, particularly since they neither expected nor wanted the women to settle. Questions of reproduction, therefore, were not initially seen as critical, especially as children could not automatically be pressed into indentureship.[21] The Government of India, however, and the imperial government, under pressure from abolitionists, insisted on the importance of a female presence. Indenture, like slavery, was thought to encourage immorality while family life, conversely, was seen as critical to the making of a healthy social body. Though recruiters were encouraged to find women of a 'better class' who were already attached to families, in practice many of those women who emigrated were single. Amongst the planters, recruiters, and immigration officers, stereotypes abounded of the low caste and 'loose nature' of Indian female migrants, their vicious and immoral character, and their propensity to move from man to man. They were castigated as mercenary and responsible for all the major social ills on the plantations.[22] An official enquiry in Fiji at the end of the nineteenth century, inspired by concerns at the murder rate amongst indentured labourers, concluded that sexual jealousy was the key. As the immigration inspector put it:

the sexual requirements of a class of men untrained in self-control—the facilities afforded by the nature of habitation and mode of life—the fact that the women are necessarily recruited from among those unsettled, and of more or less loose morals, that the men *will* satisfy their passions, and that the women *do* supply the demand—these facts show each congregation of Indians in the customary sexual proportions to be a veritable hotbed of intrigue, a nursery of jealousy and murder.[23]

---

[21] Jo Beall, 'Women under Indenture in Colonial Natal 1860–1911', in Colin Clarke and others, eds., *South Asians Overseas. Migration and Ethnicity* (Cambridge, 1990) p. 66; Verene Shepherd, 'Gender, Migration and Settlement: The Indentureship and Post-indentureship Experience of Indian Females in Jamaica, 1845–1943', in Verene Shepherd and others, eds., *Engendering History. Caribbean Women in Historical Perspective* (Kingston, 1995), p. 237.

[22] See Brij V. Lal, 'Kunti's Cry: Indentured Women on Fiji Plantations', *Indian Economic and Social History Review*, XXII, 1 (1985), pp. 55–71; and Lal, 'Labouring Men and Nothing More: Some Problems of Indian Indenture in Fiji', in Kay Saunders, ed., *Indentured Labour in the British Empire* (London, 1984).

[23] Quoted in Lal, 'Kunti's Cry', pp. 60–61.

The main employing company in Fiji often discouraged marriage amongst its employees. This was anathema to their opponents who bewailed the barrack-like housing which was provided, the lack of privacy for couples, and the consequent effects on sexual practices. At the same time, employers vociferously complained of the difficulties posed by female indentured labour. Women were more expensive to recruit, transport, and maintain, they argued, and they introduced trouble and strife on to the plantations. Women indentured labourers, like the widows who were burned, were rarely represented as agents. Rather they were seen as symbols or vessels, 'the medium through which some proscribed sexual practices—same-sex and interracial sex—were to be controlled, as well as the medium through which *other* proscribed sexual and social behaviours—for example, prostitution, promiscuity, and their alleged consequences like jealousy and violence— were introduced and proliferated'.[24] Indenture reduced all workers, whether men or women, Brahmin or low menial caste, to the status of 'coolie', the universal nomenclature. But 'coolies' were gendered and the idea of the degraded Hindu woman was central to the discourse of both the supporters and critics of indenture.

The figure of the abject Hindu woman, first imagined by the British as part of the legitimation of their rule in India, travelled across the circuits of Empire. In the mapping of difference (which was part of the construction of colonial discourses on different sites), not only between metropole and colony, but also travelling from one 'periphery' to another, she was ranked in a complex hierarchy, never fixed, which marked off the different subject peoples of the Empire. The 'Hindoo' woman was the degraded symbol of the weakness and passivity of her own culture, doomed to subjection by the Muslims or the British, but her abjection was less extreme than that of Aboriginal or 'Hottentot' women, people seen as without culture. The ways in which the British constituted subject peoples as in competition with one another has had lasting and terrible effects, whether in India, Guiana, or Fiji.

The missionary movement played a vital part in the attempt to take Christian and British values into the many parts of Empire, to rescue 'the heathen' in his or her many guises. Missions, of whatever complexion operated differently in different colonial sites. Though they went through significant changes between the late eighteenth century and decolonization,

[24] Kale, *Fragments of Empire*, p. 166.

they shared important characteristics. All were concerned with saving sinners and promoting a new way of life for their converts. The major missionary societies were founded at the end of the eighteenth century, a part of the evangelical revival, and a response to the upheavals associated with the French Revolution. In the 1820s and 1830s evangelical missionaries shared an empowering utopian vision of the changes which a small number of dedicated men and women could make in the beliefs and practices of innumerable 'heathens' across the globe.[25] At the heart of this project was the desire to turn sinners into new Christian subjects, living industrious, domesticated, and familial lives. Intimately linked to this view that all souls could be saved was the humanitarian notion that all peoples, whatever their colour or creed, were part of God's family. 'Natives' living in stages of barbarism could be improved and civilized. This was a different conception of racial difference from that which came to predominate in the late nineteenth-century Empire, when assumptions as to the fixity of racial types were much more prevalent.

In the early nineteenth century missionaries had an uneasy relation with the imperial government and its colonial officials. They were often critical of government policies and at odds with colonists. Yet they were also dependent on imperial power for protection and support in their work. This tension was particularly evident in the West Indies where many Nonconformist missionaries became powerfully identified with the struggle against slavery. In the hostile environment of Jamaica, for example, where planters were for the most part deeply antagonistic to the idea of bringing Christianity, with its dangerously radical potential, to the enslaved, missionaries often found themselves isolated. The missionaries were heavily dependent on each other, and on their supporters at home. Those who left Britain in the 1820s often had links with the anti-slavery movement and subscribed to a vision of the universal family of God. The enslaved were 'poor souls' to be rescued from sin and bondage. They were wretched victims locked in the double barbarisms of Africa and slavery. It was Britain's Christian duty, ordained by God in his providential plan for her Empire, to save these sinners. In the difficult work which missionaries faced, the family

---

[25] For a much longer discussion of the significance of the mission family in Jamaica and England, see Catherine Hall, *Civilising Subjects. Metropole and Colony in the English Imagination, 1830–1867* (Cambridge and Chicago, 2002). The utopian moment in the missionary movement could be seen as having a counterpart in the liberal project to reform India; see Metcalf, *Ideologies of the Raj*, chap. 2.

provided a haven, both in theory and practice, from the rigours of the world outside.

Most missionary societies liked their appointees to be married.[26] This reduced the risk of sexual encounters with 'native females', women who were imagined as desirable and depraved. Young single men could not be expected to withstand the alluring temptations of 'licentious savages' in hot climates. This understanding of young men's sexuality and of 'native' women's desirability was one which prevailed across the missionary societies whether working in South-East Asia, the Caribbean, or India. Although the figure of the 'native' woman would always have her specificities—the exotic beauty of the Polynesian, the ugly accoutrements of the Australian aboriginal, the sexualized body of the African—they shared the character of a degraded femininity.

Missionaries were thus best married, their masculinity tamed and domesticated to prepare them for the pitfalls of 'the field'. They needed companionate wives who would be helpmeets in the missionary enterprise. The evangelical faith which inspired these men and women was one which placed much emphasis on the religious household as the fount of morality in a wicked world. The experience of conversion, which was at the heart of evangelical faith, meant the making anew of the subject, whether man or woman. While the man was to be independent, following his vocation and supporting his wife and children, the woman was to be a wife and mother. The mission station which the couple established was at the centre of each new missionary enterprise, providing 'the object lesson of a civilised Christian home'.[27] From this base the man could organize his multiple activities: preaching, teaching, admonishing his flock, buying land, building chapels, maintaining connections with his brother missionaries, negotiating with the authorities, reporting to the home society, while his wife bore children, cared for home and family, taught the 'native' girls and women, acted as nurse, and stood in for her husband when he was away. The structure was patriarchal. It was the man who held all formal responsibilities and who was paid for his labour. His partner, in this respect similar to some other imperial women (such as wives of officials and the military), was an 'incorporated wife', central to the enterprise yet with no independent status.[28]

---

[26] See chap. by Patricia Grimshaw.

[27] Diane Langmore, 'The Object Lesson of a Civilised Christian Home', in Margaret Jolly and Martha Macintyre, eds., *Family and Gender in the Pacific. Domestic Contradictions and the Colonial Impact* (Cambridge, 1989), p. 85.

[28] Hilary Callan and Shirley Ardener, eds., *The Incorporated Wife* (London, 1984).

The idea of the mission family can be understood both as the immediate family of the missionary, and in the broader context of the linked families of all missionaries and their supporters, both on the particular colonial site and beyond. Family was associated not simply with blood but with religious belonging, and it might also be used to connote membership of the church or chapel, brothers and sisters in Christ. Thus 'native' Christians might be part of the wider Christian family, but racial hierarchies were inscribed into this notion of family, just as men and women were placed as spiritually equal but socially and politically different. St Paul's much quoted dictum, 'neither Jew nor Greek, neither male or female, ye are all one in Christ Jesus', was always in tension with the inscription of inferiority on bodies which were neither white nor male. Black people were 'babes in Christ', children who must be led to freedom, and the missionaries were their parents, exemplars, guides, and educators on the road to civilization. While the father and patriarch tended to be a somewhat distanced figure, the missionary wife was more closely identified with 'her' 'native' protégés, caught in the complexities of a maternal or sisterly role which was rooted in a shared womanhood, but marked by the axes of race and of class.[29]

In the West Indies, the moment of full emancipation in 1838 provided missionaries with extraordinary opportunities. Since many of them had been actively involved with the struggle against slavery, their contribution to emancipation was widely recognized by freed men and women, and the Baptists in particular had a period of great popularity and prosperity. The planters, however, were determined to maintain control over wages and labour. Freed men and women moved off the plantations if they could, and the Baptist missionaries in Jamaica supported them by buying land to establish free villages. For the missionaries, the dual moments of emancipation and conversion provided an unrivalled opportunity to build a new society, better even than the one they had left behind in Britain. Emancipation gave men and women their political, social, and economic freedom. Conversion gave them a new life in Christ, the possibility to be born anew. Those who had been held the property of other men were now free, they held their property in their own labour, and they could 'embrace their wives as

---

[29] On the complexities of identification and distance, see Margaret Jolly, 'Colonizing Women: The Maternal Body and Empire', in Sneja Gunew and Anna Yeatman, eds., *Feminism and the Politics of Difference* (St Leonards, 1993); Jane Haggis, ' "Good Wives and Mothers" '; on the problematic language of sisterhood, see Deborah Cherry, *Beyond the Frame. Feminism and Visual Culture, Britain 1850–1900* (London, 2001), p. 72.

their own property', as one anti-slavery enthusiast put it, rather than suffer the humiliation of seeing them at the mercy of their master.[30] Black men were to become responsible, industrious, independent, and Christian. Black women should occupy their small but satisfying separate sphere, as wives and mothers, freed from the degradation of concubinage, and the unremitting labour of the plantation. Black men should survey their families with pride, in homes and villages designed and built by their mentors, the missionaries. These free villages, many named after British abolitionist heroes, were established beyond the reach of the planters and the intention was to colonize the interior. In pride of place were the chapel, the mission house, and the school, often built at the top of a hill so that the surrounding countryside could be surveyed, displacing the great house in the imagination of the free. Laid out around them were neat homes, and tenants were encouraged to maintain standards of cleanliness and respectability, to ensure privacy of married couples' sleeping arrangements, and proper facilities for comfortable family meals. Husbands and wives would be there, 'in their proper places and the Bible on the table'.[31] Plots of land were adequate to grow food for the family but not enough to support needs without the wage labour of the man. In the vision of William Knibb, missionary leader, this land was also intended to make black men into citizens, able to claim the vote in the new Jamaica. These model communities with their new social order and their new gender order, provided the vision of the future.

The missionary dream of a new colonial order, with properly regulated gender relations and an industrious proletariat, was not confined to the Caribbean. The Cape, which came fully under British control from 1806, had a strategic British garrison, a well-established Dutch presence, and a population of mainly bonded and enslaved Africans. The early nineteenth century was a period of settler capitalism when increasing Xhosa resistance resulted in a series of wars. The agendas of governors and settlers were frequently at odds with those of the humanitarians. There was a strong missionary presence in the early nineteenth-century Cape, particularly the indefatigable Dr John Philip, local Superintendent of the London Missionary Society. He had played a critical part in a successful campaign to remove legal restrictions akin to slavery on the Khoesan. Ordinance 50 abolished pass laws and released the Khoesan from legal requirements binding them to serve the

---

[30] Cited in Catherine Hall, *White, Male and Middle-Class: Explorations in Feminism and History* (Cambridge, 1992), p. 31.

[31] The quotation is from William Knibb, cited in Hall, *Civilising Subjects*, p. 128.

colonists. Philip was celebrated at a grand dinner in 1830. On this occasion, African men were dressed in cotton trousers and waistcoats, or suits. The women were in printed calicos with white stockings, small black shoes, and neat silk handkerchiefs on their heads. By their dress and demeanour they symbolized the capacity to be both Christian and respectable, civilized people.[32] The expulsion of the Xhosa from the Kat River area by the end of 1829 gave the humanitarians a great opportunity to develop a new settlement. Respectable Africans, mainly associated with the mission stations, were encouraged to settle in Kat River with plots of land being allocated to family units. By 1833 they owned substantial numbers of horses, cattle, and sheep and some had built solid stone houses. 'The improvement of the Hottentots', triumphed their Congregational missionary, 'was such that their friends supposed them now to be taking their final exit from that state to which slavery naturally reduces a people'. Kat River was extolled in the metropole as a demonstration of the capacities of Africans to be civilized. Indeed, it was argued, the poor at home could certainly learn from these examples.[33]

In the Cape Colony slavery had existed for two hundred years when it was abolished in 1838 and, as in the West Indies, the missionaries were widely credited with having contributed to emancipation. Slavery had established its own well-defined sexual division of labour: men worked outside the home, women as domestics. Abolition brought new opportunities for the encouragement of the family. In the Western Cape, many new missions were set up, land was bought as in Jamaica, and attempts were made to establish new patterns of landownership, work, and family. The missionaries encouraged the building of 'proper' houses with gardens. Both men and women worked on the missions but with discrete spheres: where possible women withdrew from farm labour and focused on laundry, marketing clothes, and selling produce. The men frequently had to travel to find work. The result was that the missions increasingly became places for women and children. The missionaries were convinced of the importance of marriage and attempted to structure a particular kind of family, with men enjoying authority over women and children. In post-emancipation society men could claim a new masculinity while women were increasingly

---

[32] Robert Ross, *Status and Respectability in the Cape Colony, 1750–1870. A Tragedy of Manners* (Cambridge, 1999), p. 118.

[33] Alan Lester, *Imperial Networks. Creating Identities in Nineteenth-Century South Africa and Britain* (London, 2001), pp. 36–37, 118–19.

vulnerable to forms of control over their behaviour and their access to waged work.[34]

In Australia, something similar happened. While missionaries in the Caribbean had to face the horrors of slavery and the corrupt nature of plantation society, and those in the Cape experienced the depredations of settler capitalism and the military power of the Xhosa, those in New South Wales had to contend with the heathenisms and barbarisms associated with a penal colony and the fears aroused by the destruction of Aboriginal peoples. In all these instances, white society was experienced by the missionaries as quite as problematic as the 'native' population. In the 1820s, faced with evidence of a decline in the Aboriginal population, an official inquiry into indigenous needs proposed a scheme of 'missionary colonization'. Tracts of land were set aside, staffed by missionaries and their wives. Aboriginal peoples proved a much more problematic field of endeavour than the enslaved in the Caribbean. They did not welcome the missionaries, they had no fixed abodes or homes, their family and kin structures were a mystery to Europeans, and there was no system of hierarchy comprehensible to the missionaries. The hope was that the mission stations would provide an attractive place, where men could learn the cultivation of the soil, the women be initiated into some aspects of domesticity, and the children separated from their parents and put into dormitories. The missions were established in isolated places, in an attempt to limit the polluting effects of settler society, but the constant encroachment of the frontier made this an unrealistic dream. While the missionaries hoped for converts, marriages, and Christian baptisms, Aboriginal women were in constant danger of abduction by settlers and venereal disease spread at an alarming rate alongside prostitution.[35]

In the 1830s Wesleyan missionaries in New South Wales made another concerted attempt to establish new settlements which could become model communities. Joseph Orton, whose first period of service was in Jamaica where he had been persecuted for his preaching, arrived in Sydney in 1831 and from there he journeyed into Aboriginal territories. Orton was one of those 'imperial men' who worked in different sites of Empire, first, Jamaica, then Australia, from where he travelled to New Zealand. He took what he had

[34] Pamela Scully, *Liberating the Family? Gender and British Slave Emancipation in the Rural Western Cape, South Africa, 1823–53* (Cape Town and Oxford, 1997), pp. 10, 109–28.

[35] Annette Hamilton, ' "Bond-slaves of Satan": Aboriginal Women and the Missionary Dilemma', in Jolly and Macintyre, eds., *Family and Gender in the Pacific.*

leaned of 'native peoples' back to the metropole, reporting on what he had seen, commenting on the different characteristics of African, Aboriginal, and Maori peoples, helping to shape the mental maps of metropolitans about the Empire.[36] In his travels between imperial sites he also helped to build the webs of Empire which traversed the vertical connections between metropole and colony. Networks of missionaries, traders, military men, colonial officials, and settlers exchanged ideas and commodities, sharing frustrations, and sometimes building alliances.

On his journeys into the bush, Orton was shocked by the devastating effects of white settlement on indigenous peoples and believed that 'something must be done for them'. These were 'the most degraded human beings I have ever known or heard of', but they were 'part of the human family for whom Christ died'.[37] This was the moment in Britain at which humanitarian attention turned from the emancipated to the plight of 'native' peoples across the Empire. The official expression of this was the Select Committee of 1837, masterminded by abolitionist spokesman, Thomas Fowell Buxton, to which many missionaries gave evidence. The report was to emphasize British responsibility for the calamities which had beset 'uncivilized nations' in the wake of colonial expansion. Missions received government support and Orton helped to establish a model settlement in the Port Philip district. His disgust at settler behaviour, making the 'poor creatures' 'mendicants and marauders' was combined with horror at Aboriginal practices. He found the women especially degraded, 'with their clothing of animal skins from shoulders to knees, their long jet black hair decorated with kangaroo teeth and fish bones, their ears and noses pierced with small bones' and their fantastically painted faces.[38] Faced with the absolute difference between the European and the Aboriginal, missionary strategy was to focus on the children. New mission families, based in dormitories, seemed a logical step to those who believed in the importance of making new subjects, and who believed that these 'savage creatures' could be redeemed.[39]

Across the Empire, missionaries in the 1830s and 1840s established settlements built around their own families and their visions of a larger family and community, indeed empire, of respectable, industrious, domesticated Christians. By mid-century this vision was in decline, as the missionaries recog-

[36] Alex Tyrrell, *A Sphere of Benevolence. The Life of Joseph Orton, Wesleyan Methodist Missionary 1795–1842* (Melbourne, 1993).
[37] Tyrrell, *Joseph Orton*, p. 138.   [38] Tyrrell, *Joseph Orton*, p. 152.
[39] See chap. by Fiona Paisley.

nized the limitations of their own power, both over their converts, and in relation to colonists with very different aspirations. Afro-Jamaicans, for example, were building their own Creole culture which had more to do with traditions of resistance on the plantation than with Nonconformist thinking.[40] Female Christians in India used their conversion as a route into a working life, or indeed into feminism.[41] Yet the vision of the respectable family, with the industrious man and the domesticated wife and mother, had a long life, for it could be articulated to existing patterns of gender relations and reconfigure new forms of male power and female subordination.[42] While missionary expectations of a 'New Jerusalem' across the Empire were dashed, more modest missionary ventures, built on assumptions about a 'proper' gender order, had taken deep root.

In defining 'Hindoo' women as degraded, or Aboriginal peoples in need of rescue from savagery, colonial officials, planters, reformers, and missionaries, indeed all those who used this language and these stereotypes, were in part demarcating themselves from those whom they saw as inferior. In this final section, the focus is on the construction of the colonizer rather than the colonized, looking first at the centrality of gender to the early attempts to create colonies of white settlement, then at the ways of marking whiteness as masculine and feminine in the late nineteenth century, particularly in India.

   Colonial relations depended on the management of sexuality to effect racialized forms of rule. Ann Stoler privileges the 'intimate frontiers of empire' and the realm of privacy as 'dense transfer points', which connect the broad-scale dynamics of rule with the intimate realms of implementation. These are the places, she argues, where racial classifications were both defined and defied, relations between colonizer and colonized both confounded and confirmed.[43] The first phase of British colonization in areas

[40] Jean Besson, *Martha Brae's Two Histories. European Expansion and Caribbean Culture-Building in Jamaica* (Chapel Hill, NC, 2002).

[41] Haggis, ' "Good wives and mothers" '; Padma Anagol, 'Indian Christian Women and Indigenous Feminism c.1850–1920', in Midgley, ed., *Gender and Imperialism.*

[42] See, for example, Deborah Gaitskell's work on South Africa, 'At Home with Hegemony? Coercion and Consent in African Girls' Education for Domesticity in South Africa before 1910', in Dagmar Engels and Shula Marks, eds., *Contesting Colonial Hegemony. State and Society in Africa and India* (London, 1994).

[43] Ann Laura Stoler, *Race and the Education of Desire. Foucault's History of Sexuality and the Colonial Order of Things* (Durham, NC, 1995), p. 10; Stoler, 'Tense and Tender Ties: The Politics of Comparison in North American History and (Post) Colonial Studies', *Journal of American History*, LXXXVIII, 3 (2001), pp. 829–65.

such as New Zealand and western Canada was associated with white men, with exploration, and with commercial exploitation. It was often linked to hunting or seafaring. The white men in the forefront of those activities were frequently involved with indigenous women. Settler colonization, which usually involved the expropriation of land, and hence serious conflicts with indigenous peoples, signalled the arrival of larger numbers of white women and the claim by the colonizers that the place was theirs.[44] Since settlement meant the attempt to re-populate territories which were already peopled, questions of reproduction became crucial. White women as colonists 'contributed their productive and reproductive capacities to the construction of a settler society that displaced the indigenous inhabitants'.[45] White men were no longer singular agents, establishing ties with indigenous women, but were settlers with white families and households which provided a base for processes of cultural reproduction. Colonies of white settlement were organized around the double need to dispossess indigenous peoples and build a settler population in their place. 'Dispossession and settlement were and are deeply and irreparably intertwined', and it was in the realm of gender relations, the 'tender ties' that configured the intimacies both of love and care and of hatred and violence, that those relations of dispossession and colonization would be most painfully played out.[46]

Sylvia van Kirk movingly documents the effects for interpersonal relations of the shift from trading post to settlement in her history of the fur trade in western Canada. In the first phase, from the late seventeenth century to the late eighteenth century, British traders were content to live in long-term relations with 'Indian' women, ritualized with practices drawn from both cultures. The trade was based on a commodity exchange between hunters and traders, with 'Indians' and Europeans living in a mutually dependent way. Women played a significant economic role, acting as a link between traders and kin. The long-lasting unions between these men and women resulted in mixed-race children and the daughters, less 'Indian' than their mothers, became the desirable partners for officers of the Hudson's Bay and

---

[44] There were, of course, wide variations in the ways in which settler societies developed: see Daiva Stasiulis and Nira Yuval Davis, eds., *Unsettling Settler Societies* (London, 1995).

[45] Dolores E. Janiewski, 'Gendered Colonialism. The "Woman Question" in Settler Society', in Ruth Roach Pierson and others, eds., *Nation, Empire, Colony. Historicizing Gender and Race* (Bloomington, Ind., 1998), p. 57.

[46] Adele Perry, *On the Edge of Empire. Gender, Race and the Making of British Columbia 1849–1871* (Toronto, 2001), p. 19

North West Companies. James Douglas, a fur-trader who had married a mixed-race woman, was well aware of the importance of the 'tender ties' which men like himself made. 'There is indeed no living with comfort in this country', he wrote, 'until a person has forgot the great world and has his tasks and character formed on the current standard of the stage.' It was habit which made the new way of life familiar, 'softened as it is by the *many tender ties*, which find a way to the heart'.[47] By the early 1800s, white fathers reacting to metropolitan pressures became more anxious about the values of the 'great world' and less content with the standards of the outback. They aspired to make their daughters as European as possible and schoolteachers arrived to train them in proper feminine habits. The founding of Red River Colony marked the first attempt to create a place for fur traders to retire, where they could settle on land which could be farmed, after active service at the forts. Settlement also brought missionaries who were critical of the absence of Christian marriage. They blamed 'immoralities' on 'Indian' and mixed-race women who were defined as naturally promiscuous.[48]

The increased pressure to be seen as white could create terrible tensions within families. Alexander Ross, for example, had started as a clerk in the North West Company and, impressed by the virtues of the women of the Okanagan, he married the daughter of one of the chiefs in 1815. Several years later they went to live in Red River and Sally, as she was known, had thirteen children. Ross was convinced that his children were more susceptible to civilizing influences than 'pure natives' and ensured that they were well educated. One of them married the Presbyterian missionary of the settlement in 1853, to the horror of his congregation, who predicted that his unfortunate choice of 'a native for a helpmate' would have dire consequences.[49] Another daughter, Jemima, anxious to pass as white, tried to avoid riding to church with her mother to escape embarrassment. Her brother chided her: 'What if mama is an Indian? Remember the personal qualities that ought to endear mama to us. Who more tender-hearted? Who more attached to her children and more desirous of their happiness?' Was this not more important, he asked his sister, than superficial accomplishments? What was not spoken was that it was her brown skin that was the source of the problem. By mid-century white colonists wanted to be seen as

[47] Sylvia van Kirk, '*Many Tender Ties*'. *Women in Fur-Trade Society in Western Canada, 1670–1870* (Winnipeg, 1981), title page.

[48] van Kirk, '*Many Tender Ties*', p. 152.

[49] Ibid., p. 234.

part of white society across the Empire: the increased racism of white society both 'at home' and in the colonies meant that any association with 'natives' had to be denied. When Ross published his history of the settlement in 1856, the 'Indian' connections inside his own family were entirely erased.[50]

Cape Colony had a rather different history of settlement from that of western Canada. Initially the British presence was military which meant a strongly homosocial culture. Those British migrants who arrived in the 1820s, faced with established Dutch society and a large African population, were anxious to make a distinctive place and identity for themselves. Many of them were middle class, or from the lower echelons of the gentry, and they came to settle. British policy was 'to Anglicize the colony', by bringing the system of law into line with that of Britain, designating English the official language and encouraging emigration.[51] Settlers began to establish a distinctive Cape Colonial identity. Gentility and respectability were important, a respectability associated with a particular gender order, that of middle-class Britons, translated for colonial life. In Cape Town the new colonial press acted as one vehicle for the dissemination of ideas of the separate spheres of men and women. While Roman Dutch law gave women significant rights in respect to marriage and property and there had been an important female presence in the commercial activities of the city, the formalization of commerce and the increasing presence of British notions of domesticity meant a loss of influence for women. Homes were separated from workplaces and men increasingly associated with new business practices and organizations. Respectability, as in Britain, meant that married women should not be economically active and that they should take responsibility for childcare. By the 1830s Cape society had become more racially exclusive and there were many concerns over the disreputable behaviour of poor whites, especially soldiers.[52]

As the eastern frontier was driven forward and the Xhosa expelled from large tracts of land, settlers were busy creating farms and towns which looked to some like 'England in miniature'. 'The houses, the farm-yards, the cross-

[50] Ibid., pp. 33, 236.

[51] The quotation is from Wilmot Horton, Parliamentary Under Secretary for the Colonies in 1826, cited in Ross, *Status and Respectability*, p. 45.

[52] Kirsten McKenzie, ' "My Own Mind Dying Within Me": Eliza Fairbairn and the Reinvention of Colonial Middle-class Domesticity in Cape Town', *South African Historical Journal*, XXXVI (1997), pp. 3–23 and 'Of Convicts and Capitalists: Honour and Colonial Commerce in 1830s Cape Town and Sydney', *Australian Historical Studies* XXXIII, 118 (2002), pp. 199–222.

barred gates, the inhabitants in manners, dress and appearance are thoroughly English', wrote one missionary as he rode through the Eastern Cape.[53] English-style villas were built, with halls and corridors ensuring private spaces, unlike their Dutch equivalents. Urban men dressed in black broadcloth and white linen, the women in proper feminine attire, but these were not little Englands, for the dangers faced by settlers were from Africans whose lands they had expropriated. The increasing hostilities between these groups erupted periodically into serious conflicts. Settler identity became more assertive and defensive in the 1830s, increasingly distinct from missionary discourses of liberal humanitarianism except on questions of familial organization. Settlers began to construct their own history, focusing on the ways in which they had transformed, domesticated, and civilized the landscape, making it productive and profitable, bringing progress to uncivilized Africa.[54]

White women became increasingly important as boundary markers, maintaining racial authority through their differentiated ways of life. Domestic space had to be demarcated as white through specific practices and rituals, from distinctive styles of furnishing and dressmaking, to letter-writing, and tea-drinking. Antagonisms between settlers could be smoothed by the female social round and the men could bond in their common determination to defend their properties and extend the frontier. They strengthened their sense of common purpose by building networks with settlers on other sites of empire, printing each others' materials in their local newspapers, defining their differences from the colonial authorities, making political claims for themselves.[55]

While white colonial identities had a long history in the Caribbean, it was not until the mid-nineteenth century that the common tendencies across the new territories of settlement became clear. While plantation society and slavery had bred one kind of white identity, the lords and masters of creation with their indolent ladies and systems of concubinage, that of North America, Australasia, and South Africa was very different. In the second half of the nineteenth century, a particular kind of white colonial identity became increasingly distinctive across these areas of white settlement. This was a culture of sturdy manhood and domesticated femininity, of respectability,

[53] Ross, *Status and Respectability*, p. 79.

[54] Ross, *Status and Respectability*, esp. pp. 79–88, 65–66.

[55] Alan Lester, 'Settler Discourse and the Circuits of Empire', *History Workshop Journal*, LIV (2002), pp. 25–48; and Lester, *Imperial Networks*, pp. 48–77.

and of racial exclusion, marked by its contiguity to those native peoples who had been displaced for its own making. It is identifiable across these different imperial locations, always marked with the particular specificities of each site, but with values in common. Male colonists were angry at the ways in which they were denied the rights of Britons. They sought political representation and an end to the forms of autocratic government determined from the metropole. In making those claims they articulated visions of themselves as effective economic protagonists, as heads of households, as independent white men, and as worthy of respect. The winning of responsible government and the male franchise across these colonies was part of the settlement which they achieved.

This culture of respectability did not pertain everywhere and was always contested, for there were conflicting groups within all settler societies, different locations, different patterns of economic production, and different interests. The figure of the frontier man with his rough, physical forms of masculinity, often associated with working-class occupations, always provided an alternative pole. In New Zealand, for example, it was not until the 1870s that the male culture of the frontier began to decline in the face of the forces of the family and a more settled urban life.[56] In Australia, the frontier experience was paradigmatic in shaping what was to become an Australian national culture, with the central figure being that of the marauding white man.[57] In British Columbia, formally constituted as a colony in 1849 and hanging 'precariously at the edge of Britain's literal and symbolic empire', the attempts to create a 'proper colony' out of its racially plural, male-dominated, rough, and turbulent world, were doomed to very limited success.[58] British Columbia was not like England. The mixed-race children, the white fathers and 'native' mothers sharing ties, homes, and work, were a constant reminder of the ways in which the colony fell short. The sustained efforts of social reformers to regulate and reform the drinking, gambling, undisciplined workers in the gold mines and the fur trade, whose relations with Aboriginal women were constantly troubling, had little effect. There were hopes that the presence of more white women could transform and redeem the society and create a settled colony, but the refusal of working-class female

[56] On New Zealand, see Jock Phillips, *A Man's Country? The Image of the Pakeha Male. A History* (Auckland, 1987), esp. chap. 2.

[57] Marilyn Lake, 'Frontier Feminism and the Marauding White Man. Australia 1890s–1940s', in Pierson and others, eds., *Nation, Empire, Colony*, pp. 94–105.

[58] Perry, *On the Edge of Empire*, p. 3.

emigrants to behave in 'proper' ways meant that few of the reformers' hopes were realized. British Columbia remained on the edge of respectability, yet its settlers were vociferous in their claims for the privileges of whiteness.[59]

The complex mix of power and vulnerability associated with being white, being a colonizer, was painfully obvious to the British in India in the wake of the Sepoy Rebellion of 1857. 'From the rage, and fear, of 1857 emerged a new and enduring sense of the importance of the bonds of race, in contrast to those of culture.'[60] In the constant play between similarity and difference, which was so central to relations between colonizers and colonized, the focus was now on difference. This apparent difference between Britons and Indians was dramatically highlighted as supposedly docile and loyal sepoys turned upon the British and committed what was seen as unspeakable violence, particularly that associated with the supposed rapes of white women. The shift that was taking place across many sites of Empire, the shift from the liberal humanitarian idea of the educable potential of all men to a harsher view of the ineradicable nature of racial difference, was particularly pronounced in India. There the 'Mutiny', with its terrifying narratives of unspeakable things done to white women, was constantly replayed in the Anglo-Indian imagination throughout the nineteenth and early twentieth centuries.[61] The events of 1857 meant that forms of Britishness, ways of being a white man or woman in India, had to be re-made. To keep vulnerability and fear at bay, a strategy of distance and denial was employed, a constant attempt made to segregate white people from Indian others. Such a strategy could not, of course, work, since there were multiple 'contact zones' and middle and upper-middle-class Britons relied on a vast army of servants to minister to their imagined needs. The white world in India was a world of officials, merchants, traders, missionaries, and soldiers, most of whom expected to spend time there and then return home. For some it was a familial world, and increasing numbers of white women arrived after 1857. For others, particularly soldiers, it was a culture of singular masculinity, lived in the segregated world of the military cantonment with its regulated forms of sexuality.[62]

[59] Perry, *On the Edge of Empire*, esp. pp. 123, 194.

[60] Metcalf, *Ideologies of the Raj*, p. 44.

[61] There is a large literature in this field, see, for example, Nancy Paxton, *Writing Under the Raj. Gender, Race and Rape in the British Colonial Imagination, 1830–1947* (New Brunswick, NJ, 1999).

[62] See chap. 6 by Philippa Levine.

The rebellion of 1857 was 'an immensely traumatic bodily experience for the British in India'.[63] The outrage at what had been done to them, the bitterness of learning to fear those who ought to have feared them, was translated into the building of a protective racial barrier, aiming to ensure the separation of the colonizing society from that which it had colonized. First, the body itself had to be re-fashioned in a new expression of whiteness and, 'a web of Britishness' woven around it, re-imaging white masculinity and femininity. From the black frock coats of the civilian men to the deter-minedly British costume of the women, all traces of Indianness were eradi-cated. But it was the *topi*, the large protective hat, designed for a tropical climate, which was to become the lasting symbol of British prestige in India. Worn by both men and women, it signified the primacy of the racial divide in that society. Food became more British, table-wear was sent from the metro-pole, children were sent 'home' to school, hookahs and Indian mistresses went underground, there was an increase in the numbers of European women, and a tighter social code was established excluding those of mixed-race. Fears of pollution and contagion were widespread: European and Indian quarters were separated, extensive new housing in the bungalow style, with care given to ventilation and beds raised off the floor, was constructed in spacious streets.[64] Inside those homes, at least amongst the official community in India—the civil servants—a distinctive imperial way of life developed in the late nineteenth century. Homes were public places for the white community, with ever-ready hospitality and incorporated wives, who saw their work, alongside their husbands, as ruling India. Here the family business was not the mission, redeeming lost souls and bringing them to the family of Christ, rather it was the business of Empire. Imperial men needed wives who enjoyed the outdoor life, who could ride and hunt, who were practised in self-sufficiency, who could cope with running the home when their husbands were away on business, and could stand in, when necessary, for official purposes. With the children sent back to Britain for their schooling, Anglo-Indian women focused their lives on their husbands and the Empire, and derived considerable influence through this. These were partnerships which cast women in a masculine mould. Domesticated femi-nine women could not survive in this world and 'a growing approximation of femininity to masculinity... allowed Anglo-Indian women a broader scope

[63] E. M. Collingham, *Imperial Bodies. The Physical Experience of the Raj, c.1800–1947* (Cam-bridge, 2001), p. 112.

[64] Collingham, *Imperial Bodies*, esp. pp. 7, 92, 112.

for public activity in the empire'.[65] This was a different pattern from that of their metropolitan sisters.

Outside the home, the club was the place to be: a distinct Anglo-Indian version of the club, providing a home from home, including white women, integrating domestic and public life, and demarcating the boundaries between colonizer and colonized.[66] And beyond home and club there were the hill stations, established from the 1820s, havens of safety for the British and reaching the zenith of their popularity in the late nineteenth century. 'A part of England and apart from India', they were thought to be safe places for the reproduction of the race. They felt like England, with their cool evenings, more equal balance between the sexes, children at home and at school, tennis parties, village greens, English-style churches and cottages. Here the standards of home could be maintained in what was experienced as a physically and morally corrupting land.[67] Here Merivale's blood, race, and civilization seemed at one.

While family ruled in much of Anglo-Indian society, a rather different culture flourished on the northern frontier. In the period after 1857, the British mapped the races of India and contrasted 'martial races' with the non-martial, to the detriment of the latter. The men of the North, especially the Pathans, warlike antagonists of the British, were admired for their energy and independence. Seen as wild, pure-bred, and rebellious, the Islamic Pathans were favourably compared with the intelligent, educated, but effeminate Bengali middle class. In the culture of the northern frontier, where marriage ceremonies were very expensive and men tended to marry late, where women were strictly controlled and extreme risks were associated with unauthorized liaisons with unmarried women, intimate relations between men had an assured place. The homosexual culture amongst Pathan boys and young men was deeply attractive to some British officers engaged on the frontier in the late nineteenth and early twentieth centuries. Products of the public school, theirs was a masculinity in flight from domesticity, revelling in the homosocial world of Kipling's 'Great Game'. Service on the frontier was seen as the perfect training ground for disciplined, hardy, and active

[65] Mary A. Procida, *Married to the Empire. Gender, Politics and Imperialism in India, 1833–1947* (Manchester, 2002), p. 6.

[66] Mrinalini Sinha, 'Britishness, Clubbability and the Colonial Public Sphere: The Genealogy of an Imperial Institution in Colonial India', *Journal of British Studies*, XL (2001), pp. 489–521.

[67] Dane Kennedy, *The Magic Mountains. Hill Stations and the British Raj* (Berkeley, 1996), pp. 8, 105.

Englishmen. The British denounced the ferocity of the Pathans whilst admiring them as worthy and sporting adversaries. Furthermore, they could always be crushed with force, whereas the wily Bengalis posed a much more serious political threat.[68] Juxtaposed to the culture of the hill stations, this colonial economy of white male desire provides a potent reminder of the complexity of patterns of gender and sexual relations across the Empire.

The scholarship on gender and Empire is still in its infancy. This chapter has emphasized the power of Empire and of the colonizers, rather than their weaknesses, vulnerabilities, and failures. Many other stories could be told of forms of resistance across different locations, of the multiple patterns of gender relations in any given place, and of the impact of imperial encounters upon the metropole. In focusing on a particular colonial discourse, a specific colonial project, and some of the issues associated with the demarcation of whiteness, an attempt has been made to indicate both the specificities of particular locations, and the patterns across the empire. The abject Indian woman was not specific only to India, the mission family had a life in many parts of the Empire, and whiteness had to be fashioned on every colonial site. These were some of the elements of the imperial social formation in the nineteenth century.[69]

---

[68] Mukulika Banerjee, *The Pathan Unarmed: Opposition and Memory in the North West Frontier* (Oxford, 2000), pp. 35–42; John Tosh, *A Man's Place. Masculinity and the Middle-Class Home in Victorian England* (New Haven, 1999), pp. 170–94.

[69] The concept of an 'imperial social formation' is helpfully discussed in Sinha, *Colonial Masculinity*, and 'Britishness, Clubability and the Colonial Public Sphere', pp. 490–93.

Select Bibliography

E. M. COLLINGHAM, *Imperial Bodies. The Physical Experience of the Raj, c.1800–1947* (Cambridge, 2001).

JULIA CLANCY-SMITH and FRANCES GOUDA, eds., *Domesticating the Empire. Race, Gender and Family Life in French and Dutch Colonialism* (Charlottesville, Va., 1998).

FREDERICK COOPER and ANN LAURA STOLER, eds., *Tensions of Empire. Colonial Cultures in a Bourgeois World* (Berkeley, 1997).

CATHERINE HALL, *Civilising Subjects. Metropole and Colony in the English Imagination, 1830–1867* (Cambridge and Chicago, 2002).

—— ed., *Cultures of Empire. A Reader. Colonizers in Britain and the Empire in the Nineteenth and Twentieth Centuries* (Manchester, 2000).

MADHAVI KALE, *Fragments of Empire. Capitalism, Slavery, and Indian Indentured Labor Migration in the British Caribbean* (Philadelphia, 1998).

DANE KENNEDY, *The Magic Mountains. Hill Stations and the British Raj* (Berkeley, 1996).

ALAN LESTER, *Imperial Networks. Creating Identities in Nineteenth–Century South Africa and Britain* (London, 2001).

LATA MANI, *Contentious Traditions. The Debate on Sati in Colonial India* (Berkeley, 1998).

CLARE MIDGLEY, ed., *Gender and Imperialism* (Manchester, 1998).

ADELE PERRY, *On the Edge of Empire. Gender, Race and the Making of British Columbia 1849–1871* (Toronto, 2001).

MARY A. PROCIDA, *Married to the Empire. Gender, Politics and Imperialism in India, 1833–1947* (Manchester, 2002).

RUTH ROACH PIERSON and NUPUR CHAUDHURI, with the assistance of Beth McAulay, eds., *Nation, Empire, Colony. Historicising Gender and Race* (Bloomington, Ind., 1998)

PAMELA SCULLY, *Liberating the Family? Gender and British Slave Emancipation in the Rural Western Cape, South Africa, 1823–53* (Cape Town and Oxford, 1993).

MRINALINI SINHA, *Colonial Masculinity. The 'Manly Englishman' and the 'Effeminate Bengali' in the late Nineteenth Century* (Manchester, 1995).

ANN LAURA STOLER, *Carnal Knowledge and Imperial Power. Race and the Intimate in Colonial Rule* (Berkeley, 2002).

SYLVIA VAN KIRK, *'Many Tender Ties'. Women in Fur-Trade Society in Western Canada, 1670–1870* (Winnipeg, 1981).

4

Gender and Empire: The Twentieth Century

BARBARA BUSH

How can a gender perspective provide a more rounded analysis of the dynamics of the twentieth-century British Empire? Both Kathleen Wilson and Catherine Hall, in their studies of eighteenth-and nineteenth-century Empire in this volume, demonstrate how gender was integral to the articulation of whiteness and to categories of difference, strengthening race and sex borders, and defining imperial identities and national belonging. This holds equally for the twentieth century, but the rapid new developments reconfigured the intersections between gender, class, race, and nationalism in structuring imperial power relations in colony and metropole. Nationalist demands for civil liberties and political rights challenged exclusions from 'Empire Citizenship' on grounds of race, gender, and class. Class influenced men and women's interaction with imperialism, as it did the nature of participation in Empire, race attitudes, and the gendered identities of British men and women as imperial subjects. Pro-and anti-imperialist activism was largely the province of the élite and the middle classes. Most working-class men and women tended instead to experience Empire through migration to the 'white' Dominions, or as a ubiquitous theme in popular culture which informed their identities as white British citizens. Gender cannot therefore be considered in isolation but must be analysed to see how it was mediated by other social phenomena in structuring historical change.[1]

In analysing gender within this wider framework, this chapter focuses on three aspects of twentieth-century Empire; the link between social, political, and cultural change in Britain and developments in colonial societies; the gendering of colonial policy and its impact on colonial gender orders; and, finally, the significance of gender in the disintegration of Empire. The

---

[1] Himani Bannerji, 'Politics and the Writing of History', in Ruth Pierson and Nupur Chaudhuri, eds., *Nation, Empire, Colony: Historicizing Race and Gender* (Bloomington, Ind., 1998), pp. 294–95.

analysis is organized around four themes: the emancipation of women in Britain and the 'white' Dominions; and wider participation of white women in Empire as settlers, colonial wives, missionaries and welfare workers, pro-imperial activists, and academics; secondly, related transformations in imperial masculinities; thirdly, the promotion of marriage and domesticity among colonizer and colonized; and lastly, the gendered nature of imperial policy and race discourse as well as anti-imperial resistance. My starting point is the changes in British culture and society catalysed by the First World War which critically reconfigured white women's relationship to Empire and imperial gender relations.

'The British Empire, as it is today... is a [family] affair... a new commonwealth... a great experiment in progressive civilization', wrote one Empire propagandist in 1924.[2] This new imperial vision, familial and peaceable, superseded the pre-war era of bellicose, expansionist Empire. Britain acquired additional territories in the post-war peace settlement, and imperial policy now centred on consolidating Empire and making it more united and efficient. Twentieth-century Empire was defined by the strengthening of bonds between Britain and its settler 'white' Empire, the expansion of an informal 'business' Empire in China and the Far East, the emergence of a Middle Eastern Empire, and the development of the African Empire. Continuities with earlier imperial epochs persisted but twentieth-century Empire arguably emerged from the traumas of the First World War and ended with decolonization, embracing both colonial and post-colonial eras. Shaped by 'modern times', a new cultural and political ethos catalysed by war, post–1918 Empire spans what Eric Hobsbawm defines as the 'short Twentieth Century'. This 'age of extremes' was characterized by war, ideological and national conflicts, including anti-colonial nationalism, and the acceleration of modernity through scientific and technological developments. During economic depression and war the colonies remained vital to hopes of sustaining the British economy and imperial power.[3]

---

[2] Percy Hurd, The Empire: A Family Affair (being a Popular Survey of the Self Governing Dominions, Crown Colonies & Protectorates and Mandated Territories Under the British Crown and Recital of Empire Policy (London, 1924), pp. 5–6, 179–80.

[3] Wm. Roger Louis, 'Introduction', in Judith M. Brown and Wm. Roger Louis, eds., The Oxford History of the British Empire [hereafter OHBE], IV, The Twentieth Century (Oxford, 1999) pp. 4–5, 12; E. J. Hobsbawm, The Age of Extremes: The Short Twentieth Century: 1914–1991 (London, 1994), pp. 2–6.

Seminal to 'Empire strengthening' in turbulent times were developments in the discourse and culture of Empire. During the 1914–18 war, the 'Empire Family' had stood together in defence of the 'Motherland', fostering 'Empire intimacy', a domestic motif epitomized in the 'Home and Colonial' shopping chain and reflected in the advertisements of the new Empire Marketing Board. The mass democratization of Britain and its five white Dominions, now equal partners in the movement for Empire Self-Sufficiency, engendered a new sense of white 'Empire Citizenship'. The war 'enhanced the importance and popularity of Empire'.[4] Visions of a more 'participatory' and inclusive Empire were articulated through popular culture and politics, and emancipated middle-and upper-class women enjoyed an increasingly prominent profile in Empire activism.[5] Empire consciousness filtered through British and colonial society fostered by the expanding mass media, particularly the new cultural media of radio, 'Empire genre' cinema, and the rituals of Empire Day. Royalty remained the symbolic emblem of Empire unity and members of the Royal family undertook more official tours to the Colonies and Dominions. With better telecommunications, faster ships, air travel, and radio, the Empire was more tightly integrated than ever before. Empire 'globalization', facilitated by the circulation of imperial élites and the white diaspora, strengthened a unifying culture of Empire and created stronger bonds between the colonies and the metropole.

The metropolitan heartland remained the centre of economic and political power but settler politics shaped sub-imperialist centres in the white Dominions, now partners in the exercise of imperial power.[6] Intended to represent British interests, these centres of imperial power on the periphery articulated their own interests, which did not always synchronize with metropolitan imperial policy. Imperial power networks were also countered by new trans-colony, anti-colonial networks which shifted the loci of change to new centres within the periphery. Despite a rhetoric of humanitarian paternalistic governance, endorsed by the League of Nations, oppressive elements of imperial rule persisted, catalysing colonial grievances. An imperial 'colour bar' prioritized the superior white Empire over the less 'civilized' tropical branches of the imperial family, insufficiently 'adult' for self-

[4] P. J. Cain and A. G. Hopkins, *British Imperialism: Crisis and Deconstruction, 1914–1990* (London, 1993), p. 213.

[5] Andrew S. Thompson, *Imperial Britain: The Empire in British Politics c. 1880–1932* (Harlow, 2000), pp. 18, 39, 184–89.

[6] Hurd, *Empire*, pp. 5–6.

rule. Racism and lack of civil rights in metropole and colony alike exposed
the tensions between Empire and democracy, and stimulated interconnections between white anti-imperialists and anti-colonial nationalists.[7]

Important transformations also occurred in the imperial heartland as
colonial workers, students, and political activists established an extended
and permanent presence. This colonial frontier *within* Britain constituted a
new threat to imperial race borders intended to secure spatial, social, and
sexual segregation from colonized 'others' and thus bolster white power and
prestige.[8] Interracial sex, anti-imperialism, socialism, and feminism represented prime enemies of Empire 'within', which de-centred the imperial and
patriarchal certainties of the Victorian era, subverting the gendered identities
of colonizer and colonizers upon which the continuing success of the
imperial project rested.

Mounting challenges to Empire in metropolis and colonies transformed
imperial discourse, epitomized in the reconceptualization of Empire to
Commonwealth, a 'move from (masculine) power to (feminine) service'.[9]
Duty and 'service' had always characterized the public school ethos which
defined superior imperial masculinities. The 'feminization' of Empire, however, was reflected in an increasing emphasis on welfare and development,
and the growing role of gender in colonial policy and practice. Additionally,
the promotion of domesticity demanded fuller 'incorporation' of colonial
wives and, in general, a higher profile for white women in the colonies.[10]
Technologies of governance now engaged sophisticated cultural strategies,
including the stabilization of colonial gender orders and embourgeoisement
of colonial élites through education and Western domesticity. Eugenics and
the new scientific and biomedical discourse of hygiene, health, and welfare
gave greater priority to colonized mothers and to the moral and sexual health

---

[7] Leonard Barnes *Empire or Democracy: A Study of the Colonial Question* (London, 1939),
pp. 160–74.

[8] Barbara Bush, *Imperialism, Race and Resistance: Africa and Britain, 1918 to 1945* (London,
1999), pp. 205–27.

[9] Margery Perham, 'African Facts and American Criticisms', *Foreign Affairs: An American
Quarterly Review*, XXII (April 1944), p. 445.

[10] For instance, Hilary Callan and Shirley Ardener, eds., *The Incorporated Wife* (Beckenham,
1984); Nupur Chaudhuri and Margaret Strobel, eds., *Western Women and Imperialism: Compli-
city and Resistance* (Bloomington, Ind., 1992); Helen Callaway, *Gender, Culture and Empire:
European Women in Colonial Nigeria* (London, 1987); Susanna Hoe, *The Private Life of Old Hong
Kong: Western Women in the British Colony, 1841–1941* (Hong Kong, 1991); Mary A. Procida,
Married to the Empire: Gender, Politics and Imperialism, 1883–1947 (Manchester, 2002); Claudia
Knapman, *White Women in Fiji, 1835–1930: The Ruin of Empire?* (Sydney, 1986).

of colonized and colonizer.[11] Challenges to scientific racism stimulated new discourses of cultural difference as well as the growth of anthropology and sociology as academic disciplines in the service of Empire.[12]

Why and how was the Empire feminized? During the war, women had developed 'skills and character' which would be 'of immense value... to Empire' and, after 1918 they were increasingly represented as 'Empire Builders'.[13] Emancipation also reconfigured British women's relationship to Empire. By 1910 women constituted 20 per cent of university students, and the 1919 Sex Disqualification Removal Act opened hitherto male professions to women. After the passing of the 1928 Equal Franchise Act, women constituted 52.7 per cent of the electorate.[14] Elite women began to claim greater responsibility for the welfare of colonized women and to make an impact on official policy. Women's organizations (home and colonial) flourished and even the parochial Mother's Union had colonial branches and a maternalist interest in Empire. In the expanding east and southern African colonies, women, such as Ethel Tawse Jolly (1875–1950) were prominent in settler politics. The Federation of Women's Institutes in Southern Rhodesia and the East African Women's League (EAWL) actively promoted female immigration and had strong links with female dominated pro-Empire organizations in Britain and the white Dominions.[15]

[11] See chaps. by Philippa Levine and Alison Bashford in this volume. Megan Vaughan, *Curing their Ills: Colonial Power and African Illness* (Cambridge, 1991), pp. 19–23. See, also, Karen Transberg Hansen, ed., *African Encounters with Domesticity* (New Brunswick, NJ, 1992); Rosalind O' Hanlon, 'Gender in the British Empire', in Brown and Louis, eds., *OHBE, IV*, pp. 379–98; Antoinette Burton, ed., *Gender, Sexuality and Colonial Modernities* (London, 1999); Ann Laura Stoler and Frederick Cooper eds., *Tensions of Empire: Colonial Cultures in a Bourgeois World* (Berkeley, 1997).

[12] E. Barkan, *The Retreat from Scientific Racism: The Changing Concepts of Race in Britain and the United States between the World Wars* (Cambridge, 1992), esp. pp. 57, 67–89, 91.

[13] 'British Women's Emigration Association Annual Report, 1917', p. 9, Royal Commonwealth Society Collection (henceforth RCS), Cambridge University Library, R 11/16; Arthur Grimble, 'Women as Empire Builders', *United Empire*, XII (1922), pp. 196–97; D. H. Moutray Read, 'Women and Empire Consolidation', in ibid, X (1919), pp. 322–26.

[14] Susan Kingsley Kent, *Making Peace: The Reconstruction of Gender in Interwar Britain* (Princeton, 1994), pp. 114–15; Carol Dyhouse, 'The British Federation of University Women and the Status of Women in Universities, 1907–1939', *Women's History Review* (hereafter *WHR*), IX (1995), p. 469.

[15] Isak Dinesen, *Letters from Africa, 1914–31* (1982, London, 1986), p. 442; Donal Lowry, ' "White Women's Country", Ethel Tawse Jollie and the Making of White Rhodesia', *Journal of Southern African Studies* (hereafter *JSAS*), XXIII (1997), pp. 259, 272–73.

As academics, journalists, and writers, women had greater opportunities to travel and work in the Empire and to make an active contribution to imperial politics. Women MPs, Ellen Wilkinson and Eleanor Rathbone, were regularly critical of colonial policy in Parliament. Rathbone, an active feminist and humanitarian, took up the maternalist cause of oppressed Indian women in *Child Marriage: The Indian Minotaur* (1934); the socialist, Wilkinson, visited India with an India League delegation in 1932 and contributed to a report sympathetic to nationalist grievances and critical of government repression, including maltreatment of women resisters.[16] Female activists were now motivated by a humanism and/or socialism which did not separate men and women's interests. Educated middle-class women, liberal and socialist, saw themselves as 'modern', influenced by the traumas of the war and holding 'progressive' ideas on race and Empire. As activists in new anti-imperialist pressure groups, and facilitators and hosts of interracial events, they demonstrated greater empathy and understanding for the colonial oppressed than their male counterparts. The writer, Winifred Holtby, was instrumental in setting up the 'Friends of Africa' pressure group to support South African trade unionists and academic Margaret Ballinger, a Representative for disenfranchised Africans in the Union Parliament from 1938, remained a 'voice in the wilderness' fighting the cause of African rights as segregation intensified. Critics of empire and pro-imperialist women alike demonstrated a commitment to improving race relations; membership of the London-based interracial League of Coloured Peoples (founded 1931) included Winifred Holtby and the academic, Margery Perham, 'Britain's Conscience on Africa'.[17]

The pre–1914 link between imperialism and maternalism (female paternalism) persisted, tempered by the humanitarian discourse of the League of Nations.[18] The term 'imperial feminism', however, associated with pre-war strategies to establish 'fitness' for citizenship through women's active contribution to the imperial mission, no longer had the same resonance. The feminist agenda was transformed by emancipation and activism, moving

[16] Monica Whately, Ellen Wilkinson, Leonard W. Matters and Krishna Menon, *Condition of India. Being the Report of the Delegation sent to India by the India League in 1932* (London, 1934).

[17] Barbara Bush ' "Britain's Conscience on Africa": White Women, Race and Imperial Politics in Inter-war Britain', in Clare Midgley, ed., *Gender and Imperialism* (Manchester, 1998), pp. 200–22; Bush, *Imperialism, Race and Resistance*, pp. 118, 183–6, 196–97, 220–22.

[18] Susan Pedersen, 'The Maternalist Moment in British Colonial Policy: the Controversy over "Child Slavery" in Hong Kong, 1917–1941', *Past and Present* (hereafter *P&P*), CLXXI (2001), pp. 161–203.

away from the 'direct appropriation, representation and silencing' of colonized women characteristic of pre-war feminism.[19] In India, maternalism was
now tempered by white 'feminist allies' in Indian women's campaigns and, as
international feminist networks widened, British and white 'Commonwealth' feminists engaged more fully in 'cross-cultural discussions' which
muted the racial arrogance of pre-war feminists. Additionally, Australian
feminists, as both colonized and colonizing, actively defined their own
identity in relationship to Empire, whiteness, indigenous women and men,
and the metropolitan centre.[20] A minority of official wives, influenced by
feminism and/or socialism—among them novelist Stella Benson in China,
and 'Red' Hilda Selwyn-Clarke (a graduate from a working-class background) in Hong Kong—were critical of conventional expatriate society
and campaigned for reforms.[21] More conventional wives also supported
initiatives to improve race relations and emancipate their colonized sisters,
helping to 'undermine the European male world and its ethos'.[22] Missionary
women, too, extended their role in the uplift of colonized women and
'muscular Christianity' was diluted by the feminization of the missionary
project. The younger generation, influenced by 'missionary feminism', were
arguably less patronizing in their dealings with colonized women than their
pre-war counterparts, encouraging the emancipation of colonized women
through education and identifying with anti-colonial and anti-racist
struggles.[23]

These developments in the nature of white women's engagement with
Empire were matched by transformations in imperial masculinities. The

[19] Angela Woollacott, 'Inventing Commonwealth and Pan-Pacific Feminisms', *Gender &
History*, X (1998) pp. 425–28; 444–45.

[20] Marilyn Lake, 'Colonized and Colonizing: The White Australian Feminist Subject', *WHR*,
II (1993) pp. 377–86. See also Fiona Paisley, 'Citizens of the World: Australian Feminism and
Indigenous Rights in the International Context, 1920s and 1930s', *Feminist Review* (hereafter *FR*),
LVIII (1998), pp. 66–84, and Barbara Ramusack, 'Cultural Missionaries, Maternal Imperialists,
Feminist Allies: British Women Activists in India, 1865–1945', in Chaudhuri and Strobel, eds.,
Western Women and Imperialism, pp. 315–16.

[21] Hoe, *Private Life of Old Hong Kong*, pp. 181–82, 247–55.

[22] Janice Brownfoot, 'Memsahibs in Colonial Malaya: A Study of European Wives in a British
Colony and Protectorate, 1900–1940', in Callan and Ardener, eds., *Incorporated Wife*, pp. 199,
208.

[23] Jean Allman, 'Making Mothers: Missionaries, Medical Officers and Women's Work in
Colonial Asante, 1924–1945', *History Workshop Journal*, XXXVIII (1994), pp. 23–47; Deborah
Gaitskell, 'Female Faith and the Politics of the Personal: Five Mission Encounters in Twentieth-
century South Africa', *FR*, LXV (2000), p. 69.

ultra-masculine ethos of the Colonial Service was tempered as the brave
'frontier days' of the imperial 'hero' (often from a military background) gave
way to bureaucratic consolidation and development of the colonial infra-
structure. More men in the Colonial Service were now married, and the class
profile of the service changed as lower middle-class grammar school men
were recruited into the less prestigious technical grades. Wartime experiences had undermined the confident imperial masculinities associated with
nineteenth-century Empire. In the 1920s it became more difficult to recruit
élite Colonial Officers; influential pro-imperialists complained that the
'hollow men' of the post-war generation lacked a sense of adventure and
patriotism, were materialistic and selfish, and favoured the 'higher rewards'
of business over colonial service.[24] Men who had seen active service were 'no
longer satisfied with ordinary life', and suffered from restlessness, boredom,
and 'purposelessness', undermining their 'fitness' for the imperial mission.[25]
These cultural changes were reflected in the trope of the colonial 'anti-hero'
found in the inter-war writings of Graham Greene, Joyce Cary, George
Orwell, and Somerset Maugham. Maugham's fictional colonial world is
peopled by such 'anti-heroes', who, like lower-class men, lacked imperial
masculine virtues and were simultaneously weak, pathetic, neurotic, inse-
cure, brutal, and womanizing.[26]

More open homosexuality in the metropolitan centre, where it was now
marginally tolerated among certain 'cultivated élites', constituted another
facet of the cynicism, restlessness, and dissolute hedonism associated with
the perceived post-war crisis of masculinity. Although homoeroticism had
long been a facet of the colonial relationship, male homosexuals had no place
in the European colony where colonial leaders deemed it essential to uphold
superior white morality. Homosexuality subverted heterosexual white domesticity, transgressed the race boundaries on which the stability of Empire
depended, and thus weakened the foundations of colonialism. Male homosexuality remained illegal and experiences of discrimination may perhaps
have made homosexual men and women more sympathetic to colonial
grievances.[27] Lionel Fielden, an open homosexual who had a long-standing

---

[24] Lord Milner, cited in Robert Heussler, *British Rule in Malaya: The Malayan Civil Service and its Predecessors, 1867–1942* (Oxford, 1981), p. 26. See also Major Sir Ralph Furse, *Aucuparius: Recollections of a Recruiting Officer* (London, 1962), pp. 58, 286.

[25] Letter to Ingeborg Dinesen, Autumn 1921, in Isak Dinesen, *Letters from Africa*, p. 112.

[26] Heussler, *British Rule in Malaya*, pp. 320–21.

[27] Robert Aldrich, *Colonialism and Homosexuality* (London, 2003), pp. 4, 209–10, 198, 367.

relationship with an Asian man, was an 'iconoclastic, anti-colonial aesthete' at the 'centre' of the British establishment in Delhi.[28] However, as the first Controller of Broadcasting for the British Broadcasting Corporation (BBC) in India from 1935 to 1940, Fielden, who became a committed anti-imperialist in the 1940s, was not engaged directly in imperial rule of the colonized. In the imperialist mindset, the effeminate traits associated with homosexuality were negatively contrasted with the manly qualities desired of a Colonial Officer. Homosexuality thus still constituted a threat to the prestige of the Colonial Service and reprisals remained severe, as in the purge of homosexuals in government service in Malaya in the 1930s.[29]

Anxieties over the moral fibre of the post-war generation of men under-score how the 'integrity' of Empire still depended on 'superior' white masculinities cultivated through a public school education which instilled values of military discipline, duty, service, and team spirit.[30] Being 'good at sport' remained an important qualification for a job in the élite adminis-trative branches of the Colonial Service and was also valued by private companies in the colonies. Emancipated pro-imperialist women continued to admire rugged, romanticized, upper-class imperial masculinity, distan-cing themselves from feminism which they increasingly associated with new forces antipathetic to Empire. Margery Perham was ambivalent about her success in a man's world, admired superior imperial masculine virtues, and yearned for marriage to a colonial hero. Tall and athletic, Perham had all the virtues and qualities expected of, and admired in, the 'right sort' of modern colonial wife.[31]

Domesticity, marriage, and appropriate gender roles remained central to imperial stability. Eugenicists believed that single men and women who delayed marriage were failing in their racial duty to reproduce the white race. Single women were regarded as an economic and sexual threat ('amazons' and 'flappers') and masculinity was still defined through mar-riage and the paternal responsibility which conferred full adulthood.[32] In the

---

[28] Joselyn Zivin, ' "Bent": A Colonial Subversive and Indian Broadcasting', P&P, CLXII (1999), pp. 193–220, 201–04.

[29] Butcher, The British in Malaya, p. 194.

[30] Furse, Aucuparius, pp. 189–90.

[31] Described in contemporary sources cited by Procida, Married to the Empire, pp. 40–41. See also Deborah Lavin, 'Margery Perham's Initiation into African Affairs', in Alison Smith and Mary Bull, eds., Margery Perham and British Rule in Africa (London, 1991), p. 54.

[32] Katherine Holden, ' "Nature Takes no Notice of Morality": Singleness and Married Love in Interwar Britain', WHR, XI (2002), pp. 483–87; 497.

imperialist mind, feminism, unpatriotic anti-imperialism, and socialism
were conflated and associated with sexual immorality, miscegenation, and
questionable moral character. Among the wealthy 'fast' set in the metropolitan centre, illicit and interracial sex were 'chic'. Women's apparent penchant
for 'black gigolos', satirized by Evelyn Waugh in the character of Felicity
Cardover in *Decline and Fall* (1928), was used to discredit the politics of left-
wing women. Nancy Cunard was one such radical; in 1932, she privately
published *Black Man and White Ladyship: An Anniversary*, a spirited defence
of her relationship with an African–American musician.[33]

Popular narratives of miscegenation evoked images of predatory 'oriental'
men mingling on the 'dark side' of London and other British ports with the
new, sexually 'loose' flappers and degenerate 'dope' girls. The Chinese opium
dens of London's Limehouse were constructed as a site of the corruption of
white women, and the predatory sexuality of Chinese men was 'a relentlessly
reiterated theme' in popular culture.[34] Representations of Asian men as a
threat to white women were fuelled by sensational press reports of violent
abductions of European women and girls in China. Such news reports
reflected residual concerns about the white slave trade, a focus of pre-1914
reformist campaigns, which was commonly associated with 'oriental' men.
White representations of such men as inherently bestial and emblematic of
forbidden sexuality were also reinforced in the new 'desert romance' genre,
where the handsome but brutal 'oriental' forced white women into submis-
sion and sexual slavery.[35]

Conversely, the new 'Empire Romance' set in the white settler colonies
confirmed superior 'Anglo-Saxon' identities and evoked confident female
emigrants enjoying the adventure and freedom of Empire and the promise of
a husband, but free from the taint of moral and racial corruption. In contrast
to the pre-1918 masculine genre of imperial adventure, such novels focused
on heroines, emblematic of the new importance of women to the imperial
mission.[36] Female migration in the white Empire normalized and
strengthened settler societies. In contemporary pro-imperialist imagery,
virtuous white womanhood symbolized the importance of the white

---

[33] Bush, *Imperialism, Race and Resistance*, pp. 211–14.

[34] Robert Bickers, *Britain in China: Community, Culture and Colonialism, 1900–1949* (Manchester, 1999), pp. 44–45, 51–53.

[35] Billie Melman, *Women and the Popular Imagination in the Twenties: Flappers and Nymphs*
(Basingstoke, 1986), p. 137.

[36] Ibid., p. 134.

Dominions, reflecting women's central role in 'domesticating the heart of the wild', taming marauding 'frontier masculinities', and securing the stability and racial purity of the white Empire.[37]

Female emigration was thus enthusiastically promoted by the state after 1918 as a solution to the post-war 'excess of females': the 'cult of the cinema', the 'Empire Romance', and marriage to soldiers from the Dominions ensured an 'increased desire' to emigrate.[38] Such women were vital to 'Homemaking in the Dominions' and needed the skills suited to good settler wives and mothers to build up a strong white Empire. The Khaki University of Canada, the Educational Service of the Canadian Army, set up a Department of Home Economics at its London College 'to assist women [including wives of Canadian soldiers] intending to settle in Canada'. Women were offered courses in bee-keeping, dairying, poultry-keeping, gardening, dressmaking, health-care, and citizenship.[39] The moral protection of working-class female migrants remained a paternalistic priority, as emphasized in a pamphlet issued by the government in response to the 'many inquiries' at Labour Exchanges. Women were advised not to go out to the colonies alone but 'in parties in charge of a matron' (continuing the policy of chaperoning which had begun before the war), and to secure introductions through reputable organizations such as the Victoria League, which had branches in the white Commonwealth.[40]

Although emigration dwindled in the inter-war years with unstable economic conditions, pro-imperialist women continued to promote female emigration enthusiastically. In 1919, in recognition of the importance of emigration to domestic and imperial priorities, the government wrested control from older female emigration societies through their amalgamation

[37] Marilyn Lake, 'Frontier Feminism and the Marauding White Man: Australia, 1990s to 1940s', in Pierson and Chaudhuri, eds., Nation, Empire Colony, pp. 95–105; Dominic David Alessio, 'Domesticating "the Heart of the Wild"; Female Personifications of the Colonies, 1886–1940', WHR, VI (1997), pp. 239–71.

[38] Moutray Read, 'Women and Empire Consolidation', p. 322. Memorandum on Emigration Policy', enclosed in W. A. S. Hewins: General Correspondence and Papers, University of Sheffield, Official Papers, Box 81, Section 117/17/1/1–40/ 5–6.

[39] Information sheet about courses for women from Mrs Cunningham, the Khaki University of Canada (London College), 13 Dec. 1918, enclosed in Hewins papers, section 117/17/1/49–99/ 52–7; 'Homemaking in the Dominions', advertisement placed by the Emigration and Colonisation Department of the Salvation Army, United Empire, IX (Jan. 1918), p. xxi.

[40] 'The Emigration of Women: Official Statement for the use of women who may wish to Emigrate to Other Parts of the Empire After the War', 1st edn., 1919, p. 5, Hewins Papers, Box 81, Section 117/17/1/41–99.

into the Society for the Oversea Settlement of British Women (SOSBW). From 1920, this quasi-governmental organization of 'responsible' women' with 'first hand experience of... Empire migration' acted as a central advisory body on emigration and was recognized as the women's branch of the Oversea Settlement Committee.[41] Funded by an annual government grant and voluntary donations, the SOSBW was particularly active in addressing the demand for professional female emigrants in the expanding settler colonies of Southern Rhodesia and Kenya, and provided paid posts and good career opportunities for educated women, with plenty of subsidized overseas travel. From 1933, at the request of the Secretary of State for Foreign Affairs, the SOSBW also advised British women 'contemplating' marriage with foreign nationals of the 'legal and social implications... especially if their future husbands are of a different race'. Through its élite patrons, the organization was able to establish colonial branches and forge powerful links with women settlers' organizations. By 1928, the Catholic Women's League, the Church Army, the National Council of Women, the Girl Guides, the Mothers' Union, the Girl's Friendly Society, and the Young Women's Christain Association (YWCA) had representatives on the SOSBW.[42]

Elite women also worked closely with powerful male members of the Royal Colonial Institute, re-branded the Royal Empire Society (1929) and latterly the Royal Commonwealth Society (1958), name changes which reflected the evolving imperial mission. A survey of the Society's journal, *United Empire*, from 1919 reveals that women were particularly active in local branches, helped to organize conferences, engaged in public speaking, and contributed to educational schemes to promote Empire. Women were also the social facilitators of imperial 'salons' and their patronage of key organizations strengthened 'family' relationships across the Empire. Such organizations included the East West Friendship Council, founded in 1921, to provide hospitality in British homes for 'colonial and Eastern students' and the Victoria League, established in 1901 to promote 'more knowledge about Empire amongst British citizens' and foster better relationships between Britain and its white Empire.[43] Royal women were also active pro-

---

[41] G. F. Plant, *A Survey of Voluntary Effort in Women's Empire Migration* (London, 1950), pp. 95–101.

[42] SOSBW Annual Report, 1960, pp. 7–8; SOSBW Annual Report, 1928 and Annual Reports, 1919–1961, RCS, R 11/16; 'Society for the Overseas Settlement of British Women, Rhodesia Sub-Committee Report, 1935–7', RCS, −52m77, pp. 9, 11, 18–19.

[43] *Report of the Negotiations for Amalgamation between the League of Empire and the Victoria League* (London, 1909) p. 1; 'The East West Friendship Council', *The Times*, 27 Feb. 1956.

imperialists. Princess Christian was the first president of the SOSBW, patron of the Colonial Training College, president of the East African Nursing Association, and founder of the Princess Christian Cottage Hospital in Freetown, Sierra Leone. After Christian's death in 1923, Princess Marie Louise continued her charitable work for the SOSBW and as patron of the West African Nursing Service. As a grand-daughter of Queen Victoria, her African royal tours were important in securing the loyalty and consent of the colonized.[44]

With a few exceptions, elite women remained within orthodox gender bounds, concentrating on female emigration, nursing, education, guiding (under the leadership of Dame Katherine Furse), and supporting men in defending and disseminating imperial values. In academia, by contrast, women were breaching gender barriers and beginning to make their mark on colonial policy-making, anthropological studies, and critical analyses of Empire. Dr Vera Anstey (1889–1952), a lecturer in commerce at London University, was an authority on Indian development and *The Economic Development of India* (1929) was still in print in a fourth edition in 1952. Women became particularly fascinated by problems of African development. Notable here were pro-imperialists Margery Perham and Elspeth Huxley, socialist critic Rita Hinden, anthropologists Margaret Read, Lucy Mair, and Audrey Richards, and feminist and educationalist Margaret Wrong.[45]

Professional opportunities for women, however, remained limited and clearly gendered, and entry into masculine worlds triggered resentment and sexism. Women's appointment to administrative posts in the Colonial Service after 1938 evoked fears among men of a 'petticoat [colonial] Government'.[46] In a similar vein, colonial officials complained of the 'disproportionate number of women [African] experts' and an 'unhealthy... abstention of the masculine intellect', apparent until the Second World War.[47] Male anthropologists argued that women were not serious researchers, saw fieldwork as a 'sinecure' or a 'form of exotic entertainment', and believed women's 'intrusion' was undesirable; Audrey Richards' 'real work' was allegedly her

---

[44] Princess Marie Louise, *Letters from the Gold Coast* (London, 1926), pp. 24, 37–38, 106, 225.

[45] Ruth Compton Brouwer, 'Margaret Wrong's Literacy Work and the "Remaking of Women" in Africa, 1929–48', *Journal of Imperial and Commonwealth History* (hereafter *JICH*), XXIII (1995), pp. 427–52, 428.

[46] Malcolm MacDonald, MP, cited in Callaway, *Gender, Culture and Empire*, pp. 142–44.

[47] Furse, *Aucuparious*, pp. 305–06.

earlier 'welfare work', which was 'proper' women's work.[48] Professional rivalry was arguably at the root of this animosity towards Richards, who was well-connected in official circles, became a Reader in Social Anthropology at LSE in 1946 and a Fellow of Newnham College Cambridge in 1956.[49]

While men still dominated policy-making and governance, as a feminizing influence in the colonies white women made an indispensable contribution to the changing context of twentieth-century Empire. Their increased presence in the colonies after 1918 was facilitated by several factors. Marriage was now encouraged by the Colonial Office and improvements in tropical medicine, refrigeration, and transport ensured a more comfortable expatriate lifestyle for white wives in rural, as well as urban areas. Influenced by modern ideas of companionate marriage, younger officials and their wives now shared a more equal partnership in the service of the Empire.[50] Colonial development also opened up more opportunities for professional and missionary women to participate in the 'civilizing mission'. In turn, women were attracted to the Empire by improved career and/or marriage prospects, greater freedom, travel, and the adventure of the hunt, trek, and safari, 'stepping off into the blue...where no white woman had trod before'.[51] How did this increase in numbers of white women, combined with the discourse of a progressive modern Empire, affect the gendered orders of colonizer and colonized, and the articulation of race and cultural differences?

White women were seminal in the construction of whiteness and superior gender identities and the policing of sex and race borders. As an influential female Kenyan resident observed, white women should be a 'special creation', something 'infinitely higher and more remote than white men'; a powerful 'weapon' against the 'vast hordes of natives', they were crucial to white prestige.[52] White women were essential to making Empire respectable through marriage, the policing of white male sexuality, and 'moral rearmament'. The guardians of moral and physical health and hygiene in the expatriate home, white women's presence helped to secure race discipline,

---

[48] Bronislaw Malinowski to Lucy Mair, 3 July 1932; E. E. Evans-Pritchard to Meyer Fortes, 19 July 1940, both cited in J. Goody, *The Expansive Moment: Anthropology in Britain and Africa, 1918–1970* (Cambridge, 1995), pp. 69–71.

[49] Audrey Isabel Richards, 1899–1984, biographical information, British Library of Political Science Archives.

[50] Procida, *Married to the Empire*, pp. 50–51.

[51] Nellie Grant to Elspeth Huxley, 1 Feb. 1935, Elspeth Josceline Huxley Papers, Rhodes House, Oxford, Mss. Afr. S. 782, Box 1, File 3.

[52] Mrs. Hildegarde Beatrice Hinde, 'The "Black Peril" in British East Africa: A Frank Talk to Women Settlers', *The Empire Review* (1921), pp. 193, 198.

uniformity, normalcy, and order which defined visions of the European bourgeois 'colonial utopia'.[53] The parallel domestication and moralization of colonizing and colonized society were integral to the development of a modern, progressive Empire and essential to its stability and future prosperity. Domesticity stabilized white expatriate cultures creating a bourgeois social order which secured conformity to shared values and demonstrated a remarkable similarity across the British Empire. Thus, in India, the Chinese concessions, and Malaya, expatriate wives created a 'Britain in the home', a model of bourgeois white domesticity.[54] Anglo-Indian society, claimed Lionel Fielden, was increasingly defined by the 'younger sons of Clapham and Surbiton plus their suburban wives [and] stuffy drawing rooms' and even 'Darkest Africa' was now 'too suburban for words'.[55]

The domestication of the Empire to strengthen the imperial mission was, however, undermined by multiple factors: resentment of female intrusion into the masculine milieu of the newer 'frontier' colonies; the changing nature of expatriate society and white gender relations; continuing breaches in race and sex borders; the impact of women on colonial race dynamics; and the ambivalent and sometimes resistant responses of the colonized to the imposition of Western domesticity. Stable domesticity was easier to achieve in India than the rural areas of tropical Africa, where wives often stayed only for a short time, disillusioned by the 'monotonous life', the discomfort of tropical climates, and the absence of children.[56] Excess drinking, associated with the expatriate lifestyle, exacerbated the 'modern' problems of adultery and divorce and intensified white gender conflicts which further undermined the white domestic ideal.[57]

Moreover, female intrusion into a masculine world was not always welcome. In Malaya, 70 per cent of men aged thirty-five to thirty-nine were married but marriage often proved a financial strain for younger men as the 'penalties of civilization' (maintaining appropriate standards) incurred

---

[53] Ann Laura Stoler, *Race and the Education of Desire: Foucault's History of Sexuality and the Colonial Order of Things* (Durham, NC, 1996), p. 164; and Stoler, 'Making Empire Respectable: The Politics of Race and Sexual Morality in Twentieth-century Colonial Cultures', in Jan Bremen, ed., *Imperial Monkey Business: Racial Supremacy in Social Darwinist Theory and Colonial Practice* (Amsterdam, 1990), p. 48.

[54] Procida, *Married to the Empire*, pp. 50–51, 56–60; Bickers, *Britain in China*, pp. 88–90.

[55] Nellie Grant to Gervas Huxley, 19 Dec. 1934, Huxley Papers, Box 1, File 2, f. 95. See also Fielden, cited in Zivin, ' "Bent": A Colonial Subversive', p. 213.

[56] Erick Berry (Allena Champlin Best), *Mad Dogs and Englishmen* (London, 1941), p. 57.

[57] Butcher, *British in Malaya*, p. 142.

debts. Tensions also developed between white wives and male servants who had run former bachelor households 'pretty well without any feminine influence'.[58] Similarly, in Nigeria, wives 'complicated' simple masculine lifestyles with 'their curtains, their bridge parties, competitive dinners and social feuds'.[59] Women, claimed Ralph Furse, were 'apt to be a public menace in native territories', a sentiment echoed by serving officers who accused wives of creating breaches in male comradeship, and of undermining good race relations with the colonized.[60] Predictably, the élite of both sexes attributed 'narrow-minded' attitudes on race to conventional wives from 'very limited backgrounds', trapped in an 'imitation of suburban life', ignorant of local conditions, and unused to handling servants.[61] Such statements illuminate the problematic relationship between gender, class, and race, and contradictions between the ideal of domesticity generated in colonial discourse and the realities of the 'anxious and ambivalent world' which the colonizers inhabited.[62]

White gender relations and race attitudes were influenced by changes in metropolitan society and culture but also shaped by the specific conditions in the colonies. Official wives were not expected to take paid employment and therefore remained financially dependent on their husbands. A woman's status was defined by her husband's position in the colony and single women needed a husband in order to gain social acceptance.[63] In contrast, settler women saw themselves as pioneers, sharing hardships with their husbands. They developed a strong attachment to the homes they created and were proactive defenders of the settler way of life.[64] In Kenya, independent women such as Karen Blixen and Nellie Grant (mother of Elspeth Huxley) managed farms, finances, and African labour, and were the maternal powers amongst the Africans living on their land. Their menfolk tended to be dreamers, uninterested in farming, and often absent. In contrast to more conventional 'artisan' Rhodesia, 'aristocratic' Kenya was commonly represented as a

[58] Testimonies of ex-colonial wives in Charles Allen, *Tales from the South China Seas: Images of the British in South East Asia in the Twentieth Century* (London, 1983), pp. 219, 229; Butcher, *British in Malaya*, pp. 135–37, 143.

[59] Berry, *Mad Dogs*, pp. 57–59.

[60] E. F. G. Haig, *Nigerian Sketches* (London, 1931) pp. 27–32; Furse, *Aucuparius*, p. 2.

[61] Berry, *Mad Dogs*, p. 184.

[62] Stoler, *Race and the Education of Desire*, p. 169.

[63] Procida, *Married to the Empire*, pp. 15–16; Butcher, *British in Malaya*, pp. 137, 143.

[64] Deborah Kirkwood, 'Settler Wives in Southern Rhodesia: A Case Study', in Callan and Ardener, eds, *Incorporated Wife*, p. 160.

dysfunctional, hedonistic society. Fuelled by drugs, 'alcoholidays', and adultery, it was seen as a hunting ground for 'vamping women' and a 'dumping ground' for neurotics beyond the censure of conventional British society.[65] In the English imagination, Kenya offered adventure and escape from convention, as described in James Fox's *White Mischief* (1982). The growth of the tourist safari, brought to life in Ernest Hemingway's *The Green Hills of Africa* (1935), nurtured an atavistic white masculinity searching for 'virgin' hunting territory; 'safari' men yearned for adventure, not domesticity.

The imperial vision of order, permanence, and tamed masculinities through a segregated white domesticity was clearly fragile. It was impossible to exclude fully from the white expatriate home the smells, dirt, and disease that white colonial discourse associated with the colonized. Domestic life was shared with servants who witnessed the most intimate aspects of expatriate daily life, including bodily functions.[66] The continued attractions of the 'native mistress' also threatened the white home, and undercurrents of sexual jealousy complicated relationships between white and colonized women. Official strictures, the promotion of marriage, and changing demography had some success in regulating imperial male sexuality, yet in remote areas where white women were rare, single men in the Colonial African Service still kept young African women who only came in 'after dark'. Married men in India continued their 'dangerous liaisons' with 'native girlfriends', although often secretly.[67] Spirals of power fusing sex, race, money, and social advantages for powerless female (and male) 'others' weave through the history of slavery and Empire into the post-imperial era. Sex, as Philippa Levine observes elsewhere in this volume, was 'part of the politics of Empire', and the regulation of sexuality and control of prostitution and venereal diseases remained fundamental to imperial policy.

Strengthening these weak points in the sex and race borders of the Empire demanded a more strident articulation in colonial discourse of superior white masculinity, femininity, and sexuality in reference to the colonized 'other'. Imperial masculinity was characterized by moral, physical, and

[65] Dr. H. L Gordon (Kenyan 'nerve' specialist) to Nellie Grant, Nairobi, 6 Oct. 1935; Nellie Grant to Elspeth Huxley, 20 July 1933; 14 Nov. 1934; 28 Dec. 1937; Huxley Papers, Rhodes House, Oxford, Box 1, Files 2, 3, and 5. For contrasts between Rhodesia and Kenya, please see Dane Kennedy, Islands of White: Settler Society and Culture in Kenya and Southern Rhodesia, 1890–1939 (Durham, North Carolina, 1987).

[66] See, for instance, E. M. Collingham, *Imperial Bodies: The Physical Experience of the Raj, c. 1800–1947* (Oxford, 2001), pp. 169–76.

[67] Collingham, *Imperial Bodies*, pp. 184–85; Martin Lindsay cited in Charles Allen, *Tales from the Dark Continent: Images of British Colonial Africa in the Twentieth Century* (1979; London, 1987), p. 18.

intellectual superiority. Testimony analysed by John Butcher suggests that in the new 'respectable' Empire, breaches of racial borders were regarded as an 'insult to manliness and self control', and sexual laxity was regarded as an inferior trait of colonized men.[68] Sexual lapses were blamed on colonized women's naked or exposed bodies which invited 'lust [and] animal desire', a 'curse' of physical passion, stimulated by the tropical climate, and in no way comparable to 'pure love' for white women.[69] In China, Malaya, and India, interracial marriage was negatively correlated with poor white men who threatened white prestige. Men who went 'native' in Africa were commonly depicted in colonial discourse as lower class, in trade not government, and morally and physically degenerate.[70]

Through concubinage and routine day-to-day governance, which included controlling 'troublesome' women, white men had a different relationship to, and perceptions of, colonized women than did white women.[71] In white women's memoirs, African women are silent, nameless ciphers most commonly represented as beasts of burden, 'their own jailers in the subjection in which they were held'.[72] This distance increased the risk of cultural misunderstanding and reinforced white women's sense of superiority. In contrast, white women in Malaya, Hong Kong, and India were required to engage in some marginal socializing with higher-class colonized women as integral to strategies of governance. Popular representations of Asian women none the less continued to evoke the seclusion of *purdah* and passive subordination to male patriarchy; white women's emancipation and freedom was favourably contrasted with the drudgery and subservience of the mass of poorer Asian women. The gun, used for hunting and 'self-defence', and symbolic of superior imperial masculinities, became a powerful motif of emancipated imperial womanhood, enhancing white women's 'fitness to rule' over defenceless, colonized women and 'unmanly' men.[73]

[68] Butcher, *British in Malaya*, pp. 204–96.

[69] Haig, *Nigerian Sketches*, p. 232.

[70] For instance, Berry, *Mad Dogs*, p. 57; Butcher, *British in Malaya*, pp. 95–96; Bickers, *Britain in China*, pp. 97–98; Elizabeth Buettner, 'Problematic Spaces, Problematic Races: Defining "Europeans" in Late Colonial India', *WHR*, IX (2000) pp. 290–91.

[71] Analysed effectively in Patricia Hayes, ' "Cocky" Hahn and the "Black Venus": The Making of A Native Commissioner in South West Africa, 1915–46', in Nancy Rose Hunt, Tessie R. Lui, and Jean Quataert, eds., *Gender and History, Special Issue: Gendered Colonialisms in African History*, VIII (1996), pp. 364–93.

[72] Elspeth Huxley, *The Mottled Lizard* (London, 1962), pp. 123–24.

[73] Procida, *Married to the Empire*, pp. 141, 153.

Ironically, through the gender distortions of colonial society, white women were far closer to colonized men. With the exception of South Africa, where white paranoia over 'the Black Peril', and the demand for male migrant labour resulted in a complex power relationship between white 'madams' and African maids, domestic labour throughout the tropical Empire was predominantly male. Colonized men wanted to protect their womenfolk from the corrupting influences of Western culture and sexual exploitation by white men. From the white perspective, keeping black women out of the white domestic domain minimized the risks of miscegenation.[74] Women depended on favoured 'boys' for 'comfort and support' and 'houseboy stories' occupied female gossip throughout the tropical Empire.[75] On trek and in expatriate homes, women developed an unusual intimacy with the 'boys' (as did Princess Marie Louise on her royal tour of the Gold Coast in 1926) who washed and sewed their clothes, helped them dress, and arranged their hair. A trusted 'boy' was 'better than a white lady's maid', claimed Karen Blixen.[76] White women could exercise a novel, racialized power over colonized men, whereas they had little comparable power over white servants, male or female. As Blixen's critics observe, her relationship to Africans was based on paternalistic racism disguised as love, but love of a loyal dog always ready to do his mistress's bidding.[77]

Studies of gender and colonialism have focused primarily on African women, yet domestic service, incorporation into the colonial economy, and the 'demilitarization' of pre-colonial military cultures also transformed colonial masculinities with long-term repercussions for gender identities and relations. In South Africa, for instance, urban migrant workers fought to maintain their masculine identity through organizations which drew on rural cultures. The articulation of new urban black masculinities was integral to male working-class resistance and survival. Violence became an affirmation of manhood and a way of contesting white oppression, but negatively affected domestic life, intensifying violence towards women. In contrast a

[74] Elizabeth Schmidt, 'Race, Sex and Domestic Labour: The Question of African Servants in Southern Rhodesia, 1900–1939', in Hansen, *African Encounters with Domesticity*, pp. 224, 234–36; Jacqueline Cock, *Maids and Madams: Domestic Workers Under Apartheid* (London, 1989), pp. 58–65.

[75] Berry, *Mad Dogs*, p. 254; Allen, *Tales from the South China Seas*, pp. 210–16.

[76] Dinesen to Ingeborg Dinesen, 23 Sep. 1914, Dinesen, *Letters from Africa*, pp. 4, 15; Princess Marie Louise, *Letters*, pp. 75, 87–88, 101.

[77] Ngugi wa Thiong'o, 'Her Cook, Her Dog: Karen Blixen's Africa', in Thiong'o, *Moving the Centre: The Struggle for Cultural Freedoms* (London, 1993), p. 133.

minority of conservative rural chiefs collaborated with white men; white and
black patriarchies came together as 'convergent masculinities' to reconfirm
power over colonized women and subordinate men. Similar transformations
occurred elsewhere in colonial Africa.[78]

In addition to the collaborative traditional élites, the only colonized men
to retain white respect were those admired for their military prowess and
rugged independence, evoking white male nostalgia for frontier masculinities. Rationality, financial prudence, sexual control, authority, and responsibility— virtues deemed lacking in colonized men—defined a superior white
masculinity. The feminization of Asian men and infantilization of African
'boys' sealed their inferiority and neutralized their sexual potency in 'quies-
cent' colonies. In turbulent India, however, memories of the 1857 Mutiny
lingered, nourished by stories of the desecration of white women still in
circulation; one English female visitor to the Mutiny memorial at Cawnpore
described it as a 'deadly place... full of sinister ghosts', and expressed fears
for her own safety.[79] In the African white settler colonies, the alleged black
male sexual threat to white women was commonly evoked to strengthen
white racial solidarity. The rhetoric of this 'Black Peril' had little correlation
with incidences of rape, reflecting instead fluctuating levels of white anxiety.[80]

White constructions of colonial masculinities and femininities, and related perceptions of inferior colonial gender relations, domesticity, and
sexuality informed colonial policy and practice. The link between civilization and domesticity can be traced back to the nineteenth-century campaigns of evangelical missionaries to civilize the 'heathen'.[81] After 1918,
'modernization' of colonial gender orders was given greater priority in
colonial policy as cultural and political transformations resulting from
accelerated developments in colonial economies posed new threats to the
colonial order. If the colonized shared 'modern', Western notions of domesticity, colonial societies would be stabilized and greater consent secured for
the imperial 'civilizing' mission. 'Remaking' the 'primitive' African man

---

[78] Robert Morell, 'Of Boys and Men: Masculinity and Gender in Southern African Studies',
Journal of Southern African Studies, XXII (1998), pp. 619–44, 629.

[79] 'Tour from Nagpur to Delhi', Diana Hartley Papers, RCS, Mss 22, Addenda 1, File 1, 'Diaries
etc.', p. 4.

[80] Stoler, *Race and the Education of Desire*, pp. 46–47. For a more detailed discussion, see Jock
McCulloch, *Black Peril, White Virtue: Sexual Crime in Southern Rhodesia, 1902–1935* (Bloomington, Ind., 2000).

[81] See chap. by Catherine Hall in this volume.

centred on 'moralizing' migrant workers through philanthropic initiatives such as the South African Bantu Men's Social Clubs which emphasized superior white masculine values.[82] Similarly, in India, the Purity Mission set up by the Central Labour Board in Bombay helped the labourer 'give up his habits of vice, including drink and gambling and live an honest life'.[83] The young colonized were socialized into Western gender roles and value systems through the Girl Guides and Boy Scouts Movement.[84] Domestic science education trained Indian and African women to be good modern wives and mothers who would act as stabilizing influences on men.[85]

Christian conversion, education, a stable family life, improved health and welfare, and the 'uplift' of colonized women were part of a 'raft of strategies' employed to inculcate 'civilized values' and to provide an 'antidote to subversion'.[86] These new colonial policies were implemented primarily by female missionaries, nurses, doctors, welfare workers, and teachers. From 1919, the Overseas Nursing Association (a modernized version of the Colonial Nursing Association established in 1895) played an active role in training nurses and developing health services. Diana Hartley (1894–1986), a nurse-midwife, was appointed the first full-time general secretary of the Trained Nurses' Association of India from 1935 to 1944 to promote nursing education for Anglo-Indian and Indian women. The increase in indigenous nurses, who were paid far less than their white counterparts, added a new dimension to the articulation of race, gender, and class divisions in colonial cultures.[87]

Although there were common threads in gendered colonial policies, specific strategies varied according to different representations of female colonial subjects. In Africa, migration and urbanization evoked the spectre of unregulated male sexuality, prostitution, and venereal diseases. Female urban migrants, superfluous to the urban male workforce and

---

[82] Bush, *Imperialism, Race and Resistance*, pp. 153–55.

[83] Rajani Palme Dutt, *India Today* (London, 1940), p. 370.

[84] See chap. by Fiona Paisley in this volume.

[85] For instance, LaRay Denzer, 'Domestic Science Training in Colonial Yorubaland, Nigeria', in Hansen, ed., *African Encounters with Domesticity*; Mary Hancock, 'Gendering the Modern: Women and Home Science in British India', in Burton, ed., *Gender, Sexuality and Colonial Modernities*, pp. 148–61.

[86] Stoler and Cooper, 'Between Metropole and Colony: Rethinking a Research Agenda', in Stoler and Cooper, eds., *Tensions of Empire*, pp. 26, 31.

[87] For a seminal study, see Shula Marks, *Divided Sisterhood: Race, Class and Gender in the South African Nursing Profession* (London, 1995). See also 'Miss Hartley's tours, Nov. 24, 1937–Jan. 5, 1939', Hartley Papers, File 1, 'Diaries etc; "Printed Items" (including *Nursing Journal of India*), ibid., File 5.

outside traditional gender discipline, were anathema to colonial authorities
and threatened the 'vista of masculine ethnicity' defended by indigenous
élites.[88] In Australia and New Zealand, 'native' women's apparent greater
autonomy and unregulated sexuality was also regarded as a major threat to
the stability of colonial society and to racial 'pollution' through 'miscegenation'. Similarly, African–Caribbean women continued to be associated with
'heathen practices' stemming from slavery and associated with promiscuity,
rejection of Christian marriage, and 'mother-headed' families.[89] Colonial
policies, supported by missionary initiatives, focused on two key strategies:
the strengthening of indigenous patriarchy to control both female migration
and sexual autonomy and the promotion of Christian marriage, and 'home
life' education emphasizing health, cleanliness, and hygiene. Colonialism
now 'entered some of the most intimate aspects' of the lives of African
women, who, unlike Indian women, had attracted negligible attention before
1918.[90] Interventions in gender roles and childbearing practices, however,
provoked ambivalent and complex responses mediated by education, class
position, and levels of Westernization.[91]

   In British Asia, there was a well-established pattern of intervention by
metropolitan imperial feminists to emancipate oppressed Asian women
from what they believed was a barbaric, patriarchal Asian culture. After
1918, campaigns to control child marriage in India and the sale of young
Chinese girls in Hong Kong, had more influence on colonial government,
which implemented modernizing reforms.[92] From the perspective of the

[88] Bruce Berman and John Lonsdale, *Unhappy Valley: Conflict in Kenya and Africa, II*
(Oxford, 1992), p. 381; see also Elizabeth Schmidt, *Peasants, Traders and Wives: Shona Women
in the History of Zimbabwe* (London, 1992), pp. 98–106; Jean Allman, ' "Rounding Up Spin-
sters": Gender Chaos and Unmarried Women in Colonial Asante', *Journal of African History*,
XXXVII (1996), pp. 195–214.

[89] Contemporary observations cited in Barbara Bush, ' "Lost Daughters of Afrik"? Caribbean
Women, Identity and Cultural Struggles in Slavery and Freedom', in Maire ni Flathuin, ed., *The
Legacy of Colonialism* (Galway, 1998) p. 34; Christine Choo, *Mission Girls: Australian Aboriginal
Women on Catholic Missions in the Kimberley 1900–1950* (Crawley, WA., 2001), pp. 71, 86, 116:
Kuni Jenkins and Kay Morris Matthews, 'Knowing their Place: The Political Socialisation of
Maori Women in New Zealand through Schooling Policy and Practice, 1967–69', *WHR*, XVII
(1998) pp. 85–106.

[90] Nancy Rose Hunt, 'Le Bébé en Brousse (the baby in the bush): African Birth Spacing and
Colonial Intervention in Breast Feeding in the Belgian Congo', in Stoler and Cooper, eds.,
Tensions of Empire, pp. 307–08.

[91] Allman, 'Making Mothers', pp. 31, 37.

[92] Pedersen, 'The Maternalist Moment', pp. 163, 184–87, 194. See also Antoinette Burton, *Burdens
of History: British Feminists, Indian Women and Imperial Culture, 1865–1914* (Durham, NC, 1994).

colonial intelligentsia, however, the rhetoric of imperial feminism was deeply problematic. Particularly controversial was Katherine Mayo's *Mother India* (1928) which perpetuated stereotypes of passive, repressed Asian women, yet was highly influential in official circles. Nationalist C. S. Ranga Iyer criticized her argument scathingly in *Father India: a Reply to Mother India* (1928). Educated Indian feminists also resented metropolitan maternalist interventions. Although influenced by Western feminism, they now claimed greater autonomy, supporting Indian nationalism, and actively campaigning in favour of such measures as the 1929 Child Marriage Restraint Act.[93]

Mother India is emblematic of a gendered colonial discourse on Indian disease, poverty, and backwardness which prioritized reproductive practices. Mayo paints a grim picture of the traditional childbirth customs of 'unclean' *dhais* (midwives) of the untouchable class.[94] In the 1930s, birth control and development experts also targeted female reproductive practices and high birth rates—which they regarded as a consequence of the inferior position of women—as a prime barrier to development. Despite high infant and maternal mortality rates, they argued, India was experiencing a 'population explosion' which was the cause of poverty, malnutrition, and famine, a deterministic explanation evading any critique of imperial rule.[95] From the 1930s, sterilization and birth control were promoted by health visitors attached to welfare centres, 'spray dry skimmed milk' was distributed to children in famine areas, and Mothercraft nurses taught modern Western practices. Particular attention was paid to the training of *dhais*.[96] White intervention in indigenous reproductive practices was to have an ambivalent outcome which highlights the complex relationship between gender, class, culture, and health. Diana Hartley recorded that missionaries, nurses, and midwives faced 'colossal' challenges to breaking down 'bad habits' and traditional customs which persisted even amongst the 'fairly well to do'.[97]

---

[93] Mrinalini Sinha, 'The Lineage of the "Indian" Modern: Rhetoric, Agency, and the Sarda Act in Late Colonial India', in Burton, ed., *Gender, Sexuality and Colonial Modernities*, pp. 207–21. See also Introduction to Sinha ed., *Mother India* (Ann Arbor, 2000).

[94] Katherine Mayo, *Mother India* (New York, 1928), pp. 91, 109.

[95] Birth Control International Information Centre, *Birth Control in Asia* (London, 1935), and official government publications critiqued in Palme Dutt, 'Overpopulation Fallacies', *India Today*, pp. 60–64.

[96] 'Notes of the Development of Nursing in India, 1947', published as 'Babies in India', *Mothercraft Magazine*, 1947, Hartley Papers, File 1, 'Diaries etc.'.

[97] Ibid.

Overall, improvements in maternal and child welfare and the promotion of bourgeois domesticity were undermined by indigenous female resistance to cultural interventions and the dissonance between the rhetoric of welfare and the economic pragmatics of Empire. In urban and rural India, all family members had to work to survive. Poor women worked in factories and on tea plantations for lower wages than men, and were also exploited by indigenous élites. Malay and Tamil women laboured on Malayan rubber plantations, and white Kenyan farmers exploited the labour of women and children living on their farms.[98] The heavy-handed treatment of colonized women, as resistance to colonialism intensified, also undermined the image of colonial governments as supporters of women's progress. In India, women joined in boycotts, led processions, distributed 'subversive' literature, and made provocative speeches against colonial rule which resulted in official violence against women and unprecedented jail sentences.[99] The colonial authorities in Southern Nigeria shot and killed over forty women in 1929 during mass protests against the extension of taxation to market women and the erosion of women's traditional rights. African gender relations arguably deteriorated under colonialism and women's struggles for survival in a male-oriented colonial economy frequently led to their victimization by the authorities.[100]

Anti-colonialism and nationalism also reconfigured colonial masculinities as male activists reclaimed control over the domestic sphere as central to nationalist ideology and to the revalidation of culture and related gender identities. In India, nationalist writers had claimed the right to organize the domestic domain since the nineteenth century. The 1937 election manifesto of the Indian National Congress now pre-empted the Government of India's role as protector of women's welfare, and committed itself to the 'removal of all sex disabilities'.[101] Missionary campaigns against female circumcision in Kenya in the 1930s intensified the conflict inherent in 'two opposed male sexualities' and conceptions of correct gender orders which stimulated anti-colonial nationalism. Male anti-imperialists, although critical of missionary

[98] Kennedy, *Islands of White*, pp. 141–42; Butcher, *British in Malaya*; Palme Dutt, *India Today*, pp. 45–47, 54–55, 354–56, 360–61.

[99] Suruchi Thapar-Bjorkert, 'Gender, Nationalism and the Colonial Jail: A Study of Women Activists in Uttar Pradesh', *WHR*, VII (1998), pp. 583, 591, 602–05.

[100] Bush, *Imperialism, Race and Resistance*, pp. 64–65.

[101] Palme Dutt, *India Today*, pp. 459–61, 500–01. See also Dipesh Chakrabarty, 'The Difference-Deferral of a Colonial Modernity: Public Debates on Domesticity in British Bengal', in Stoler and Cooper, eds., *Tensions of Empire*, pp. 373–406.

activities and supportive of African nationalism, shared a desire to reform African gender orders. Fenner Brockway, invited to East Africa by the Kenyan African Union in the 1950s, advised Kikuyu men to embrace Western concepts of 'equal marriage' and adopt a 'new attitude' to Kikuyu women whom Brockway regarded as primitive 'beasts of burden' with 'no feminine appeal'. In response to such white cultural interventions, the Kikuyu nationalist, Jomo Kenyatta, defended traditional gender relations in *Facing Mount Kenya; The Tribal Life of the Kikuyu* (1938), and African gender discipline, rights, and duties became central to Mau Mau ideology and the re-conceptualization of citizenship after independence.[102]

The heroic literature of independence and nationalism was predominantly a masculine discourse and prioritized a reactive 'hyper-masculinity' as central to post-colonial modernity.[103] Most colonized women were marginalized from the agenda of 'progressive' colonial policies which were directed to securing a collaborative male élite. In India, a minority of educated women was enfranchised in 1935; West African women's political rights were not considered until after the Second World War and their 'community of women' was mobilized without any Western feminist consciousness-raising.[104] This gendering of nationalist discourse by colonized men, the colonial authorities, and metropolitan anti-imperialists, male and female, obscured women's significant contributions to, and experiences of, nationalist struggles. Prioritizing the alternative female voice, feminist historians have established that women were equal participants in mass nationalist movements, including armed struggles, as in the Mau Mau uprising in Kenya (1954–60). In India, poor rural women's active agency in trade unions and as freedom fighters demonstrated that they were not invisible but obscured between 'layers of historical misconception and distortion'.[105] Involvement

---

[102] Berman and Lonsdale, *Unhappy Valley*, II, pp. 385–86; Fenner Brockway, *African Journeys* (London, 1955), pp. 93–97, 114, 195–260.

[103] Frances Gouda, 'Gender and "Hypermasculinity" as Post-colonial Modernity during Indonesia's Struggle for Independence, 1945 to 1949', in Burton, ed., *Gender, Sexuality and Colonial Modernities*, pp. 161–75.

[104] Cheryl Johnson Odim, 'Actions Louder than Words: The Historical Task of Defining Feminist Consciousness in Colonial West Africa', in Pierson and Chaudhuri, eds., *Nation, Empire, Colony*, pp. 77–93.

[105] Aloka Parashar, 'Women in Nationalist Historiography', in Leela Kasturi and Vina Mazumdar, eds., *Women and Indian Nationalism* (New Delhi, 1994), p. 26. See also Cora Ann Presley, *Kikuyu Women, the Mau Mau Rebellion and Social Change in Kenya* (Denver, Colo., 1993); Susan Geiger, *Tanu Women: Gender and Culture in the Making of Tanganyikan Nationalism, 1955–1965* (Portsmouth, NH, 1997).

in anti-colonial resistance and nationalist protest subverted white representations of colonized women and transformed colonial gender identities,
catalysing important changes in the discourse and practice of imperialism.[106]
These developments, combined with impact of the Second World War,
contributed to the end of Empire.

The fall of Singapore, Hong Kong, and Malaya to the Japanese in 1941–42,
and the subsequent internment of British men and women, seriously damaged British prestige and accelerated the end of Empire in India and the Far
East. Colonial participation in the war effort further undermined colonial
power. African and Caribbean men, banned from bearing arms in the First
World War, now became active servicemen and fighter pilots, and Caribbean
women joined the Women's Royal Army Corps. 'Small . . . slender [and]
graceful' Indian women were transformed into "tough" soldiers, 'crack rifle-
men who were expert with a savage kind of knife'.[107] Wartime conditions also
catalysed mass nationalist movements and the increased numbers of black
workers and servicemen in Britain, including US military personnel, re-
energized moral panics over breaches in sex and race borders.[108] Never before
had Britain and its Empire been so threatened yet, simultaneously, so
dependent on its colonial resources and subjects. This dependency, combined with post-war political priorities, stimulated colonial reforms to pacify
nationalist demands which paved the way for self-rule. Empire was transformed, in rhetoric if not in practice, into a multiracial Commonwealth of
'equal' citizens and development extended under the 1940 Colonial Welfare
and Development Act.

How can a gender dimension enhance understanding of the complexities
of the end of Empire? Additional to the gendering of nationalism and
resistance, four key themes emerge: the enhanced importance of the African
Empire; the continuing feminization of imperial discourse and practice; the
mobilization of élite women and settlers in the defence of Empire; and the
gendering of immigration discourse in post-colonial Britain. Sir Malcolm
Hailey's officially-commissioned *An African Survey; A Study of Problems
Arising in Africa South of the Sahara* (1938; 1957) marked a turning point in
African governance and the re-appropriation of African studies as a respect-

---

[106] See chap. by Mrinalini Sinha in this volume.

[107] Ethel Mannin, *Jungle Journey* (London, 1949) pp. 125–26. See also Ben Bousquet and Colin
Douglas, *West Indian Women at War: British Racism in World War Two* (London, 1991).

[108] Sonya Rose, 'Race, Empire and British Wartime National Identity, 1939–45', *Historical
Research*, LXXIV (2001) pp. 220–38.

able area of élite masculine enquiry, although Margery Perham retained her position as a foremost expert on 'progressive' imperialism. Colonial policy was reoriented towards accelerated modernization, 'managed' mass nationalism, improved welfare and education programmes, and economic development. Policies remained gender-biased, prioritizing men.[109] Economic development, however, compounded pre-war anxieties about the stability of colonial orders as, in Margery Perham's words, 'raw tribesmen turned proletariat' and 'runaway tribal girls' were allegedly transformed into 'prostitutes'.[110] Official fears that wartime disruptions and 'the effect of western civilization' would intensify social deviance and urban disorder resulted in the inauguration of the Colonial Social Science Research Council (CSSRC) in 1944.[111] Interventions in colonial gender orders to promote Western gender values were intensified and Homecraft Clubs, directed at sustaining colonialism through incorporation of the wives of élite African men, flourished.[112]

Areas of academic expertise in which women had made a mark, namely the 'new' disciplines' of sociology and cultural anthropology, were more in demand in the new CSSRC. Council members included the anthropologist, Professor Audrey Richards, already drafted on to the Colonial Research Committee, Professor Ida Ward, an expert in teaching English in the Gold Coast, and Margaret Read, who was in charge of postgraduate training. A number of women made applications for the twenty-five Colonial Research Fellowships on offer. Rather than opening up opportunities for women, however, the CSSRC facilitated male appropriation of the social sciences, as an increasing number of 'distinguished academic workers' were attracted to colonial research and development. The male-dominated Council favoured research proposals from men, and prejudice from colonial officials and male academics was evident. Sir Frank Stockdale, representing

---

[109] Joan E. Lewis, 'Tropical East Ends and the Second World War: Some Contradictions in Colonial Office Welfare Initiatives', *JICH*, XXVIII (2000), p. 47.

[110] Margery Perham, 'The Colonial Dilemma', *Listener*, 15 July 1949, reproduced in Margery Perham, ed., *Colonial Sequence, 1930–1949: A Chronological Commentary upon British Colonial Policy, Especially in Africa* (London, 1967), p. 335.

[111] CSSRC: minutes of first meeting 17, July 1944; agenda of second meeting, 5 Sept. 1944, British Library of Political and Economic Science (BLPES), London School of Economics, Colonial Research, Section 8/1. 8/4.

[112] Sita Ranchod Nillson, 'Educating Eve: The Woman's Club Movement and Political Consciousness among Rural African Women in Southern Rhodesia, 1950–1980', in Hansen, ed., *African Encounters with Domesticity*, p. 195.

the government of Jamaica, opposed a proposal to research into 'development and welfare relief' submitted by the Jamaican anthropologist, Edith Clarke, who had studied at the London School of Economics and carried out research in Africa in the 1930s. Despite Audrey Richards' support, Stockdale objected to Clarke's bid on the grounds that she had allegedly criticized the government for 'lack of knowledge of local conditions', and her proposed study was likely to have a negative impact on the 'smooth working' of the scheme 'under discussion'.[113] It was four years later, in 1948, that Clarke finally secured CSSRC funding for the two-year field study on which she based her influential, but controversial, *My Mother Who Fathered Me: A Study of the Family in Three Selected Communities in Jamaica* (1957).

Discrimination against female academics was counterbalanced by the expanding opportunities for professional women in education, health, social welfare, and the Colonial Administrative Service, reflecting the increasing feminization of colonial policy. Additionally, colonial wives now wanted to work as equals with their husbands in developing the colonies, and demonstrated greater interest in welfare and education of African women. New organizations such as the Women's Corona Society, founded in 1950, the female branch of the Corona Society for top colonial officials, reflected the greater autonomous presence of women.[114] These changes refigured white gender relations and identities, and relationships with the colonized. Allegedly, white women were no longer seen by colonial officials as a hindrance but 'far more go-ahead' than men, 'anxious to improve [race] relations' and to develop social relationships with non-Europeans.[115]

In the metropolitan heartland, the activities of pro-imperialist women were directed towards smoothing the transition from Empire to Commonwealth and retaining British imperial influence. From the 1930s the Victoria League was involved in supervision and guidance of colonial students in the UK. In the 1950s the organization changed its name to the Victoria League for Commonwealth Friendship, and extended its hospitality, formerly restricted to white Commonwealth and overseas visitors, to Africans and Asians in recognition of the need to placate a race-conscious nationalist

[113] Memo by Miss E. Clarke, enclosed in fifth minutes CSSRC, 5 Dec. 1944; CSSRC, 8/4: agenda of second meeting of CSSRC, 5 Sept. 1944; minutes of third meeting, 29 Sept. 1944 (for details of female applicants for fellowships); minutes of first meeting 17 July 1944, Colonial Office, CSSRC /44: 8/1; general survey of minutes and other papers of the CSSRC, 1944–1963.

[114] Cecillie Swaisland, *Forty Years of Service: The Women's Corona Society 1950–1990* (London, 1992).

[115] Governor Bernard Bourdillon (Nigeria), cited in Callaway, *Gender, Culture and Empire*, p. 239.

intelligentsia.[116] The SOSBW also responded to the transition from Empire to Commonwealth. In the 1950s it became the 'woman's branch' of the migration section of the Commonwealth Relations Office, focusing increasingly on African welfare work. The 1955 Annual Report claimed that social workers settled by the SOSBW were making 'valuable contributions' to the rehabilitation of Kikuyu women and children displaced during the Mau Mau emergency.[117] There is, of course, no mention of the terrible conditions Kikuyu women and men suffered in internment camps and 'protected' villages.[118]

False optimism about the continued viability of African settler colonies was premised on a settler discourse which erased acts of white violence against indigenous populations. Increasing pressure from African nationalism, however, forced white settlers to develop defensive survival strategies.[119] Settler women made a proactive and prominent contribution to this change. In the 1950s, the EAWL consolidated its position in settler politics and launched the *Kenya Women's News* to defend the settler way of life. *Home and Country: The Official Journal of the Federation of Womens' Institutes of Southern and Northern Rhodesia* (Salisbury, 1962–) served a similar function. Pre-war policies to diffuse African discontent through the spread of domesticity were also intensified. The Kenyan Government appointed a Provincial Homecrafts Officer and male domestic servants now received formal training. The EAWL established an African welfare section which initiated uplift schemes for African women, including homecrafts courses and 'Better Homes' competitions. The hope was that, once trained, women would share their new knowledge with others. Nellie Grant, who ran homecraft summer schools on her farm complained, however, that the women did not do so.[120] Domestication projects mostly failed; wives did not 'tranquilize' their menfolk, and visions of transforming 'boys' into men who conformed to the white model of responsible husbands and workers, did not quell political discontent or the growth of Mau Mau.[121]

[116] 'Leading Article', *The Times*, 4 May 1956: 'Victoria League', ibid, 8 June 1957. See also 'Supervision and Guidance of Colonial Students in the UK: Victoria League', The National Archives of the UK [NA]: Public Record Office, London, Colonial Office (CO) 323/1531/5, 1938–9.

[117] SOSBW Annual Report, 1955, p. 11.

[118] As revealed in oral researches by Caroline Elkins in 'Kenya: White Terror', Correspondent, *BBC2*, 17 Nov. 2002.

[119] See chap. by Jock McCulloch in this volume.

[120] Nellie Grant to Elspeth Huxley, 24 Aug. 1953, Huxley Papers, Box 3, File 6.

[121] Luise White, 'Separating the Men from the Boys: Colonial Constructions of Gender, Sexuality and Terrorism in Central Kenya, 1930–1959', *International Journal of African Historical Studies*, XXXIII (1990), p. 19.

For Kenyan settlers, Coronation Year (1953) was disquieting and un-stable, marred by drought, viruses, and what settlers regarded as horrific murders of whites by Mau Mau, disrupting royalist celebrations. African discontent threatened the very heart of the settler home as houseboys were increasingly feared by whites as surly, disobedient, and untrust-worthy, and were implicated in attacks on white families. *Mau Mau: A Pictorial Record: A Collection of Photographs recording Kenya's Battle Against Mau Mau* represented Kikuyu men as degenerate and ugly, em-phasizing their 'savage' barbarism. Antagonisms between colony and metropole over African political representation intensified with the pres-ence in Kenya of British soldiers during the Emergency and found gen-dered expression in comparisons between strong, colonial womanhood and 'weak', duplicitous, and degenerate metropolitan manhood. Nellie Grant complained bitterly about the 'foul' Lancashire Fusiliers, who allegedly wrote home about white brutality to Africans. The soldiers '[could] not be kept out of the *bibis*' [women's] huts', had 'permanently tight [drunk] officers', and were awful in their behaviour towards 'boys'.[122] Metropolitan anti-imperialists such as Fenner Brockway when visiting Kenya in 1950 and 1952 also encountered hostility. A settler delegation, chaired by a leading female farmer who gave the impression of 'strength, will and competence', opposed Brockway's presence in Kenya, accusing him of communist beliefs.[123]

The Mau Mau Emergency was only suppressed with the help of the metropolitan armed forces. Proportionately very few whites died, in contrast to thousands of colonized men and women, but in settler propaganda the Mau Mau uprising was represented as a brutal threat to white order and domesticity.[124] Both white men and women were memorialized as heroic in defending their property against insurgents. In this era of uncertainty, settler women were key publicists and defenders of Empire. From the 1930s women pioneered a pro-settler literary genre glorifying the early pioneers, male and female, which confirmed settler myths about their frontier history and defined an identity separate from the metropolis. The Rhodesian settler activist Jeannie M. Boggie's 'true accounts' of pioneer women, published in

---

[122] Nellie Grant to Elspeth Huxley, 16 March; Aug. 24, 1953, Huxley Papers, Box 3, File 6. See also *Mau Mau: A Pictorial Record* (Nairobi, Kenya Colony, n.d.), enclosed ibid., Box 3, File 7.

[123] Brockway, *African Journey*, pp. 111, 118–24.

[124] Wendy Webster, *Imagining Home: Race, Class and National Identity, 1945–64* (London, 1997), p. 54.

1938, were reissued in revised format in 1940 and 1953.[125] In her *Random Collections of A Pioneer Settler* (1975), Eleanor Cole vindicated 'the proud best of our settler period', and Elspeth Huxley, awarded a CBE in 1962, collated material for a 'Pioneers' Scrapbook; Reminiscences of Kenya, 1890 to 1968', based on the experiences of EAWL members. Her fictionalized memoirs gained a mass audience when Hayley Mills played Tilly (Huxley's mother, Nellie) in the televised version of *The Flame Trees of Thika: Memories of an African Childhood* (1959).[126] Karen Blixen's *Out of Africa* (1937) was likewise republished and made into a film in 1985.

Such imperialist nostalgia sanitized the uglier side of settler life and captured the popular imagination as confident British identities were undermined. But the settler dream was over. In the 1960s metropolitan priorities shifted from the Empire to Europe, independence came rapidly to most British colonies, and the settler cause seemed increasingly anachronistic. The SOSBW, rebranded in 1961 as WOMAS (Women's Migration and Oversea Appointments Society) was still settling women in Southern Africa, but in 1963, after cuts in the government grant, the organization was phased out.[127] As Empire waned and 'New Commonwealth' migration to Britain increased, attention was refocused on 'the Empire within', race problems, and perceived threats to British cultural identity, as reflected in Elspeth Huxley's *Back Streets: New Worlds; A Look at Immigrants in Britain* (1964).

Competing visions of colonial gender orders, which contrasted superior white domesticity and sexual regulation with the repressive patriarchal Asian family or the problematized, mother-headed, black 'non family', persisted into the post-colonial era. Gender is thus important to interpreting migrant experiences. Homogenizing colonial stereotypes of black women as primitive, sexualized, and unruly, and Asian women as passive and repressed, shaped popular British perceptions of female migrants. Many Caribbean women, for example, entered Britain as independent migrants and had high rates of economic activity, but nonetheless had to adopt 'postures of

---

[125] *Experiences of Rhodesia's Pioneer Women: Being a True Account of the Adventures of Pioneer White Women Settlers in Rhodesia from 1890, Elicited and Arranged by Jeannie M. Boggie* (Bulawayo, 1938): *First Steps in Civilizing Rhodesia: Being a True Account of the Experiences of the Earliest White Settlers—Men, Women and Children—in Southern and Northern Rhodesia Elicited and Arranged by Jeannie M. Boggie* (1940, 2nd Rhodes Centenary edn., Bulawayo, Southern Rhodesia, 1953).

[126] Correspondence relating to the televising of *The Flame Trees of Thika*, Huxley Papers, Box 16, File 1, ff. 26–35; Box 28, File 8.

[127] WOMAS Annual Report, 1963, pp. 7, 23.

servility'. They were relegated to low-paid unskilled work and carried the dual burdens of sexism and racism.[128] Stereotypes of inferior colonial masculinities persisted but 'coloured' male migrants were also perceived as a threat to the moral and racial stability of the imperial centre. In the novel *City of Spades* (1958), which *The Times* equated to a 'sociological study', Colin MacInnes fictionalized popular representations of black men in London as pimps, drug addicts, dealers, and criminals. Black men's sexuality and their 'corruption' of white women threatened white domesticity, racial purity, and thus British culture and identity.[129] These concerns resulted in white interventions in black 'family problems' to moralize and stabilize black sexuality and domestic life, and to reduce interracial sexual relations, but interracial relationships persisted, negatively affecting black gender relations and fuelling popular white antipathy well into the post-colonial era.[130]

As in the inter-war years, pro-imperialists conflated anti-colonialism, socialism, and sexual breaches in racial borders as threats to Empire. Such attitudes, in effect, suggest white women's continued affinity for the colonial oppressed reflected in membership of new organizations such as the Movement for Colonial Freedom, the Campaign Against Racial Discrimination, and the Anti-Apartheid Movement. The expanding field of 'race relations', directed to stabilizing new social configurations created through decolonization and migration, also attracted a disproportionate number of women academics; one of the most influential academic studies of the era on both sides of the Atlantic was Sheila Patterson's, *Dark Strangers: A Study of West Indians in London* (1963). Influenced by 'progressive' colonial anthropology, Patterson and other social scientists were committed to the assimilation of migrants into British culture, rejecting scientific racism.[131] *Dark Strangers* affords important insights into the ways in which colonial discourse on domesticity, culture, and modernity was reformulated in the metropolitan context. The common thread linking these themes was the implicit assumption of the superiority of 'civilized' white domesticity and gender roles.

[128] Carol Boyce Davis, *Black Women, Writing and Identity: Migrations of the Subject* (London, 1994), p. 99. For a critique of stereotypes of Asian women, see Avtar Brah, *Cartographies of Diaspora: Contesting Identities* (London, 1996), pp. 72–75.

[129] Webster, *Imagining Home*, pp. xii, xviii, 59, 62. See also 'New Fiction', *The Times*, 5 Sep. 1957, p. 11.

[130] S. Ruck, ed., *The West Indian Comes to England: A Report Prepared for the Trustees of the London Parochial Charities by the Family Welfare Association, London* (London, 1960), pp. 119–37.

[131] Chris Waters 'Dark Strangers in Our Midst: Discourses on Race and Nation in Britain, 1947–1963', *Journal of British Studies*, XXXVI (1997), p. 218–19.

Gender and race were central to the redefinition of British national identities as the Empire fragmented after 1945. Decolonization and 'New Commonwealth' (a euphemism for non-white) immigration had important and
irreversible ramifications for imperial and colonized gender relations. Loss of
Empire created a crisis in British masculinities and, as nationalism transformed colonial masculinities, the 'emasculation' of Empire accelerated.
Insecurity stemming from the erosion of imperial power enhanced by black
migration stimulated a new configuration of race and nation. White gendered
identities and domesticity now became fundamental to redefining national
identities leading to a 'feminization' of the nation.[132] Developments in British
society, particularly the sexual revolution, the iconoclastic Sixties, and
second-wave feminism accelerated these transformations. In the African
white settler colonies, however, an anachronistic, rugged imperial masculinity
was reaffirmed to strengthen besieged settler societies; nostalgia for Empire
and lost imperial masculinities, was evoked in films such as *Lawrence of Arabia*
(1962).[133] In Britain gendered representations of the colonized continued to
determine public policy towards Black and Asian migrant communities.

By virtue of geographical scope and complexity of Empire, this survey has
had to be selective. It has not addressed the Middle East, and China and the
Caribbean have received only brief mention. Much more could have been
said about the contentious link between gender, class, and race, and the
gendering of the colonial economy. Indeed, rich archival and other sources
uncovered in researching this article suggest fruitful areas for further
in-depth research. As this overview has demonstrated, a gendered analysis
of colonial discourse and practice can provide a richer and more nuanced
understanding of late imperialism. Gender and Empire were intimately
interconnected in the domestication of Empire in the inter-war years and
the management of decline after the Second World War. Superior imperial
masculinities and femininities and white domesticity were central to white
prestige and power and the strengthening of racial boundaries. Key defining
features of twentieth-century Empire include the 'feminization' of imperial
policy and the wider participation of emancipated white women. Although
all white women remained privileged by race, as relations between colonizer

---

[132] Ibid., p. 212.

[133] Graham Dawson, *Soldier Heroes: British Adventure, Empire and the Imaginings of Masculinities* (London, 1994), p. 218.

and colonized were transformed by 'modern times', a minority of women became genuinely committed to improving race relations and colonial reform.

Social and cultural change catalysed by two world wars and the unprecedented scale of anti-racist and anti-colonial challenges to Empire are also distinguishing features of twentieth-century Empire. These developments stimulated a dynamic re-articulation of gender, class, race, and nationalism spanning the metropolitan heartland and imperial hinterland. Nationalism subverted white gendered stereotypes of the colonized and end of Empire eroded confident imperial identities. Additionally, however, the modernizing project of 'progressive' scientific imperialism disrupted colonial cultures, and its most ubiquitous impact was arguably on gender relations and the intimate domestic sphere. Colonial discourse relating to gender and domesticity proved highly durable, influencing the reception of colonial migrants in Britain and gendered aid and development projects in the Third World. The primacy of Western cultural values and whiteness has been one of the most enduring legacies of the formal age of Empire in the post-colonial era. Echoes of Empire still reach into the everyday mundane, the familial, sexual, and gender relations which define culture, identity, and belonging.

Select Bibliography

BRUCE BERMAN and JOHN LONSDALE, *Unhappy Valley: Conflict in Kenya and Africa*, 2 vols. (Oxford, 1992).

ROBERT BICKERS, *Britain in China: Community Culture and Colonialism, 1900–1949* (Manchester, 1999).

ANTOINETTE BURTON, ed., *Gender, Sexuality and Colonial Modernities* (London, 1999).

BARBARA BUSH, *Imperialism, Race and Resistance: Africa and Britain, 1919 to 1945* (London 1999).

—— ' "Britain's Conscience on Africa": White Women, Race and Imperial Politics in Inter-war Britain', in Clare Midgley, ed., *Gender and Imperialism* (Manchester, 1998).

JOHN G. BUTCHER, *The British in Malaya, 1880–1941: The Social History of a European Community in Colonial South East Asia* (Oxford, 1979).

HELEN CALLAWAY, *Gender, Culture and Empire: European Women in Colonial Nigeria* (London, 1987).

NUPUR CHAUDHURI and MARGARET STROBEL, eds, *Western Women and Imperialism: Complicity and Resistance* (Bloomington, Ind., 1992).

KAREN TRANBERG HANSEN, ed, *African Encounters with Domesticity* (New Brunswick, NJ, 1992).

SUSANNA HOE, *The Private Life of Old Hong Kong; Western Women in the British Colony, 1841–1941* (Hong Kong, 1991).

DANE KENNEDY, *Islands of White: Settler Society and Culture in Kenya and Southern Rhodesia, 1890–1939* (Durham, NC, 1987).

ROSALIND O' HANLON, 'Gender in the British Empire', in Judith M. Brown and Wm. Roger Louis, eds., *The Oxford History of the British Empire: The Twentieth Century* (Oxford, 1999).

RUTH ROACH PIERSON and NUPUR CHAUDHURI, eds., *Nation, Empire, Colony: Historicising Race and Gender* (Bloomington, Ind., 1998).

MARY A. PROCIDA, *Married to the Empire: Gender, Politics and Imperialism, 1883–1947* (Manchester, 2002).

ANN LAURA STOLER, *Race and the Education of Desire; Foucault's History of Sexuality and the Colonial Order of Things* (Durham, NC, 1996).

—— and FREDERICK COOPER, eds., *Tensions of Empire: Colonial Cultures in a Bourgeois World* (Berkeley, 1997).

5

Medicine, Gender, and Empire

ALISON BASHFORD

Health and ill-health were both problems and imperatives of Empire. The author of *Health and Empire* (1912), for example, wrote of the need to secure 'the utmost physical efficiency and therefore welfare for the 4,000,000,000 inhabitants of the British Empire ... the health of the people is the supreme law'.[1] A healthy Empire was an ambition of colonial officials, especially in the century between the 1850s and 1950s. This was the broad period in which 'public health' itself was being institutionalized at home and in the Empire, and after which the idea of 'world health' gained strength alongside decolonization. Medicine, public health, nursing, and the clinic were themselves instruments and sites of colonial governance. These fields of expertise and practice put into place institutions, therapies, and sanitary infrastructures, many of which have come to be considered desirable and beneficial by any criteria in the post-colonial world. The process of global human movement and displacement, however, which characterized the British Empire through exploration, slavery, indentured labour, transportation, settlement, migration, and travel, also produced real problems of health. One aim of British medicine historically, then, has been to solve health problems created by imperialism itself.

Wherever indigenous and British health was of concern to colonial and imperial governments, it was not just individual therapy, health, or ill-health which were at issue. Rather, medical and especially sanitation measures were part of the ensemble of governing instruments and powers which rendered groups of people known and knowable as aggregate populations. Medicine and public health were crucial means by which the quantification, classification, and bureaucratic knowledge of imperial administration took place, from data on vaccination and communicable diseases across the Empire, to the health returns of the Colonial Office detailing longevity and

---

[1] Francis Fremantle, *Health and Empire* (London, 1912), pp. 348–49, p. 368.

fecundity as well as mortality and morbidity rates for a myriad of sub-populations classified by sex, race, region, occupation, age, religion, and more.[2] These were the vital statistics of Empire.

In assessing health and ill-health in any context, sexed and sexualized difference and its social significance (that is, gender) need to be taken into consideration. Medicine in its broadest sense manages bodies, which are always themselves gendered. In greater or lesser ways, gendered bodies matter in the experience of, and intervention into, communicable diseases, reproduction and its regulation, injury and therapeutics, public health and sanitation, health education, and propaganda. Moreover, the post-Enlightenment and colonial dominance of Western biomedicine as the discourse of truth on sex, sexuality, gender, and race, brought changing understandings of each of these, often authorizing and naturalizing their inter-relations. Medicine and its experts, therefore, also managed gender itself.

The complicated relations between colonialism, medicine, and the production of knowledge about gender are illustrated in the first section of this chapter, through the specific problem of inoculation versus vaccination, an ongoing medical and governmental problem throughout the eighteenth and nineteenth centuries. Revolving around the figures of Lady Mary Wortley Montague and Dr Edward Jenner, are connected histories of medicine, colonial culture, and imperial law and policy. Through this case study, we see the history of imperialism implicated in the production of knowledge about gender, and, conversely, in the gendering of biomedical knowledge. In the following section, practitioners of health and medicine as both gendered and 'raced' subjects in the Victorian Empire are examined. Critics and advocates of women practitioners often discussed femininity in the context of potential or actual work in the Empire, but men's imperial practice was equally gendered. Analyses of three domains of health and medical intervention follow: childbirth and population management, communicable diseases, and the medical problem of white conduct in the tropics. Each analysis treats medicine as a form of colonial rule and the significance of gender is discussed in its historical context.

The rise of biomedical science as a modern discourse of truth actively produced certain understandings of 'natural' sex, sexuality, and gender. The engagement between natural philosophy, medicine, and imperial

---

[2] U. Kalpagam, 'The Colonial State and Statistical Knowledge', *History of the Human Sciences*, XIII (2000), pp. 37–55.

knowledge-gathering on 'Nature', on 'Man' and on 'Evolution', meant that 'sex' and 'race' became biologized ideas with strong reference to one another.[3] This knowledge often relied on problematic cultural practices of objectification, whereby women and non-British people were similarly (but not identically) placed as objects, not subjects of control, activity, and desire; as objects of a masculine and colonial gaze.[4] Objectivity was increasingly written into the technical procedures and the epistemology of scientific medicine itself. Thus, British doctors displayed women and men (always distant from themselves in class or race terms) as cases for the learned societies in a stark relation of activity (on the part of the subject–scientist) and passivity (on the part of the object–patient–body–specimen). The Royal Society of London heard a talk in 1864: 'On the Brain of a Bushwoman; and on the Brains of Two Idiots of European Descent'.[5] Similarly, medical men's interest in the 'last' Tasmanian Aboriginal woman, her display in both life and death, brought together a colonial and a scientific capacity to objectify. A generation of feminist philosophers and historians have offered important ways of understanding this relation of subject and object as in itself gendered: that is to say, the attributes (and capacity) of observing and reasoning, of discerning knowledge from an 'other' object, were explicitly established by early British natural philosophy and by liberal theorists as masculine capacities.[6]

This gendering of medical and scientific knowledge might seem to be the scholarly business of epistemologists and philosophers, yet it needs to be integrated with the historical analysis of imperial engagements and as part of colonial discourse. The history of inoculation and vaccination practices in the eighteenth century, and their revision in the nineteenth century, suggests how this might be so. Lady Mary Wortley Montague 'discovered' the practice of inoculation amongst women and children, during her years as wife of the

[3] Londa Scheibinger, 'Mammals, Primatology and Sexology', in Roy Porter and Mikulas Teich, eds., *Sexual Knowledge, Sexual Science: The History of Attitudes to Sexuality* (Cambridge, 1994), pp. 184–209; Anne Fausto-Sterling, 'Gender, Race and Nation: The Comparative Anatomy of "Hottentot" Women in Europe, 1815–1817', in Jennifer Terry and Jacqueline Urla, eds., *Deviant Bodies* (Bloomington, Ind., 1995), pp. 19–48.

[4] Gyan Prakash, 'Science "Gone Native" in Colonial India', *Representations*, XLIX (1992), pp. 153–78.

[5] John Marshall, 'On the Brain of a Bushwoman; and on the Brain of Two Idiots of European Descent', *Philosophical Transactions of the Royal Society of London* (1864), pp. 501–58.

[6] Genevieve Lloyd, *The Man of Reason* (London, 1984); Ludmilla Jordanova, *Sexual Visions* (London, 1989).

British Consul in Constantinople in the 1720s. Eventually receiving considerable medical favour in England, the practice of inoculation (with actual smallpox matter) was later set against Edward Jenner's work on vaccination (with cowpox matter) from the 1790s. In theory, inoculation gave the child a mild case of smallpox, while vaccination infected the child with the milder cowpox disease. The two procedures were understood as very different preventive practices. Over time the former was increasingly associated with feminine and feminized folk tradition, and the latter heralded as one of the great discoveries of modern science in a strongly masculine tradition. By the 1860s, inoculation was outlawed while vaccination, in some parts of the Empire, was so favoured by government as to be compulsory. Throughout the nineteenth century there was endless quantification and tabling of smallpox rates either to verify or protest the two methods, nearly always drawing on the figures of Montague and Jenner. Indeed the 'Inoculation Period' and 'Vaccination Period' were sometimes summarized as the period of 'Montague' and of 'Jenner'.[7] The history of Montague and Jenner, of inoculation versus vaccination, is a history of England on the cusp of modernity, about feminine, 'Eastern', folk knowledge and masculine, 'Western', expert knowledge, about gender and colonialism.

Indian practices of inoculation against smallpox were studied and recorded closely in many English texts of the eighteenth century, in a period when learned Indian medicine commanded considerable respect. One 1767 text, for example, thought there would be 'great benefit . . . to mankind from a knowledge of this foreign method, which so remarkably tends to support the practice now generally followed with such marvellous success'. By this the author meant the inoculation method Montague had introduced into England. In this rendition, the practices of learned Indian men, consistently weighted as ancient, as 'having the sanction of remotest antiquity', lent an authority to the other source of the practice 'blundered upon' by Montague amongst women in the Orient.[8] Despite such weighting, inoculation was never fully accepted in England as a proper medical procedure. No matter how common the practice of inoculation became in England, its foreign origins were sustained, often through the story of Montague herself. Its

---

[7] Ernest Hart, 'A Memorandum of the Influence of Vaccination in the Prevention and Diminution of Mortality from Small-pox', in Australasian Sanitary Conference, *Report and Minutes of Proceedings* (Sydney, 1884), p. 62.

[8] J. Z. Holwell, *An Account of the Manner of Inoculating for the Small Pox in the East Indies* (London, 1767), pp. 2–3.

connections with the East as well as with Indian medicine were newly drawn
by anti-inoculation, pro-vaccination commentary in the Victorian period.
Alternatively, for the growing ranks of anti-vaccinationists, inoculation was
simply the precursor to vaccination, both equally nasty practices 'grafted
upon Western medicine . . . from the East'.[9] Under the Vaccination Acts in
1840 and 1853, the Imperial Vaccination Act (1867), and various local ordinances, British imperial powers declared inoculation illegal in England and
Wales, and in colonies where it was traditionally practised: replacing inoculation with vaccination was part of the mission of imperial medicine.[10]

Inoculation was feminized through its 'Eastern-ness' and through its
strong and lasting association with Montague, herself often 'orientalized'
and turbanned in public representation.[11] Importantly also, inoculation was
connected with the femininity of the inoculators in eighteenth-century
Constantinople: the 'Bedouin female servant', a 'woman from Morea' and
another from Bosnia were the source of Montague's knowledge.[12] There was
(and is) a deep investment in constructing it so, for this feminization of
inoculation as Eastern and as a folk practice of women simultaneously
constructed 'vaccination' as masculine, expert, and modern. Inoculation
(deliberate infection) came to be understood by British experts as a dangerous technique, largely undertaken by mothers. For example, the author of
The Conquest of Disease (1925) wrote of the 'ignorant' practice of mothers'
deliberate infection of their children as a preventive measure. Such deliberate
infection no doubt went on: it still does, for better or worse. Here the concern
is with the comprehension of this practice within a long-lasting modern
story of orientalism and gender: 'If any one is to be blamed in the matter, it
appears to be the Turks, who were practising this method of voluntary
infection long before the people in England thought of it'.[13] For the English,
vaccination as opposed to inoculation was a domestic idea and, if originally
an English folk practice, none the less was rendered 'expert' by a distinguished man of science, Jenner. In Jenner's science, women were very clearly

---

[9] Charles W. Forward, *The Golden Calf: An Exposure of Vaccine-Therapy* (London, 1933), p. 17.

[10] David Arnold, 'Smallpox and Colonial Medicine in Nineteenth-century India', in Arnold,
ed., *Imperial Medicine and Indigenous Societies* (Manchester, 1988), pp. 45–64.

[11] For representation of Montague, see Wendy Frith, 'Sex, Smallpox and Seraglios: A Monu-
ment to Lady Mary Wortley Montague', in G. Perry and M. Rossington, eds., *Femininity and
Masculinity in Eighteenth-century Art and Culture* (Manchester and New York, 1994), pp. 99–122.

[12] See Peter Razzell, *The Conquest of Smallpox* (Firle, 1977), pp. 2–6.

[13] David Masters, *The Conquest of Disease* (London, 1925), p. 36.

the objects not the subjects of knowledge-production, the patients and not the practitioners.

Inoculation's connections with the 'East' and its associations with feminine (or feminized indigenous) medical practice made it unscientific in contrast to Jenner's vaccine. Inoculation and vaccination were thus entwined with gendered and colonial histories of modernity, medicine, and Empire in which British, expert (masculine) practices were, in effect, defined and authorized by their opposite, the Eastern, traditional, and indigenous practices, diminished in the Victorian era as feminine or feminized pre-modern traditions. This encapsulates the significance of a gendered comprehension of medicine and modernity, women's and men's authority in medical knowledge-production, and the changing English assessment of, and interventions into, indigenous practices.

There was a logic to modernizing medicine which dovetailed neatly with the logic of Empire and that of expansionist evangelical mission. Medicine, especially scientific medicine of the later nineteenth century, was itself expansionist; its modern practices, research, and ideas were to be progressively disseminated, displacing older, traditional, and folk techniques associated with unregulated women's and men's practice, and increasingly with indigenous practice. Medical ideas were to spread as the humanitarian imperatives of Christian mission but also as part of the imperatives of modernity. Medicine imagined itself as a civilizing mission most markedly in its encounter with indigenous people and spaces.[14] 'Civilization was equated less with political freedom than with a clean water supply and a society educated in sanitary principles.'[15] Even as medicine and public health brought desirable new effects in terms of better individual health and public works, they were instruments through which indigenous men and women were managed by missions and by government. Colonial public health and sanitary reform also aimed to change conduct and personal habits at the most intimate levels. Instilling cleanliness and order along with industry and moral conduct, *was* to civilize and modernize in the minds of experts, colonial governors and their agents, British philanthropists, and missionaries. Given the significance of the domestic in nineteenth-century sanitary reform and in twentieth-century maternal and infant health and welfare, this

[14] John and Jean Comaroff, *Ethnography and the Historical Imagination* (Boulder, Colo., 1992), pp. 215–34.

[15] E. B. van Heyningen, 'Agents of Empire: The Medical Profession in the Cape Colony, 1880–1910', *Medical History*, XXXIII (1989), pp. 451–52.

often involved encounters between indigenous women and British women, as missionaries, doctors, wives of managers on indigenous reserves, and in particular, as nurses. The literal whiteness of late nineteenth-century British nurses symbolized and embodied a moral cleanliness and ordering: a racialized bourgeois culture where cleanliness was whiteness.[16] The expansionism (and activism) of imperialism, medicine, and Protestant mission afforded many British men and women an enormous field of opportunity for practice. The Empire was conversely a 'cultural and social space for the making of Victorian medicine'.[17]

Large numbers of British medical men took imperial posts, attached to a trading or shipping company, or in civil administration. Men worked through the Army Medical Department, the Indian Medical Service, or the Naval Medical Service. Sometimes medical practice was a private enterprise, often one shaped by individual imperial connections and introductions, and by a persistent hierarchy of institutional training and patronage. In the 1890s the Colonial Office under Joseph Chamberlain systematized salaried imperial medical posting within the all-male Colonial Medical Service and mandated instruction for colonial medical practice in the new London School of Tropical Medicine, founded in 1898.[18] If being a professional medical man in the nineteenth and twentieth centuries meant expertise, control, and decision-making over the bodies and lives of others, even others socially superior to oneself, in the imperial context these qualities of masculinity were significantly amplified by the racial difference of the colonial encounter. Socially precarious (in class terms), British medicine none the less came to be a kind of mastery at the level of individual doctor–patient clinical encounter. By the early twentieth century, this was a mastery of the social world, whereby biomedical expertise was authoritative over any number of social, legal, and political issues. Although the historiography on medicine and masculinity is sparse, some historians have pointed to the significance of codes of gentlemanly behaviour and male honour as the crucial means by which the clinical encounter was authorized, the boundaries of the profession were secured, and the informal means by which women and non-British or non-European men were marginalized even after the formal rules for their

---

[16] Sheryl Nestel, '(Ad)ministering Angels: Colonial Nursing and the Extension of Empire', *Journal of Medical Humanities*, XIX, (1998), p. 259.

[17] Douglas Haynes, *Imperial Medicine: Patrick Manson and the Conquest of Tropical Disease* (Philadelphia, 2001), p. 8.

[18] Ibid., pp. 126–74.

inclusion were relaxed.[19] The everyday encounters of imperial medical practice, especially for the young, British, single men consistently sought by the Colonial Office, shaped and sustained experiences and meanings of authoritative masculinity.

Histories of masculinity make possible the interpretation of imperial medical ventures as expressions of an enterprising and adventurous Victorian masculinity: Dr David Livingstone is a good example. Yet expressions of masculinity (and femininity) are often more everyday than this, and, by their very normativity have great purchase. For example, a major aspect of masculinity under question for many imperial medical men was a seemingly mundane fiscal one. By the 1860s, general practice in Britain had come to be a heavily over-stocked occupation for middle-class men: a lucrative or even a moderate practice was often hard to come by. Although imperial posts were typically low-paid and low-status, they none the less offered *some* opportunity for general practice and perhaps even research. Not infrequently, under-employed general practitioners as sons, fathers, or husbands sought opportunity in the Empire to provide for family or to secure enough money to move from bachelorhood to marriage.[20] In strongly gendered household and family economies, to provide and thus to enable the dependence of others, *was* to be masculine: to be unable to provide, to *be* dependent correspondingly undercut masculinity.[21]

This was precisely the situation of the young Dr Patrick Manson (1844–1922). Unable to find appropriate employment in Scotland or England, his post at Amoy in China provided the prosperity required to marry well in England. His wife brought him in return, and amongst other things, social capital in his colonial life. The imperial doctor *par excellence*, Manson made his (troubled) research reputation first through work on elephantiasis in China, then by mining the British Museum as a colonial resource.[22] He collaborated with Ronald Ross in India on malaria research and ushered Ross's work through the elaborate systems of Victorian medical knowledge-production. Returning permanently to London, Manson had direct access, unlike Ross, to the learned Societies, the Colleges, the journals, and the contacts. In concert with Chamberlain and the Colonial Office, Manson

[19] Robert A. Nye, 'Medicine and Science as Masculine "Fields of Honor" ', *Osiris*, XII (1997), pp. 68–69.

[20] Haynes, *Imperial Medicine*, pp. 127–29.

[21] Nye, 'Medicine and Science', pp. 68–69.

[22] Haynes, *Imperial Medicine*, p. 30.

established the London School of Tropical Medicine as a training and research institution. It was Manson's position as masculine and as British which facilitated his education, which gained him imperial posts and authority over local medical men and indigenous patients, which gave him the social capital to know the masculine rules of engagement with the learned societies, and to engage in the contest of research which needs to be analysed as both expressive and formative of professional masculinity.[23] All this was critical to the identity and authority of the doctor as a middle-class British man, and precisely because of this, the gender of British medical men, always in play, was rarely explicitly discussed.

For women practitioners, however, gender was always a problem, and one partly solved for them by the fact of Empire. There were any number of ways in which women who wanted to practice medicine conventionally, and wanted to do so in the Empire, approached the problems of the exclusivity of male medical and imperial appointments and practice. Mary Seacole (1805–81) was a Creole woman from Jamaica known, like her mother, as a 'doctress'. She practised traditional medicine as well as surgery, and was knowledgeable in epidemic management, these skills being sought officially by the military at various points. Seacole's well-known autobiography details her medical work as well as her travels, and was written to establish herself as an Englishwoman within, and in the service of, the Empire; her book valorizes the colonial mission and Englishness.[24] Yet those who 'owned' Englishness with greater certainty than Seacole placed her on the margins. She was for example, not among the contingent of nurses sent to the Crimean War under Florence Nightingale. Seacole was refused this association, but famously set herself up independently in the Crimea, treating soldiers surgically and medicinally, and nursing them. As a Creole and a woman, her position was always a liminal one in an imperial setting, constrained by forces well beyond her control. As the daughter of a Jamaican doctress, however, she was trained in medical skills and expertise which permitted her a place to practice unconventionally on the imperial stage, in a way which, in the medically unregulated 1850s, was still recognized and valued.

British-born women saw in the Empire an opportunity for types of work unavailable to them at home. One such, Lucy Osburn (1835–91), was poised

[23] Nye, 'Medicine and Science', p. 78.
[24] Mary Seacole, *The Wonderful Adventures of Mrs Seacole in Many Lands* (London, 1858).

to take a position with the Delhi Medical Mission as a female medical practitioner. She had spent some years assisting in surgery and hospital work in Jerusalem, and explained away her interest in surgery and medicine (as opposed to nursing) to the disapproving Florence Nightingale saying: 'in as far as it was *medical* work in *India* I did not object' [emphasis in original].[25] In other words, being a lady-doctor specifically to Indian women was as much a mission–philanthropic endeavour as a medical one. But she was snapped up and remoulded by the canny Nightingale, herself an influential commentator and policy-maker on things medical and colonial, and instead of working in India Osburn entered into a contract between the Nightingale Fund and the Government of New South Wales to reform its hospitals and asylums.[26] Expressions of a civilizing medical modernity often took the form of conspicuously large and grand asylums and charitable hospitals, built in colonies of white settlement. These not only differentiated British methods of health, welfare, and philanthropy from indigenous customs, but also marked cities such as Christchurch, Cape Town, Ottawa, or in this case Sydney, as places of proper Victorian government. Part of the rationale for Osburn's appointment was a bourgeois 'feminizing' of such institutions signalling order, cleanliness, sanitation, and modern reform.

Another option for women's practice in colonial health-care—although a most unusual one—was to re-invent one's own gender. Thus, rather than pressing politically the male exclusivity of various colonial and medical institutions, as various British feminists did from the middle of the nineteenth century, at least one woman slipped unnoticed inside the norms of gender, and passed for most of her life as James Barry (?–1865). Barry was a successful army surgeon, a 'medical man' educated in Edinburgh and posted to the Cape Colony, British North America, and the West Indies.[27] This kind of hyper-masculine imperial–military–medical career was only possible for a British man, and Barry's case encapsulates the contrived exclusivity of the conventions of medical, educational, and military institutions. Her performance of masculinity shows how entirely necessary it was for that career and life. Her male colleagues at the medical school and in the military also

[25] Lucy Osburn to Florence Nightingale, 23 Oct. 1866, Nightingale Correspondence, Greater London Record Office, H1/ST/NC2/V/6/66.

[26] Alison Bashford, *Purity and Pollution: Gender, Embodiment and Victorian Medicine* (London, 1998), pp. 88–89. Osburn never worked in India.

[27] Rachel Holmes, *Scanty Particulars: The Strange Life and Astonishing Secret of Victorian Adventurer and Pioneering Surgeon, James Barry* (London, 2002).

performed masculinity, even if they (and subsequent historians) merely assumed the codes of behaviour, modes of conduct, and styles of authority as the repertoire of British middle-class masculinity, stylized in these cases by the costumerie and conventions of the Army. The discovery of Barry's sex after death, in 1865, coincided with other kinds of interventions into the question of gender, medicine, and imperial practice, which played gender more conventionally but at the same time politically.

A major part of the push from the 1860s to gain women places within conventional medical training was the argument that indigenous women of the Empire, in particular Indian women, desperately needed formally trained women doctors, nurses, and midwives, as they would not be examined by men.[28] In sharp contrast to Barry's strategy of passing as a man, these arguments traded on, but also pressed, conventional femininity. Activist Victorian sensibilities allowed that a morally and philanthropically driven female practice in the Empire was tolerable and even desirable. In the process, such arguments constructed British women's practice *against* the passivity and need of Indian women, and constructed British men's and women's medical practice as, almost necessarily, different.

Unlike Seacole or Barry, Dr Mary Scharlieb (1845–1940) was both all-English and all-woman, but the Empire was similarly her ground. As a woman, her professional identity was more like Osburn's and Seacole's than Barry's. Placing herself under the tutelage of the Madras Surgeon-General, and the Matron and Superintendent of the Madras Lying-In Hospital, she trained in midwifery practice. Later, she received the Licentiate of Medicine, Surgery and Midwifery from the Madras Medical College, largely on the argument of the needs of Indian women. Yet she was determined to extend Indian practice well beyond obstetrics and gynaecology.[29] In London, in addition to her private practice (which included wealthy Indian women travelling specifically to consult her), she was also associated with Elizabeth Garrett Anderson and her New Hospital for Women. From her own experience, she argued 'the great advantages, social, political and religious, that must accrue from a supply to India of well-educated, enthusiastic and devoted medical women'. Yet Scharlieb kept religion and medicine separate, clearly distinguishing herself from the tradition of female medical missionaries.[30]

---

[28] Maneesha Lal, 'The Politics of Gender and Medicine in Colonial India: The Countess of Dufferin's Fund, 1885–1888', *Bulletin of the History of Medicine*, LXVIII (1994), pp. 29–66.

[29] Mary Scharlieb, *Reminiscences* (London, 1924).

[30] Ibid., pp. 154, 162–23.

Together, the patterns of these lives illustrate how women practitioners, mainly but not always British, circulated around the Empire, through, within, and sometimes against, its medical, educational, governmental, and mission institutions. They also illustrate how women crossed over and between the different modes of practice—nursing, medicine, midwifery, traditional therapeutics—modes which only became firmly distinguished from the late nineteenth century.

For indigenous people, the means to enter into British allopathic medicine were, needless to say, markedly different for men and women, and different again from their British counterparts. Some men entered fully into the masculine institutions of Victorian British medical education. S. C. G. Chuckerbutty (1826–74), for example, was educated at Calcutta Medical College and sent to England for higher studies in 1845.[31] More typically, however, indigenous people entered British medical institutions and training in supervised auxiliary roles. In the late 1850s, a British surgeon in Rajasthan established an institution to train locals in European medicine, who then worked mainly in supervised roles in district dispensaries. In East Africa in the 1930s, African men were sought and trained as dressers, hospital assist-ants, vaccinators, assistant surgeons, and laboratory assistants. Their access to such positions depended largely on the nature, quality, and simple availability of a colonial education. For women, this was more difficult as education was less readily available. Indeed the problem of improving health was often linked to the problem of women's education and training.[32] Often it was less through government than missionary endeavours that women received their earliest entry into Western nursing and midwifery practice.[33]

There was a difference between indigenous people being trained in British institutions and medical ways, and them sustaining or hybridizing trad-itional methods. The effects of Empire on traditional practice has required historians to recognize not just the relation between British and traditional medicine, but rather a more complicated negotiation between learned indi-genous traditions (usually men's), on the one hand, and folk or popular

[31] Deepak Kumar, 'Unequal Contenders, Uneven Ground: Medical Encounters in British India, 1820–1920', in Andrew Cunningham and Bridie Andrews, eds., *Western Medicine as Contested Knowledge* (Manchester, 1997), pp. 172; 175.

[32] George O. Ndege, *Health, State and Society in Kenya* (Rochester, 2001) pp. 86–87.

[33] Jane Haggis, ' "Good Wives and Mothers" or "Dedicated Workers": Contradictions of Domesticity in "The Mission of Sisterhood", Travancore, South India', in Kalpana Ram and Margaret Jolly, eds., *Maternities and Modernities: Colonial and Postcolonial Experiences in Asia and the Pacific* (Cambridge, 1998), pp. 92–123.

therapeutics (often women's), on the other.[34] These traditions became 'problems' for imperial authorities in different ways, at different times. The desire to sustain traditional therapies and knowledges sometimes politicized medical men into anti-colonial nationalism. By the second half of the nineteenth century, the learned Indian traditions of Yunani and Ayurverdic medicine, once respected, were being marginalized by British medical personnel in India. Despite, or because of, this marginalization, schools (for men) in Yunani and Ayurvedic medicine were defiantly reinvigorated from the 1880s, alongside new journals in the traditions, and newly translated texts. The success of the associated hospitals, schools, and texts prompted the Government of India to pass a new medical Licensing and Registration Act in 1912 which excluded the indigenous system from state patronage. The two prominent figures who led the re-institutionalization of learned indigenous medicine were Ajmal Khan (1868–1927) of Delhi who promoted Yunani knowledge, and P. S. Verier (1869–1958) who promoted the Ayurvedic system. Both grafted their project and their protest on to the nationalist movement.[35] A series of events around questions of practice, ownership, and access to knowledge, to income, to the manufacture of medicines, took place between Englishmen and Indian men. This was the public sphere at work: political and epistemological engagement between élite men, although they were placed on uneven ground and unequally contending.[36]

Childbirth engaged many imperial practitioners, with local women as both patients and as midwives. It also engaged colonial observers. The rituals and practices around the experiences of pregnancy, labour, and breast-feeding are highly culture-bound and therefore historical processes, but interest in childbirth has not necessarily been constant. In the early centuries of North American contact, the traditional culture of childbirth was largely overlooked by British colonist-observers, but in medical and anthropological texts of the late eighteenth and nineteenth centuries, the birth practices of Aboriginal and Native women were a common object of inquiry. In particular, the question of indigenous women's experience of pain compared to British women's became part of philosophy on 'Nature' and evolutionary

---

[34] Helen Lambert, 'Plural Traditions? Folk Therapeutics and "English" Medicine in Rajasthan', in Cunningham and Andrews, *Western Medicine as Contested Knowledge*, p. 191.

[35] Kumar, 'Unequal Contenders', pp. 180–81.

[36] Kumar's 'Unequal Contenders' details this engagement at the turn of nineteenth century, but not in terms of masculinity.

theory on sex and racial difference.[37] Such descriptions were often denigrat-
ing, representing indigenous practice as inadequate or dangerous, and in the
cases of abortion and infanticide, criminal.[38] Such representation became
increasingly common when British childbirth began to shift from folk
midwifery practices and local management to biomedical expertise, and
especially with a growing state interest in standardization, regulation, and
licensing.

For most British women, white settler women, and indigenous women in
the Empire, birth was likely to be a traditional or domestic, rather than an
institutional, event, until well into the twentieth century. None the less,
government interest in childbirth, reproduction, and population brought
major changes. In the Malayan colonies, Malay and some Chinese women
were trained in Western midwifery, for employment within government
systems of home-care, dispensaries, and hospitals from 1905.[39] In many
contexts, the success of new maternity wings in existing hospitals and
separate institutions for confinement depended almost entirely on the availability of women as medical and nursing staff. In Kenya in the 1930s the
availability of British nurses prompted European-style pre-and post-natal
maternity care in villages and on reserves. Additionally, maternity wings
were added to many government as well as mission hospitals. With these
services in place—often strongly sought by locals—hospital births increased
dramatically in the 1930s.[40] Maternal and infant morbidity and mortality
improved in this major twentieth-century shift, but traditional ways were
also challenged.[41] For indigenous women in Canada and Australia, moreover, this institutionalization and increasing state interest in childbirth in the
inter-war period was of considerable concern because it coincided with
assimilationist programmes of removal of children.[42]

The reshaping of maternal institutions and experiences was deeply connected to the project of modernity, itself a highly gendered process, in part
because of the historic casting of women, and in particular non-European

[37] Patricia Jasen, 'Race, Culture, and the Colonization of Childbirth in Northern Canada',
Social History of Medicine, X, (1997), pp. 383–400. See chap. by Kathleen Wilson.

[38] Margaret Jolly, 'Colonial and Postcolonial Plots in Histories of Maternities and Modernities', in Ram and Jolly, eds., *Maternities and Modernities*, p. 4.

[39] Lenore Manderson, 'Shaping Reproduction: Maternity in Early Twentieth-century
Malaya', in Ram and Jolly, eds., *Maternities and Modernities*, pp. 36–37.

[40] Ndege, *Health, State and Society in Kenya*, pp. 88, 120.

[41] Manderson, 'Shaping Reproduction', p. 33.

[42] See chaps. by Fiona Paisley, Patricia Grimshaw, and Catherine Hall.

women, as more traditional and 'religious', most remote from, and therefore in need of, a rational, scientific, and modern approach.[43] In that indigenous maternal practices were associated with native women, they encapsulated tradition perfectly in the joint scheme of modernity and medicine. Women's transformation through missions, and especially through government projects, effectively signalled hygiene, civilization, reform, improvement, and latterly, development. The modernizing history of sanitation and hygiene is a colonial one, involving both Christianity and science in shaping relations across races. Precisely because of the dominance of hygiene as a marker of modernity and development, it has historically also shaped expressions of class and caste difference into the post-colonial period. For example, in south India, Nada Bible-women were converts under the auspices and training of the lady missionaries of the London Missionary Society. With 'improving' aspirations, their Christianity but also their training in Western hygiene, nursing, and midwifery came to be their entrée into middle-class and later professional status. In present-day south India, midwives in Christian clinics have directly inherited this use of the Western medical and nursing tradition and the imperative of hygiene as a way to distinguish themselves from local and traditional fisherwomen–midwives.[44]

In terms of imperial (and national) histories in the modern period, historical policies and practices around women and reproduction are nearly always linked to policies on population. For modern liberal strategies of governance, the quality, quantity, efficiency, fecundity, and health of the population is a prime aspiration. Of course, how governments differentiated and categorized different populations over time, and what they problematized about them, altered markedly. For British governments during and after the Anglo-Boer War of 1899–1902, for example, the quantity as well as the health of the domestic British population mattered for the continuance of the Empire: crudely, white British women should reproduce more (and better) individuals for the 'expansion of England', for the imperial race.[45] In the same period, in Canada and Australia (settler societies which imagined

[43] Antoinette Burton, 'Introduction: The Unfinished Business of Colonial Modernities', in Burton, ed., *Gender, Sexuality and Colonial Modernities* (London, 1999), pp. 1–16.

[44] Kalpana Ram, 'Maternity and the Story of Enlightenment in the Colonies: Tamil Coastal Women, South India', in Ram and Jolly, eds., *Maternities and Modernities*, pp. 131–32; Haggis, 'Good Wives and Mothers,' pp. 81–113.

[45] Anna Davin, 'Imperialism and Motherhood', in Frederick Cooper and Ann Laura Stoler, eds., *Tensions of Empire* (Berkeley, 1997), p. 93.

themselves as 'British', that is to say, 'white') government and medical interest in infant and maternal mortality, in regulating methods of contraception, and in new welfare endowments for mothers, was similarly driven by race-based nationalisms, and anxiety over falling birth-rates among white women. In other parts of the Empire, however, interventions into reproduction were driven by quite different problems, which involved increasing the indigenous birth-rate and health. In the Straits Settlements, the infant and maternal mortality rate, and therefore the arrested population growth, was of concern to British governing and business interests, because of the labour needs of plantations and mines.[46] By contrast, in Fiji the concern of governing experts was to reverse the threatening tragedy of indigenous depopulation. Between 1893 and 1896 a Commission of Inquiry was held on the 'Decrease of the Native Population', as depopulation did not fit (in this instance) with colonial discourses of improvement.[47] In other instances, notably Australia, 'improvement' was precisely about implementing bio-medically authorized policies of native depopulation. What remains constant through these examples is governmental, medical, and public health interest in motherhood and its management as a way to secure population ambitions based on race in imperial and colonial locations.

British medicine aimed to solve or prevent certain bodily conditions and illnesses which imperial expansion, in many cases, had produced in the first place: in particular the introduction of communicable diseases to isolated communities: smallpox, tuberculosis, measles, whooping cough, and more. Sexually transmitted infections (in earlier nomenclatures, venereal or contagious diseases) were major problems in nearly all colonies and remained health problems from the seventeenth to the twentieth century. The scale of the problem, and the chronic nature of syphilis and gonorrhoea, made these diseases serious threats for the military institutions of the Empire.[48] Sexually transmitted infections chronically disabled indigenous communities, and in particular affected women's fertility.[49] As diseases known to be transmitted

---

[46] Manderson, 'Shaping Reproduction', pp. 35–36.

[47] Margaret Jolly, 'Other Mothers: Maternal 'Insouciance' and the Depopulation Debate in Fiji and Vanuatu 1890–1930', in Ram and Jolly, eds., *Maternities and Modernities*, pp. 177–212.

[48] Philippa Levine, 'Venereal Disease, Prostitution, and the Politics of Empire: The Case of British India', *Journal of the History of Sexuality*, IV (1994), pp. 580–81.

[49] Margaret Jolly, 'Desire, Difference and Disease: Sexual and Venereal Exchanges on Cook's Voyages in the Pacific', in Ross Gibson, ed., *Exchanges: Cross-cultural Encounters in Australia and the Pacific* (Sydney, 1996), pp. 185–217; Ndege, *Health, State and Society in Kenya*, p. 120. Philip

sexually, the preventive and treatment strategies were thoroughly shaped by understandings, based on race, of gender, and of sex.

Preventive strategies had particular ramifications for women, whom experts typically considered to be both the source and the major conduit of sexually transmitted diseases. Female prostitutes, as opposed to their military or civil male clients, were, in the main, targeted as a public health danger. In Madras, Bombay, and Bengal, early colonial systems of 'lock hospitals' for the compulsory isolation, detention, and treatment of Indian prostitutes were periodically in operation in the first three decades of the nineteenth century. Vigorous debate in the 1830s over financial costs, medical efficacy, and the ethical nature of the coercion of the women, saw the Lock Hospitals formally closed, but a similar surveillance of women continued informally. All of this colonial activity anticipated both the passing of the British Contagious Diseases (CD) Acts from 1864, which re-opened the compulsory lock hospitals, and the subsequent domestic campaign to abolish them. In India, compulsory detention and treatment of prostitutes was reintroduced informally as part of the increasing rigidity of racial hierarchies and heightened concern for the health of British troops after the Indian Rebellion, and once again formally with the passing of the Indian CD Act in 1868.[50] Historians commonly see the Contagious Diseases Acts as 'spread[-ing] beyond Britain to the Empire'.[51] In some instances, such as New Zealand's 1869 Act, this was the case. As the situation in early nineteenth-century India suggests, and as Levine's work has shown, colonial experiences of preventing venereal diseases through the compulsory detention, examination, and treatment of prostitutes as much informed British domestic legislation and policy as derived from it. Indeed, the management of venereal diseases (VD) in India continued to be a political problem for both British and Indian governments, well after the repeal of the CD Acts in Britain.[52]

Largely as a legacy of the repeal campaign, an array of pre-war and inter-war anti-VD associations in the twentieth century explored a 'British' style of

W. Setel and others, eds., *Histories of Sexually Transmitted Diseases and HIV/AIDS in Sub-Saharan Africa* (Westport, Conn., 1999).

[50] Douglas Peers, 'Soldiers, Surgeons and the Campaigns to Combat Sexually Transmitted Diseases in Colonial India, 1805–1860,' *Medical History*, XLII (1998), pp. 137–60.

[51] Milton Lewis, *Thorns on the Rose: The History of Sexually Transmitted Diseases in Australia in International Perspective* (Canberra, 1998), p. 94.

[52] Philippa Levine, 'Venereal Disease, Prostitution, and the Politics of Empire', pp. 579–602; and Levine 'Re-reading the 1890s: Venereal Disease as "Constitutional Crisis" in Britain and British India', *Journal of Asian Studies*, LIV (1996), pp. 585–612.

non-coercive management of sexually transmitted infections. Their objects were often the variants of CD legislation still in operation in various colonial locations. The confluence of policing and medical personnel and powers played out powerfully in colonial contexts where both indigenous women and women of the diaspora were already subject to a certain surveillance, intervention, and spatial management by virtue of their race. Public health detention of women in particular (because of the anti-CD Act campaign), came to be viewed by British commentators as an uncivilized, pre-modern practice. 'A Threat of Compulsion!' was the title of the exclamatory leader of a 1937 issue of the British Social Hygiene Council's organ, *Health and Empire*: 'a voluntary scheme is in line with British tradition, which puts great stress on personal liberty'.[53] Just how the Crown Colonies, the Protectorates, the self-governing colonies, and the new nations of the Commonwealth approached VD signalled the global and imperial progress or regress of the mission of Empire and of the extension of liberal British rule. This was paralleled with British opposition to certain colonial governments' insistence on the compulsory detention of people with leprosy.[54] The Social Hygiene Council expressed the keen sense of responsibility held in Britain for the health of Empire and the Commonwealth. Its aims were to educate both British and imperial subjects in sexual behaviour and the self-governance of men and women, as the major route to the prevention of venereal (and other) diseases. Its Propaganda Committee engaged constantly with its counterparts in the colonies on matters of public health and sex reform, circulating anti-VD films, posters, and educational texts.

In certain colonies epidemic communicable disease reduced the possibility of reproduction so severely that communities never recovered their populations. Smallpox was a significant depopulating disease. A chronic disease such as gonorrhoea, while rarely a cause of death, was also a depopulating disease because it often rendered women infertile. In some colonial situations, decisions to leave gonorrhoea in indigenous women untreated was seen as a means to reduce that population. Dr Cecil Cook, Protector of Aborigines and Chief Medical Officer in Australia's Northern Territory, told an inter-war government conference that with no medical intervention, 'the

---

[53] Anon., 'A Threat of Compulsion!', *Health and Empire*, XII (1937), p. 1.

[54] In particular, the work of the British Empire Leprosy Relief Association. See Michael Worboys, 'The Colonial World as Mission and Mandate: Leprosy and Empire, 1900–1940', *Osiris*, XV (2000), pp. 207–18; Jane Buckingham, *Leprosy in Colonial South India: Medicine and Confinement* (London, 2002); Alison Bashford, *Imperial Hygiene* (London, 2004).

aborigines would probably be extinct in Australia within 50 years'. Rather than arguing for improved health-care, Cook saw this as an opportunity to solve a threatening race problem, for if there *was* concerted medical intervention to increase women's fertility, there would be 'a black race numbering about 19,000 and multiplying at a rate far in excess of the whites...their numbers will increase until they menace our security'.[55] Cook, an expert on venereal disease and leprosy amongst Aboriginal communities, was a strong advocate of segregation on complex and connected race and health grounds. He addressed the race problem, in the first instance, through women's fertility and the social engineering of sex and reproductivity.[56]

In colonial contexts, spatial segregation on public health grounds often dovetailed with already existing spatial management of people through racial rationales: indigenous people in various systems of reserves and mission stations. There is now a substantial historiography which links the histories of colonialism, race, and medicine with histories of formal and informal segregation.[57] An analysis of the subsequent segregation by sex, which was an important expression of the management of colonial 'problem populations' especially in institutions, remains underdeveloped. Separating men and women was a way of minimizing sex and reproduction, and of producing internal order and discipline. For example, those with leprosy isolated on Robben Island off Cape Town were segregated by sex.[58] The disease was strongly associated with sexuality—for some experts it *was* a sexually transmissible disease—and thus both the race segregation and subsequent sex segregation on Robben Island were represented as public health measures. In this instance, as in others, public health management was indistinguishable from measures of colonial race management.[59]

---

[55] Cecil Cook in *Aboriginal Welfare: Initial Conference of Commonwealth and State Aboriginal Authorities* (Melbourne, 1937), pp. 13–17.

[56] Patricia Jacobs, 'Science and Veiled Assumptions: Miscegenation in Western Australia 1930–37', *Australian Aboriginal Studies*, II (1986), pp. 15–23.

[57] For example, Harriet Deacon, 'Racism and Medical Science in South Africa's Cape Colony in the Mid-to Late Nineteenth Century', *Osiris*, XV (2000), pp. 190–206; Suzanne Saunders, 'Isolation: The Development of Leprosy Prophylaxis in Australia', *Aboriginal History*, XIV (1990), pp. 168–81.

[58] Harriet Deacon, 'Outside the Profession: Nursing Staff on Robben Island 1846–1910,' in Anne Marie Rafferty and others, eds., *Nursing History and the Politics of Welfare* (London, 1999), pp. 80–107; and Deacon, 'Leprosy and Racism at Robben Island', *Studies in the History of Cape Town*, VII (1994), pp. 45–83.

[59] Bashford, *Imperial Hygiene*, chap. 6.

The idea that climate and the physical environment affected the bodily and mental constitutions of individuals was deeply ingrained in British medical theory and practice. Thus, being 'out-of-place' was understood as a biological and medical (and later a psychological) problem, literally productive of disease or ill-health.[60] Unsuitability of certain peoples to particular climatic conditions proved to be a long-lasting political and legislative rationale for controlling non-white peoples' movement in the Empire and Commonwealth: it was used, for example, to limit African–American entry to Canada, and in negotiations between Australian and British authorities in Singapore over Chinese people on Christmas Island. The same set of climatic theories, however, established British-white presence in tropical places as a health problem. Experts in 'the diseases of warm climates' (later institutionalized as tropical medicine) dealt with the difference between British morbidity and mortality (usually of men in the military) and indigenous morbidity and mortality.[61] They were also concerned with mortality differences between British women and men. In India by the end of the nineteenth century, mortality was significantly higher for British women than for British military men, in large part because of puerperal fever.[62] Governments in India and in colonies such as the Gold Coast (the 'White Man's Grave') were keen to make residence safer for British women, but also to make it appear safer in the British imagination.

Tropical medicine of the late nineteenth and twentieth centuries involved laboratory research into parasites, human and animal physiology, and pathology. It was also about tropical 'hygiene', about racial and gendered conduct in the tropics, about how to govern oneself safely and responsibly as a white person 'out-of-place'. Tropical hygiene texts were essentially conduct manuals for British men and women. Conversely, conduct books for the tropics were health and hygiene manuals. For British women in India, in Queensland, in Singapore, or in Jamaica, tropical hygiene involved detailed sanitary instruction in management of the private and the domestic: in dress, rest, eating, confinement, sleeping, in the discipline and management of infants and children, and of servants, in the arrangement of furniture, in the disposal of waste. As in British sanitary reform, experts recognized the

[60] Warwick Anderson, *The Cultivation of Whiteness: Science, Health and Racial Destiny in Australia* (Melbourne, 2002).

[61] Trevor Burnard, 'The Countrie Continues Sickly: White Mortality in Jamaica 1655–1780', *Social History of Medicine*, XII (1999), pp. 45–72; Peers, 'Soldiers, Surgeons', p. 137.

[62] Mark Harrison, *Public Health in British India* (Cambridge, 1994), p. 50.

significance of women in the creation of a healthy and productive, clean and ordered, private and familial sphere. Again, however, like sanitary reform, the effects of this went well beyond the object of public health, and created subjectivities and social relations both gendered and based on race.

It was not just indigenous people and white women who came to be objects of a conflated imperial and medical gaze. The malleability and limits of the male body which made up the British Army, or the capacities of a white male labour force, were equally part of the colonial business of tropical medicine. In the Australian case managing the male body was the explicit business of government. Australian governments had legislated for Chinese exclusion and the deportation of Islander indentured labour from the 1880s, as part of the bid for a 'White Australia'. Yet the tropical environment left doctors, scientists, and government with the unsettling question: 'Is White Australia Possible?' Given centuries of medical work on the difficulties of tropical climate for the British, could white men labour productively, especially on the tropical sugar plantations in the north? White male bodies were specific research objects of government-funded tropical medicine. The tools of biomedical research became increasingly refined, involving cellular-level physiological and biochemical investigation, and experiment on working-class men, specifically investigating their *whiteness*. In the process, colonial and racial masculinities were imagined and lived.

If imperial rule was about knowing and managing populations in other parts of the world, medicine and public health were part of the same project. Medicine, like the 'gentlemanly' imperial power of the late nineteenth century, was often the perfect governmental combination of assistance and rule. Medicine was also part of imperial rule as mission, as part of the imperial gesture of care, protection, and improvement. As mission and as government, medicine and public health were important vehicles for imperial aspirations to modernize and civilize: a process which has been called 'sanitizing-colonizing'.[63] This is not to suggest that medicine, public health, and the associated practices and expertise were not beneficial to individuals and populations. Indeed, colonized groups often argued strongly for more and better institutions, greater funding, more personnel, and the services of British medicine, especially in the twentieth-century Empire by which time health and welfare had become firmly recognized as government responsibilities. Just as sanitary reform in Manchester or London from the 1830s was

---

[63] Nicholas Thomas, *Colonialism's Culture* (Cambridge, 1994), p. 116.

deeply connected with Poor Law administration, with the management of class and gender as well as ideas about hygiene, whiteness, and race, so imperial health and hygiene, medicine, and nursing, were often politicized endeavours, interested in managing colonial individuals and populations. Each of these aspects of a connected medicine and imperialism was gendered.

Select Bibliography

ALISON BASHFORD, *Imperial Hygiene: A Critical History of Colonialism, Nationalism and Public Health* (London, 2004).

—— ' "Is White Australia Possible? Race, Colonialism and Tropical Medicine', *Ethnic and Racial Studies*, XXIII (2000).

DEA BIRKETT, 'The "White Woman's Burden" in the "White Man's Grave": The Introduction of British Nurses in Colonial West Africa', in Nupur Chaudhuri and Margaret Strobel, eds., *Western Women and Imperialism* (Bloomington, Ind., 1992).

ANTOINETTE BURTON, 'Contesting the Zenana: The Mission to Make "Lady Doctors for India," 1874–1885', *Journal of British Studies*, XXXV (1996).

HARRIET DEACON, 'Midwives and Medical Men in the Cape Colony before 1860', *Journal of African History*, XXXIX (1998).

MARY ANN JEBB, 'The Lock Hospital Experiment: Europeans, Aborigines and Venereal Disease', *European-Aboriginal Relations in Western Australian History*, VIII (1984).

SUSANNE KLAUSEN, 'The Imperial Mother of Birth Control: Marie Stopes and the South African Birth-Control Movement, 1930–1950', in Gregory Blue and others, eds., *Colonialism and the Modern World* (New York, 2002).

PHILIPPA LEVINE, *Prostitution, Race, and Politics: Policing Venereal Disease in the British Empire* (New York, 2003).

VICKI LUKERE and MARGARET JOLLY, eds., *Birthing in the Pacific: Beyond Tradition and Modernity?* (Honolulu, 2001).

LENORE MANDERSON, *Sickness and the State: Health and Illness in Colonial Malaya* (Cambridge, 1996).

SHULA MARKS, *Divided Sisterhood: Race, Class and Gender in South African Nursing* (New York, 1994).

PHILIPPA MEIN SMITH, *Mothers and King Baby: Infant Survival and Welfare in an Imperial World: Australia 1880–1950* (London, 1997).

—— 'New Zealand Milk for 'Building Britons', in Bridie Andrews and Mary Sutphen, eds., *Medicine and Colonial Identities* (London, 2003).

6

Sexuality, Gender, and Empire

PHILIPPA LEVINE

Much of Britain's Empire between the eighteenth and twentieth centuries was located in tropical and semi-tropical zones, from the sugar plantations of northern Australia to the cotton-growing regions of India, from the coffee zone of the West Indies to the veldt of sub-Saharan Africa. Heat and vegetation marked these out for the British as fecund environments, a metaphor not just for the local flora but also for local sexual customs and preferences. Colonial environments came to be seen as sexually distinct from Britain: sexually loose, sometimes predatory, and frequently excessive. Sex in colonial surroundings needed greater regulation and control than in temperate Britain where reason outswayed passion, and where the curbing of sexual appetite was, by the nineteenth century, a mark of good breeding and proper behaviour.

This chapter will argue that sex was a significant imperial policy issue and a 'key site of colonial anxieties'.[1] Unlike Ronald Hyam, who argues that the opportunities for sexual contact in the Empire made a difficult environment more attractive to colonists, I see sex as part of the politics of Empire.[2] Sex was something that needed regulating and managing. Unrestrained sexuality was an unending threat to Empire; it undermined notions of British moderation and rationality, it produced inter racial liaisons and sometimes offspring; it encouraged and facilitated unauthorized sexual behaviours considered dangerous or unseemly. These were not minor considerations, but central to the functioning of imperial governance. Sex always threatened

---

[1] Pamela Scully, 'Rape, Race and Colonial Culture. The Sexual Politics of Identity in the Nineteenth Century Cape Colony, South Africa', *American Historical Review*, C, 2 (1995), p. 338; see too Dagmar Engels, 'History and Sexuality in India: Discursive Trends', *Trends in History*, IV, 4 (1990), p. 17.

[2] Ronald Hyam, 'Empire and Sexual Opportunity', *Journal of Imperial and Commonwealth History* (hereafter *JICH*), XIV, 2 (1986), pp. 34–90; and Hyam, *Empire and Sexuality. The British Experience* (Manchester, 1990).

the bulwarks of Empire and civilization, needing to be restrained and reined in.

A vast range of regulations governed sexuality, far more in imperial settings than in metropolitan Britain. In the domestic arena, a powerful rhetoric of non-intervention dominated the language of government by the mid-nineteenth century. This did not mean that sexuality remained unregulated. Powerful social mores as well as concrete laws and policies stigmatized children born out of wedlock, same-sex practices, and paid sex. By the close of the nineteenth century, concern over the age at which women in particular should be permitted to engage in sexual activity had become of significant concern, many experts arguing that class substantially affected sexual development. If proletarian sexuality was regarded as obscene by the ruling classes, however, the allegedly unbridled and over-heated sexuality of colonial peoples was far worse.

The idea of sexual vice was an important frame for much of the legislation. It was commonly assumed that 'native' peoples were characterized by sexual deviance and vice. An 1853 report in Natal condemned 'the Kafir character' as akin to 'other savages, debased and sensual to the last degree'.[3] Missionary Joseph Salter spoke of the 'vices of the various heathen systems in which the Asiatic is...brought up'.[4] Social purity activist, W. N. Willis, thought 'the microbe of Eastern immorality' devastating to the white race.[5] Colonists in Africa, in Asia, and in the Caribbean shared this homogenized view of non-Western peoples as morally lax and sexually unencumbered. A perceived lack of bodily shame in the non-Christian (and non-Islamic) world signified immorality alongside ignorance. As Christian missionaries gained access to the colonial world, they sought to cover and hide 'native' bodies, to inculcate the biblical concepts of bodily modesty and of carnal shame so fundamental to Western Christianity.

These aspirations to control and to change non-Western sexualities were vital components of imperial rule, and by no means exclusive to missionaries. Colonial governments actively legislated in these areas, with the support of the imperial Parliament in London. The control of sexual practices was

---

[3] *Report of the Commission appointed to inquire into the Past and Present State of the Kafirs in the District of Natal* (1853), quoted in Julian Riekert, 'Race, Sex and the Law in Colonial Natal', *Journal of Natal and Zulu History*, VI (1983), p. 83.

[4] Joseph Salter, *The Asiatic in England. Sketches of Sixteen Years' Work Among Orientals* (London, 1873), p. 22.

[5] W. N. Willis, *Western Men with Eastern Morals* (London, 1913), p. 73.

not only central; it was also definitive. Bad sex, wrong sex, deviant sex defined, described, and characterized those in need of the civilizing hand of colonialism. The argument of altruism—that a British presence was an educative, progressive, and civilizing force in primitive or degraded societies—made the control of sexuality not just acceptable but imperative.

At the same time, the 'Orient' had long been the site of European sexual fantasy.[6] Titillating descriptions and illustrations of semi-clothed peoples on tropical islands was standard literary fare, encouraging popular equations between body and sexuality. Since the days of the Crusades, translations of Arabic and Indian sex manuals had been collectors' items among Europeans.[7] The myth of the harem as a place of sexual adventure and intrigue found expression in art, poetry, and prose, as well as in pornography. Pornography, of course, boomed with the growth of cheaper printing as well as growing literacy, phenomena that speeded its increase in the colonies and not just in Europe.[8] The advent of photography made cheap depictions of the nude 'savage' more common, reinforcing the gap between the clothed and proper English and the barely clad and shameless 'primitives' they ruled.

Fundamental to readings of sexuality as revealing a society's moral character was the principle of racial difference. Race and sex were never far apart politically.[9] Nineteenth-century biological theories of racial hierarchy were not new in stressing racial difference. In the sixteenth and seventeenth centuries, trading intensified contact between Europeans and other peoples. Race and sex—'the whiteness of English women and the blackness of African men'—became a concern.[10] Scientists saw racial difference vividly illustrated in sexual characteristics. Larger genitals were equated with smaller brain size. Sexual excess became the mark of inferiority.

[6] Ann Laura Stoler, 'Making Empire Respectable: the Politics of Race and Sexual Morality in Twentieth-Century Colonial Cultures', *American Ethnologist*, XVI, 4 (1989), p. 635; Michael Sturma, *South Sea Maidens. Western Fantasy and Sexual Politics in the South Pacific* (Westport, Conn., 2002).

[7] V. G. Kiernan, *The Lords of Human Kind. European Attitudes to the Outside World in the Imperial Age* (Harmondsworth, 1972), p. 139.

[8] Charu Gupta, '(Im)possible Love and Sexual Pleasure in Late-Colonial North India', *Modern Asian Studies* (hereafter *MAS*) XXXVI, 1 (2002), p. 197.

[9] Joanna de Groot, ' "Sex" and "Race": The Construction of Language and Image in the Nineteenth Century', in Susan Mendus and Jane Rendall, eds., *Sexuality and Subordination. Interdisciplinary Studies of Gender in the Nineteenth Century* (London, 1989).

[10] Kim F. Hall, *Things of Darkness. Economies of Race and Gender in Early Modern England* (Ithaca, NY, 1995), p. 9. See also the essays collected in Margo Hendricks and Patricia Parker, eds., *Women, "Race", and Writing in the Early Modern Period* (London, 1994).

Yet at the same time, these widely perpetrated ideas demonstrate many of the contradictions imminent in the imperial project. The Empire, as this volume amply demonstrates, was perceived as a fundamentally masculine enterprise. In Britain, masculinity connoted sexual dominance and power. Women's alleged nature had transformed over time from lustful and insatiable to quietly passive. Women's nature was to desire children rather than sex, while men's nature was more directly sexual. And in as masculine an environment as the Empire, male sexuality was an issue governments could ignore only at their peril. If man's nature was so powerfully sexual, then the sensuality of the colonial environment might unhinge him from the British path of civilized moderation. Over-sexedness, associated with colonial peoples, was feared as an unmanning threat which might lead to effeminacy, enervation, and weakness. Masturbation and other solitary forms of sex, too much sex, sex too early were all signs of endangered masculinity. Where was the line to be drawn between master and subject? Regulation and management of sex were key to maintaining and perpetuating the idea and the practice of British superiority.

Assuring that the rulers would remain uncontaminated by local excess was even more critical than effecting change in native behaviour. While missionaries focused mostly on changing native practice and custom, official policies stressed the protection of colonists from the local environment. As a result, there was far more regulatory activity around practices which might harm or jeopardize the standing of the Empire or its maintenance than around those harmful to colonized women. Thus while prostitution was, in almost the whole Empire, subject to stringent management, the trafficking of women for sexual gain was of only nugatory interest to the imperial state. Various subject peoples—the Chinese, and certain Indian 'tribes' or 'castes', for example—were condemned as sexual slavers, but no serious measures ever addressed the problem. Instead, colonizers shrugged off sexual brutality as another indigenous failing.

Most striking was the malleability of representations of female sexuality. On the one hand, women were regarded as licentious temptresses drawing men away from better and more important pursuits. On the other, they were a beneficent domesticating presence without which men would run wild. Colonial authorities supported female emigration schemes as likely to produce more orderly behaviour among frontier men.[11] In the Andaman Islands,

[11] Adele Perry, *On The Edge of Empire: Gender, Race and the Making of British Columbia, 1849–1871* (Toronto, 2001).

the site for Indian convict prisons, women's presence was seen as taming the wildness of convict men.[12] Yet women convicts transported to Australia were routinely assumed to be all of loose morals. In British India, women were regarded both as a nuisance and a necessity.[13] Circumstance and context were everything in the political representations of female sexuality.

One of the earliest sexual encounters between colonizer and colonized was concubinage between local women and British men. Common in the Caribbean, India, parts of Africa, and the Pacific in the eighteenth century, the arrangement sometimes allowed women to rise in status or wealth. Mimicking the formal marriages of the West but without benefit of clergy, women provided domestic and sexual services, often bore a man's children, and were sometimes supported materially after men returned to Europe. As armies became the dominant European presence, concubinage became a less and less workable arrangement. Though in the Dutch East Indies, concubinage survived as 'the dominant domestic arrangement' into the twentieth century, enjoying formal 'recognition in the civil law code', this was not so in British colonies.[14] The East India Company prohibited senior employees from marrying Indian women by 1835.[15] Still, concubinage had its advocates. The commander of the Meerut division in India informed the government in 1870 that 'Military Commanders advocate every possible encouragement to the practice.'[16] Missionaries actively campaigned against concubinage, often publicly shaming offenders.[17] In Hong Kong, marriage between government

[12] Satadru Sen, 'Rationing Sex: Female Convicts in the Andamans', *South Asia*, XXI (1998), p. 36.

[13] Mary A. Procida, 'All in the Family: Marriage, Gender and the Family Business of Imperialism in British India', in Gregory Blue and others, eds., *Colonialism and the Modern World. Selected Studies* (Armonk, NY, 2002), p. 170.

[14] John Ingleson, 'Prostitution in Colonial Java', in David P. Chandler and M. C. Ricklefs, eds., *Nineteenth and Twentieth Century Indonesia. Essays in Honour of Professor J. D. Legge*, (Clayton, Victoria 1986), p. 124; Hanneke Ming, 'Barracks-Concubinage in the Indies, 1887–1920', *Indonesia* XXXV (1983), pp. 64; 70; Ann Laura Stoler, *Race and the Education of Desire. Foucault's History of Sexuality and the Colonial Order of Things* (Durham, NC, 1995), p. 45; and Stoler, 'Making Empire Respectable', p. 637.

[15] Douglas Peers, 'The Raj's Other Great Game: Policing the Sexual Frontiers of the Indian Army in the First Half of the Nineteenth Century', unpublished paper, p. 2. I thank the author for permission to quote from unpublished work.

[16] M. M. Court, Commander, Meerut Division to C. A. Elliott, Officiating Secretary to Government of Northwest Provinces, 25 Aug. 1870, National Archives of India (hereafter NAI), New Delhi, Home Department Proceedings, Public A, 1870.

[17] Margaret Jolly and Martha Macintyre, 'Introduction', in Jolly and Macintyre, eds., *Family and Gender in the Pacific. Domestic Contradictions and the Colonial Impact* (Cambridge, 1989), p. 3.

servants and local women was not formally forbidden, but there were enough disincentives to forestall all but the most determined.[18] The India Secretary candidly admitted to the Indian Viceroy in 1901 that were 'public attention called to the sexual relations existing between Civilians and Burmese women, I should be compelled to condemn it (sic) publicly'.[19] By the late nineteenth century, a local mistress could cost a government servant his promotion. In 1909, Lord Crewe, Secretary of State for the Colonies, warned those unwilling to forego local concubines that 'disgrace and official ruin... will certainly follow'.[20] While early imperialists had seen concubinage as a valuable path to understanding and knowing local culture, changing technologies of information alongside the hardening of racial segregation told against its continuance.

Mixed-race relations were no less common in white settler colonies. In Australia, for example, white working-class men frequently entered into relationships with Aboriginal women, and in Canada with Native Americans, arrangements often favoured because they could be more easily abandoned than those with white women.[21] In the early years of the Canadian fur-trade, traders commonly married local women who brought to the marriage valuable trading networks as well as critical survival skills in a hostile climate. By the end of the eighteenth century, they favoured instead mixed-race women who moved more easily between the indigenous and the settler communities. By the middle of the nineteenth century, such partnerships were giving way to marriages between European men and women, as the idea of mixed-race

---

[18] Norman Miners, *Hong Kong Under Imperial Rule 1912–1941* (Hong Kong, 1987), p. 81.

[19] Lord Hamilton to Lord Curzon, 15 Aug. 1901, Oriental and India Office Collections (hereafter OIOC), Mss. Eur. C.126/3, f. 357. For a detailed account of the formal condemnation of the practice in Africa, see Ronald Hyam, 'Concubinage and the Colonial Service: The Crewe Circular (1909)', *JICH*, XIV, 3 (1986), pp. 170–86; Dan Jacobson, 'Going Native: The Exploits of Silberrad,' *London Review of Books* (25 Nov. 1999), pp. 27–30.

[20] Hyam, 'Concubinage,' p. 184.

[21] Annette Hamilton, 'Bond-Slaves of Satan: Aboriginal Women and the Missionary Dilemma', in Jolly and Macintyre, eds., *Family and Gender in the Pacific*, pp. 252–54; Su-Jane Hunt, 'Aboriginal Women and Colonial Authority. Northwestern Australia 1885–1905', in Judy Mackinolty and Heather Radi, eds., *In Pursuit of Justice. Australian Women and the Law 1788–1979* (Sydney, 1979), p. 37; Ann McGrath, ' "Spinifex Fairies": Aboriginal Workers in the Northern Territory, 1911–39', in Elizabeth Windschuttle, ed., *Women, Class and History* (Melbourne, 1980), pp. 249–50; Windschuttle, 'The White Man's Looking Glass: Aboriginal-Colonial Gender Relations at Port Jackson', *Australian Historical Studies*, XXIV (1990), p. 190; Perry, *On The Edge of Empire*, p. 62.

sex became less and less palatable among both metropolitan and colonial whites.[22]

As a liaison between a local colonized woman and a colonizing man, concubinage in no way disrupted the existing racial or sexual power base. Sexual contact between a white woman and a non-white colonial man, however, was always and everywhere troubling. The idea that a white woman would consent to such a relationship was, for most colonists, unimaginable, and it is in this arena that one of the few instances of a policy around sexual violence appears in the colonial record. The 1926 White Women's Protection Ordinance in Papua New Guinea and the 1903 Criminal Law Amendment Ordinance in Southern Rhodesia made non-white male assaults on white women capital offences.[23] Southern Rhodesia also prohibited 'illicit' sex between white women and black men in that same year. White women everywhere were effectively excluded from white society if they chose an inter-racial liaison.[24]

As racial attitudes hardened, the prospect of mixed-race progeny was increasingly unpalatable. There was a constant fear that mixed-race women would attract white men and the resulting sexual liaisons would dilute the racial stock, with babies ever less English.[25] As early as the eighteenth century the East India Company was sifting Eurasians out of their employ.[26] This fear of racial dilution was frequently cast in protective and health terms; Nott and Gliddon's 1857 treatise on the world's races claimed 'the union of south (*dark*) Europeans with negresses or squaws [resulted in] a hardier animal', than a union with northern whites.[27]

Inter-racial sex was unfortunate, but inter-racial marriage was unimaginable. Such marriages were certainly not common; the social banishment they entailed ensured their rarity. There are a few instances in which élite colonial

[22] Sylvia Van Kirk, *Many Tender Ties: Women in Fur-Trade Society, 1670–1870* (Norman, Okla., 1983).

[23] Amirah Inglis, *The White Woman's Protection Ordinance. Sexual Anxiety and Politics in Papua* (New York, 1975); Jock McCulloch, *Black Peril, White Virtue: Sexual Crime in Southern Rhodesia, 1902–1935* (Bloomington, Ind., 2000).

[24] Janice N. Brownfoot, 'Memsahibs in Colonial Malaya: A Study of European Wives in a British Colony and Protectorate 1900–1940', in Hilary Callan and Shirley Ardener, eds., *The Incorporated Wife* (London, 1984), p. 205.

[25] Lionel Caplan, 'Iconographies of Anglo-Indian Women: Gender Constructs and Contrasts in a Changing Society', *MAS*, XXXIV, 4 (2000), p. 872.

[26] Sudipta Sen, 'Colonial Aversions and Domestic Desires: Blood, Race, Sex and the Decline of Intimacy in Early British India', *South Asia*, XXIV (2001), p. 27.

[27] J. C. Nott and G. R. Gliddon, *Indigenous Races of the Earth* (London, 1857), p. 357.

men married white brides, but women making such marriages lost status in white eyes. In its early years the East India Company had encouraged inter-marriage, since 'importing' white women was a costly undertaking.[28]

The colonial state frequently intervened in marriage practices, affecting contracts between husband and wife as well as with their kin, the status of wives, the property that accompanied marriages, and age of marriage. When the state intervened, it led invariably to the consolidation and conservation of husbandly power. In many instances, colonial intervention worsened women's lot. The 1856 Widow Remarriage Act in India, which attempted to facilitate women re-marrying when widowed, assumed high-caste Hindu practice to be widespread. Yet though the high-caste Hindu widow was expected to live in chastity and seclusion following the death of her husband (a situation that often led to poverty and isolation for women likely to have been married at a very young age), other Hindus rejected the practice. As a result of its focus on the high-caste, the Act hurt poorer women hitherto unaffected by these constraints, and whose re-marriages were now under British scrutiny.[29]

Women none the less found outlets for exerting power in marriage even as male authority was strengthened; in parts of Africa, for example, the West-ernizing of marriage gave women access to law courts where they sought redress for such insults as desertion or assault.[30] While they might not enjoy equality within marriage, women creatively wielded the colonial system to bring neglectful or abusive husbands to heel. In other instances, however, government intervention proved useless. The state's attempt in 1864, for example, to prohibit polygamy in Lagos was futile.[31]

The British view of marriage as a Christian covenant between one man and one woman—enshrined in Hardwicke's Marriage Act of 1753—was not always shared by their colonial subjects. That Act was not operable in the colonies, though missionaries tried hard to promote the Western view of marriage as an exclusive, sanctified, heterosexual union. In many settings, however, the temporary marriage was a more convenient and logical

---

[28] Sen, 'Colonial Aversions', p. 30.

[29] Lucy Carroll, 'Law, Custom and Statutory Social Reform: The Hindu Widow's Remarriage Act of 1856', in J. Krishnamurty, ed., Women in Colonial India (Delhi, 1988).

[30] Jane L. Parpart, 'Sexuality and Power on the Zambian Copperbelt: 1926–1964', in Sharon B. Stichter and Jane L. Parpart, eds., African Women in the Home and the Workforce (Boulder, Colo., 1988), pp. 125 ff.

[31] John C. Caldwell and others, 'The Destabilization of the Traditional Yoruba Sexual System', Population and Development Review, XVII, 2 (1991), p. 253.

arrangement, although dubbed immoral by the British.[32] As urban populations grew, the emerging male-dominated labour environment led to short-
term marriages, both heterosexual and homosexual, especially in colonial
Africa.[33] Marriage in many cultures was not regarded as a match between two
people, but rather as a kin or family affair, designed to benefit larger numbers
of people than merely the married couple. Living arrangements and dowry
distribution suggest the wider social significance of marriage in many parts
of the world. Yet the increasing romanticization of marriage in Britain, which
ignored how often it was a carefully managed business arrangement, made
such alternative ideas of marriage seem barbaric and unnatural, evidence of a
lesser sensibility.[34]

Legislation on the age of consent in some places was directly focused on
debates, around another related marriage issue, that of infant marriage. In
India the age of female consent was raised from ten to twelve in 1891 to
prevent the consummation of child marriages before puberty. Stiff opposition from protesters claiming that this was an attack on Hindu marriage
conventions made the law untenable, though a similar and successful law, the
Infant Marriage Regulation Act, was passed in the princely state of Mysore in
1893. It was 1929 before female age of consent in India was raised to fourteen.
In white settler colonies, by contrast, consent was raised to sixteen, and even
older, and unlike the Indian context was debated as an issue about sexual
behaviour, and not marriage. The lower age in India reflected not only
religious protest but assumptions about 'native' attitudes to, and propensity
for, sex at an early age.

Women's labour was, in the eyes of colonizer, also symptomatic of their
sexualization. Colonial non-white women worked in industries that in
Britain would have been closed to them, such as construction work and
other heavy manual labour. One of the things that set them apart from male
workers, their smaller pay packets aside, was their vulnerability to male
sexual demands. Employers, overseers, and other workers often made
demands upon women which they repelled sometimes at risk to their
livelihoods. In other instances, suspicions about working-class female sexu-

---

[32] Barbara Watson Andaya, 'From Temporary Wife to Prostitute: Sexuality and Economic
Change in Early Modern Southeast Asia', Journal of Women's History, IX, 4 (1998), pp. 11–34.

[33] Parpart, 'Sexuality and Power'; Luise White, 'Domestic Labor in a Colonial City: Prostitution in Nairobi, 1900–1952', in Stichter and Parpart, eds., African Women, pp. 139–60.

[34] Pervez Mody, 'Love and the Law: Love-Marriage in Delhi', MAS, XXVI, 1 (2002),
pp. 223–56.

ality deprived women of their jobs. At the Fort William cantonment in India, the grass-cutters petitioned in 1897 for the return of women's jobs. Husbands and wives traditionally worked alongside one another and the male grass-cutters insisted that their wives were 'of good character' and that without their wages, 'we cannot possibly earn enough'.[35] Officials none the less suspected husbands of selling and soliciting their own wives, and not just in India. At Beagle Bay, on the West Australian coast, Daisy Bates found 'four Manilamen ... married to native women. By tribal custom the women had all been betrothed in infancy to their rightful tribal husbands. They were therefore merely on hire by their own men to the Asiatics, and in spite of the church marriage [to the 'Asiatics'], remained, not only their husband's property, but that of all his brothers, and all of the Manila husband's brothers.' The evil was, thus, multifarious. Christian marriage had become a mockery, and women, thought Bates, were passed around from one man to another. Little wonder she concluded that 'the association of the Australian native with the Asiatic is definitely evil', condemning two races for their immorality at one stroke.[36]

The image of sexual slavery implicit in these views of women sold by greedy husbands was a powerful one. Colonial officials condemned a wide range of colonial cultures for their alleged sexual enslavement of women. The Chinese were said to enslave poor women in brothels, the Indians in temple prostitution. And in the years before the institution of slavery was abolished in the British Empire, abolitionists found the rhetoric around coerced sex a valuable weapon. Much of their stark imagery was based on fact, for slave women were indeed vulnerable to sexual abuse.[37] Certainly they learned to use their sexuality as a commodity to improve their own situation and that of their kin, but slavery relied heavily on their coerced availability across a wide range of sexual partnering over which they had little or no control.[38]

Plantation overseers frequently treated indentured women workers in a similar fashion, sleeping with them when they desired and requiring sexual services on demand.[39] Florence Garnham found the Fiji plantations in 1918

[35] Grass Cutter's Petition, 1 June 1897, OIOC, P/5248.

[36] Daisy Bates, *The Passing of the Aborigines. A Lifetime spent among the Natives of Australia* (London, 1944), p. 12.

[37] Barbara Bush, *Slave Women in Caribbean Society, 1650–1838* (Kingston, 1990), p. 113.

[38] See chap. by Kathleen Wilson.

[39] Brij V. Lal, 'Kunti's Cry: Indentured Women on Fiji Plantations', *Indian Economic and Social History Review* (hereafter, *IESHR*) XXII, 1 (1985), pp. 58; 64.

an 'unspeakably corrupt' environment in which it was 'quite impossible...
for a woman to preserve her chastity'.[40] For some women, slave and indentured, this was a useful route to small privileges; for others, it was a torment.

'What is a common prostitute?' asked a colonial civil servant in 1870. In
answering his own question, he provided a glimpse of how prostitution was
defined in terms which condemned large swathes of colonial subjects as
immoral:

The women who walk the road every evening to the west of the Cawnpore
Cantonment, the coolie women and milk sellers, who are employed at the barracks
in the day time, all of them married women, and by repute respectable household
women, are as much common prostitutes as the most habitual professionals.[41]

This reading of prostitution as commonplace and unremarkable was a clear
marker of the sexual inferiority of colonial societies. Australian settlers
thought 'the Gins [Aboriginal women] are simply prostitutes'.[42] A senior
civil servant at the Colonial Office claimed that 75 per cent of Chinese women
in Hong Kong were prostitutes.[43]

By the middle of the nineteenth century, systems for regulating prostitution were widely formalized throughout most of the Empire.[44] The system
centred mainly on controlling the brothel trade, a tactic that, in the metropolis, would have provoked significant protest as sanctioning 'vice' but
which was acceptable on colonial terrain. Routinely, brothels were required
to register with the requisite authority. They were usually racially segregated,
and women working in brothels for white men were forbidden to accept
other clients. By the late nineteenth century, European prostitutes worked in
many areas of the Empire, and though few were apparently English, there was
always alarm that 'native' men would regard white, and above all English,

[40] Florence E. Garnham, *A Report on the Social and Moral Condition of Indians in Fiji, Being
the Outcome of an Investigation set on Foot by Combined Women's Organisations of Australia*
(Sydney, 1918), p. 14.

[41] F. O. Mayne, Commissioner, 4th Division to C. A. Elliott, Officiating Secretary to Government, Northwest Provinces, 20 Aug. 1870, NAI, Home Department, Public. Consultations.
A Proceedings, 1870.

[42] Sergeant F. J. O'Connor, Boulia Sub District to Inspector of Police, 20 Dec. 1898, Queensland State Archives, Brisbane, COL/144, 12886.

[43] C. P. Lucas to F. Meade, 6 May 1879, National Archives Public Record Office, (hereafter
PRO), London, Colonial Office (hereafter CO) 129/184, 6690.

[44] Philip Howell, 'Prostitution and Racialised Sexuality: The Regulation of Prostitution in
Britain and the British Empire before the Contagious Diseases Acts', *Environment and Planning
D: Society and Space*, XVIII (2000), pp. 321–39.

women as sexually available. In 1902 legislation in Cape Colony forbade white prostitutes to accept black clients. White colonial customers disliked the idea that the women they purchased might service men of other races. 'Soldiers or sailors, and other Englishmen, educated or uneducated, who enter a brothel and find "niggers" there, at once proceed to turn them out ... racial animosity is bred and fostered day by day and night by night in the brothels'.[45]

By the 1920s attempts to suppress prostitution became more common as regulation proved unwieldy, unsuccessful, and unpopular. The growing interest of bodies such as the League of Nations in stemming prostitution and the sexual trafficking of women strengthened the hand of those who opposed reglementation. In India, in the Malay peninsula, and in Hong Kong, the laws shifted from toleration to crackdowns on commercial sex. In India, additionally, the anti-*nautch* movement gained strength, leading in many places to a ban on the raising of female children as *devadasis*, women married to the temple gods and in some instances earning their keep through sex.[46]

The control of women's bodies because of their reproductive capacities has, of course, a lengthy history. It was no less an issue in the colonial period than in other eras. One of the salient characteristics of the imperial period is the capture of this debate by medicine and science. By the early twentieth century, the moral lobby competed in particular with the champions of eugenics, who promoted a science of 'good breeding', explicitly racial in its terminology and its philosophy. Though employing the vocabulary of science, eugenics mirrored earlier concerns about reproductive capacity. Clearly, the appearance of a new generation was all that ensured the longevity of a people, and in non-industrial arenas, in particular, the fertility of women was symbolically linked to the fertility of the land. A society's well-being, its wealth, its ability to feed and clothe itself, its very future, were frequently perceived as directly related to women's ability to bear healthy children. And

---

[45] John Cowen, 'Report of A Visit to the Two Great Brothel Areas of Singapore in the Autumn of 1915', PRO, CO273/452 (60716), p. 10, reprinted in an amended and abridged version in *The Shield*, Third Series, I, 3 (Oct., 1916).

[46] Frédérique Apffel Marglin, *Wives of the God-King. The Rituals of the Devadasis of Puri* (Delhi, 1985); Mrinalini Sarabhai, *The Sacred Dance of India* (Bombay, 1979); Amrit Srinivasan, 'Reform and Revival: The Devadasi and Her Dance', *Economic and Political Weekly*, XX, 44 (1985), pp. 1869–1876; and Srinivasan, 'Reform or Conformity? Temple "Prostitution" and the Community in the Madras Presidency', in Bina Agarwal, ed., *Structures of Patriarchy. State, Community and Household in Modernising Asia* (New Delhi, 1988), pp. 175–98.

as racial hierarchies rigidified through colonial contact and scientific data, which claimed to prove that race was biological, women's fertility was increasingly linked to racial purity. In white settler lands and in the metropolis, woman's duty was represented as upholding and uplifting the race, ensuring its longevity and its purity.[47] This eugenics-inflected fear of racial mixing increasingly affected the tenor of debates over reproduction.

Even fear at the thought of apparent racial degradation could not, however, make birth control a polite topic. Only in the 1920s could the issue, frequently re-named 'family limitation' in a bid for respectability, finally be discussed publicly, and even then it was risqué. In earlier eras those who publicized birth control methods, or even general discussions of the issue, were liable to prosecution. Feminist groups on the whole gave the topic a wide berth, being unwilling to risk their own claims to respectability. None of this, of course, slowed an age-old 'grapevine', especially strong amongst women, about controlling conception. People from all walks of life quietly prevented conception and spaced births in spite of public disapprobation.

The advent of barrier methods associated with the vulcanization of rubber medicalized birth control. In the nineteenth and twentieth centuries, throughout the Empire, new laws limiting the dispensing of contraceptive devices to the medically qualified robbed women of control, though they may also have offered more reliability. Women who had traditionally dispensed advice and products became liable to punishment. In some instances, local reformers embraced the new medical methods. In the 1920s in India, groups such as the Hindu Malthusian League, based in Madras and limited in the main to educated men, publicly advocated birth control. A decade later, Indian women became involved in the campaigns. Most were well educated, and they moved cautiously in recognition of the local moral climate. Birth control faced no legal impediment in British India, but women's sexuality was tightly controlled and procreation was regarded as a fundamental duty of wives, and wifehood as women's highest calling.[48] The first attempt, in 1931, by Rani Lakshmi Rajwade to secure birth control as an

---

[47] Anna Davin, 'Imperialism and Motherhood', *History Workshop Journal*, V (1978), pp. 9–65; Marianna Valverde, ' "When The Mother of the Race Is Free": Race, Reproduction and Sexuality in First-Wave Feminism', in Franca Iacovetta and Mariana Valverde, eds., *Gender Conflicts. New Essays in Women's History* (Toronto, 1992), p. 16.

[48] In Britain, by contrast, contraception faced legal barriers. There, too, it might be worth noting, the unmarried woman was stigmatized.

agenda item at the All India Women's conference was a failure.[49] The following year the conference agreed to take on the issue, and new women's organizations interested in 'social hygiene' also began to get involved. By 1936, the year Margaret Sanger visited India, there were a handful of privately run clinics in Bombay and Calcutta, though municipal authorities refused to provide public clinics. The new clinics often had trouble attracting a clientèle since their *raison d'être* was still seen by many as not respectable and as dangerous. Campaigners emphasized birth spacing over prevention, to signal that the adoption of birth-control techniques did not represent women's defection from the bearing and raising of children.

In the early 1930s birth-control clinics began to open in the burgeoning cities of South Africa where, as urbanization took root and despite the growing separation of labouring men from their families, the birth rate had soared.[50] Some of this increase in fertility was certainly an effect of the social and familial disruptions caused by migration, and by the erosion of both the use of traditional herbal potions and the practice of pre-marital intracrural sex, between the thighs and without vaginal penetration.

Inevitably increased birth rates were accompanied by a rising clamour for terminations. Patent medicine abortifacients abounded as advertising proliferated. Abortion, too, was subject to an increasing medical monopoly as herbal traditions gave way to surgical techniques. Unlike contraception, abortion was commonly criminalized, as in the Indian Penal Code (1860) and in Fiji (1902). In part this was the result of missionary horror, but it also paralleled a metropolitan crackdown on abortion; abortion was first criminalized in England and Wales in 1803, with tighter versions of the law following in 1828 and 1837.[51]

Substantial difference in how cultures understood the foetus meant that abortion and contraception had many different meanings. Inducing menstruation was in many cultures acceptable where termination was not, even though their technical difference may be ambiguous. In the metropolis, the

[49] Barbara N. Ramusack, 'Embattled Advocates: The Debate Over Birth Control in India, 1920–40', *Journal of Women's History*, I, 2 (1989), p. 41.

[50] Susanne Klausen, 'The Imperial Mother of Birth Control: Marie Stopes and the South African Birth Control Movement, 1930–1950', in Blue and others, eds., *Colonialism and the Modern World*, p. 184; Helen Bradford, 'Herbs, Knives and Plastic: 150 Years of Abortion in South Africa', in Teresa Meade and Mark Walker, eds., *Science. Medicine and Cultural Imperialism* (New York, 1991), p. 131.

[51] Angus McLaren, *Reproductive Rituals. The Perception of Fertility in England from the Sixteenth to the Nineteenth Century* (London, 1984), p. 114.

law defined the foetus as alive and requiring legal protection after quickening, and thus at about four months, but elsewhere this seemed arbitrary.[52] Abortion laws often imposed alien definitions alongside tightening public control of women's reproduction. And as abortion became more difficult to obtain, more women despatched unwanted babies immediately after birth, exposing themselves to criminal prosecution for infanticide. Again, local culture shaped women's choices; in nineteenth-century Jamaica, the social pressures that pushed women elsewhere to infanticide or to concealing births were absent.[53]

In many settings, controversy over abortion was linked to other arenas of female sexuality which highlighted its central role as a mechanism of patriarchal control. Critics in South Africa lambasted the new birth-control clinics of the 1930s for encouraging white women to sidestep maternity, thus endangering future white supremacy.[54] In India, where abortion was illegal but tolerated in many quarters, Indian reformers linked abortion to what they saw as the evils of Hindu widowhood and to the female infanticide that they claimed was common in some communities.[55] Ishwar Chandra Vidyasagar, the leading campaigner for widow re-marriage, argued that permitting widows to re-marry rather than to remain in chaste seclusion would reduce the rate of abortion.[56] Though little hard evidence supported his claim, it resonated with fears of women not under the control of a male figurehead and running rampant sexually.

It was this same and age-old fear of the consequences of untrammelled female sexuality that linked abortion to the controversy over female circumcision in East Africa in the late 1920s. Despite pressure from feminists in Britain, the Colonial Office and local colonial authorities in Africa were mostly reluctant to endorse or initiate aggressive anti-circumcision campaigns.[57] In the Meru district of central Kenya, however, an altogether

[52] Bradford, 'Herbs, Knives and Plastic,' p. 124.

[53] Persis Charles, 'The Name of the Father: Women, Paternity and British Rule in Nineteenth-Century Jamaica', *International Labor and Working-Class History*, XLI (1992), pp. 4–22.

[54] Klausen, 'Imperial Mother of Birth Control', p. 184.

[55] Tapan Raychaudhuri, 'Love in A Colonial Climate: Marriage, Sex and Romance in Nineteenth-Century Bengal', *MAS*, XXXIV (2000), p. 365.

[56] Supriya Guha, 'The Unwanted Pregnancy in Colonial Bengal', *IESHR*, XXXIII, 4 (1996), p. 420.

[57] On feminist campaigns, see Susan Pedersen, 'National Bodies, Unspeakable Acts: The Sexual Politics of Colonial Policy-making', *Journal of Modern History*, LXIII, 4 (1991), pp. 647–80; on colonial reluctance, see Heather Bell, 'Midwifery Training and Female Circum-

different approach unfolded. Alarmed by a low birth-rate and by active pre-marital female sexual activity, local African leaders and white district officials decided that female circumcision was the lesser evil. They embarked on a campaign (not endorsed by the Nairobi authorities) to encourage pre-pubertal circumcision (labial excision), believing that this initiation into adulthood would result in earlier marriages and therefore fewer abortions. Traditional practice in the district had been to excise only after the onset of menses and preferably after betrothal.[58] Evidence that young women aborted pregnancies in their pre-initiation years overrode the usual Western indignation at female circumcision. Since it was customary, officials reasoned, undertaking the practice earlier would have beneficial effects on the district's birth-rate and social stability. It also curtailed the freedoms of women at an even earlier age.

Though the Meru policy of encouraging excision was unusual, there was none the less a significant gap between public condemnation of female circumcision and an active policy to end the practice which was common-place not just in parts of British Africa (such as the Sudan and Kenya) but in Britain's Malayan territories too. Female circumcision was usually debated as a health issue, amongst feminists as much as officials and doctors. In so far as government did intervene to limit or prevent excision, the basic justification was that cutting was a health problem imperilling women's reproductive capacities. Inevitably the practice was also popularly associated with back-wardness and savagery, an example of the primitive sexuality of colonized peoples and their cruelty to women. The continued use of female circumci-sion at this juncture in the 'advanced' civilization of the United States was seldom mentioned.[59]

Government's stance on the circumcision issue effectively demonstrates the close connection of politics and sexuality in colonial governance, for in many instances, colonial authorities were reluctant to move against the practice for fear of losing ground with local male power bases. In the

cision in the Inter-War Anglo-Egyptian Sudan', *Journal of African History* (hereafter *JAH*), XXXIX (1998), pp. 293–312.

[58] Lynn M. Thomas, 'Imperial Concerns and "Women's Affairs": State Efforts to Regulate Clitoridectomy and Eradicate Abortion in Meru, Kenya, c. 1910–1950,' *JAH*, XXXIX (1998), p. 125.

[59] Ornella Moscucci, 'Clitoridectomy, Circumcision and the Politics of Sexual Pleasure in Mid-Victorian Britain', in Andrew H. Miller and James Eli Adams, eds., *Sexualities in Victorian Britain* (Bloomington, Ind., 1996); Andrew Scull and Diane Favreau, 'The Clitoridectomy Craze', *Social Research*, LIII (1986), pp. 243–60.

Sudan, for example, where a British-dominated Anglo-Egyptian Con-
dominium ruled from 1898, officials were anxious not to antagonize Islamic
leaders and local élites.[60] The Mahdist jihad of the 1880s was a reminder to
the British that there were other powers in the colonies which had to
be accommodated. At the Kabare station in Kenya's South Nyeri district,
the local church, anxious not to lose Christianity's hold, in 1929 helped
to introduce a Christian circumcision practice and ceremony for the young
of both sexes.[61] It was women's lives which were sacrificed to political
necessity.

The reluctance of the imperial government to become involved when
controversy erupted in central Kenya in the 1920s reflected their concurrence
with African male rulers that the control of women's bodies fundamentally
'belonged' to the men of a society.[62] The issue was more complicated, for
missionary activity had also catalysed native critiques of colonial authority
which officials on the ground could not countenance.[63] As was so often
the case, questions around sexuality proved politically potent, not only
in highlighting the state's investment in particular forms of sexuality
and in maintaining prescribed gender roles, but because such issues also
frequently brought about critiques of, and dissatisfactions with, colonial
rule, and its imposition of alien religious and cultural values. In
the case of female circumcision, it was not women's pain or pleasure
but their reproductive capacity and their freedom of choice that were
seen as critical issues which could destabilize colonial power, just as abortion
was seen as jeopardizing a labour supply and undercutting the idea of
women as tied to a single male sexual partner. In colonial societies, seen as
simultaneously highly sexed and unusually prudish, these controversial
topics became thus deeply political issues at the heart of proper colonial
governance.

Governments, moreover, were not wrong in their assessments of the
unrest that might ensue if they moved to obliterate circumcision. In Meru
the practice was outlawed in 1956, but adolescent women, unwilling to
abandon their formal initiation into womanhood, excised one another in

---

[60] Bell, 'Midwifery Training', p. 307.

[61] Jocelyn Murray, 'The Church Missionary Society and the "Female Circumcision" Issue in
Kenya', *Journal of Religion in Africa*, VIII, 2 (1976), p. 100.

[62] Pedersen, 'National Bodies, Unspeakable Acts', p. 665.

[63] Penelope Hetherington, 'The Politics of Female Circumcision in the Central Province of
Colonial Kenya, 1920–1930', *JICH*, XXVI, 1 (1998), p. 93; Thomas, 'Imperial Concerns', p. 130.

defiance of the law.[64] The women's stand became entwined with the growing Mau Mau resistance movement, symbolizing a rejection of Western values.

The Empire, for white colonizers, was always and in most places a predominantly male environment, in settler and dependent colonies alike. Imbalance in sex ratios was typical of many colonial environments. Pioneer white colonies were overwhelmingly male in their early years and in many cases schemes to bring in white women were regarded as critical for the colony's long-term survival. For colonized peoples, too, demographic unevenness was common. Colonies where white populations remained the minority relied on young, migrant, male labour and it was well into the twentieth century before the proportion of men to women began to even out. Convict colonies invariably had more men than women. In these circumstances, an undercurrent of fear around male homosexuality profoundly influenced colonial governments. Though colonial environments were often seen as unfit for women, there was anxiety lest their small numbers or absence encourage men to seek sexual relief from one another. The protector of Chinese at the Straits, William Pickering, thought regulated prostitution a vital defence against homosexuality.[65] A committee reporting to the Government of India in 1917 warned that 'the vice of homo-sexualism has invariably made its appearance among collections of male human beings deprived of access to women'.[66]

Many a Briton regarded same-sex liaisons as another example of non-British perversity, claiming that Indians, Arabs, and Africans were devotees of practices increasingly criminalized under British law, judgments resting on profoundly different ideas about the meaning and nature of human sexual relations. Just as the British persistently misunderstood marriage and heterosexual activity across the Empire, they were mystified, shocked, and often fearful of the more expansive sexualities they sometimes encountered, and were quick to condemn them as immoral or amoral. They were, moreover, unwilling to imagine the ways in which their own colonial policies might produce the very practices they so abhorred.

---

[64] Lynn M. Thomas, ' "*Ngaitana* (I Will Circumcise Myself)": The Gender and Generational Politics of the 1956 Ban on Clitoridectomy in Meru, Kenya,' in Nancy Rose Hunt, and others, eds., *Gendered Colonialisms in African History* (Oxford, 1997), pp. 16–41.

[65] R. N. Jackson, *Pickering. Protector of Chinese* (Kuala Lumpur, 1965), p. 93.

[66] 'Report of the Committee appointed by the Local Government to Advise on Certain Questions Concerning Brothels and Prostitutes in Rangoon', Nov. 1917, OIOC, L/P&J/6/1448 (2987).

A case in point is the 'mine marriage' between older and younger males in African mining communities.[67] Such temporary arrangements were often valuable in providing not only companionship in a harsh environment but could also form the basis for the younger man to accrue assets in anticipation of a later heterosexual marriage.[68] The British saw this easy shift between different expressions of sexuality as especially perverse. Gender roles and sexual preference were, in Western culture, regarded as fixed and not fluid, and the heterogeneity of sexuality they found in other cultures was an index of savagery, proof that passion not reason dominated.

Needless to say, given the Western reading of female sexuality as passive and passionless, the existence of same-sex liaisons between women in colonial environs aroused far less consternation or interest. The existence in Africa of female husbands (an arrangement sometimes dubbed 'mummy-baby' marriage, reflecting an age stratification similar to men's mine marriages) on the whole escaped colonial notice.[69] Such relationships did not necessarily preclude sexual relations with men, and this evidence of fluidity was grist to the moral mill.[70] Though women often escaped attention men were liable to prosecution, even as early as the eighteenth century.[71] In the 1890s, prosecutions for 'unnatural offences' were frequent in southern Rhodesia, for example, and the vast majority of the defendants were African.[72] White mens' transgressions, while often more shocking, were frequently covered up.

In India, patterns of migration and urbanization also altered sex ratios, and while same-sex relations are not just the product of opportunity, changing demographics which disrupted traditional family patterns certainly highlighted long-standing practices. The steady growth of

[67] Marc Epprecht, ' "Good God Almighty, What's This!": Homosexual "Crime" in Early Colonial Zimbabwe', in Stephen O. Murray and Will Roscoe, eds., *Boy-Wives and Female Husbands. Studies of African Homosexualities* (New York, 1998), pp. 197–221; Patrick Harries, 'Symbols and Sexuality: Culture and Identity on the Early Witwatersrand Gold Mines', *Gender & History*, II, 3 (1990), pp. 318–36.

[68] Harries, 'Symbols and Sexuality', p. 329; Deborah Pellow, 'Sexuality in Africa', *Trends in History*, IV, 4 (1990), p. 82.

[69] Joseph M. Carrier and Stephen O. Murray, 'Woman-Woman Marriage in Africa', in *Boy-Wives and Female Husbands*, pp. 255–66; Pellow, 'Sexuality in Africa', pp. 84–85.

[70] Margaret Strobel, 'Women's History, Gender History, and European Colonialism', in Blue and others, eds., *Colonialism and the Modern World*, pp. 53–54.

[71] Robert Ross, 'Oppression, Sexuality and Slavery at the Cape of Good Hope', *Historical Reflections*, VI (1979), p. 431.

[72] Epprecht, 'Good God Almighty', p. 205.

nationalism, and the expressions of sexuality and of gender roles nationalism enshrined, frequently produced conservative readings of sexual role and practice. Indian nationalism increasingly relied on an invocation of Indian male virility and female purity, and on a critique of Western degradation. In such an environment, male–male relations were seen as an ugly Western import which would feminize and weaken male strength.[73] The British had decried especially Bengali men as effeminate and ineffectual through too much sex, at an early age or without a partner.[74] The nationalist ethos replaced that image with an idea of India which, though it rejected much of British culture, incorporated a 'natural' union of female chastity and male virility, in which there was no room for same-sex arrangements.

Even amongst otherwise sympathetic colonial voices, ideas about native sexuality tended to set the indigenous apart from and below Western values. Anthropologist Tom Harrisson, who spent a number of years living in the New Hebrides in the 1930s and was frequently critical of imperial practice, noted the absence of masturbation, of same-sex relations, and of other sexual practices considered problematic in the metropolis. 'The general absence of perversion', he thought, 'corresponds with the absence of revolutionary artists and genii.'[75] Sexuality clearly occupied a central if troubling place in colonial rule, something it was not always easy to talk about but which none the less needed constant management.

Colonialism both accommodated pre-existing sexual codes and intervened to alter them. In cases where local practice, even if regarded as abhorrent and fundamentally antipathetic to Western values, none the less allowed colonial rule to function smoothly, such practices were often permitted, or even encouraged. The unwillingness to alienate local chiefs and religious leaders in Africa over the issue of female circumcision, and the continued legality of child marriage in India and of polygamy in a number of environs are good examples. Where, however, moral consternation did not interfere with rule, more strenuous official opposition could be entertained. Policy, like sexual practice, was never homogenous; it was piecemeal and frequently opportunistic. Despite a tenacious rhetoric of essentialism which saw sexuality as a natural and unhistorical human attribute, actual practice

[73] Gupta, '(Im)possible Love', p. 200.

[74] Mrinalini Sinha, Colonial Masculinity. The 'Manly Englishman' and the 'Effeminate Bengali' in the Late Nineteenth Century (Manchester, 1995).

[75] Tom Harrisson, Savage Civilization (New York, 1937), p. 363.

suggests rather the deeply historical and always changing ground of sexuality, as much a cultural and historical product as a biological urge.

Connectedly, and in the context of Western notions of property as well as propriety, much of the colonial policy-making around sexuality derived from ideas of property. In particular, when we consider the criminalization of a wide range of sexually connected practices, the motive of property becomes apparent. When women disposed of either foetuses or small children, they were stealing from fathers and husbands and could be condemned as thieves. Likewise, a rapist was guilty of theft; the brutalization of a woman's body was in some cases secondary to the damage rape (and other forms of unsanctioned sex) did to a family or a man's honour and prestige. Age of consent laws, similarly, never really addressed the consent of individual women, dealing rather with the age at which daughters might be given in marriage so designating the passing of property from fathers to husbands.

In all these instances, colonial policy stressed control in a variety of forms. In some instances, it was the assertion of male control over wayward female sexuality; in others, it was controlling unbridled native lust. In all cases, however, controlling sexuality was seen as critical colonial practice. While it may seldom have captured press headlines, sexuality was a central concern that surfaced over and over in both the Westminster Parliament and in local colonial governance. The control of white colonial sexuality was just as critical as the managing of indigenous mores. Colonial power cannot be reduced to a mere one-sided form of oppression. In this instance, the adherence of colonizers to the forms and propriety of their native Britain was crucial. In the intensifying discouragement to concubinage, in the often Draconian policing of interracial sex, lay fears about miscegenation and the dilution of racial superiority. The collapse of racial difference—in the scientific parlance of the time, palpably achievable if the races intermingled sexually—could spell not just the end of European superiority or distinctiveness but, more pressingly, the end of Empire.

Select Bibliography

KENNETH BALLHATCHET, *Race, Sex and Class Under the British Raj. Imperial Attitudes and Policies and their Critics, 1793–1905* (London, 1980).

PHILIP HOWELL, 'Prostitution and Racialised Sexuality: The Regulation of Prostitution in Britain and the British Empire before the Contagious Diseases Acts', *Environment and Planning D: Society and Space*, XVIII (2000), pp. 321–39.

RONALD HYAM, *Empire and Sexuality. The British Experience* (Manchester, 1990).

AMIRAH INGLIS, *The White Woman's Protection Ordinance. Sexual Anxiety and Politics in Papua* (New York, 1975).

PHILIPPA LEVINE, *Prostitution, Race, and Politics: Policing Venereal Disease in the British Empire* (New York, 2003).

ANNE McCLINTOCK, *Imperial Leather. Race, Gender and Sexuality in the Colonial Context* (New York, 1995).

ANN LAURA STOLER, 'Making Empire Respectable: the Politics of Race and Sexual Morality in Twentieth-Century Colonial Cultures', *American Ethnologist*, XVI, 4 (1989), pp. 634–60.

—— *Race and the Education of Desire. Foucault's History of Sexuality and the Colonial Order of Things* (Durham, NC, 1995).

LUISE WHITE, *The Comforts of Home. Prostitution in Colonial Nairobi* (Chicago, 1990).

7

Gender and Migration

A. JAMES HAMMERTON

The history of migration has in some respects been the 'poor relation' of imperial history generally, and more specifically of gender and Empire. Until about the last four decades, the study of migration shared the prevailing gender blindness in academic disciplines, and as gender emerged as a category of analysis, migration tended to be eclipsed by focus on issues such as gender and ethnic relations, employment, health, and reproduction.[1] British imperial migration, moreover, has often had a lesser profile compared to other aspects of imperial history because of its focus on regions of white settlement at a time of profound concern with race and race relations. The gendered character of the migration process, despite its obvious centrality to settler societies' relationships with indigenous populations, has until recently been overshadowed by the history of other parts of the Empire.[2]

Although historians were slow to register it, the gendered dimensions of migration have always been fundamental to its character, reflecting dominant sexual ideologies and assumptions in Britain and in the evolution of settler societies. The very act of transplanting communities and creating new societies has invariably brought into focus preferred forms of social and family formation, most explicitly where governments intervened directly in settlement patterns as in colonial Australia and New Zealand. In its most extreme form this led to an imperial impulse towards 'social engineering', for example to control sex ratios and to ensure male settler access to the services—domestic, sexual, and reproductive—of women. The actual historical experience is a more complex matter. Migration has shared with war a capacity to reinforce contemporary gender ideologies and practices, while at

---

[1] Katie Willis and Brenda Yeoh, eds., *Gender and Migration* (Cheltenham, 2000), pp. x–xxii.

[2] For example, Nupur Chaudhuri and Margaret Strobel, eds., *Western Women and Imperialism: Complicity and Resistance* (Bloomington, Ind., 1992); Clare Midgley, ed., *Gender and Imperialism* (Manchester, 1998).

the same time creating conditions for their subversion, and much of its history focuses on these tensions.[3]

Most work charting the sometimes tenuous connections between gender ideology and practice in migration has shared three characteristics: it has emerged from national–historical perspectives rather than imperial ones; it has focused on the nineteenth and early twentieth centuries; and it has been disproportionately preoccupied with the experience of single women rather than with more inclusive gender dynamics.[4] One result of this has been a relatively meagre output of studies of migration and masculinity, and migration and marriage. Most relevant recent work has emerged from the experience of Australia, Canada, and New Zealand, in the modern period the numerically predominant imperial destinations of British emigrants. 'Empire migration', though, is not confined to the long 'British Diaspora'; post-1945 reverse migration from former colonies to the old imperial centre has recently redefined the notion of Empire and Commonwealth migration. Gender elements in these patterns are now being reflected more explicitly in historical writing.

The largest emigration flow from Britain in the eighteenth century was, of course, that to colonial America, commonly associated with the importation of indentured labour. Its story has most often been told as one of young single males escaping poverty, reflecting the greater preponderance of single male migration and the demand for male over female labour.[5] A gradual shift away from poor and unskilled migration favoured the skilled and lower middle-ranks, while the prevalence of female black servants and slaves dampened demand for female servants. On the eve of the Revolution, the motivation for migration shifted from the push factor of distress towards the pull factor of greater opportunity, a shift which seems to have applied equally to both sexes. Once migrant communities were established, single women, although clearly in smaller numbers and more likely to travel with family groups, were no less likely to be attracted by the promise of better conditions than young men. At the same time indentured labour migration, mainly

---

[3] Marilyn Lake and Joy Damousi, *Gender and War: Australians at War in the Twentieth Century* (Melbourne, 1995), pp. 4–5.

[4] On 'female aware' and 'gender aware' migration models, see Sylvia Chant and Sarah A. Radcliffe, 'Migration and Development: The Importance of Gender', in Chant, ed., *Gender and Migration in Developing Countries* (London, 1992), pp. 1–29.

[5] James Horn, 'British Diaspora: Emigration from Britain, 1680–1815', in P. J. Marshall. ed., *The Oxford History of the British Empire* (hereafter *OHBE*), II, *The Eighteenth Century* (Oxford, 1998), pp. 35–36.

from London and the Home Counties, was accompanied by regionally differentiated family migration, mainly from Scotland and northern England, in which the quest for land predominated.[6]

Apart from indications that men and women approached migration with similar motivations, our understanding of how gender dynamics informed eighteenth-century experience is limited. The prominent role of women in the 'refinement of America', in urban and rural regions, was likely to appeal to upwardly mobile immigrant families.[7] The process of the advancement of gentility—the 'softening' of American culture—paralleled social changes in Britain, but was likely to be more realizable in non-frontier colonial conditions.[8] It foreshadows the powerful nineteenth-century association of migration with the self-improvement ethos for both men and women. Similar patterns are evident in the numerically smaller eighteenth-century British migration to the Caribbean.[9]

After 1815, as old mercantilist hostilities to emigration yielded, first to an impulse to seize a 'safety valve' for relieving distress in Britain, and later to the urge for healthy peopling of the Empire with British stock, gender associations in migration debates began to loom large. In Australia the conditions for anxious public discussion were ripe and ensured that issues of sex ratios, marriage prospects, and sexual morality would dominate public discourse. By the 1830s four decades of convict transportation had created a sharp sex imbalance in the white population. As British interest in Australia shifted from penal outpost to settlement colony the fashion emerged for 'theories of colonization', which carefully articulated the importance of gender balance and proper gender roles in new colonies. The most prominent of these theorists was Edward Gibbon Wakefield, whose views were influential in both Australian and New Zealand migration practice. Best known for his attack on the supposed practice of 'shovelling out paupers' in his elaborate theory of 'systematic colonization', Wakefield placed gender issues and the role of women at the centre of discussion; his arresting aphorisms, and his increasing preoccupation with the role of female immi-

---

[6] Bernard Bailyn, *Voyagers to the West: Emigration from Britain to America on the Eve of the Revolution* (London, 1986), pp. 129–41.

[7] Richard Bushman, *The Refinement of America: Persons, Houses, Cities* (New York, 1993).

[8] Leonore Davidoff and Catherine Hall, eds., *Family Fortunes: Men and Women of the English Middle-Class, 1780–1850* (London, 1987).

[9] Bridget Brereton, 'Text, Testimony and Gender: An Examination of Some Texts on the English-speaking Caribbean from the 1770s to the 1920s', in Verene Shepherd and others, eds., *Engendering History: Caribbean Women in Historical Perspective* (New York, 1995), pp. 63–93.

grants, have been quoted extensively ever since.[10] To make a colony attractive to men, it was enough to 'take care to make it attractive to women'; unlike the masculine spheres of trade, war, and politics, in colonization 'women have a part so important that all depends on their participation'. Imperial expansion and English salvation were to be ensured by transforming the colonies into 'an immense nursery'.[11]

Like most early emigration theorists, Wakefield took for granted a pioneering model of colonization and migration in which new settlements, conveniently cleared of aboriginal occupiers, are founded and rendered habitable by men; they are then followed by women, the civilizers, who enable family formation and replication of the structures and morals of the founding society. The nineteenth-century version of this model took for granted the export of domestic ideology to the colonies, where the promise of prosperity implied its more successful practice. It also rested on idealized visions of hard-working, breadwinning manhood and domesticated womanhood. The role of women as wives for settlers was therefore never far from public debate, and at times this lent itself to both idealization and crude caricature on themes of 'matrimonial colonization'.[12]

From the beginning of government action, however, actual practice pointed in different directions. From 1832 experiments in mass female emigration to Australia, with convict-like shiploads of up to 300 single women, were designed to remedy the gender imbalance. But matrimonial rhetoric was outweighed by colonial demands for female servants in both bush and urban locations. This theme continued beyond the colonial period in Australia and New Zealand, so that the histories of single female migration and of domestic service are inseparable. The associated links between urban migration and highly mobile female servants in Britain are well known.[13] We know that emigrant servants to Australia preferred urban employment, but eligible male bachelors were more numerous in remote bush locations. At times the demand for servants in the country was so difficult to meet that

[10] A. James Hammerton, *Emigrant Gentlewomen: Genteel Poverty and Female Emigration, 1830–1914* (London, 1979), pp. 44–47; Rita S. Kranidis, ed., *Imperial Objects: Victorian Women's Emigration and the Unauthorized Imperial Experience* (New York, 1998).

[11] Edward Gibbon Wakefield, *A View of the Art of Colonization* (London, 1849), pp. 137, 156, 413.

[12] Hammerton, *Emigrant Gentlewomen*, pp. 105–06, 124.

[13] Theresa M. McBride, *The Domestic Revolution: the Modernisation of Household Service in England and France, 1820–1920* (London, 1976), p. 34; Jan Gothard, *Blue China: Single Female Migration to Colonial Australia* (Melbourne, 2001), p. 13.

immigration authorities resorted to making work in rural areas a condition of the assisted passage. The continued preference of servants for town employment, however, points to the ways in which the primary goals of migrating women related to employment rather than marriage, which mirrored their mobility patterns in Britain.[14] Not surprisingly, vast numbers of single women did marry, but their goals were much closer to those of men—focusing on employment and self-improvement—than colonial theorists and propagandists understood.[15] In New Zealand, too, immigrant servants were 'autonomous actors, not followers', with 'limited and pragmatic' aspirations, akin to those of men.[16] At the same time, women's high valuation of kinship networks could highlight their unique role in maintaining international kinship connections. In the crude, isolated, gold-mining settlements of Western Australia, Irish women, often transmigrants via the eastern Australian colonies, fostered complex transnational family linkages. Here it was vital for migrants to construct 'complex webs of association, stretching from Nelson Creek [New Zealand] to Ballarat [Australia], and from south Westland [New Zealand] to distant parishes in County Clare [Ireland]'.[17]

Idylls of colonial bachelors in the bush awaiting willing wives, who otherwise faced starvation and moral ruin in Britain, died hard. They were boosted in the 1850s by the surge in emigration numbers associated with the gold rushes, the consequent revival of fears of sex imbalance, and the high profile intervention of philanthropists. Foremost among the latter was Caroline Chisholm, famous for her characterization of women as colonial civilizers: ' "God's police"—wives and little children—good and virtuous women'.[18] Relentless harping on the theme of marriage and respectability probably exerted more influence on the image of Australia as an acceptable destination for women and families than it did on actual immigrant for-

[14] For scepticism about narrow preoccupation with colonial sex ratios, see Charlotte Macdonald, 'Too Many Men and Too Few Women: Gender's "Fatal Impact" in Nineteenth-Century Colonies', in Caroline Daley and Deborah Montgomerie, eds., The Gendered Kiwi (Auckland, 1999), pp. 17–35.

[15] Gothard, Blue China, pp. 12– 13.

[16] Charlotte Macdonald, A Woman of Good Character: Single Women as Immigrant Settlers in Nineteenth Century New Zealand (Wellington, 1990).

[17] Lyndon Fraser, ' "No One But Black Strangers to Spake to God Help Me": Irish Women's Migration to the West Coast, 1864–1915', in Lyndon Fraser and Katie Pickles, eds., Shifting Centres: Women and Migration in New Zealand History (Dunedin, 2002), p. 56.

[18] Hammerton, Emigrant Gentlewomen, p. 101.

tunes. By the time Chisholm, Dickens, and the periodical press had finished with their pro-Australian and New Zealand propaganda in the mid-1850s, the way was open to more extensive projects to assist women to emigrate to increasingly urbanized antipodean colonies.[19]

The course of social engineering in the service of domestic ideology, however, rarely ran smooth. Large-scale programmes of immigration, in-cluding refugee flows, have always been controversial, inspiring criticism from sceptics in the sending countries and from dissatisfied employers, officials, or settled populations in receiving societies. The perceived failings of immigrants can relate to age, and inappropriate skills and education, but most often are linked to issues of ethnicity and gender. This was especially acute in colonial Australia. Suspicion of Irish Catholic immigrants domin-ated colonial discourse on migration, and frequently this was bound up with wider hostility towards the 'quality' of the women who landed. The first venture in mass female emigration in the 1830s provoked hysterical criticism of the women's alleged unsuitability. Depraved morals, ignorant pauper backgrounds, alien Irish ignorance, and lack of domestic skills were just a few of the charges, and there were perennial lofty claims, especially from Emigration Commission officials, that a woman's willingness to emigrate alone implied evidence of dubious moral character.[20] Young Irish orphans came in for particular criticism; in addition to dubious morals and unsuitable qualifications for service, they menaced 'the future of Anglo-Saxon society' in Australia.[21] At times the resulting controversies were intense enough to cause the suspension of ambitious schemes to correct sex imbalances. While most of the women obtained employment soon after arrival, confounding settler allegations that they were unemploy-able, the criticisms of women's morals and qualities continued to restrict attempts to recruit a larger number of female than male assisted emigrants.[22] One criticism arose from colonial suspicions that British authorities deliberately aimed to solve their own problems by shipping out unemployable paupers at colonial expense (passages were subsidized by the proceeds of colonial land sales). The other complaint dwelt on the

---

[19] Coral Lansbury, *Arcady in Australia: The Evocation of Australia in Nineteenth-Century English Literature* (Melbourne, 1970); Hammerton, *Emigrant Gentlewomen*, p. 92–117.

[20] A. James Hammerton, ' "Without Natural Protectors": Female Immigration to Australia, 1832–36', *Historical Studies*, XVI, 65 (1975), p. 560.

[21] Patrick O'Farrell, *The Irish in Australia* (Kensington, NSW, 1986), pp. 74–75.

[22] Hammerton, "Without Natural Protectors", pp. 559–61.

moral risks of the long voyage for unprotected females and fears of corruption of the innocent.

The 'shovelling out paupers' argument has long dominated discussion of colonial assisted emigration to all parts of the white settlement Empire. Most historians have assumed that, in Australia, despite stringent official procedures, the 'tyranny of distance' from Britain, which placed the antipodes at a disadvantage compared to North America, forced settlers to endure the 'best available' immigrants.[23] In most cases this meant the sweepings of workhouses, men without experience in farm work, and women of low morals. This picture was an exaggeration. The Colonial Land and Emigration Commission selected those for assisted passages for Australia with scrupulous care, and soon learned to resist the blandishments of parishes eager to rid themselves of those least fitted for colonial life. Careful selection ensured that assisted migrants had higher rates of literacy than their peers in Britain. They had better qualifications for rural and domestic occupations, and they showed particular initiative in seeking sponsors to subsidize their journey. Compared with the emigrants crossing the Atlantic, and to the unassisted hordes of male gold-seekers of the 1850s, they were uniquely qualified as young settlers. And while this requires further research, many of those noted for their literacy, and possibly for taking the initiative to move their families around the world, were women. Their global mobility was often an extension of their propensity to internal mobility, so that mobile, literate women may have been 'prime-movers in the push to seek a livelihood abroad, intent on invigorating their own and their families' future prospects'.[24] Even Irish orphan girls often entered workhouses intent on selection for an assisted passage, and many prospered in Australia well beyond their dreams.[25] Again, the attitudes of women and men migrants had more in common than has been supposed.

Much has been made of the elaborate arrangements put in place to ensure protection of women during long voyages to the antipodes. Historians of shipboard practices note that the mobile 'total institution' during the three-month voyage reflected gender hierarchies and practices more generally. Single women were in effect valuable commodities, to be transported and

---

[23] The classic statement of this thesis is R. B. Madgwick, *Immigration into Eastern Australia, 1788– 1851* (London, 1937).

[24] Robin Haines, *Emigration and the Labouring Poor: Australian Recruitment in Britain and Ireland, 1831–60* (Basingstoke, 1997), pp. 72, 256–57.

[25] Ibid., p. 257.

delivered to employers untainted. From the 1830s there had been well-documented abuses, in which senior crew members chose concubines from the passengers, and these events were used to justify the powerful campaign to end convict transportation.[26] Having suffered once from lax supervision, the Colonial Office went to great lengths to ensure that in future women migrants, and their reputations, warranted conditions of the strictest security and protection. Stringent rules of spatial segregation would henceforth govern ship design below decks, and carefully chosen matrons and surgeon-superintendents would patrol the boundaries. Caroline Chisholm purported to do the job better by using respectable families as protectors of single women throughout the voyage, and no voluntary female emigration organization in future was able to proceed without elaborate and widely publicized arrangements for supervision and protection.[27]

There was a short distance, however, between protection and control. Shipboard protection practices replicated and magnified the control of women and their incarceration at home under conditions of separate spheres, which is evident in shipboard diaries.[28] Even middle-class cabin passengers could experience the cabin as a homely place of confinement if they were female; as on land, too, men might see the floating 'home' as a natural and pleasant refuge, as Robert Gouger recorded in 1836: 'we have found it a most delightful retreat; in proof of which I may say truly that we have not been more than four hours a day out of it, while Harriet has not been more than half that time'.[29] The more overt segregation and supervision of single women in steerage conditions, in part a mechanism for policing sexuality, could, however, be experienced as severe repression. The matron— the sole woman with shipboard authority—was gaoler as well as supervisor; she held the keys to the women's compartment and locked them in at night. Dissidents seeking greater freedom were punished for disobedience, which extended until the 1840s to head-shaving and being placed in irons, and later to deprivation of exercise time on deck.[30]

---

[26] Hammerton, 'Without Natural Protectors', pp. 558–59.

[27] Gothard, *Blue China*, pp. 95– 101.

[28] Andrew Hassam, *Sailing to Australia: Shipboard Diaries by Nineteenth-Century British Emigrants* (Melbourne, 1995), pp. 68–73; Sue Rowley, 'The Journey's End: Women's Mobility and Confinement', *Australian Cultural History*, X (1991), pp. 69–83; David Hastings, 'Women at Sea, 1870–1885', in Fraser and Pickles, *Shifting Centres*, pp. 29–43.

[29] Hassam, *Sailing to Australia*, p. 69.

[30] Ibid., pp. 70–71.

Spatial arrangements for passengers reflected gender as well as class stratification, echoing the structure of an idealized, heterosexual family unit. In steerage, single men occupied the forward section under the crew's quarters, families were amidships, and single women were in the stern beneath the cabins. Ideas of sexual propriety were reflected in the fact that men were allocated single hammocks or bunks while women were assigned shared bunks.[31]

These practices denote the obvious association of confinement with victimization. Indeed, on the surface the history of women's shipboard experience, if not their migration experience more generally, is invariably told as a victim's story. Before extensive supervision became standardized, licentious male crew or passengers preyed on helpless women. Strict surveillance then replaced sexual danger with virtual imprisonment, and on those occasions when discipline broke down chilling cases of exploitation— extending to pack rape—could result.[32] At each stage, migration decisions were evidently made for women rather than by them. For both women and men, however, the history of migration includes a countervailing and complex story of agency, which is particularly apparent on the voyage. Women's incarceration, unsurprisingly, was often met by defiance, with cross-dressing, the passing of notes to the men, attempted fraternization, and their rough handling of doctors. Transgressing of spatial boundaries was standard fare among the litany of complaints about the women's behaviour, and resistance was invariably interpreted as a function of the coarseness of inferior class status.[33] Moreover, while confinement below decks is a clear-cut case of the gender hierarchy at work through spatial arrangements, the uses made of the most privileged space on the ship, the poop deck, presents a more complicated picture.

For reasons of comfort, the poop had long been the most socially prestigious outdoor space on passenger ships, traditionally reserved for the most élite cabin passengers. On emigrant ships, however, the desire to segregate the unmarried led to the women being given access to the poop, well away from the single men's space on the lower decks.[34] There was a neat symbolic symmetry to this, since the poop was also the site where hens were caged, and

[31] Ibid., pp. 69–70.

[32] Marion Diamond, *Emigration and Empire: The Life of Maria S. Rye* (New York, 1999), pp. 144–45.

[33] Hassam, *Sailing to Australia*, pp. 70–73.

[34] Gothard, *Blue China*, pp. 134–43.

the hencoops were considered to be the finest seats on board. While women's use of this privileged space did not encompass complete freedom, however, it belied any hint of caging metaphors. The matron was tasked with rigorous supervision of women's conduct on the poop, but sharing of the space led to challenges to her authority by men and women alike. The site of wheel and compass, the poop was shared with the captain and ship's officers as well as the surgeon-superintendent and cabin passengers. The resulting challenges to the matron's authority were often encouraged by the women, so that the poop became 'a highly visible, indeed an elevated, stage for contests over social authority'.[35]

If the prospect of women's agency and defiance simmered throughout the tightly controlled surveillance of the voyage, the more fluid conditions of female employment and married life in the colonies magnified the opportunities for immigrant autonomy. While colonial domestic service could mean relentless underpaid drudgery, isolation, and subordination, most accounts emphasize the relative mobility and bargaining power of servants in colonial conditions compared with those in Britain.[36] Indeed, scarcity value could give colonial servants an employment advantage over unskilled male immigrants, who, for long periods, faced an unstable casual labour market.[37] Beyond these sweeping evaluations, it is difficult to assess the meaning of immigrant agency, 'success', and more particularly 'empowerment' in gendered terms. Part of the problem is that gender difference in fulfilment was rarely spelled out at the time beyond the promise of greater ability to assume conventional roles in a prosperous family; for white British immigrants this could encompass an understated mission of imperial destiny, which intensified by the late nineteenth century. Historians are, moreover, heavily reliant on the few surviving but often unrepresentative collections of emigrant letters. For men, the explicit understanding was that emigration afforded a greater opportunity for realization of the deeply embedded British ethos of self-improvement: enhanced earning capacity, better opportunities for self-instruction (often associated with religious enthusiasm) and above all, fulfilling headship of a respectable and functioning family unit.[38] For women, the meaning of self-improvement was rarely

[35] Ibid., pp. 136–37.

[36] Anthony Trollope, *Australia* (1873; St Lucia, 1967); Beverley Kingston, *My Wife, My Daughter and Poor Mary Ann* (Melbourne, 1975), pp. 30–31.

[37] Gothard, *Blue China*, pp. 24–25

[38] Trygve R. Tholfsen, *Working-Class Radicalism in Mid-Victorian England* (London, 1976).

articulated so clearly, but the 'God's police' rhetoric of women's civilizing mission as wives and mothers left little to the imagination.

For the mid- to late-nineteenth century, the Irish–Australian case provides the most dramatic illustration of a relative similarity of men's and women's attitudes and experiences around migration. David Fitzpatrick has proposed the 'unimportance of gender in explaining post-Famine Irish emigration', a claim most powerful for Australia but applicable in various degrees to other destinations.[39] It rests upon both demographic and qualitative evidence, although it traverses only marginally the different meanings that migration might carry for men and women across the entire life cycle. Male and female numbers were roughly equal, with women often in a significant majority (more so than among the English). They showed a marked preference for urban occupations.[40] There was no evident tendency to female passivity in initiating emigration decisions; women, once settled, were equally active, at times 'more generous' than men, in promoting chain migration among extended family and community, by arranging prepayments and nominations. While married women were prominent in this process, female immigrant servants also had better saving capacities than men in unskilled labour or construction work; and practiced persuasive skills equally upon men and women in Ireland. Women's and men's letters underscore these trends. Fitzpatrick notes that 'men and women alike were portrayed as rational beings, seeking betterment overseas, without betraying the interests of the dispersed family'.[41]

The correspondence of Isabella Wyly underlines the point vividly.[42] Isabella Wyly, a penniless Anglican orphan who emigrated to Adelaide in 1851, had the relative advantage of a background of 'reduced gentility' in Newry, County Down. Although entered as a 'servant' on the ship's list, she promptly used a letter of reference to gain local patronage and obtain an assistant's position in a drapery. There she rapidly overcame her initial loneliness and homesickness and prospered beyond her dreams. An energetic businesswoman and a devout Wesleyan convert, she married her

---

[39] David Fitzpatrick, 'The Unimportance Of Gender In Explaining Post-Famine Irish Emigration', in Eric Richards, ed., *Visible Immigrants Four: Visible Women, Female Immigrants in Colonial Australia* (Canberra, 1995), pp. 145–67.

[40] James Jupp, *Immigration* (Melbourne, 1998), p. 44.

[41] Fitzpatrick, 'Unimportance of Gender', p. 166.

[42] David Fitzpatrick, *Oceans of Consolation: Personal Accounts of Irish Migration to Australia* (Ithaca, NY, 1994), pp. 96–138.

employer, produced ten children, and fostered chain migration of extended family members. Her enthusiastic contrasting of her fortunes in Ireland and Australia served to inspire others: 'I never have had one reason to complain yet. It is like a new world to me. Everything seems to go well with me as it went ill with me atome' [sic]. Most revealing was her account of her choice of husband: 'You will see [?] I was determined to have my own country man. It is the first offer I have had from an Irish *man* but plenty of English which I expect Aunt will tell you of but as I told you before I waited until *Mr Write would come* and he has *at last*.'[43]

Isabella Wyly's determined choice of her own 'country man' was not one that all Irish women in Australia could achieve. Poorer, Catholic immigrants, mostly from peasant backgrounds, frequently married out of their religion and ethnicity, if only 'in order to marry at all'.[44] However painful for a traditionally endogamous community conscious of the loss of ethnic continuity into an 'alien network', these trends marked fundamental departures for poor women immigrants.[45] With old constraints on marriage partners loosened, women had an increasing role in that long process of ethnic amalgamation which helped to produce a unique Australian identity, distinct from its foundational Englishness, by the end of the nineteenth century. In the new country, too, the old Irish property match was virtually unheard of; tolerance of disparities of wealth among marriage partners signalled not only greater social mobility but a wider scope for women's agency in determining their fate. Marriage remained an unequal partnership, but women's choices undoubtedly widened once they disembarked from the ship. Isabella Wyly was convinced of this and not only on her own account. Commenting on her cousin's marriage to an Englishman, she wrote that she had nevertheless 'made a very comfortable home' and was 'very much altered for the better, and is quite a *little Mother*'.[46]

The concept of empowerment for women here was of motherhood in strictly traditional terms, but Isabella Wyly's more diverse career as businesswoman, wife, and mother shows how migration could open up opportunities for women which approximate to conventional notions of the meaning of migration for men. Recent research has probed this issue in greater depth.[47] The stereotypical success story has to be seen alongside the personal tragedies. Colonial suicides attributed to temporary insanity,

---

[43] Ibid., p. 101.   [44] O' Farrell, *The Irish*, p. 116.   [45] Fitzpatrick, *Oceans*, pp. 592–93

[46] Ibid, p. 593.

[47] For Australia, see Gothard, *Blue China*, pp. 203–08.

'eccentricity', or 'melancholia' could be traceable to events with their roots in pre-migration experiences as well as migration itself.[48] Despite greater egalitarianism in the colonies domestic service could remain a punishing experience, often affording few options for friendship and advancement. In New Zealand it inhibited 'the growth of a non-domestic culture for women'.[49] There are signs that by the late nineteenth century, however, domestic service skills could also serve as a basis for the adventurous female sojourner's global peregrinations, traversing familiar colonial destinations from Australia to New Zealand and Canada. In this way the possibilities of emigration for women, as well as men, began to merge into the rather different narrative of adventure and travel. Sensing this, outside observers began to characterize shiploads of women rather differently as, for example, 'free agents these domestic damsels'.[50] 'Domestic damsels', perhaps, were becoming less willing to be made the butt of critical and patronizing colonial authorities, as women's letters attest.[51] Women's determination to escape from old constraints, and to exploit new opportunities, indicate crucial parallels with men's migration experience.

The nature of the cultural impact of male excess in antipodean populations has yet to be resolved. In New Zealand, uncontrolled incursions of gold miners in the 1860s had a substantial impact; they disturbed small, newly settled communities preoccupied with the preservation of social order, and prompted a degree of demonization of single male labourers.[52] Jock Phillips attributes the early masculine character of white New Zealand society to the male majority, although, as in most contemporary settler societies, the sex ratio was more unbalanced in the frontier regions than in the towns.[53] Stereotypes of frontier colonial masculinism have thus obscured more conventional versions of masculinity in urban locations. Most significant is the way propagandists of migration began to promote it as a means for men to realize their traditional manhood, as opposed to an emasculating and effeminate suburban existence in Britain. The migration promoter and New Zealand enthusiast, Charles Hursthouse, appealed to lower middle-class men in 1857:

---

[48] Ibid., *Blue China*, pp. 204–05.

[49] Macdonald, *Woman of Good Character*, pp. 189–93.

[50] Gothard, *Blue China*, p. 203.   [51] Ibid., p. 208.

[52] Jock Phillips, *A Man's Country: The Image of the Pakeha Male, A History* (Auckland, 1987), p. 48.

[53] Ibid., pp. 6–11.

rather than grow up here wanderer of the earth with no better chance than that of finding myself some day behind the counter with a bonnet on, measuring tape and bobbins to morning misses, or becoming the snubbed clerk with the pale wife and the seedy children, nailed to the dingy desk for life for £60 a year, I would turn and breast the current; pull off my coat, take six months at some manly handicraft, and then, despite the dark warnings of Aunt Tabitha, spite the twaddle of my male friends in petticoats, I would secure cheap passage to Australia or New Zealand and taking ten pounds and my trade, common sense, common energy, common industry for my arms, would trust to God and myself to achieve a happy escape and a good deliverance from that grinding social serfdom, those effeminate chains, my born and certain lot in England.[54]

This rhetoric, although unusual among promoters of emigration, was to become more common later in the century, when scorning of lowly white-collar males became a literary convention. Mid-Victorian discussion of migration and renewal invited the characterization of an idyll of separate spheres where men could be men and women could be women.[55] New Zealand, with its reputed openings for aspiring farmers, remained a convenient literary escape route to sturdy manhood and traditional womanhood. A popular novel of 1907, drawing on the genre of the demeaning stereotype of white-collar and suburban life for men, offered New Zealand farming, where the hero could be 'more of a man', as a panacea for the discontented clerk's bleak existence in England.[56] How far this imagined utopia reflected the lives of most New Zealand immigrants, who sought modest prosperity in the towns, is another question.[57] Constructions of rural, frontier, and domestic urban versions of colonial masculinity were routinely in conflict throughout the Empire. The threat of masculine independence on the goldfields, for example, was regularly juxtaposed against familial ideals, and goldminers themselves commonly wrote of their yearning for a 'settled life' with wife and family.[58] Frontier masculinity was no less complex and contradictory than urban versions.

[54] Charles Hursthouse, *New Zealand or Zealandia: the Britain of the South* (1857) quoted in Phillips, *A Man's Country*, p. 4.

[55] See John M. Robson's discussion of the debate on marriage, celibacy, and emigration in *Marriage or Celibacy? The Daily Telegraph on a Victorian Dilemma* (Toronto, 1995).

[56] Shan Bullock, *Robert Thorne: The Story of a London Clerk* (London, 1907), pp. 188, 288–91; Phillips, *A Man's Country*, pp. 5–6, cites a fictional example of 1889.

[57] Phillips, *A Man's Country*, p. 5.

[58] David Goodman, *Gold Seeking: Victoria and California in the 1850s* (St Leonards, 1994), pp. 152–87.

The Canadian migration experience often diverged sharply from the antipodean, if only because of longer but regionally variable stages of settlement and development. The British government had an interest in exporting 'British stock' to Canada after the 1759 conquest, which raised questions of how to populate former French territories. The process lacked the social engineering imperatives of Australasian migration, it was rarely as state-directed as in the antipodes, and is thus less systematically documented. Apart from independent migration, larger schemes tended to be managed by land companies and charities. Despite extensive working-class migration, more is known about the gendered dimensions of the relatively smaller-scale movement of what Wakefield called the 'uneasy' middle-class, and particularly half-pay officers and their families.

Credit for this historiographical imbalance is due to the acclaimed literary output of the Strickland sisters, especially Susanna Moodie, who settled in Upper Canada during the 1830s and 1840s.[59] Moodie's writing affords unusual insight into married women's experiences of migration. In contrast to heroic tales by men extolling Canada's virtues as an emigrant's paradise, Moodie conveyed a grim picture of the alienating experience of migration for middle-class women. As the wife of a half-pay officer settling in the bush, her experiences speak for a small minority of Canadian immigrants, but she was an acute observer of others, even in her litany of grievances. For her own uneasy middle class, she admitted that emigration was at best a necessity rather than choice, 'an act of severe duty' to escape economic pressure at home, with little of the promise held out for lesser ranks. Her descriptions ranged across diseased cities, loss of the virtues of civilization in the bush, alienation from genteel society, social disorder, class and gender inversion, and a relentless battle between colonial barbarity and British hierarchy and civility.[60] An early observer of the unruly independence and social defiance of colonial servants, she was most shocked by the overt class antagonism of lower-class women, who now felt free to release their 'long locked-up hatred'. The resentful speech of the Canadian, Mrs Joe, as she watched Moodie wash clothes for the first time, conveyed a chilling sense of class inversion. 'I am glad to see you brought to work at last. I hope you may have to work as hard as I have ... I hate you all, and I rejoice to see you at the wash-tub, and I wish

---

[59] Susanna Moodie, *Roughing it in the Bush* (London, 1852); Catherine Parr Strickland, *The Backwoods of Canada* (London, 1846).

[60] Sherrie A. Inness, ' "An Act of Severe Duty": Emigration and Class Ideology in Susanna Moodie's *Roughing It in the Bush*', in Kranidis, ed., *Imperial Objects*, pp. 190–210.

that you may be brought down 'pon your knees to scrub the floors'.[61] For Mrs Joe, that moment no doubt represented a triumphal sense of empowerment. For Moodie, it was a sign of colonial social breakdown and barbarism.

In her bitter denunciation of the breakdown of class relations, Moodie inverted most of the hallowed gender myths of migration as self-improvement. Colonial bush life degraded rather than rejuvenated British men, who easily adopted the 'profitless accomplishments' of hunting and fishing, drinking and smoking. Far from allowing men to develop their natural manliness to the full, the bush undermined their agency, prompting them to denigrate British values such as education, while women, faced with daily material challenges, became more self-reliant.[62] Here the power of the bush and frontier to undermine male agency was seemingly beyond the restorative capacity of the feminine civilizing mission. Colonial migration, almost by definition, threatened conventional gender norms. It is no surprise, then, to find Moodie urging her middle-class compatriots to eschew emigration, and to learn of the Moodies' return to England. The same grievances that alienated her from the Canadian 'prisonhouse', however, provided the attraction of emigration for poorer women like Mrs Joe.[63]

If the nexus between colonial migration, gender, and race is understated in much of the accompanying rhetoric and historiography, colonial British Columbia provides an illuminating corrective. Mid-nineteenth century British Columbia displayed all the features of frontier gender and race disruption *in extremis*. Its racial pluralism was marked by dramatic outnumbering of whites by indigenes; white men similarly outnumbered white women, a male homosocial culture thrived, and sexual relations between white men and indigenous women were common. The resulting race and gender hierarchies were typical of frontier conditions, but the smallness and apparent vulnerability of the white community heightened the awareness, in Britain and the Colony, of the perceived threats to Victorian norms and the difficulty of creating a respectable white settler colony. Alarmists were quick to promote the familiar panacea of female immigration for these social evils.[64]

---

[61] Ibid., p. 203.

[62] Ibid., p. 198. For a similar account from colonial Australia, see Katherine Kirkland's story, in A. James Hammerton, ' "Out of Their Natural Station": Empire and Empowerment in the Emigration of Lower Middle-Class Women', in Kranidis, ed:, *Imperial Objects*, pp. 143–69, esp. 159–60.

[63] Inness, 'Act of Severe Duty', p. 204.

[64] Adele Perry, *On the Edge of Empire: Gender, Race and the Making of British Columbia, 1849–1871* (Toronto, 2001).

This homosocial culture extended well beyond the conventional stereotypes of pioneer men as depraved frontier outcasts and marauding males.
The backwoods enabled all-male households—mostly but not exclusively
miners—'to create and maintain a social life revolving around same-sex ties
and practices'.[65] The more complex construction of colonial masculinity
could encompass the proud acquisition of domestic skills, and echoed that
in the antipodes in the 1850s, but it also celebrated a white male identity and
fostered sexual relations with indigenous women. Its very existence resisted
imperial designs to found a white settler colony on normative standards of
domesticity and respectability.[66]

Predictable calls to remedy this 'evil' of sexual relations with indigenous
women by importing 'fair ones of a purer caste into the Colony' testified to
the high expectations customarily attached to shipments of female immigrants.[67] The familiar 'God's police' rhetoric was calculated to attract respectable white women and convert footloose men into settled colonists,
agents of a thriving, British, agricultural colony. The goal was only ever
achieved in the most tenuous of ways. Some female immigrants, far from
serving as 'boundary markers between races and as symbols of Imperial
authority', pursued their own interest oblivious of their intended destiny.[68]
Like the men they too often posed threats to colonial respectability rather
than serving as its agents. Most women did in time enter dependent and
often vulnerable marriages, reaping a meagre dividend as beneficiaries of
white imperial control, but there were enough well-publicized examples of
aberrant behaviour and immigrant autonomy—from work as teachers,
dressmakers, midwives, servants, dancers, and publicans to prostitutes—to
sap faith in female immigration 'because it suggested the possibility, and
sometimes delivered the disturbing presence, of working-class female independence'.[69] Moreover, the concerted attempts to socially engineer whiteness
and Britishness by means of planned immigration were mostly defeated by
the 'hybrid collections' of Asians, Europeans, Australasians, and Africans
who settled in the Pacific Northwest.[70]

Much discussion of gender and Empire has dwelt on complex ways in
which white women activists in imperial spheres were both empowered by,
and then shared responsibility for, imperial rule.[71] Perry demonstrates that,

---

[65] Ibid., p. 30.   [66] Ibid., pp. 20–47   [67] Ibid., p. 138.
[68] Ibid., p. 193.   [69] Ibid., p. 192.   [70] Ibid., pp. 139–93, 200.
[71] Antoinette Burton, *Burdens of History: British Feminists, Indian Women, and Imperial Culture, 1865–1915* (Chapel Hill, NC, 1994).

whatever degree of empowerment colonial rule afforded to white women, the shape and direction of imperialism was not their doing. This is especially true of women migrants, 'a handful of relatively powerless settler women', who managed to turn colonial circumstances, and aboriginal dispossession, to their advantage.[72] It applies equally to those numerous middle- and upper-class women who, in the later nineteenth century, seized on migration promotion as a field for their philanthropic or entrepreneurial endeavours.

Heightened imperial enthusiasm for the mission of white women's colonial settlement offered a fruitful field for dedicated feminists, imperialists, and philanthropists, who have been dubbed, awkwardly, 'emigrators'. The years of high imperialism coincided with the period when newly self-governing colonies took responsibility for promotion and selection of their own migration programmes. It is no accident that some women who served these colonies as paid emigrant selection agents in Britain were also powerful propagandists and organizers of female emigration societies.[73] Initially the main rhetoric and energy went into finding colonial outlets for under-employed and socially displaced middle-class women in Britain, but before long domestic servant emigration came under the same umbrella. All this was justified with heady imperial rhetoric linked to racial duty and the promotion of colonial motherhood to check alien influences of foreign immigrants or indigenous populations. This was most pronounced in South Africa, which enjoyed heightened attention from female emigration propagandists, and a surge in female emigration, after the Boer War.[74] Here the links between migration, race, and gender were more palpable than ever before, especially when white women servants and educated 'lady helps', were intended to supplant black workers. Even the language used to entice women to leave borrowed substantially from the masculine framework of adventure and mission, although with due concessions to the discourse of femininity. Women of 'honest mettle' had noble work awaiting them: 'The trials and the unexpected she must meet in the spirit of courage and good sense, and delight in the charm of sun and clear air,

---

[72] Perry, *On the Edge of Empire*, p. 199; Julia Bush, *Edwardian Ladies and Imperial Power* (New York, 2000).

[73] Maria Rye was a prominent example. Diamond, *Emigration and Empire*, pp. 157–80.

[74] Cecilie Swaisland, *Servants and Gentlewomen to the Golden Land: The Emigration of Single Women from Britain to Southern Africa, 1820–1939* (Oxford, 1993).

fruit and luxuriant flowers, and the sense of expansion that belongs to a colony'.[75]

The goals of these imperial enthusiasts had much in common with former projects designed to buttress stable colonial extensions of British society based on familial ideals. A generation of 'women's movement' debate and activity brought new meaning to these late-Victorian and Edwardian female migration projects. 'Emigrators' such as Maria Rye, Ellen Joyce, and Elizabeth Blanchard came from diverse backgrounds, from socially conservative Evangelical to liberal feminist, but they all sought to remedy the predicament of underemployed single women while promoting the wider export of domestic servants. Historians have studied the work of 'emigrators' in their 'quest for independence' extensively.[76] By the Edwardian period, their rhetoric was linked powerfully to the eugenically based racial duty of 'Imperial motherhood'. Ellen Joyce's regular reminders that 'English women make homes wherever they settle all the world over and are the real builders of Empire' were designed to inspire potential emigrants, but Joyce also had a shrewd eye on the support of male Empire-builders. Male patrons of female emigration societies such as Lord Milner, Robert Baden-Powell and Lord Lyttleton were quick to seize on the promising rhetoric of 'imperious maternity' to promote white settlement, but the more pivotal role of women in the wider cause was uniquely empowering for its architects.[77] It also tied women, more explicitly than ever before, to the project of Empire settlement, in sharp contrast to non-Empire migration to destinations such as the United States; the 'real builders of Empire' now had a patriotic mission closely linked to their eugenic mission as 'mothers of the race'. Actual prosecution of imperially minded female emigration, though, was still beset by colonial suspicions of British manipulation. Maria Rye was sufficiently disillusioned to turn to young girls' migration to Canada, where she shrewdly evaded objections to female immigrants while still populating Canada with potential British—and Protestant—wives.[78]

[75] Julia Bush, ' "The Right Sort of Woman": Female Emigrators and Emigration to the British Empire, 1890–1910', *Women's History Review*, III, 3 (1994), p. 395.

[76] For example Andrew Yarmie, ' "I Had Always Wanted to Farm": The Quest for Independence by English Female Emigrants at the Princess Patricia Ranch, Vernon, British Columbia, 1912–1920', presented at Canadian Studies migration conference, Institute of Commonwealth Studies, London, 2002; Susan Jackel, ed., *A Flannel Shirt and Liberty: British Emigrant Gentlewomen in the Canadian West, 1880–1914* (Vancouver, 1982).

[77] Bush, 'Right Sort', pp. 394–400; Hammerton, *Emigrant Gentlewomen*, pp. 148–78.

[78] Diamond, *Emigration and Empire*, pp. 181–280.

The peak years of imperial migration for women coincided with the era of enthusiasm for 'Empire settlement', a period associated with Imperial federation preoccupations from the 1870s and land settlement projects between the wars. The new eagerness coincided with growing racial exclusiveness in settler colonies; the explicit desire to build a 'white Australia', for example, was marked by racially restrictive colonial legislation in the 1880s, effectively the reverse side of the coin of ardour for white settlement.[79] From this perspective, Empire-building rhetoric was crucial for all potential migrants. It was deployed effectively, for example, to urge emigration upon élite men, trained for Empire in the public schools.[80] John Tosh has associated this late imperial élite urge to emigrate with a masculinist 'flight from domesticity', in which the attractions of Empire overshadowed the family-oriented sentiments of the mid-Victorian generation.[81] There was undoubtedly a surge in élite male emigration from the 1870s, especially to Western Canada, stimulated by the attraction of imperial adventure and land availability, as well as declining gentry incomes and entry restrictions to the professions.[82] The extent of male migration's association with a decided rejection of domestic values in Britain remains, however, uncertain. Many upper-class men adapted to the rigours of emigration only with great difficulty, their determination to cling to an old-country upper-class identity easily made them the butt of colonial scorn; it could inspire hostility to the English, especially at a time when many white settlement colonies were developing a more robust awareness of their national identities.[83] Moreover, élite men were no less susceptible to the same ambivalence towards independence and domesticity as mid-century gold-miners, and there was no doubt a continuum between the two, conditioned in part by age.

If upper-class emigration can be associated with a 'flight from domesticity' only in the most tenuous of ways, it seems even more remote from the post First World War practice of imperial land settlement. Combined support from Britain and the Dominions resulted in an unprecedented equality in the number of assisted male and female emigrants, and a surge in family

---

[79] Jupp, *Immigration*, pp. 72– 78.

[80] Patrick Dunae, *Gentlemen Emigrants: From the British Public Schools to the Canadian Frontier* (Vancouver, 1981).

[81] John Tosh, *A Man's Place: Masculinity and the Middle-Class Home in Victorian England* (New Haven, 1999), pp. 170–94.

[82] Dunae, *Gentlemen Emigrants*, pp. 7–8.   [83] Ibid., pp. 123–47.

migration.[84] This might suggest that the family-oriented rhetoric of migration propaganda was persuasive, but the outcomes of inter-war migration were frequently disappointing to men and women alike, especially in the highly promoted land settlement schemes designed to settle ex-servicemen and their families. The allocated land was usually inferior, the settlers poorly equipped and qualified; not surprisingly the schemes were frequently judged to be disastrous failures. Where they did endure, it was after great hardship, and often at the expense of women, who frequently bore the brunt of the struggle to ensure family survival.[85]

The dismal outcome of the land schemes mirrors the more general gloomy course of inter-war migration history, when British enthusiasm for emigration declined dramatically. One much canvassed reason for the change was that British social insurance innovations deterred family-minded Britons from transplanting themselves to less welfare-oriented dominions. Critics suggested a decline in the manly pioneering spirit, a result of the degenerative and enervating influence of urbanization.[86] But the worldwide depression was enough to explain the ultimate downturn, when countries such as Australia experienced net population outflows. Emigrants frequently found themselves worse off in the promised land; men's voices of despair readily associated their disappointment with failure to fulfil their familial role. An Australian immigrant complained in 1931: 'Give me a chance to keep my wife and child and myself that is better than living in charity and also help me to regain my manhood.'[87]

After 1945 the disruption of war, reconstruction, and pent-up dissatisfactions stimulated a new surge in emigrant aspirations. These were complemented by urgent development agendas in white settlement countries, precipitating bidding wars for the most suitable emigrants. Old imperial agendas promptly reappeared, as demands for ethnically based population transfers again took on a gendered character. To compete with the might of the superpowers, the White Dominions needed the strengthening infusion of an 'interchange of blood'. 'Emigrating British stock' was to be the defining

[84] Stephen Constantine, 'Introduction: Empire Migration and Imperial Harmony', in Constantine, ed., *Emigrants and Empire: British Settlement in the Dominions Between the Wars* (Manchester, 1990), pp. 15–16.

[85] Marilyn Lake, *The Limits of Hope: Soldier Settlement in Victoria, 1915–38* (Melbourne, 1987).

[86] Constantine, ed., *Emigrants and Empire*, pp. 14–15

[87] Michael Roe, ' "We Can Die Just as Easy Out Here": Australia and British Migration, 1916–1939', in Constantine, ed., *Emigrants and Empire*, p. 116.

goal of the new migration schemes.[88] Recruitment propaganda targeted primarily young, ambitious, nuclear families made up of white, skilled male workers, accomplished housewives, and promising children, vital ingredients for rapid socio-economic development and the preservation of British cultural norms in the Dominions.[89]

Belatedly, with the aid of oral testimony, we are learning more about the post-war generation of migrants than we could ever know about their forebears. For all the well-known hazards of retrospective memory sources, the massive output of oral history projects is beginning to provide insights into the intricate subtleties of gender difference in migration experience. Many of the themes to emerge both confirm and confound earlier impressions of migrant experience, as they do the urgent ideological pronouncements of the post-war social engineering architects. In the 1950s generation, familiar gendered divisions between the enthusiastic husband and his reluctant migrant wife appear routinely. Reluctant wives, however, often transformed themselves into the most enthusiastic new citizens; many, too, reversed roles and persuaded reluctant or compliant husbands to risk the unknown for the sake of a new beginning. A woman who lured her husband to Australia this way recalled: 'I could see that our future was pretty ordinary and so my hidden agenda I suppose was to drag him out to Australia and hope that both our lifestyles would improve and there would be new opportunities'.[90] Men, too, reflected a post-war preoccupation with family centredness at the expense of career interests. The narratives of these skilled and semi-skilled men hint at shifts in working-class respectability; many emigrated just as they were rejecting their fathers' values, determined to be good fathers and husbands, or, as one put it, to insist that 'family comes first'.[91] The insights now emerging from migrant testimony may echo more explicitly what is occasionally only hinted at in the fragmentary written record from earlier periods, that some nineteenth-century women were initiators of family migration rather than stereotypical 'reluctant migrants'.[92]

[88] Kathleen Paul, *Whitewashing Britain; Race and Citizenship in the Post-War Era* (Ithaca, NY, 1997), pp. 25–63.

[89] Ibid., p. 50; R. T. Appleyard, *The Ten Pound Immigrants* (London, 1988), pp. 9–14.

[90] Interview, Joanna White, in A. James Hammerton. ' "Family Comes First": Migrant Memory and Masculinity in Narratives of Post-war British Migrants', in Hammerton and Eric Richards, eds., *Speaking to Immigrants: Oral Testimony and the History of Australian Migration* (Canberra, 2002), p. 30.

[91] Interview, Leonard Hedges, in ibid., pp. 34–37.

[92] Haines, *Emigration and the Labouring Poor*, pp. 256–57.

The complexities of experience and relationships evident in oral testimony suggest a similar range of practices in earlier generations.

Gender complexities are more pronounced in studies, mostly based on oral testimony, of mass post-war migration from the imperial periphery to Britain, and increasingly in complex population movements between old colonies of subjugation and settlement.[93] Research by social anthropologists and cultural historians, preoccupied with concepts of diaspora and transnationalism, is redefining our understanding of gendered migration patterns.[94] Work on Caribbean migration, for example, explores family migration dynamics and behaviour as 'ways in which the transnational family contributes to a mobile individual identity'.[95] Traditional male patterns of migrant life, focused on expectations of adventure, lucrative employment, and return, were invariably confounded for post-war immigrants to Britain by financial imperatives, limited horizons, and the difficulty of return. The new experience carried widely different meanings for men and women, evident in complex readings of migrant memories. Noting the stereotypical Caribbean tendency for migrant men to look beyond the family for their autonomy while women sought theirs through the family, Mary Chamberlain asks whether 'men *expressed* their autonomy through migration; women *achieved* theirs through migration?'[96]

Chamberlain's question could be posed usefully for all the phases of Empire migration surveyed here. The themes of exile, alienation, and opportunity, which have for so long dominated the history of migration, were all deeply gendered, even though the structures of emigrant decision-making and aspirations could be gender neutral. The opportunity to probe these questions for more recent generations has now been expanded with the aid of the simple interview. The awareness of the transnational family as a product of modern migration and mobility also provides research opportunities which are beyond reach for earlier periods. There are lessons here for the relationship of gender to the writing of migration history more generally. At a time when historians seek increasingly to privilege migrant voices, and to employ diasporic and transnational frameworks, existing histories of

[93] Colin Holmes, 'Historians and Immigration', in Colin G. Pooley and Ian D. Whyte, *Migrants, Emigrants and Immigrants: A Social History of Migration* (London, 1991), pp. 191–207.

[94] Mary Chamberlain, 'Gender and the Narratives of Migration', *History Workshop Journal*, XLIII (1997), p. 90; and Chamberlain, *Narratives of Exile and Return* (London, 1997).

[95] Chamberlain, 'Gender', p. 107.

[96] Ibid., p. 105.

gender and Empire migration already have much to offer. The insights and methods employed by gender historians are well-placed to resist the temptation to celebratory studies, or a simple approving acknowledgment of the inherent drive for self-improvement in migrant narratives.[97] The Empire migration of the last two-and-a-half centuries has constituted one of the most complex diasporas in recent history; it spawned a dizzying network of transnational families, lone sojourners, and communities. An awareness of gender dynamics offers the most promising prospect for understanding these patterns, as it does for tapping the raw emotions, the gains and losses which are intrinsic to migrant experience.

[97] For example, Horn, 'British Diaspora', p. 51.

Selected Bibliography

R. T. APPLEYARD, *The Ten Pound Immigrants* (London, 1988).

BERNARD BAILYN and BARBARA DEWOLFE, *Voyagers to the West: Emigration from Britain to America on the Eve of the Revolution* (London, 1986).

JULIA BUSH, *Edwardian Ladies and Imperial Power* (New York, 2000).

MARY CHAMBERLAIN, *Narratives of Exile and Return* (London, 1997).

STEPHEN CONSTANTINE, ed., *Emigrants and Empire: British Settlement in the Dominions Between the Wars* (Manchester, 1990).

MARION DIAMOND, *Emigration and Empire: The Life of Maria S. Rye* (New York, 1999).

PATRICK DUNAE, *Gentlemen Emigrants: From the British Public Schools to the Canadian Frontier* (Vancouver, 1981).

DAVID FITZPATRICK, *Oceans of Consolation: Personal Accounts of Irish Migration to Australia* (Ithaca, NY, 1994).

LYNDON FRASER and KATIE PICKLES, eds., *Shifting Centres: Women and Migration in New Zealand History* (Dunedin, 2002).

JAN GOTHARD, *Blue China: Single Female Migration to Colonial Australia* (Melbourne, 2001).

A. JAMES HAMMERTON, *Emigrant Gentlewomen: Genteel Poverty and Female Emigration, 1830–1914* (London, 1979).

—— and ERIC RICHARDS, eds., *Speaking to Immigrants: Oral Testimony and the History of Australian Migration* (Canberra, 2002).

ANDREW HASSAM, *Sailing to Australia: Shipboard Diaries by Nineteenth-Century British Emigrants* (Melbourne, 1995).

RITA S. KRANIDIS, ed., *Imperial Objects: Victorian Women's Emigration and the Unauthorized Imperial Experience* (New York, 1998).

CHARLOTTE MACDONALD, *A Woman of Good Character: Single Women as Immigrant Settlers in Nineteenth Century New Zealand* (Wellington, 1990).

KATHLEEN PAUL, *Whitewashing Britain: Race and Citizenship in the Post-War Era* (Ithaca, NY, 1997).

ADELE PERRY, *On the Edge of Empire: Gender, Race and the Making of British Columbia, 1849–1871* (Toronto, 2001).

ERIC RICHARDS, ed., *Visible Immigrants Four: Visible Women, Female Immigrants in Colonial Australia* (Canberra, 1995).

CECILLIE SWAISLAND, *Servants and Gentlewomen to the Golden Land: The Emigration of Single Women from Britain to Southern Africa, 1820–1939* (Oxford, 1993).

8

Nations in an Imperial Crucible

MRINALINI SINHA

The scholarship on nationalism and the nation in the British Empire has been critically shaped by a broader scholarship that sees the nation as a historically fashioned construct rather than a timeless community.[1] In recent years, moreover, gender has clearly emerged as an important 'category of analysis': not only a constitutive element of social relationships based on perceived differences between sexes, but also a primary way of signifying relationships of power.[2] The dominant trend in both these areas of scholarship has been to suggest that both genders and nations are socially constructed around ideological systems of 'difference' that implicate them in relations of social power. The result has been an emerging, and still fragile, scholarly consensus that modern discourses of gender and of the nation have mutually informed and shaped one another. The 'new imperial histories' of the past decade or so have further informed, and been informed by, this historiographical convergence in the study of gender and nation. Its role in bringing the study of the imperial metropole and its colonies within the same field of analysis has been to demonstrate the intersection of various national histories in the combined, but uneven, evolution of an imperial system whose political, economic, and ideological reach has been world-wide for several centuries.

This essay is dedicated to Professor Bernard Semmel, exemplary teacher and mentor, whose contributions to British imperial history remain an inspiration for bringing together the domains of the 'domestic' and the 'imperial'.

[1] There has been a vast amount of scholarship summarizing this literature: see Peter Alter, *Nationalism* (London, 1994); John Hutchinson and A. D. Smith, eds., *Nationalism* (Oxford, 1994); Geoff Eley and Ronald Grigor Suny, eds., *Becoming National* (New York, 1996); Gopal Balakrishnan, ed., *Mapping the Nation* (London, 1996); A. D. Smith, *Nationalism and Modernism: A Critical Survey of Recent Theories of Nations and Nationalisms* (London, 1998).

[2] Joan Scott, 'Gender: A Useful Category of Historical Analysis', in *Gender and the Politics of History* (New York, 1988), pp. 28–52.

The contemporary scholarly attention to nations as gendered formations was pioneered by scholarship on anti-colonial nationalisms. Until recently, scholarship on gender and on the nation had developed in the main along separate and independent lines. Most theorists of nationalism were content with an apparently gender-neutral analysis of the subject which underestimated the contribution of women, whether in nationalist movements or in the construction of national identities, and assumed that the experience of modern nationhood was similar for men and women. This scholarship treated men and masculinity as 'universal' categories, ignoring the ways in which nationalism helped shape both men and women.[3] It was scholars writing about anti-colonial nationalisms who took the lead in making gender significant. Frantz Fanon drew attention early to the gendered dimension of both colonial and anti-colonial national politics.[4] Though theorists of nationalism were generally slow to follow Fanon's lead, his pioneering insights on gender and national politics are finding new currency in contemporary scholarship.

If until recently the scholarship on the nation had ignored gender as a category of analysis, feminist scholarship was equally guilty of neglecting the nation and nationalism. This was especially true in feminist scholarship that assumed the apparent naturalness of the nation for women in North America and North-Western Europe: '[A]s a woman I have no country. As a woman I want no country. As a woman my country is the whole world'.[5] Virginia Woolf's remark, of course, invoked the experience of British women who had waged a bitter struggle for the right to vote and to be included as formal citizens of the nation. But her words also suggest that feminism as a historical movement developed with an apparently natural antipathy for, and an ability to transcend, the nation. Feminist scholarship that took this history as axiomatic tended to dismiss the salience of the nation and nationalism for the history of both women and feminism. Since women's participation in nationalist struggles against colonialism often produced a very different trajectory for feminism in the 'third world' (the colonized and semi-peripheral regions of the world), the precedence for engaging nationalism as a feminist concern came from such works as Kumari Jayawardena's

---

[3] For a critique of this literature, see Nira Yuval-Davis, *Gender and Nation* (London, 1997).

[4] See esp. Frantz Fanon, 'Algeria Unveiled', in *A Dying Colonialism* (1959: Harmondsworth, 1970), pp. 35–69. For an assessment of Fanon's treatment of gender, see Madhu Dubey, 'The "True Lie" of the Nation: Fanon and Feminism', *Differences*, X (1998), pp. 1–29.

[5] Virginia Woolf, *Three Guineas* (1938; London, 1947), p. 197.

Feminism and Nationalism in the Third World (1986). At roughly the same time as Woolf was writing, for example, the anti-colonial nationalist struggle in India produced a relatively favourable dynamics for bourgeois women's investment in the nation, nicely captured in the popular nationalist slogan: 'India cannot be free until its women are free and women cannot be free until India is free'. In many colonized and semi-peripheral areas of the world, the struggle for women's emancipation arose in tandem with nationalist activism. It should come as no surprise, therefore, that third-world feminist scholarship was at the forefront in engaging with the phenomenon of nationalism. By now, there is a considerable body of feminist scholarship that takes seriously the study of the nation and its investment in, and relation to, gender identities and gender relations even in the older nation states of the world.

The integration of an imperial framework into the study of gender and nation has several important implications. It has cleared the ground for a global history of nations and nationalisms. It thus suggests that the history of the modern nation in Britain cannot be examined apart from the project of colonial expansion and domination, for emerging ideas about national and gender difference in the imperial metropole were elaborated and tested in a variety of colonial sites. The 'rule of colonial difference'—a supposedly essential difference between the rulers and the ruled—served to reconcile the growth of democratic ideals at home with the despotic rule of Empire abroad.[6] By the same token, an imperial framework also revises such influential accounts of the global history of nationalism as Benedict Anderson's *Imagined Communities*, which assumes that anti-colonial nationalisms in the empire simply replicated the 'modular' form of the nation as it was once imagined in Europe and the New World.[7] Anti-colonial nationalism, precisely because it was a belated and 'derivative discourse', was elaborated not through an identification with, but through a difference from, the modern West.[8] The imaginative labour of anti-colonial nationalism, therefore, often lay in constructing its project as 'different-but-modern' in relation to the

---

[6] The following is from Partha Chatterjee, *The Nation and its Fragments: Colonial and Postcolonial Histories* (Princeton, 1993), p. 10.

[7] Benedict Anderson, *Imagined Communities: Reflections on the Origin and Spread of Nationalism* (London, 1983).

[8] This critique of Anderson is from Partha Chatterjee, 'Whose Imagined Community?' in Balakrishnan, ed., *Mapping the Nation*, pp. 214–25. For his argument about anti-colonial nationalism, see also Chatterjee, *Nationalist Thought and the Colonial World: A Derivative Discourse?* (London, 1983).

West. Even in places that were not formal colonies, where the national imagining was not necessarily elaborated around anti-colonialism, the relation to European or Western culture was seldom straightforward.[9] The point of a global history of nations, whether in the imperial metropole or in the colonial and semi-peripheral regions of the world, then, is to recognize the connected, yet also differently constituted, nature of national projects on different sides of the imperial and colonial divide.

The imperial framework also serves as a reminder that the ideological work of gender does not rest on the construction of sexual difference *per se*. For gender itself is constituted by other forms of difference such as class, race, ethnicity, religion, sexuality, as well as colonizer and colonized. For example, the creation of the Commonwealth of Australia in 1901, out of a federation of six former British colonies, was seen as the coming of age of a white Australian masculinity.[10] A populist narrative of the nation around the 'mateship' of rough and virile men in a white frontier society represented Australia's difference from the 'mother country'. The nation was thus shaped around a white masculinity that privileged white 'bushmen' at the expense of both non-Aboriginal and Aboriginal women, as well as Aboriginal men. At the same time, however, white Australian women were enfranchised only one year after the creation of the Commonwealth, well before women in Britain. The incorporation of white Australian women as 'citizen mothers' was closely tied to a desire to maintain a 'white' Australia. The heavily masculinist rhetoric of the nation was thus tempered by the imperatives of a colonial settler society. This example illustrates the pressure of various forms of difference—colonizer versus colonized, élitist versus populist, urban versus rural, settlers versus indigenous populations, and men versus women—on the gendered construction of the nation and the nation-state in Australia. By the same token, this example also highlights that nations are not only gendered, but are simultaneously constituted by other axes of difference. The discourse of 'race' is no less important than that of gender in the construction of nations.[11] To ignore the various ways of organizing 'differ-

[9] The point is made in Afshaneh Najmabadi, 'The Erotic Vatan [Homeland] as Beloved and Mother: To Love, To Possess, and To Protect', *Comparative Studies in Society and History*, XXXIX (1997), pp. 442–67.

[10] This discussion draws on Marilyn Lake, 'Frontier Feminism and the Marauding White Man: Australia, 1890s to 1940s', in Ruth Roach Pierson and Nupur Chaudhuri, eds., *Nation, Empire, Colony: Historicizing Gender and Race* (Bloomington, Ind., 1998), pp. 94–105.

[11] Etienne Balibar, 'The Nation-Form', in Balibar and I. Wallerstein, *Race, Nation, Class: Ambiguous Identities* (London and New York, 1991), pp. 86–106.

ence' in the articulation of the nation, therefore, would simply reproduce the 'gender blindness of previous historians of nations and nationalism in another key'.[12] The further point is that these various modes of organizing 'difference' are not only mutually constitutive, but also *differently* constituted: that is, they are neither equivalent nor identical. The ways they reinforce or de-stabilize one another cannot be predicted *a priori*. The expanded imperial context thus cautions against privileging gender, even when it incorporates divisions of class, race, ethnicity, and so on, over other forms of organizing difference in the production and reproduction of the nation.

The multiple and changing historical contexts of various imperial arrangements underscore another crucial point: the importance of specific historical contexts and locations. If nations and national identities are continuously formed and reformed, their gendered articulations, no less than their articulation in other forms of difference, take effect only in concrete historical situations. Hence the gendered politics of the nation may be subject to change and rearticulation over time. So, for example, the cultural-nationalist elaboration of the 'modern woman' as signifying the nation's difference from the modern West in late-nineteenth-century India was reconfigured in the period after the First World War. The post-war experiment with colonial self-government in a 'non-white colony' of the British empire, as well as the shift in the 1920s from a cultural to a 'new political nationalism' in India, was mediated by a different elaboration of the modern woman.[13] The imperatives of a political nationalism whose unit was no longer the discrete community but the individual Indian citizen—no longer bound by caste and religious community—allowed for a new subject-position for women within Indian nationalism. A nascent Indian feminism in the 1920s and 1930s constructed women as a universal and homogenous gender category, not as markers of 'community' identity but as citizens of a modern nation-state.[14] The re-shaping of the late-nineteenth-century cultural-nationalist construction of the 'modern woman' in the new

[12] Catherine Hall, quoted in Ruth Roach Pierson, 'Nations: Gendered, Racialized, Crossed with Empire', in Ida Blom and Karen Hagemann eds., *Gendered Nations: Nationalisms and Gender Order in the Long Nineteenth Century* (New York and London, 2000), p. 42.

[13] See Gyanendra Pandey, *The Construction of Communalism in Colonial North India* (1990: Delhi, 1997), esp. chap. 7.

[14] The following is from Mrinalini Sinha, 'Refashioning Mother India: Feminism and Nationalism in Late-Colonial India,' *Feminist Studies*, XXVI (2000), pp. 623–44.

elaboration of 'Indian woman' as citizen illustrates the importance of specific historical conjunctures in an exploration of the gendered politics of the nation.

The insights that follow from adopting an imperial framework for the study of gender and nation come together in Catherine Hall's exemplary study of the passage of the English Parliamentary Reform Act of 1832.[15] The Act was framed by two preceding events: Catholic Emancipation in 1829 (followed by the Irish Coercion Act of 1833 and the attempt to reform the Irish church), and the 1831 slave rebellion in Jamaica, also known as the 'Baptist War', which was followed by Britain's abolition of slavery in 1833. The settlement of 1832, shaped by these events, entailed new definitions of citizens and subjects and different modes of belonging to, and identifying with the nation and the Empire. We thus see a variety of intersecting, but uneven, modes of identification with and belonging in the imperial-nation: Protestant women claimed their right to participate in the public sphere by signing petitions to Parliament opposing Catholic emancipation; Catholic Irish women succeeded in campaigning on behalf of their men in the passage of the Catholic Emancipation Act; Catholic men gained the right to enter some public offices at the same time as many Irish Catholic men lost the franchise; former slave men and women were partially freed, becoming apprentices for a fixed term until they could 'learn' to be free; freed black women became the property of their husbands; working-class men and women actively participated in reform demonstrations and female political unions; and new groups of men claimed their political fitness by asserting their manly independence against the effeminacy of the aristocracy. It is against these multiple definitions of citizen and subject in relation to class, gender, ethnicity, and race that the settlement of 1832 acquires its full significance. The Reform Act articulated a masculine form of rule, specifying for the first time that only men could vote in elections and be political citizens of the nation. Property remained the basis for the franchise, but female property owners were denied the right to vote. This specific act of excluding women would also put the question of women's suffrage on the national agenda in succeeding decades.

This multi-layered analysis of the 1832 Reform Act exemplifies the potential of an exploration of gender and nation in the context of Empire. As a densely historicized analysis of how gender and nation work together, it makes visible the multiple, and often uneven, ways in which particular forms

[15] Catherine Hall, 'The Rule of Difference: Gender, Class and Empire in the Making of the 1832 Reform Act', in Blom and Hagemann, eds., *Gendered Nations*, pp. 107–36.

of difference inform, and are produced by the nation at a given historical moment. At its best, the scholarship on gender, nation, and empire suggests that attempts to universalize the gendered production of nations—outside of specific historical situations—are futile.

Though universalizing patterns are unhelpful, one can still draw attention to the cumulative effect of more than a decade of scholarship on the inter-connectedness of discourses of gender and nation. The challenge posed by this scholarship has to do not just with the visibility of women, but with the constitution of the nation itself in the 'sanctioned institutionalization of gender *difference*'.[16] The discourses of the nation in turn have been vehicles for the consolidation of dichotomized notions of 'men' and 'women' and of 'masculinity' and 'femininity'. This is the sense in which ideas about gender and the nation have been seen as symbiotic: national narratives rely heavily on the supposedly natural logic of gender differences to consolidate new political identities around the nation; yet the discourse of nationalism itself provides legitimacy to normative constructions of masculinity and feminin-ity.[17] The implications of this scholarship may be seen in three broad areas of inquiry: (1) the construction of nations through gender differences; (2) the impact of gendered modes of belonging on 'men' and 'women'; and (3) the complex relationship between feminisms and nationalisms.

Nations have typically been imagined as 'domestic genealogies'.[18] Terms such as motherlands or fatherlands; mother-tongues; mother-cultures; 'founding fathers', and 'mothers of the nation' are used to capture the relations of peoples to specific lands, languages, cultures, or shared histories. Critical attention to these kinds of gendered and familial imagery around the nation reveals much about the nature of the nation as a historical project consti-tuted in the crucible of empire.

What recent scholarship has begun to reveal is that the family—con-structed as 'natural,' heterosexual, and patriarchal—crucially services how the nation is constituted. Its first, and perhaps most obvious function, lies in representing the nation as an organic community whose members, like those

---

[16] Anne McClintock, ' "No Longer in a Future Heaven" ', in McClintock and Aamir Mufti, eds., *Dangerous Liaisons: Gender, Nation and Postcolonial Perspectives* (Minneapolis, Minn., 1997), p. 89.

[17] Tamar Mayer, 'Gender Ironies of Nationalism: Setting the Stage', in Mayer, ed., *Gender Ironies of Nationalism* (London and New York, 2000), pp. 1–24.

[18] Anne McClintock, *Imperial Leather: Race, Gender and Sexuality in the Colonial Context* (New York, 1995), p. 357.

of the family, share 'natural' rather than accidental or optional ties. The familial imagery thus offers the 'invented' nation a powerful legitimizing language of naturalization. In order to do so, however, the institution of the family itself has first to be removed from history and made into a supposedly timeless and natural unit of social organization. In the discourse of the nation, the family is de-politicized, constructed as prior to history and immune to political challenge or change.[19]

The history of the modern nation, nonetheless, has been closely associated with a particular historical form of the family—the heterosexual, bourgeois, nuclear family—and the normative constructions of sexuality and gender identities that sustain this family-form. The so-called 'gender revolution' of the later eighteenth century, the elaboration of fixed and essential notions of gender difference, and the corresponding code of a bourgeois 'respectability' that emphasized the control of sexual passions by both men and women and presented marriage as the only acceptable sexual relationship emerged alongside, and intersected with, new constructions of the 'nation' and national difference.[20] In eighteenth-century Britain, this emerging mesh of ideas was both established and de-stabilized in the crucible of colonial contact.[21] By the nineteenth century, the relationship between nationalism and bourgeois 'respectability' in the imperial metropole had reached new heights. If its constitution as a 'national' project helped spread the norms of bourgeois respectability across classes, then the norms of bourgeois sexual respectability, in turn, helped in the construction of the national community as a virile homosocial community whose 'proper' male homosocial relations were secured through the identification and exclusion of homosexuality, often figured as 'effeminacy' or deviance.[22] The norms of sexual respectability also helped differentiate 'pure' from 'fallen' women, the former constructed as the symbolic signifiers of the nation and deployed in the service of the nation in their 'naturally' subordinate roles as dutiful mothers, wives, and daughters.[23] In contrast to the 'normal' sexuality of respectable men and women of the nation, European national projects now associated 'abnormal'

[19] McClintock, ' "No Longer in a Future Heaven" ', pp. 90–91.

[20] Kathleen Wilson, The Island Race: Englishness, Empire, and Gender in the Eighteenth Century (London, 2003); Thomas Laquer, Making Sex: Body and Gender from the Greeks to Freud (Cambridge, Mass. 1990).

[21] See chap. by Kathleen Wilson; and Wilson, The Island Race.

[22] This discussion is drawn from George L. Mosse, Nationalism and Sexuality: Middle Class Morality and Sexual Norms in Modern Europe (Madison, Wis., 1985).

[23] See chap. by Urvashi Butalia.

sexuality with a variety of 'others'—Jews, Africans, homosexuals—in their midst. This was the sense in which the project of modern nationalism sustained, and was itself sustained by a particular racialized, bourgeois, heterosexual, and patriarchal family form that was naturalized in the context of empire and imperialism.

The norms of bourgeois domesticity and the resulting construction of gender difference in the colonies further helped construct and maintain the ideological, economic, and political power of imperialist-nationalist projects. The Western bourgeois ideal of gender difference now became the yardstick of 'civilization' and any deviation from it 'proved' the backwardness of indigenous peoples. Hence alongside the *zenana*, the secluded female quarters in certain élite households in north India, British social reformers and missionaries directed their zeal to the *Marimakkathayam*, or matrilineal traditions of the Nairs in southern India. The *Marimakkathayam* were considered 'primitive' for not conforming to the 'proper' patriarchal gender-roles of the Victorian bourgeois family.[24] The imposition of a Western bourgeois ideology of gender and family similarly informed such colonial initiatives as British slave emancipation at the Western Cape of South Africa, where 'liberating the family' allowed newly freed African men to assume their 'proper' roles as fathers and as heads of households, while freed African women were, as wives and mothers, brought under the natural authority of the male head of the family.[25] The pervasiveness of this ideal, to which many freed African men and women contributed, helped to maintain the power of former slave owners, missionaries, and the colonial state over African men and women even after emancipation. The marriage between modern nationalisms and bourgeois respectability was thus cemented not just in Europe, but also in the process of the 'domestication of the empire'.[26]

Interestingly, various anti-colonial nationalist projects also deployed the bourgeois nuclear family (often constructed as distinctive through a selective appropriation of bourgeois Western forms and the adaptation of certain indigenous traditions) in its own discourse. These narratives were often

[24] The following discussion is from Janaki Nair, 'Uncovering the Zenana: Visions of Indian Womanhood in Englishwomen's Writings, 1813–1940', *Journal of Women's History*, II (1990), pp. 8–34.

[25] The following discussion is from Pamela Scully, *Liberating the Family? Gender and British Slave Emancipation in the Rural Western Cape, South Africa, 1823–1853* (Portsmouth, NH, 1997).

[26] The phrase is from the title of Julia Clancy-Smith and Frances Gouda, eds., *Domesticating the Empire: Languages of Gender, Race, and Family Life in French and Dutch Colonialism* (Charlottesville, Va., 1998).

transparently rooted in the structural transformations of élites. For bourgeois norms in the Third World did not get universalized across classes in the same way as in the nineteenth-century metropole. The origin of modern Egyptian nationalism, for example, was closely intertwined with the transformation of élites in late nineteenth- and early twentieth-century Egypt.[27] The model of the bourgeois family, following the demise of harem slavery that had been the mainstay of élite Ottoman–Egyptian households, was the key to both these processes. On the one hand, the new familial discourse reflected a new élite consolidation that was the result of the upward mobility of native Egyptian élites and the 'Egyptianizing' of older Ottoman–Egyptian élites. On the other, it was also the 'building block' of the modern Egyptian nation. The bourgeois family, especially through an emphasis on motherhood, offered a shared national narrative to Egyptian Copts and Muslims, and a myth of continuity for modern Egypt to the 'Golden Ages' of the Pharaonic past. The specifically bourgeois aspect of this process was, arguably, more visible in the context of Third-World nationalisms than in nineteenth-century European nationalisms.[28]

The interconnection between national, gender, and sexual identities in a range of nationalist projects has proved mutually reinforcing, rendering the above identities as natural and innate. Indeed, at moments of perceived crisis the defence of national and of normative gender and sexual identities often become closely intertwined. When scholars ignore the significance of the trope of the family for nationalist discourse, therefore, they not only foreclose an examination of the intersection of national, gender, and heterosexual identities in sustaining one another. They also underestimate the force of representing the nation, like the family, as timeless, natural, and organic.

The second, and related, function of the representation of nations as domestic genealogies—replete with a cast of fathers, mothers, sons, and daughters of the nation—lies in providing the nation with its 'instrumental passions'.[29] The nation, for all its foundational ambivalence, has the capacity to inspire enormous passion and devotion. Indeed, what intrigues scholars about nationalism is that so many men and women have been willing not

---

[27] The following discussion is from Beth Baron, 'The Making of the Egyptian Nation', in Blom and Hagemann, eds., *Gendered Nations*, pp. 137–58.

[28] For this point, see Ranajit Guha, *Dominance Without Hegemony: History and Power in Colonial India* (Cambridge, Mass., 1997).

[29] G. Kitching, 'Nationalism: The Instrumental Passion', *Capital and Class*, XXV (1985), pp. 98–116.

only to kill, but to die for their nation. Hence nationalism, as some scholars suggest, resembles less such modern political ideologies as liberalism or conservatism, than it resembles religion with its promise of immortality, or the discourse of kinship and ethnicity which emphasizes the inevitable, as opposed to the merely accidental or chosen connections between members of the collectivity.[30] The language of kinship plays a very important role in allowing the nation to appropriate for itself the kind of elemental passions hitherto associated with blood ties. Thus the nation in the form of an abused or humiliated mother appeals to her sons and daughters, although often in differently gendered ways, to protect her and to restore her honour. Similarly the nation as fatherland calls upon its sons and daughters to obey the father and to fulfill their respective gendered duties to the nation. The representation of the nation through a language of love, an 'eroticized nationalism', has often entailed the mapping of heterosexual desire on to political desire as *amour patrie*, love of country.[31] The nation becomes that for which modern people die, and kill, by the millions.

The further ideological work of the family has been to make the various forms of hierarchies within the nation and between nations seem 'natural'. Since the family is idealized as a domain in which individual members willingly subsume their interests to the supposedly unified interests of the family (represented by the male head of household), the family becomes a signifier of 'hierarchy within unity' for the nation.[32] The myth of the family as a fundamental 'unity' is sustained, of course, in part through a belief in the allegedly natural subordination of women and children to adult men within the family. The nation's identification with the family to signify the fundamental 'unity' of its own members similarly constructs the hierarchies of gender, class, race, ethnicity, and so on, within the national community as natural and thus without a history. The familial discourse leaves the fundamental 'unity' of the nation unchallenged even as actual social relations of power and exploitation divide the members of the nation.

This 'family romance' glosses over relations of domination within the family as much as within the nation.[33] The age and gender hierarchies within

---

[30] Anderson, *Imagined Communities*.

[31] 'Introduction', in A. Parker and others, eds., *Nationalisms and Sexualities* (New York, 1992) p. 1.

[32] McClintock, *Imperial Leather*, p. 45.

[33] The phrase is from the title of Lynn Hunt, *The Family Romance of the French Revolution* (London, 1992).

the family were also frequently used in the context of a developmental narrative of colonial superiority to legitimate imperial domination abroad. Colonized peoples were often represented as 'children', needing the benevolent and natural protection of European fathers, and occasionally of European mothers. European imperialism and colonialism was incorporated within a familial discourse which saw imperial nations as stern, but kindly, guardians over peoples as yet lacking requisite political maturity.

The nation, moreover, 'presents itself both as a modern project that melts and transforms traditional attachments in favour of new identities, and as a reaffirmation of authentic cultural values culled from the depths of a presumed communal past'.[34] The temporal contradiction of the nation—its paradoxical function as a force for both change and continuity—is negotiated, often in very complex ways, via the medium of gender difference. One resolution of this 'temporal anomaly', the representation of the nation as both the bearer of tradition *and* the agent of modernity, has been through the identification of women with the 'authentic body of national tradition' and of men with 'national modernity'.[35] Yet the figure of the 'woman', especially in Third World nationalisms, has occupied a more variable position. Womanhood has sometimes been used to signify the continuity and authenticity of national tradition; at other times, it has represented the backwardness of a past to be eschewed by the modernizing project of the nation.[36] The gendering of tradition and modernity has produced considerable flexibility in the metaphorical role of women in national projects.

The complex ways in which the problem of tradition and modernity is recast in the context of colonialism and anti-colonial nationalism has provided women (more often than not) with the intricate burden of representing the colonized nation's 'betweenness' vis-à-vis pre-colonial traditions and 'Western' modernity.[37] For the dilemma of anti-colonial nationalisms was simultaneously to appropriate post-Enlightenment ideas of modernity and progress and to assert the nation's cultural difference from the West.[38] This

[34] D. Kandiyoti, 'Identity and its Discontents: Women and the Nation', *Millennium: Journal of International Studies*, XX (1991), p. 431.

[35] McClintock, *Imperial Leather*, p. 359.

[36] This point is made in Valentine M. Moghadam, 'Introduction and Overview: Gender Dynamics of Nationalism, Revolution and Islamization', in Moghadam, ed., *Gender and National Identity: Women and Politics in Muslim Societies* (London, 1994), p. 4.

[37] Winifred Woodhull, 'Unveiling Algeria', *Genders*, X (1991), esp. p. 113.

[38] The discussion is from Partha Chatterjee, 'The Nationalist Resolution of the Woman Question', in K. Sangari and S. Vaid, eds., *Recasting Women: Essays in Indian Colonial History*

process entailed, as in the case of nineteenth-century Bengal, the construction of a spatial dichotomy in nationalist discourse between an inner and spiritual world, where the cultural authenticity of the nation was located, and an outer and material world, where the nation acknowledged its subordination to, and the need to borrow from, the modern West. This spatial division acquired a gendered dimension in the division between the 'Home' and the 'World'. Yet the 'home', as the locus of the nation's authentic identity, was never in any simple way the site of static pre-colonial traditions. Instead, the middle-class Bengali 'home' was subject to reforming interventions that included selective appropriations of Western bourgeois domestic norms. In this context, the Bengali *bhadramahila* (respectable woman) was assigned a *new* identity in nationalist discourse, defined against both the excesses of modernization associated with the Western and Westernized woman, and the backwardness associated with peasant and lower-caste/class women in India. Only the reformed and modern woman, and not the 'traditional' woman, could truly embody the cultural identity of the new nation-in-the-making.

In various Third World nationalist projects, therefore, nationalism both initiated women's access to modernity and set the limits of desirable modernity for women.[39] In this context, several early twentieth-century feminists, such as Huda Sha'rawi in Egypt or Sarojini Naidu in India, constructed dynamic public roles as a duty to the nation rather than as a right. As signifiers of the nation, women needed to be modern, but could not break completely from tradition. The woman of the Third World nationalist imagination, then, was not necessarily the 'traditional' woman. She was more likely the 'modern-yet-modest' woman, both symbolizing the nation and negotiating its tension between tradition and modernity.[40] The identification of women as the 'true essence' of national and cultural identity (whether as signifiers of tradition or of modernity) underscores the significance of gender in the constitution of nations. The familial and gendered imagery of the nation reveals the crucial investment of the nation in the ideology of gender difference, which was itself shaped in a transnational context of imperialism and colonialism.

(New Brunswick, NJ, 1990), pp. 233–53; See also Chatterjee, *Nation and its Fragments*. For a sustained critique of the explicitly patriarchal dimension of the politics of domesticity in Bengali nationalism, see Tanika Sarkar, *Hindu Wife, Hindu Nation: Community, Religion and Cultural Nationalism* (New Delhi, 2001).

[39] This point is made in Kandiyoti, 'Identity and its Discontents', p. 442, n. 17.
[40] A. Najmabadi, cited in Kandiyoti, 'Identity and its Discontents', p. 432.

If the ideology of gender difference has been important in the constitution of the nation, then the nation has been equally important for the construction of gender and the 'performance' of masculinity and femininity. For national projects themselves entail repeated performances of certain gendered norms, such as militarism and sacrifice, honour and shame, sexual purity and impurity.[41] Since scholars have begun to call into question the necessity and inevitability of the link between masculinity and the biological 'male', or between femininity and the biological 'female', and to suggest more historical and contingent foundations for these links, the role of the gendered discourse of nationalism in grounding notions of masculinity and femininity around attributes of biological maleness and femaleness respectively has begun to receive considerable attention.

The focus on the nation as a site for the construction of gender difference has, first of all, called attention to the hitherto neglected question of the construction of 'men' and 'masculinity' in nationalist discourse. The nation itself is largely modelled as a brotherhood or a fraternity, which has never, of course, included all men. The homosociality of the national brotherhood has depended in large part on the exclusion of homosexuals and of men otherwise constructed as deviants. The nation is not only imagined typically as fraternal, it is defended and administered through predominantly homosocial institutions. In numerous ways, then, nationhood relies on particular constructions of masculinity, and thus becomes an important site for the enactment of masculinity. The military, an increasingly masculine arena from which women who traditionally accompanied soldiers to provision, cook, clean, and tend to the wounded were gradually excluded, has enjoyed a privileged place in the construction of both modern masculinity and the modern nation.[42] In many cases, political rights for men have flowed directly from their eligibility to shed blood for the nation. Yet masculinity, however defined, is always elaborated in relation to, and as a complement to, the proper 'feminine' roles of women.

---

[41] See Mayer, 'Gender Ironies of Nationalism', pp. 1–24.

[42] Ida Blom, 'Gender and Nation in International Comparison', in Blom and Hagemann, eds., Gendered Nations, p. 15; Cynthia Enloe, Bananas, Beaches and Bases: Making Feminist Sense of International Politics (Berkeley, 1989); Karen Hagemann, 'A Valorous Volk Family: The Nation, the Military, and the Gender Order in Prussia in the Time of the Anti-Napoleonic Wars, 1806–15', in Blom and Hagemann, eds., Gendered Nations, pp. 179–206. For Britain, see Linda Colley, Britons: Forging the Nation, 1707–1837 (New Haven, 1992).

The production of nationalist masculinity is often enacted via the control and protection of women. The politics of 'colonial masculinity' that informed both colonizers and colonized in the British Empire illustrates the multiple dimensions at work in the performance of masculinity.[43] Elite 'white' British masculinity was constructed both through its difference from feminized or effeminate native men and through its role as benevolent protector of women. The protection of 'Oriental' women was an important component of white British masculinity in the colonies. The real or imagined threat to white women from native men provided, perhaps, the most dramatic demonstrations of white imperial masculinity in the colonial domain. Even rumours of attacks on white women, as for example, during the Rebellion of 1857–58 in India, produced a call to arms to white men to avenge British 'honour'.[44] At the same time, 'native' men also sought to reclaim their honour and their masculinity—from negative representations in colonial discourse—by claiming the right to control and protect native women from foreigners and foreign influence. The rhetoric of the protection of women as well as the protection of the nation (often represented as a woman) was thus an important component in defining nationalist masculinity.

Equally significant is the nationalist construction of 'women' and of 'femininity', and women's own role in these constructions. Despite the historical marginalization of women in formal national politics, the construction of the nation has seldom precluded the active participation of women.[45] Nationalist projects assign women roles not just in biological reproduction, but in the larger social and cultural reproduction of the national collectivity. As such, women have been called to perform important nationalist tasks such as the preservation and transmission of the national language, the 'mother tongue', and the national culture. Women have emerged in national projects as mothers, educators, workers, and fighters. At times, women's contributions to the nationalist struggle have been more radical than men's. During the Irish Land War (1881–82), the uncompromising stand of Anna Parnell's Ladies Land League, with a membership extending from Catholic middle-class to peasant women, against evictions

[43] Mrinalini Sinha, *Colonial Masculinity: The 'Manly Englishman' and the 'Effeminate Bengali' in the Late Nineteenth Century* (Manchester, 1995).

[44] Jenny Sharpe, *Allegories of Empire: The Figure of Woman in the Colonial Text* (Minneapolis, Minn., 1993).

[45] For the many ways in which women contribute to the nationalist project, see Nira Yuval-Davis and Floya Anthias, eds., *Woman-Nation-State* (New York, 1989), p. 7.

and in favour of Irish self-determination, became an embarrassment to male leaders ready to compromise with the British. In Kenya, women fought alongside men as guerrillas in the Land and Freedom Army during the Mau Mau uprisings of the 1950s.[46] At the same time, nationalist projects have also invoked the supposedly 'traditional' roles of women as mothers, as objects of reverence and of protection, and as signifiers or markers of a group's innermost identity.

The construction of femininity within nationalist discourse, moreover, has had important implications for women. The pervasiveness of powerful female figures, especially the figure of the mother, in the discourse of nationalism provides an important context for understanding the co-operation and complicity of women with such constructions. The image of 'motherhood', both in the cultural representation of the nation as 'mother' and in women's roles as 'mothers of the nation', is among the most powerful and exalted images of the feminine in nationalist discourse. The dominant construction of women as mothers, as objects of both national reverence and protection, has thus been the most important way in which women have been integrated into nationalist projects. Yet this glorification of mother-hood in nationalist discourse has also justified the exclusion of women from the civic virtues that made formal political participation in national politics possible.[47] Nationalist projects demonstrate a tension between the exaltation of powerful female figures and the marginalization of women in national politics.

The relationship between the exaltation of feminine images and the marginalization of women in nationalist projects, however, is not always straightforward. Women have also successfully mobilized the construction of 'motherhood' to stake their claims in national politics, both constructed by, and themselves constructing, the meaning of motherhood in nationalist discourse. And the meaning of motherhood is, of course, different in different arenas. In South Africa, despite superficial similarities, 'mother-hood' meant different things in the racially exclusive Afrikaner nationalist project and in the multiracial nationalism of the African National

---

[46] Margaret Ward, 'The Ladies Land League and the Irish Land War 1881/1882: Defining the Relation between Women and Nationalism', in Blom and Hagemann, eds., *Gendered Nations*, pp. 229–48; Cora Ann Presley, *Kikuyu Women, the Mau Mau Rebellion and Social Change in Kenya* (Boulder, Colo., 1992), p. 136.

[47] For 'republican motherhood' in America, see Linda K. Kerber, *Women of the Republic: Intellect and Ideology in Revolutionary America* (New York, 1980).

Congress.[48] In the former, motherhood remained limited to the domestic domain and did not encompass broader issues. Women in the African National Congress, however, used the focus on motherhood to raise general concerns about women's emancipation. Women in both camps were not only active themselves in the articulation of motherhood, but also used it to sanction their own participation in nationalist movements. In this sense, then, the construction of powerful female figures in nationalist projects has empowered some women.

To the extent that constructions of 'women' and of 'femininity' are closely bound up with considerations of national and cultural identity, however, they have important implications for women's experience of nationhood. For the sake of the nation, for example, women are often at the receiving end of a wide range of nationalist policies and practices, especially at moments of perceived national crisis. The emergence of the discourse, and at times the deliberate strategy, of the rape of 'enemy' women serves as the most criminal illustration of the consequences for women of being symbols of national culture, vulnerable to violation by national enemies. There are numerous other ways, however, in which national concerns about the health, the demographic future, the racial composition, or the cultural identity of the nation have entailed the adoption of policies that target women. By the beginning of the twentieth century in Britain, maternal and infant health and mortality were central to imperial–national concerns. The demographic emphasis on the reproduction of the 'imperial race' made concern with motherhood in Britain a priority.[49] For women, nationalist projects have often entailed a transition from a 'private patriarchy', where women are under the control of individual heads of families to a 'public patriarchy', where women experience the patriarchal control of a larger community of men.[50] The nationalist construct of 'women', therefore, produces an anomalous experience of nationhood for women.

Finally, nationalist projects construct 'women' primarily through a heterosexual relationship to men that emphasizes a supposedly 'natural'

---

[48] The following discussion is from Deborah Gaitskill and Elaine Unterhalter, 'Mothers of the Nation: A Comparative Analysis of Nation, Race and Motherhood in Afrikaner Nationalism and the African National Congress', in Yuval-Davis and Anthias, eds., *Woman-Nation-State*, pp. 58–78.

[49] Anna Davin, 'Imperialism and Motherhood', in A. Stoler and F. Cooper, eds., *Tensions of Empire: Colonial Cultures in a Bourgeois World* (Berkeley, 1997), pp. 87–151.

[50] Sylvia Walby, 'Women and Nation', in Balakrishnan, ed., *Mapping the Nation*, pp. 235–54.

hierarchy between men and women. The identification of women mainly with the private and familial sphere has been the basis for the exclusion of women as citizens or from full membership of the community. The most obvious of these, of course, is the denial of political rights to women as citizens. In most states in Europe and the Americas, women's suffrage followed well after most men's; most of these states only granted national female suffrage in the twentieth century. Many Asian and African states, however, extended universal suffrage to men and women simultaneously, during the period of national independence in the twentieth century. Yet the political disabilities in women's status as citizens goes beyond the denial of the right to vote. The history of discrimination against women in relation to education, professional employment, economic independence, rights within marriage, divorce, inheritance, and the custody of children have disqualified women from a variety of public roles and constructed them as dependent on fathers and husbands. The legacy of this residual construct of dependence has haunted women's relation to the nation and to the state long after the granting of formal legal equality to women.

The anomalous status of women as citizens is reflected in the dual construction of women as individuals in their own right who are subject to the general laws of the state and as men's legal appendages, subject to special laws. The nationality and immigration laws in Britain, for example, have long been based on the model of the heterosexual nuclear family, with a male head of household under whom women are subsumed as dependants. Until the Second World War, European countries other than the Soviet Union, did not give married women equal access to nationality and citizenship. A married woman's citizenship typically derived not from her father or from the country of her birth, but from her husband's citizenship. When women married foreign men, they lost their natal nationality and had to take up the nationality of their husband. In the event of a divorce, these women often found themselves 'stateless'. The anomalous position of married women's nationality and citizenship was addressed only in the context of international concern over the so-called 'white slave trade' in the inter-war period.[51] As large numbers of European women began to emigrate in the last quarter of the nineteenth century in search of more opportunities, many landed in

---

[51] The following discussion is from Donna Guy, ' "White Slavery". Citizenship and Nationality in Argentina', in Parker and others, eds., *Nationalisms and Sexualities*, pp. 201–17. For the British Empire, see Philippa Levine, 'The White Slave Trade and the British Empire: Crime, Gender and Sexuality in Criminal Prosecutions', *Criminal Justice History*, XVII (2002), pp. 133–46.

brothels and bordellos in foreign ports. Their sexual availability to foreign, often racially diverse, men galvanized many European nation-states to 'protect' the sexual virtue of their national women, who were now re-constructed not as prostitutes but as 'white slaves' in need of protection. The so-called rescue of these women, regardless of their desire to be rescued, created an international movement that came up against the anomalous nature of married women's nationality and citizenship. Ironically, therefore, the movement concerned about the sexual virtues of 'bad women' opened the way for a reconsideration of married women's citizenship rights in a number of Latin American and European countries. Nationality and immigration legislation have been important means through which nation-states have maintained and preserved a gender-based as well as racialized community of citizens.[52]

In many Third World countries, the duality in the construction of women as citizens is reflected in the tension between secular law and religious/communal law.[53] In many cases, for example, the domain of family legislation and of personal law that affects marriage, divorce, child-custody, and maintenance and inheritance, is based on canonical law even when other legal codes are fully secular. The domain of personal law usually privileges the heterosexual patriarchal family and the rights of men over those of women. The nation-state, therefore, ends up reinforcing the patriarchal family in circumscribing women's legal equality as citizens of the state. The Constitution of independent India, despite its commitment to the adoption of a uniform Civil Code, compromised with the colonial legacy of the separation between secular law and religious-based personal laws to subordinate the rights of women as citizens to that of 'community' rights.[54] The recognition of women as citizens in their own right in a variety of nationalist projects is often compromised by the construction of women primarily through a heterosexual relationship to men. Nations, themselves shaped by the dynamics of imperialism, have thus been deeply implicated in the construction and preservation of particular gendered identities.

The contemporary scholarship on gender, nation, and empire belies any easy generalizations about the compatibility of feminisms and nationalisms.

[52] Frances Klug, ' "Oh to be in England": The British Case Study', in Yuval-Davis and Anthias, eds., *Woman-Nation-State*, pp. 16–35.

[53] Kandiyoti, 'Identity and its Discontents', pp. 436–40.

[54] Nivedita Menon, 'State/Gender/Community: Citizenship in Contemporary India', *Economic and Political Weekly*, XXXIII (31 Jan. 1998), pp. PE-3-PE-10.

Scholars have sometimes assumed that the exclusion of the 'woman question' by and large from the early nationalist projects in Europe, produced a necessarily antagonistic relationship between European feminisms and nationalisms.[55] While early European feminisms may have aligned with radical ideologies that were often explicitly international, and even anti-national, in their orientation, this does not mean that European feminists were not staunchly nationalist, or were not invested in the racial and imperial politics of their nations. In Europe and the United States, feminists articulated explicitly racialized and imperialist feminisms to gain acceptance and inclusion in the imperial nation. Victorian and Edwardian British feminists, for example, framed their demand for suffrage in terms of women's imperial-nationalist responsibility. When British feminists elaborated the image of the supposedly helpless and degraded Indian woman, this was not incidental to their feminist project. Rather the plight of the Indian woman justified their own claims—as bearers of the 'white woman's burden'—for political inclusion in the imperial-nation.[56] The internationalism of first-wave feminists did not necessarily entail the transcendence of nationalist politics. Notwithstanding the inhospitable climate for feminism in many nationalist projects, the feminism of middle-class, white feminists was informed by the racial and imperial politics of their respective projects of nationhood.

However, the development of feminism alongside nationalism, as in many colonized and semi-peripheral parts of the world, did not necessarily provide any safeguards.[57] While these nationalist projects often stimulated the transformation of women's position as part of a broader concern with national rejuvenation and social reforms, often by turning to a 'golden age' in the ancient past where women supposedly enjoyed equality with men, the results were decidedly mixed. In many Third World nationalist projects, the articulation of women's interests was often subordinated to the interests of the nation. Feminist demands, for example, were framed only within the parameters of anti-colonial nationalism. In some nationalist movements, moreover, feminists were advised to shelve their demands until the nationalist emergency ended; feminists were told 'not now, later'.[58] In other cases, feminists were

[55] Gisela Kaplan, 'Feminism and Nationalism: The European Case', in Lois A. West, ed., *Feminist Nationalism* (New York, 1997), pp. 3–40.

[56] This discussion draws on Antoinette Burton, *Burdens of History: British Feminists, Indian Women, and Imperial Culture, 1865–1914* (Chapel Hill, NC, 1994), esp. pp. 171–205.

[57] Kumari Jayawardena, *Feminism and Nationalism in the Third World* (London, 1986).

[58] Enloe, *Bananas, Beaches and Bases*, p. 62.

portrayed as 'traitors' to the nation, and feminism identified as a bourgeois and Westernized project, irrelevant to the more urgent concerns of the nation. In still others, the hospitable climate for feminism created during nationalist liberation struggles evaporated with the attainment of independence, as happened in Ireland. The commitment to a progressive gender-politics, as well as the contributions of Irish women in the nationalist struggle, was conveniently forgotten in the repressive gender-regime instituted by the Irish constitution of 1937.[59] To conclude from this that anti-colonial nationalist projects have simply manipulated women cynically to garner support for nationalism, however, would be to underestimate the importance of the 'woman question' in the self-representation of anti-colonial nationalisms.

Here is the key: *nowhere has feminism ever been autonomous of the national context from which it has emerged.* This national positioning has been clearly evident in the history of the international feminist movement. The major liberal-feminist international organizations of the early twentieth century were dominated by women from the United States and North West Europe, many of whom not only assumed feminism's transcendence of national politics, but were invested in an ideology that insisted on the apparent separation of feminist from nationalist concerns.[60] This view was widely contested and exposed by feminists from other parts of the world. Indian feminists such as Kamaladevi Chattopadhyay, Shareefah Hamid Ali, Dhanvanthi Rama Rau, and others, never missed an opportunity to raise the question of the struggle against imperialism at international feminist conferences throughout the inter-war period.[61] Feminists from different parts of the world not only challenged the 'maternalism' that often underwrote the ideology of the international feminist movement, but also insisted on making national self-determination into a feminist issue.[62]

---

[59] Breda Gray and Louise Ryan, 'The Politics of Irish Identity and the Interconnections between Feminism, Nationhood, and Colonialism', in Pierson and Chaudhuri, eds., *Nation, Empire, Colony,* pp. 121–38.

[60] Leila J. Rupp, *Worlds of Women: The Making of an International Women's Movement* (Princeton, 1997).

[61] Mrinalini Sinha, 'Suffragism and Internationalism: The Enfranchisement of British and Indian Women Under an Imperial State', in Ian Fletcher and others, eds., *Women's Suffrage in the British Empire* (London, 2000), pp. 224–40.

[62] The phrase is from Barbara Ramusack, 'Cultural Missionaries, Maternal Imperialists, Feminist Allies: British Women Activists in India, 1865–1945', in Nupur Chaudhuri and Margaret Strobel, eds., *Western Women and Imperialism: Complicity and Resistance* (Bloomington, Ind., 1992), pp. 119–36.

This brief survey of the scholarship points not only to the ways in which modern discourses of gender and the nation have sustained one another, but also to their elaboration and consolidation within an imperial context. Hence its implications for the understanding of the British Empire and its legacy. When imperialism itself is revealed as a constitutive site in, and against, which modern gender and national identities were consolidated around the world, the legacy of the British Empire, much wider and deeper than is often assumed, continues to cast its shadow long after the formal dismantling of the empire itself.

Select Bibliography

MARGOT BADRAN, *Feminism, Islam, and Nation: Gender and the Making of Modern Egypt* (Princeton, 1995).

IDA BLOM and KAREN HAGEMANN, eds., *Gendered Nations: Nationalisms and Gender Order in the Long Nineteenth Century* (New York and London, 2000).

ANTOINETTE BURTON, *Burdens of History: British Feminists, Indian Women, and Imperial Culture, 1865–1914* (Chapel Hill, NC, 1994).

PARTHA CHATTERJEE, *The Nation and its Fragments: Colonial and Postcolonial Histories* (Princeton, 1993).

KUMARI JAYAWARDENA, *Feminism and Nationalism in the Third World* (London, 1986).

ANNE MCCLINTOCK, *Imperial Leather: Race, Gender and Sexuality in the Colonial Context* (New York, 1995).

VALENTINE M. MOGHADAM, ed., *Gender and National Identity: Women and Politics in Muslim Societies* (London, 1994).

ANDREW PARKER, M. RUSSO, D. SOMMER and P. YAEGER eds., *Nationalisms and Sexualities* (New York and London, 1992).

RUTH ROACH PIERSON and NUPUR CHAUDHURI, eds., *Nation, Empire, Colony: Historicizing Gender and Race* (Bloomington, Ind., 1998).

TANIKA SARKAR, *Hindu Wife, Hindu Nation: Community, Religion and Cultural Nationalism* (New Delhi, 2001).

KATHLEEN WILSON, *The Island Race: Englishness, Empire, and Gender in the Eighteenth Century* (London and New York, 2003).

NIRA YUVAL-DAVIS, *Gender and Nation* (London, 1997).

—— and FLOYA ANTHIAS, eds., *Woman-Nation-State* (New York, 1989).

9

Legacies of Departure:
Decolonization, Nation-making, and Gender

URVASHI BUTALIA

Decolonization and nation-making have traditionally been parallel and sometimes overlapping processes. As the colonial power departs, colonized peoples come into their own. Because the process of nation-making is so marked by the excitement and euphoria that inevitably accompanies it, histories that threaten to rupture this narrative, particularly those that speak of violence, are often silenced, a silence that sometimes lasts for many years. Where they have to do with actors who already occupy the margins of history and historiography, such as women, children, minorities, the poor, the silence is even deeper. Further, it is a silence on which, all too often, both histories from within (which find it difficult to acknowledge the violence of a moment that should, rightly, have been a moment of celebration) and from without (the received wisdom about the British Empire in India is that this was an unusually benevolent encounter, not marked by any 'real' violence) are in agreement, each for reasons of their own. In India, such histories have only recently begun to emerge.[1] Many of them have to do with the British decision in 1947 (perhaps the single most crucial one they took, once it became clear that they would have to leave) to partition the old Empire into two: India and Pakistan.

Women have traditionally had little or no say in the decisions about borders and nations and yet gender and sexuality, more particularly notions

I am grateful to Philippa Levine for suggesting, and then gently bullying me, into writing this essay. Her comments, and those of the participants at the authors' meeting in Los Angeles, which have been extremely useful. I would also like to thank Uma Chakravarti for commenting on various drafts, and encouraging me to look at related areas.

[1] Urvashi Butalia, *The Other Side of Silence: Voices from the Partition of India* (Delhi, 1998); Ritu Menon and Kamla Bhasin, *Borders and Boundaries: Women in India's Partition* (Delhi, 1998); Gyanendra Pandey, *Remembering Partition* (Cambridge, 2001).

of femininity and masculinity, of pollution and purity, remain central to the processes of decolonization and nation-making. At such moments, women are called upon to mark and recreate the boundaries of ethnic or national groups. It is they who must remain pure, and it is their responsibility to reproduce the ideological community, so central to the nation. Women carry the responsibility—most often on their bodies—of acting as symbols of both ethnic and national communities.[2] They symbolically embody the pure nation, the pure community; the violation of their bodies, as if by tacit agreement between the warring factions, becomes one with the violation of the nation. The nation itself, however, even if imagined as maternal, remains the responsibility and creation of men. This process of gendering is carried through into issues of citizenship—also central to nation-making—where women are invariably assigned different, and frequently lesser, citizenship rights than are men.[3]

In India, the hard-won fight for Independence was a victory not only for nationalist fighters, but also for the idea of 'Mother India', the nation. The partitioning of the country which accompanied independence, however, represented more than just a loss of territory. At a symbolic level, it represented the severing of the body of Mother India. Men, who held themselves responsible for the protection of Mother India, were shamed and humiliated at having 'allowed' themselves to accept the partitioning of the country, a decision they came to see as the price of independence, though not of their own making. Inside the Constituent Assembly, in the press, and elsewhere, men referred to themselves as emasculated and weak for being unable to protect the nation. An article in *The Organiser*, the mouthpiece of the Rashtriya Swayamsevak Sangh, spoke of the challenge of rehabilitating millions of refugees:[4]

Their early and effective absorption in the economy and society of the regions of their adoption is the primary duty of every national of Hindustan. The task is not

[2] Nira Yuval-Davis and Floya Anthias, *Woman-Nation-State* (New York, 1989), p. 6.

[3] See D. Kandiyoti, 'Identity and its Discontents: Women and the Nation', *Millenium, Journal of International Studies*, XX, 3 (1991).

[4] Founded in 1925, the *Rashtriya Swayamsevak Sangh* (RSS) provides the ideological grounding for the politics of the Hindu Right. RSS cadres are trained in its skewed version of nationalism (read majoritarianism) which includes and actively encourages violence towards the 'other' (the Muslim, the Christian, and others). The RSS poses as a 'cultural' organization, but it is from its cadres that the membership of its electoral sister organizations is largely drawn and its leadership feels it has a right to be heard on any decisions these organizations take.

easy. It bristles with difficulties. That is obvious. But no less obvious is the fact that the problem is *a challenge to our manhood, no less than to our nationalism* (my emphasis).[5]

For women, however, the creation of two new nations came to acquire many other meanings. Although the history of the mass rape of women on both sides is by now well known, it bears repetition here. In the violence of Partition, as people fled in fear from places where they had lived and made their homes but which became unsafe as new definitions of home and nation acquired currency, thousands of women, Hindu and Muslim, were raped and abducted. Estimates vary, but about 100,000 women were subjected to rape and abduction. The large-scale rape of women as a weapon of war or genocide is now widely recognized; indeed in wars and conflicts the world over it has become an almost commonplace occurrence. Women's mass abduction, however (for kidnapping and abduction were not new to women generally), was something that was specific to the circumstances of Partition, as was the marking of their bodies with symbols of the other religion. There are innumerable instances of women who had their breasts cut off, or whose bodies, particularly the genitalia, were tattooed with symbols of the 'other' religion. Women were abducted and sold into slavery or sexual service. Some changed hands many times, others were 'kept' by one man, and several acquired the 'legitimate' role of wives. I have dealt in detail with the fate of raped and abducted women elsewhere.[6] Here, I want to draw attention particularly to what this occurrence meant for the women them-selves (about which, until recently, little was known even though their fate formed the substance of many discussions at the time), and for men (whose opinions, not surprisingly, fill many pages of the records of the Constituent Assembly), and how this otherwise 'shameful' chapter in India's history provided one of the first challenges to the Constitution of the new nation-state on what is perhaps the most important question to face any newly forming nation, the basis of citizenship. Were women in the new Indian state fully fledged citizens? Were they 'direct' citizens, or was citizenship mediated for them through their men and their families? What was the fate

[5] Urvashi Butalia, 'Muslims and Hindus, Men and Women: Communal Stereotypes and the Partition of India', in Tanika Sarkar and Urvashi Butalia, eds., *Women and the Hindu Right: A Collection of Essays* (Delhi, 1995), p. 69.

[6] Urvashi Butalia, 'Community State and Gender: On Women's Agency During Partition', *Economic and Political Weekly*, XXVIII, 17, 24 April, 1993. See also Butalia, *The Other Side of Silence*, and 'Muslims and Hindus'.

of women who did not fit the norm? How, in the wake of decolonization and independent self-government, did the fledgling state deal with such questions?

The scale of women's 'disappearances' became clear within a few months after Partition, as family after family began to report the loss of their women. A unique—and completely unexpected—problem now forced both new states to act. By and large, abducted women now living in one or other country, were seen to belong to the other country. The majority of abducted women found in India were Muslim, and therefore assumed to belong to Pakistan, just as the majority of abducted women found in Pakistan were Hindu and Sikh, and likewise, therefore, belonged to India. Indian law could not apply to women who were seen to be citizens of Pakistan, or the other way round. Clearly, some other form of action 'suitable' to this unusual situation had to be found. Mridula Sarabhai, an articulate, influential woman politician, swore an affidavit testifying to the terrible conditions in which abducted women found themselves. Her class and influence ensured that she was given a hearing, and as a result, the two governments came together to discuss the problem. They arrived at an understanding (later given legal shape) to set up search parties, made up of women social workers and police, authorized to look at reports and go into clearly demarcated 'interior' areas in search of abducted women. Women thus located had to be brought back to what was defined as their 'home'. Hindu women were to be brought back to India, and Muslim women to Pakistan, no matter that this might not correspond to their real homes. It was a curious paradox for the Indian state, for India perceived itself as a secular, rational, modern nation, and religion was not what defined its identity. Yet women, theoretically equal citizens of this nation, were being defined in terms of religious identity. Thus the 'proper' home for Hindu and Sikh women presumed to have been abducted was India, home of the Hindu and Sikh religion, and for Muslim women it was Pakistan, home of the Muslim religion. In neither case was the home these women might actually have chosen a consideration. At Partition, every citizen theoretically had a choice as to which nation he or she wished to belong; it was a choice unavailable to abducted women.

Within the Constituent Assembly, the abduction and rape of women was a subject of considerable discussion. Accusations were levelled at the Indian Government that it was too 'soft' on Pakistan because India had recovered 'more' Muslim women than Pakistan had recovered Hindu and Sikh women. By 29 February 1952, 7,981 abducted persons had been recovered in Pakistan, and 16,168 in India.[7] Their recovery raised a slew of questions. Could the 'recovered' Indian women be re-integrated into society? How could this be done? They had, after all, crossed the borders of permitted sexual mores by having sexual contact with men of the 'other' religion, and by the tenets of the Hindu religion, they had been rendered 'impure' or 'polluted'. In several instances, recovered women could not be re-integrated into their families because the families now refused to take them back. Worse was to follow, for many abducted women, when they were found (often many years later), refused to return, perhaps out of fear of rejection by their families, or because they were now in contractual, marital, and sometimes even voluntary relationships with men, or were pregnant or had had children with the men with whom they now lived. In other words, whatever their circumstances, they had—literally and metaphorically—crossed the boundary that the new process of nation-making had created and laid down for them. Desiring women, women who refused to be 'recovered' and rejected the 'necessity' of returning to the nation, women who asserted their right to live with a man of another religion, women who had sex with men of the other religion, these were all women who represented, in many ways, a sexuality gone, or threatening to go, out of control, a sort of sexual chaos. They had, somehow, to be brought back within the boundaries set by the nation, the community, and the family.[8]

The drawing of external boundaries also had the effect of hardening or making more rigid other boundaries in the lives of women, particularly inside families and communities. If abducted and raped women represented one kind of danger, the *possibility* of abduction and rape for women represented quite another. At the time of Partition, many communities and families, particularly among the Sikhs and Hindus, killed their women to prevent them from being raped and perhaps impregnated by men of the other religion. There are many stories in which women were coerced into 'becoming martyrs', into taking their own lives for the sake of the purity of the religion. In the village of Thoa Khalsa in Rawalpindi district, some eighty

---

[7] Criminal Appeal No. 82 of 1952, The State of Punjab–Appellant–v Ajaib Singh and another–Respondents, 182, 1953, *Criminal Law Journal* (hereafter *CLJ*), p. 1319.

[8] Often the considerations governing recovery were more material. The legendary story of Zainab and Buta Singh (Butalia, *The Other Side of Silence*, pp. 127–31) is one such example. Zainab, a Muslim woman, was abducted, then sold to Buta Singh, a Sikh, and the two later married and had a family. Several years later, Zainab was forcibly recovered by the police and sent to Pakistan where, it is said, her uncle's family wished her to marry their son so that property in her name could then be joined with theirs.

women were said to have jumped into a well and taken their own lives because they, and their families and communities, feared rape, conversion, and impregnation at the hands of the Muslims. There is no way of reading back into this conflicted history how much this extreme step had to do with the women's own agency, and how much with coercion or social pressure. Such incidents took place on both sides. Several men killed women and children of their families for the same reason, disguising these killings as martyrdom. Not a single one of them was ever brought to book, because these killings fell into a different realm: one that privileged 'honour' rather than law.

These brief descriptions in no way do justice to the complex experiences of women during and in the aftermath of Partition. They do, however, draw attention to how the process of packing up a history and leaving, otherwise known as decolonization, had more than narrow political ramifications. Rather, its impact was felt deep in the lives of ordinary human beings, and in specific ways in the lives of women. For the British, Indian men were in many ways lacking, and were often described as effeminate, a justification for their subjugation under British rule. The fact of Partition, that is, the loss of one part of the territory of India to another nation, and to one whose men, moreover, were identified as masculine, aggressive, libidinous, and possessing a rampant sexuality, only affirmed British perceptions of Indian men. The rape and abduction of women came to represent a sort of failure on the part of Indian men to 'protect' their women. Over time, as it became clear that many women were now asserting their right to choose the kind of life they wanted, it became correspondingly important for Indian men, or at least those represented in the Assembly, to see themselves as capable of 'rescuing' and 'recovering' their women, even if it meant doing so by force.

From these larger beginnings, I want now to turn to the smaller histories, and to a specific and landmark case which came before the courts in the early 1950s. This locating of the small against the large, and vice versa, has the advantage of 'relocating the enquiry from reified structures to actual men and women engaged in concrete acts and relationships'.[9] It is important to ask how these broad sweeps of state intent and action worked themselves out in the lives of women and men. The attempt here to answer this question will refer only to the Indian legislative provisions applicable to abducted women. One of the legacies of decolonization in divided countries is the partial access

---

[9] Tanika Sarkar, *Hindu Wife, Hindu Nation* (Delhi, 2002), p. 3.

scholars have to information and knowledge across borders. As an Indian scholar, I know little or nothing about Pakistani legislation and how it worked, nor is there any way in which this information can become easily accessible to me, hence its absence from my work.

In order to set in motion the recovery operation (known as the Central Recovery Operation), representatives of the two governments met in December 1947, and set up groups of recovery police and social workers who soon began functioning in agreed geographical areas. In November 1948, this initial arrangement was given formal shape in an Inter-Dominion Agreement signed by both countries and, a few months later, in January 1949, an Ordinance for the Recovery of Abducted Persons was promulgated. In December 1949, the Ordinance was replaced by the Abducted Persons Recovery and Restoration Act. This was to remain in force till the end of October 1951, but was extended by a year.

Why, one might well ask was this legislation necessary at all? And further, why was it limited only to certain areas?[10] By 1949, the pace of recovery had slowed considerably and, apart from dealing with pending cases in court, the legislation served little purpose. The situation was, without doubt, unusual and unprecedented, and the general feeling was that the state had to act in whatever way possible. Extraordinary situations, it was said, merited extraordinary solutions. The ordinary law of the land was not adequate to deal with the situation and 'the two governments had to devise ways and means to check the evil'.[11]

Of the several cases of abduction with which the courts concerned themselves under this Act, only one will be considered here. The facts of *Ajaib Singh v State of Punjab* were as follows: on the 17 February 1951, Major Babu Singh, Officer Commanding, No. 2 Field Co., Faridkot, reported that one Ajaib Singh had three abducted persons (women) in his possession. On the

[10] The United Provinces, the Provinces of East Punjab and Delhi, the Patiala and East Punjab States Union, and the United States of Rajasthan. Interestingly, the Act did not extend to Bengal and East Pakistan which were also affected by abductions. Historians have yet to offer an explanation for this. Abduction itself was not new or unusual. The interesting paradox is that while the courts in areas covered by the Act dealt with cases of abduction under the dispensation of the Act and not the ordinary law of the land, other courts, in other parts of the country which did not come under the ambit of the Act, dealt with and ruled on what were presumably more 'normal' and more 'routine' abductions under the Criminal Procedure Court. How did this difference play itself out? A comparison could yield interesting insights.
[11] Criminal Appeal No 82 of 1952, The State of Punjab–Appellant v. Ajaib Singh and another–Respondents, 182, 1953, *CLJ*, Supreme Court, p. 1319.

basis of his report, the recovery police of Ferozepur raided Ajaib Singh's house four months later, taking into custody a young girl, Mukhtiar Kaur, alias Sardaran. She was handed over to the officer-in-charge of the Muslim transit camp at Ferozepur, from where she was taken to the Recovered Muslim Women's Camp in Jullundur. A sub-inspector of police, Nihar Dutt Sharma, deputed to make enquiries into the facts of the case confirmed that the girl had been abducted during the violence in 1947. Fearing that she would be sent away, Ajaib Singh filed a writ of *habeas corpus* in the Division Court, asking that the girl not be removed from Jullundur until the disposal of the petition. He obtained an interim order that Sardaran should not be removed from the High Court, to whom the case was referred. Further enquiry by two superintendents; one each from India and Pakistan, confirmed that she was an abducted woman. In the course of their enquiry, they questioned the girl's mother; her uncle, Ghulam Rasul, the girl herself, and others. In their report dated 17 November 1951, the police recommended that the girl be restored to her family (in other words, that she be sent to Pakistan). In view of the interim order of the High Court, they suggested that their recommendation be held in abeyance until the court reached its final decision.

The next step in this saga took place before a tribunal made up of two superintendents of police, one from Pakistan and the other from India, under Section Six of the Act. They, likewise, recommended Sardaran's 'return' to Pakistan, taking not even a full day to reach this decision. When the *habeas corpus* petition came up for hearing before Justices Bhandari and Khosla, however, key questions were raised about the validity of the Act of 1949, particularly whether some sections violated the provisions laid down in India's new Constitution, and about what constituted 'arrest', 'detention', and 'deportation'. The judges referred these questions to a full Bench, making it clear that the Bench would not be obliged to confine itself within the narrow limits of the phraseology of the said questions.

Mukhtiar Kaur/Sardaran's case was, in its facts, not all that different from the many others that came before the courts. The timing of the case, however, lends it some peculiar significances. In 1952, the 1949 Act was up for renewal, the pace of the Central Recovery Operation had slowed, and the authorities were increasingly faced with women's 'resistance' to being rescued or recovered; their refusal to 'return' to their families. There were many reasons women were reluctant to return: fear of rejection as polluted through sexual contact; fear of separation from their children; fear of further dislocation.

Furthermore, by 1952, the rights and privileges of Indian citizens had been defined by the Indian Constitution, a secular, liberal, modern document. Yet the cases of abducted women pending in the Indian courts, continued to provide challenges to constitutional guarantees and citizenship rights. And while the passport system now in place between the two countries should have further helped defined citizenship, the presence of a number of abducted Muslim women within the territory of India continually threw the question of female citizenship into sharp relief. Were these women Indian citizens or Pakistani citizens? Much of the time, they 'belonged' to someone (a person) but had no documentation that established their allegiance to something as nebulous as a particular 'nation'. This ambivalence, and the very public nature of the question of abducted women, represented just the kind of rupture that a newly forming nation-state could do without.

Indeed, the continuing evidence that there were abducted women in India threw several of the certainties of citizen, state, nation, and liberty into question. Because the women 'arrested' under the Act of 1949—all picked up within the territory of India—were Muslim, this question became even more fraught. Muslim women abducted by Hindu men were assumed, by virtue of their belonging to Muslim families, to be from across the border, and if they were to be restored to their kin, this meant sending them to Pakistan. Given that their relatives, possibly their parents, were now (presumably) Pakistani citizens, these women, no matter that they might have been adults, were also assumed to have taken on the citizenship of their parents. And further, given this Kafkaesque reality, could they then lay claim to any of the rights guaranteed by the Indian Constitution even if they had been 'captured' within the territory of India? Article 19 of the Indian Constitution specified, for example, that every citizen of India had the fundamental right to stay within the territory of India and to carry on any occupation, trade, or business. How, then, could the Indian state deal with these women, caught in the liminality of disputed citizenship, for even if some or all of them knew themselves to be Indian citizens, the Indian (secular) state thought otherwise, just because they belonged to a 'different' religion?

Young Mukhtiar Kaur/Sardaran (for she was only twelve or fourteen years old at the time) could hardly have known that her situation would lead to a major debate on constitutional questions. As her case came up for argument, the judges decided to consider other similar cases pending before them in which relatives of abducted women had claimed that the provisions of the Act of 1949 violated the Articles of the Indian Constitution, in particular

Articles 19 and 22. Could the courts uphold the legality of an Act whose very provisions could be seen to be violate the Indian Constitution? What was the status of such enactments *vis-à-vis* the Constitution, especially if they were found to be in opposition? The arguments were not simple. Caught between their loyalties to the new state, their commitment to the Constitution, and the varying needs of the women and their families, as well as their own socialization as men, the judges had some hard decisions to make.[12] As the case moved from the specific to the general, the court ordered that Sardaran 'be set at liberty', and specified that no matter what answers they came up with, this would not affect the young girl's release.

The first point for discussion related to the right conferred by the Act on the police, to take into 'custody' any person who, in the opinion of the officer, 'is an abducted person and deliver or cause such person to be delivered to the custody of the officer in charge of the nearest camp with the least possible delay'. How were officers to determine who was abducted? Could such persons be either male or female? For this, the judges turned once again to the Act which defined an abducted person as 'a male child under the age of sixteen years or *a female of whatever age* (my emphasis) who is, or immediately before the first day of March, was a Muslim and who, on or after that day and before the first day of January 1949, has become separated from his or her family and is found to be living with or under the control of any other individual or family, and in the latter case includes a child born to any such female after the said date'. Clearly, a male person could be a free agent once he reached the age of consent (at that time, sixteen years) but a female, no matter what her age, was, in certain circumstances at least, incapable of making an independent decision.

Indeed, throughout the course of the arguments in the courtroom and elsewhere, women continued to be constructed as helpless victims, in need of the parental (read patriarchal) support of the state. India, Justice Bhandari pointed out in his arguments, had suffered many losses as a result of Partition, but 'there was no loss that was felt more keenly than the loss of their women—their wives and sisters and daughters—who had been snatched

---

[12] The Hindu and male bias of the judges is evident in the text of the judgement. Not only are women not deserving of full citizenship rights in their own right, but Muslim women are even less so. It is worth noting that Justice Khosla is probably the person who conducted a government enquiry into the communal disturbances of 1947, and whose report displayed a particular bias: G. D. Khosla, *Stern Reckoning: A Survey of the Events Leading up to and Following the Partition of India* (1949; Delhi, 1989).

away by ruffians of an alien race'. It was perhaps the loss of its own women that made the Indian state, according to the Indian judiciary, so sensitive to the fate of abducted Muslim women.[13]

And yet, how helpless were these women really? Given that they are mere shadows in court records (we know Sardaran/Mukhtiar Kaur's name, for example, and her approximate age, but very little else about her) and virtually absent in other records, it is difficult to construct a picture of the women whose lives were on the line here. Other sources, more specifically accounts by women social workers, tell a more nuanced story. Damyanti Sahgal, who worked in different camps for abducted women, describes the case of Satya, a Hindu woman in Pakistan, whom she helped to recover. 'Two young men reported to me that their sister, Satya, whose marriage they had been preparing, had been abducted. They suspected Pathans had picked her up.' Damyanti Sahgal managed to track Satya down, but when she tried to bring her away, the 'Pathans followed us and appealed in court saying we're not prepared to give up this woman, she's been a Muslim from the start'. Such was the pressure on Damyanti from the Pathans, and so strong was the girl's own resistance, that Damyanti had to call upon the good offices of Raja Ghaznafar Ali Khan, the Pakistan Minister for Refugees, who stopped his train at Gujrat to talk to her. At the station, the Minister asked that the woman, Satya, be produced before him. Here is how Damyanti Sahgal describes the scene. 'The police came with the girl *in handcuffs* (my emphasis). I was standing here, he was there. The girl shouted: "Who has come to take me? This bastard woman? . . . This woman has come to take me away? I will not go." ' So saying, Satya pulled out her slipper and brandished it at Damyanti, threatening to hit her with it.[14] This is hardly the image of the docile, oppressed, unable-to-think-for-herself woman.

---

[13] Despite its secular self-image the Indian state was often discriminatory towards its minority population, particularly Muslims. An interesting case (Criminal Appeal No 459 of 1956, against the acquittal by Magistrate 1st Class, Rohtak, Camp Sonepat, D/-26-6-1956, State v. Abdul Hamid, A[ll] I[ndia] R[eporter] 1957, Punjab 86, State vs. Abdul Hamid, AIR, 1957) concerned Abdul Hamid and his wife Latifan, who both claimed to have been separated as minors from their parents during Partition, and that they had therefore lived in India and were Indian citizens. They were denied citizenship because the judges believed that their parents must have gone to Pakistan, and argued that international law asserts that a child acquires the nationality of a parent. Since their parents were 'certainly' in Pakistan, the 'children' by default, assumed their nationality. The courts also refused to accept a judgement of the Pakistan court that Abdul Hamid was an Indian citizen, saying that a foreign judgement was not binding on 'this court'.

[14] Damyanti Sahgal, personal interview, quoted in Butalia, *The Other Side of Silence*, p. 142.

Anis Kidwai, another social worker who worked with abducted women, offers a different reason—and one which probably has a great deal of truth in it—for women seeming helpless in the face of their abductors:

There were some women who had been born into poor homes and had not seen anything other than poverty. A half-full stomach and rags on your body. And now they had fallen into the hands of men who bought them silken salwars and net dupattas, who taught them the pleasures of cold ice cream and hot coffee, who took them to the cinema. Why should they leave such men and go back to covering their bodies with rags and slaving in the hot sun in the fields? If she leaves this smart, uniformed man, she will probably end up with a peasant in rags, in the filth, with a danda on his shoulder. And so they are happy to forget the frightening past, or the equally uncertain and fearful future, and live only for the present.[15]

Clearly, these were not the helpless women described in the court records whose fate formed such an important subject for discussion in the Constituent Assembly.[16] Equally, however, they were not 'free' to make decisions about the life choices they were faced with; free neither in the kind of environment in which Satya found herself, nor where she was eventually taken (the Indian recovery workers took no account of her protests, and Damyanti records that she lost track of her afterwards), not in the atmosphere described by Anis Kidwai, nor indeed in the camps heavily guarded by armed police to 'protect' the women in order to enable them to exercise choice freely.[17]

Let us now return to the judgment in Sardaran/Mukhtiar Kaur's case. The full Bench discussed the case in the High Court of Punjab. Section 4 of the Act of 1949 empowered the police to take into custody any abducted person. Such taking into custody effectively amounted to arresting a person, though no criminal charges were to be laid against her. Nor generally was the detainee—in this case, the abducted woman—produced before a magistrate within twenty-four hours as mandated by the Constitution. Rather, all too

[15] Ibid., p. 150.
[16] See Constituent Assembly of India (Legislative) Debates, various years, starting 1949 and up to 1955.
[17] Interestingly, there was much ambivalence and many contradictions in the stands taken by the courts. In Bhopan v Chhotey, in the Allahabad High Court (Criminal Revn No. 1218 of 1947, decided 14 June 1948, Bhopan–Applicant v Chhotey–Opposite Party, 1949, *CLJ*, p. 50) the judge ruled that Bhagwati, wife of Chhotey, presumed to have been abducted by Bhopan, was not really abducted because, 'when a woman of her own free will desires to keep away from her husband and to stay with the accused, there can be no detention in any sense of the word'.

often, she was simply 'conveyed' out of the country. Did this not, the judges asked, violate Article 19 of the Constitution, which specified that any citizen of India who is arrested or taken into custody must be produced before a magistrate within twenty-four hours?

They debated the pros and cons of this question: 'abducted' women were not being arrested for, after all, they were not criminals. How then could they be produced before a magistrate? Instead, they were lodged in transit camps and then 'conveyed' out of the country. On the face of it, however, these were clear cases of violation of the rights of these women. How could this seeming 'arrest' be explained away? The court found an ingenious way out. The judges ruled that: 'This Act does not deal with punitive or preventive detention, *but with a new kind of detention which may be called 'protective detention'* [my emphasis]. And because the implication was that the person being thus protected was being held for her own good, therefore, 'a citizen of India,' they went on to say, 'who has been detained in a camp under S. 4 [of the Act] cannot complain that he has been deprived of the rights guaranteed by Art. 19.'

However, if the detention was 'protective'—in other words, for the woman's own good—her 'deportation' or being 'conveyed' to another country did not meet the approval of the judges. Every Indian citizen, they held, has the right to stay within the territory of India (Article 19, clause g) and 'for all practical purposes a person who is conveyed out of India under the provisions of Section 7 [of the Act] is deprived of the rights guaranteed to her by Article 19 (1) (g) of the Constitution.'[18] If this was the case, what was the validity of the Act which specifically stipulated that abducted persons had to be conveyed out of the country? The judges went on to say, in no uncertain terms, that the Indian State was not bound by every treaty entered into by the Indian Government. 'There is no provision in the Constitution of India which declares that all treaties to which the Government of India is a party shall be vested with statutory authority.'[19] Even extraordinary conditions, and it was widely acknowledged that the Abducted Persons legislation had to be enacted because of the extraordinary conditions that obtained at the time, 'cannot create or enlarge Constitutional authority and cannot justify action outside the sphere of such authority.'

[18] Unless otherwise specified, all quotations from the judgement are taken from Ajaib Singh vs. State of Punjab (Criminal Writ No. 144 of 1951), Ajaib Singh, Lehna Singh, Petitioner, v The State of Punjab and another, Respondent, 1952, *CLJ* 1952, pp. 1313–39.
[19] Ibid.

Detention and deportation were not the only issues before the bench. Other difficult questions remained to be tackled. Did the Act discriminate against people (read women) on the grounds of religion? After all, it was only Muslim women who were being 'conveyed out of the country' and who were not being given the choice of saying no. After some discussion, the judges quoted Article 15 of the Constitution which deals with discrimination 'only' on the basis of religion:

The word 'only' is important and it is clear that what Article 15 says is that a person shall not suffer merely because he belongs to a particular religion, race or caste vis-à-vis another person similarly circumstanced. The persons who come under the mischief of the Abducted Persons (Recovery and Restoration) Act have other *qualifications* [my emphasis] besides the qualification of religion. Religion alone is not the ground upon which the distinction is based. The abducted person may not even be a Muslim at the time of his or her being taken into custody. He must have been separated from his family between the 1st of March 1947 and the 1st of January 1949 and he must be living under the control of any other individual or family. *These additional factors are a necessary incidence of an abducted person and thus there is no discrimination on grounds of religion* [my emphasis].

At issue also were the children of these mixed unions: to whom did they belong? Who had more right over them, the mother or the father? How much freedom should the woman have in deciding the fate of her children? Interestingly, the debate related to persons the politicians saw as Indian women, that is, Hindu and Sikh women abducted in Pakistan who were being rescued and brought 'back' to India, but the politicians were not blind to the significance of their arguments for Muslim (read Pakistani) women abducted and kept in India. We hear very little about what was to be the fate of their children but, given that India saw itself as a secular, democratic State with a Constitution that upheld these principles, it was necessary that even citizens of the 'other' country be seen as having freedom of choice, something a little difficult to prove in light of the strict and rigid controls put on abducted women's freedom of movement and choice in the Act of 1947. Thus one of the questions with which the Bench was concerned was women's liberty. As early as 3 March 1948, Jawaharlal Nehru had written to K. C. Neogi, the Minister for Relief and Rehabilitation:

I have just had a telephone message from Sushila Nayyar from Patiala. She told me that a great majority of the (Muslim) women recovered refused to leave their new homes, and were so frightened of being taken away forcibly that they threatened to commit suicide. Indeed, last night, 46 of them ran away from the camp through some back door. This is a difficult problem. I told Sushila that she can assure these women that no one is going to send them forcibly to Pakistan, but we thought it desirable for them to come to Delhi so that the Pakistan High Commission and others could then find out what their desires were. This would finally settle the question. In any event I assured her that we would not compel any girl to be sent to Pakistan against her wishes.[20]

In the Sardaran/Mukhtiar Kaur case, the arguments made by the judges were wide-ranging but their conclusion was clear. The provisions of the Act of 1949, they ruled, did not deprive the abducted person of her liberty, except perhaps briefly and for a limited period. What the Act actually did, they went on to say, was to deprive the abducted person of his or her personal liberty only 'from the moment he is taken into custody and taken to the camp, up to the time when is he allowed to go away or conveyed out of India'. Clearly, for the Bench, a temporary deprivation of liberty, even a temporary arrest masquerading as 'protective detention', did not constitute a violation of individual liberty. A variety of arguments supported their case. A woman presumed to be abducted was taken away from what were seen as surround-ings where she could not make a free choice. The idea of putting her in a camp was not to confine or incarcerate her, but to keep her in 'friendly surroundings' where the police guarded the gates for her protection. It was only after she had been kept in such surroundings that 'she dared to disclose her identity and became eager to contact her own relations.' The mental condition of abducted women was,' the judges opined, 'no better than that of a person who has been shell shocked on the battle front'. The idea behind such a move, then, was to restore, as far as possible, 'the atmosphere in which they were brought up before they were abducted, to encourage them to give expression to their own feelings and desires and to enable them to decide for themselves'. It was of little consequence that the 'atmosphere in which they were brought up' might have been both oppressive and violent; the judges were not interested in that, for it was, after all, one nation that was being pitted against the other here, and bigger issues were at stake.

Citizenship, rights, movement, liberty, choice—the Abducted Persons Recovery and Restoration Act of 1949 raised all these issues and presented them as challenges to the Indian Constitution. Preoccupied with dealing with the massive aftermath of the violence of Partition, the Indian state had

---

[20] *Selected Works of Jawaharlal Nehru*, Second Series, V, (Delhi, 1987), p. 114.

to address these questions, and the courtrooms became a critical arena for debate. The halls of the Constituent Assembly as well as the press offered similar debates on these issues. What of the women themselves? Where were their voices in all of this? Court records for many of the cases that came up under this Act are remarkably silent where the views of the women are concerned. Although camps and other institutions were presented as places where the women could think and decide in a free and friendly atmosphere, it is well known that this was hardly the case. Many women tried to escape and were forced to return. Despite being guarded by troops of soldiers, the camps were often attacked by men trying to get 'their' women back.

The perception of the woman as victim, as helpless and unable to make her own decisions, also guided the state's attitude to women as citizens. 'Normal' women, those located inside families, were legitimate citizens of the new nation-state, although even for them, as for abducted women, citizenship had to be mediated through the family. Women were not seen as direct citizens of the state. This is what made it all the more necessary that abducted and recovered women be relocated inside families if they were to be seen as 'real' citizens. The urgency of keeping the legislation in place, and indeed of extending it as far as possible, and the skilful ways in which constitutional questions on the nature of citizenship were handled, were all part of this perception. The courts thus succeeded in doing several things at once: establishing the female citizen as the indirect, mediated-through-the-family citizen, establishing themselves as modern and open in taking up constitutional questions, and, in the end, keeping up the illusion of democracy by setting the women whose cases were pending before them, free.

In discussing the many issues before it, the Bench referred to Magna Carta, and to the definition of fundamental rights in the United States, seeking to learn from both. Yet, in the end, we must ask what it meant for women like Sardaran to be set at 'liberty'? Where could a twelve or fourteen year old go? If she was a Muslim, and all indications are that she was, would liberty for Sardaran mean going back to her captors? What kind of life awaited her there? These are questions for which we will never have answers, for young Mukhtiar Kaur's legacy is that while she herself has disappeared from the pages of the archives, like many of her counterparts, the questions raised by her 'capture', her arrest, detention, and then release, remain to dog women as citizens of the now decolonized, more than half-century old, free, nation-state. So-called deviant women still continue to be held in 'protective' custody, rape and abduction loom large, new nationalisms first target women and draw them in, and women still remain unequal citizens of a democratic state that they can claim as their own but which continues to deny them their rights. It is these women who are the casualties of the long arm of decolonization and nation-making.

Select Bibliography

JASHODHARA BAGCHI and DASGUPTA SUBHORANJAN, *The Trauma and the Triumph: Gender and Partition in Eastern India* (Calcutta, 2003).

ANTOINETTE BURTON, *Burdens of History: British Feminism, Indian Women and Imperial Culture 1865–1915* (Chapel Hill, NC, 1994).

URVASHI BUTALIA, *The Other Side of Silence: Voices from the Partition of India* (Delhi, 1998).

UMA CHAKRAVARTI, *Rewriting History: The Life and Times of Pandita Ramabai* (Delhi, 1998).

P. K. DUTTA, *Carving Blocs: Communal Ideology in Early Twentieth–Century Bengal* (Delhi, 1999).

MUSHIR-UL HASAN, ed., *India Partitioned: The Other Face of Freedom* (Delhi, 1995).

RITU MENON and KAMLA BHASIN, *Borders and Boundaries: Women in India's Partition* (Delhi, 1998).

KUM KUM SANGARI and SUDESH VAID, *Recasting Women: Essays in Colonial History* (Delhi, 1993).

10

Empire and Violence, 1900–1939

JOCK MCCULLOCH

The Age of Empire saw the rise of new forms of power at the imperial centres and the employment of old forms of power at their margins. Weapons were among the tools of conquest, and violence was an essential element in the management, of all modern empires including that of Britain. The high tide of imperialism was framed on either side by global conflicts: the First World War saw Germany lose her empire and the Second World War heralded the end of the British, French, and Dutch systems. In the case of The Netherlands, France, and Portugal, decolonization was intensely violent. And for that reason, within political discourse, imperialism has been almost a synonym for violence. Britain's success in dismantling its Empire relatively peacefully has encouraged the idea that its imperial rule was also benign.[1] Such judgements assume that this history is well understood, and that there is agreement about what constitutes violence.

From the early 1960s feminist historians began to expand the definition of violence, most notably by defining sexual crime in terms of power. That process has been furthered by recent literatures on the labour process and commodity markets. These literatures need to be considered in any imperial reckoning. The picture of Britain as a benign power also changes if the famines, orchestrated by the Raj between 1876 and 1902 and in which millions died, are included in the imperial balance sheet.[2] Further removed again from familiar inventories are assaults of the kind documented by Alfred Crosby upon landscape, flora, and fauna in Southern Africa, the Pacific, and Australasia. Definitions of violence are always contested, and boundaries can shift as different political orthodoxies become ascendant. There is no discrete

---

[1] For a collection of essays which rejects the idea that Britain decolonized in a peaceful and orderly manner, see Robert Holland, ed., *Emergencies and Disorders in the European Colonial Empires after 1945* (London, 1994).

[2] See Mike Davis, *Late Victorian Holocausts: El Niño Famines and the Making of the Third World* (New York, 2001).

literature on empire and violence; and the problems of configuring that field are compounded by the politically sensitive nature of the material and by the relative lack of documentation.

The end of Empire in Malaya, Kenya, Cyprus, and Aden was violent but, with the exception of the South African War (1899–1902), Britain engaged in no protracted conflicts on the scale of the French wars in Indo-China or Algeria.[3] No graduates of Sandhurst, for example, could match the active service of their French contemporaries. Colonel Raoul Salan, a graduate of St Cyr, fought in the Second World War against Germany. He then fought against the Viet Minh in Indo-China where he participated in the humiliating defeat at Dien Bien Phu. He fought, too, in Algeria, where he eventually led the notorious *Organisation Armée Secrete* (OAS) in its futile attempt to prevent the emergence of an independent Algeria. Also in contrast to the French at Setif (1945) and in Malagasy (1947), British troops did not commit large-scale massacres of civilians.

Between 1871 and 1914 there was no war in Europe and the only fighting the troops of Britain, France, and Germany did was on the colonial frontiers. Military violence is supposed to be decisive, with neatly defined means and ends. While that may be true of some wars, colonial or 'small wars' were particularly messy. The opponents of Empire were neither governments nor armies, but communities. And the destruction of cattle, crops, and villages was often used to intimidate entire populations. The wars were masculine enterprises, in that in the main men did the fighting, but through the destruction of households the impact was often felt most severely by women.

In the three decades before the First World War, there was armed resistance at numerous sites in British Africa including Southern Rhodesia, South Africa, and Nyasaland.[4] At the beginning of 1896 a war of resistance or *chimurenga* erupted in Southern Rhodesia and by the end of March, 122 white men plus five women and three children had been killed. The eventual total was around 10 per cent of the European population, in a rebellion that was arguably the most serious single blow to colonization in southern Africa. The nascent colonial state of the British South Africa Company, aided by imperial troops, responded with Maxim guns and the slaughter of thousands of civilians. Using similar methods, in the period from 1895 to 1905, the

[3] On the massacre at Setif in Algeria, see Alistair Horne, *A Savage War of Peace: Algeria 1954–1962* (London, 1977), pp. 23–43.

[4] See Shula Marks, *Reluctant Rebellion: The 1906–8 Disturbances in Natal* (Oxford, 1970), and T. O. Ranger, *Revolt in Southern Rhodesia 1896–7: A Study in African Resistance* (London, 1967).

British established the beginnings of a colonial economy in Kenya in a series of military incursions that cost hundreds of lives.[5] Subsequent resistance to colonial rule took many forms including desertion from underpaid labour, theft, cattle maiming, and the avoidance of taxation.

The distinction between 'small wars' and peace was not always clear, nor did the emerging colonial states enjoy a monopoly of violence, so that reprisals could continue long after military operations had ended. The conduct of colonial wars was also distinctive: the use of Gattling and Maxim guns and dum-dum bullets, the shelling of civilians, killing of the wounded on the battlefield, and shooting prisoners all occurred in West African wars in the late nineteenth century.[6] Machine guns had not at that time been used against European troops, in part because of conventions about the proper conduct of wars. Those conventions did not apply on the imperial frontier.[7] A number of historians have argued that since 1914 there has been a regression in the standards of civility and that, in contrast to what had gone before, wars in the twentieth century were waged against civilian populations. Those strategies were first applied in the imperial world.[8]

There is no neat sequence to imperial violence: for example with armed resistance and state incursions, which marked the beginnings and endings of Empire, being separated by a period of tranquillity. In a series of books published since 1981, historians, including Noel Butlin and Henry Reynolds, have revised the story of Australia's colonization, discarding the idea that Aboriginal peoples were the passive victims of white settlement. In their wars against squatters, which began in the late eighteenth century and lasted until the early years of the twentieth, blacks destroyed white property and stole or killed cattle, horses, and sheep. Aborigines also killed between 2,000 and 2,500 Europeans, in a series of wars in which as many as 20,000 blacks died.[9] Until recently, white historians did not see such conflict as political resistance

---

[5] For a catalogue of state violence in that period, see Table 2.2, 'British Military Operations in the Kenya Highlands 1893–1911', in Bruce Berman and John Lonsdale, *Unhappy Valley: Conflict in Kenya and Africa: Book One: State and Class* (London, 1992), p. 28.

[6] See Jaap de Moor and H. L. Wesseling, eds., *Imperialism and War: Essays on Colonial Wars in Asia and Africa* (Leiden, 1989).

[7] For a history of the use of such weapons in small wars, see John Ellis, *The Social History of the Machine Gun* (New York, 1975), pp. 79–109.

[8] E. J. Hobsbawm, *The Age of Extremes: A History of the World, 1914–1991* (New York, 1994).

[9] Noel Butlin, *Our Original Aggression* (Sydney, 1984) and Henry Reynolds, *The Other Side of the Frontier: Aboriginal Resistance to the European Invasion of Australia* (Melbourne, 1982).

in defence of land and the communities it sustained. The re-writing of that history is part of an ongoing revision of imperial pasts.

The literature on violence falls across a number of disciplines, each of which uses distinct concepts of power. In her survey of Western philosophy, Hannah Arendt argues that political violence is the preserve of the state and is distinguished by its purely instrumental character.[10] Where violence loses that quality it grades into criminality. Norbert Elias, writing before Arendt, also distinguishes between violence that is rationally chosen in pursuit of a goal and violence engaged in as an end in itself. In *The Civilizing Process*, Elias argues that the rise of instrumental and the waning of expressive violence within European societies is one of the most distinctive features of modern states. Philosophers, including Arendt, have generally agreed that there is an inverse relationship between the use of violence and power. Violence may be a manifestation of power but power does not grow from violence: on the contrary, tyranny is the most violent and the least powerful form of government. Arendt notes that because violence is the last resort of regimes seeking to retain power, it sometimes appears as if violence is the prerequisite of power and that power itself is nothing but a façade. Arendt and Elias were both writing specifically about western European states and it is difficult to translate their work into an historical context outside of those social systems. In contrast to the imperial world, modern states display high degrees of consensus between governments and their publics, which normally precludes the need for states to use violence against their citizens. Arendt is adamant that politics is the preserve of states and governments. As a consequence she pathologizes the violence of the stateless and assumes that violence in civil society is apolitical. Problems arise, however, where such violence is systemic or is linked strategically to political dominance or the management of an economy. The conceptual frameworks Arendt and Elias employ are implicit in much of the historiography on empire, which limits discussion of violence to the establishment and dissolution of imperial systems.

Surprisingly, the term violence is not cited in the subject index of the standard works on imperialism, nor does it appear in *The Encyclopaedia of the Social Sciences* (1967). Within sociology and political science, violence is usually judged to be expressive of class interest, national enmity, or political frustration but in itself is assumed to have little valency. The silence about

---

[10] Hannah Arendt, *On Violence* (London, 1970).

imperialism and violence is less easy to explain. The literatures on imperialism that enjoyed such a vogue during the 1960s and 1970s had their origins in two books, both of which were written in response to wars. Hobson's *Imperialism: A Study* (1902) was inspired by his opposition to the South African War. And in Lenin's *Imperialism: The Highest Stage of Capitalism* (1916), the author argues that the territorial division of the globe between the Great Powers was a prime cause of the First World War. The nationalist generation that emerged in Africa and South-East Asia after 1945 wrote little about violence, perhaps because from their side of the imperial divide imperialism and its instruments were too closely allied to separate. The notable exceptions are the Martiniquan authors Aimé Cesaire and Frantz Fanon, who argued that fascism was born in Europe's empires and like a virus was imported back into the metropoles where it infected political life. But only Fanon (who died in 1961) theorized violence as being a central element in both the creation and maintenance of imperialism, and as being essential to the nationalist struggles for independence. Fanon's writing was in many ways heterodox, being so much informed by his psychiatric work and his involvement in the Algerian war, a war in which as many as one million people died.

The history of violence is difficult to recover. The people who used violence denied they did so and those who were subject to violence are often invisible in the archival record. The sexual assault of indigenous women was a feature of colonial regimes, and in 1902 the death penalty for the crime of attempted rape was introduced in Southern Rhodesia. Although the legislation was colour-blind, only black men were executed under that law. And, as elsewhere in the British Empire, it was rare for a white man to be convicted of rape.[11] In 1912 a South African government commission into sexual assault on women was appointed. Although the terms of reference included assaults upon all women the commission dealt almost exclusively with assaults on white women by 'coloured' men; as if such crimes were common, which they were not.[12] The commission's hearings (like the final report) were shaped by mythologies about the sexuality of black men and ignored assaults carried out by white males. In Australia, the Pacific, and Africa where political struggles are still being fought over identity and land, recovering lost voices is a task for historians drawn from indigenous com-

[11] Jock McCulloch, *Black Peril, White Virtue: Sexual Crime in Southern Rhodesia, 1902–1935* (Bloomington, Ind., 2000).

[12] *Report of the Commission Appointed to Enquire into Assaults on Women* (Cape Town, 1913).

munities. It is possible, however, to identify the structural features that encouraged the use of violence.

In addition to war and its sexual toll on women, there were other spheres in which violence was characteristic of imperial rule. Charles van Onselen's 1979 study of forced labour in Southern Rhodesia examines the brutalities of gold-mining and, in particular, the toll of life caused by entirely preventable diseases such as scurvy and infectious pneumonia. More recent work by Allen Isaacman on cotton cultivation in adjacent Mozambique has identified further linkages between land alienation, migrant labour, and even sexual abuse.[13] Such studies reveal competing moral universes; the one of imperial ideology and the other of labour markets shaped by greed and Draconian law. The prospect for comparative research on the labour process has been opened up by the pioneering work on masters and servants legislation by Douglas Hay and Paul Craven, research which has the merit of encompassing most of Britain's Empire.[14]

The use of violence against workers was widespread in British Africa and sometimes assaults were so severe they resulted in death. On 4 May 1908, William Laidlaw, a farmer in Kinvarra in Southern Rhodesia, faced trial in the Salisbury High Court for the murder of a 'houseboy' named Neti.[15] The evidence showed that when he discovered Neti without a pass, Laidlaw beat and kicked him to death. Laidlaw was found guilty of assault and sentenced to six months hard labour. At that time the average sentence for an African convicted of stealing a bicycle was between three and nine months. The High Commissioner, Lord Selbourne, was shocked by the verdict but chose not to intervene and the sentence stood.[16] Five months later, four white men were charged with culpable homicide. The case, which followed the deaths of two workers named Mangesi and Sixpence at the Battlefields gold mine, was heard in November 1908. Battlefields was typical of mine life: brutal managers, violent compound police, and theft.

---

[13] See Charles van Onselen, *Chibaro: African Mine Labour in Southern Rhodesia, 1900–1933* (Johannesburg, 1980); Elizabeth Schmidt, *Peasants, Traders and Wives: Shona Women in the History of Zimbabwe, 1870–1939* (Oxford, 1992); and Allen Isaacman, *Cotton is the Mother of Poverty: Peasants, Work and Rural Struggle in Colonial Mozambique 1938–1961* (Oxford, 1996).

[14] Douglas Hay and Paul Craven, 'Master and Servant in England and the Empire: A Comparative Study', *Labour/Le Travail*, XXXI (Spring 1993), pp. 175–84.

[15] *The Rhodesian Herald* published a full transcript of both the magistrate's hearing and the trial.

[16] Letter from Selbourne to Resident Commissioner, 14 July 1908, Administrator's Office: Special Juries, Zimbabwe National Archives (hereafter ZNA), A3/21/87.

Mangesi, Sixpence, and a fellow worker named Jack were arrested by compound police for stealing a watch, and over a period of three days they were flogged with a *sjambok*, or heavy whip, to force a confession. During their ordeal both Mangesi and Sixpence fainted and before the final beating Mangesi tried to kill himself. Within twenty-four hours Mangesi was dead; Sixpence survived a week. According to the district surgeon, who almost certainly committed perjury, the deaths were due to a combination of shock and a chill that caused pneumonia. To the jury, the floggings were born of frustration at chronic thieving and they sympathized with the accused. After ten minutes of deliberation, the jury returned a verdict of not guilty and the men were released. The verdict brought protests in the British House of Commons, and the Rhodesian Missionary Conference suggested it showed the unfitness of colonists to manage their own affairs.[17] After prevaricating, Selbourne eventually made an official protest to the Resident Commissioner. That brought no change: in the next six months nine cases involving the murder, culpable homicide, or serious assault of a black man were heard in the Umtali and Salisbury High Courts. The assaults occurred on farms, mines, and in domestic service and in every instance the relationship between the assailant and the victim was that of employer and employee. Invariably the accused was found not guilty or, at worst, given a suspended sentence and a fine. With rare exceptions the offenders were males, as were their victims. So too were the juries, the judiciaries, and the medical experts who gave evidence at the trials. It is significant that defence counsel presented such crimes in gendered ways, akin to the beatings fathers inflict upon disobedient children.

Flogging and caning were standard forms of punishment in British Africa and employers used instruments and methods that the state also favoured. Only men were subjected to such treatment; indigenous women and juveniles were exempt. In the period from 1911 to 1914, just under 4,000 men each year received cuts or lashes in South Africa with the average sentence being nine strokes. There were heavier sentences in the Cape and Natal where flogging was used as a punishment for stock theft.[18] In 1921 the Kenyan administration held a Commission into Native Punishment. The oral and written evidence taken in a number of towns, and from a range of white

[17] Letter to the editor from G. A. Wilder, Chairman, Rhodesian Missionary Conference, *Rhodesian Herald*, 4 Dec. 1908.

[18] Martin Chanock, *The Making of the South African Legal Culture, 1902–1936: Fear, Favour and Prejudice* (Cambridge, 2001), pp. 104–05.

witnesses, suggests that flogging was used routinely by employers; and that District Commissioners, the Native Affairs Department, and the Government condoned the practice.[19] Employers told the Commission that it was too expensive and time-consuming to pursue infractions of the pass and masters and servants ordinances through a magistrate's court and so they preferred to mete out their own punishments.

There is ample evidence from Southern Rhodesia that in the period before 1914 flogging was the unofficial policy of the Native Affairs Department. In the space of a decade, as many as seven officers were dismissed for that reason. Most offenders claimed they were forced to resort to violence.[20] Byron de Laessoe, the Native Commissioner for Belingwe who, in March 1907, was charged with forced labour and flogging, resorted to the *sjambok*, so he told the department, because his office carried no authority.[21] In fact, his superiors praised him for having imposed his will on the local community even as they censured him for using 'unsound methods', the very criticism made by the colleagues of Joseph Conrad's Captain Kurtz.[22] It was the weakness of the state that, according to de Laessoe, made him take matters into his own hands. The same justification was used repeatedly in cases of culpable homicide including Laidlaw and Battlefields. The verdicts in those trials, like the crimes themselves, were a form of revenge against a work-force impervious to legislative control and imperial authorities that refused to discipline labour, but behind Laidlaw and Battlefields lay a paradox: employers wanted the state to provide the land, workers, and subsidies which were necessary for their economic success but in their treatment of workers they did not want to be subject to state regulation.

Assaults upon workers had their own political economy. Small farmers like Laidlaw had to compete against indigenous producers who were more competent in growing crops and managing cattle. They also had to compete against the gold mines for a limited pool of labour upon which they were dependent. Unstable markets, droughts, and cattle disease increased the woes of white farmers and their families. Many of them failed and those

[19] See 'The Native Punishment Commission, October 1921', chaired by Justice J. W. Barth, Kenya National Archives (hereafter KNA), AG5/240.

[20] J. J. Taylor, 'The Emergence and Development of the Native Department in Southern Rhodesia, 1894–1914', unpublished Ph.D. dissertation, University of London, 1974, p. 173.

[21] See evidence of the Belingwe enquiry heard at Bulawayo before Justice Vintcent in 'Report of the Belingwe Enquiry', Correspondence, Resident Commissioner, ZNA, RC 3/4/1.

[22] 'Report of the Belingwe Enquiry', Correspondence, Resident Commissioner, ZNA, RC 3/4/1.

who did succeed only managed to scrape a meagre living. The situation in the mining sector was little better. Before the First World War, mining was dominated by numerous small companies, many of which lacked expertise and capital. To turn a profit, employers sought to reduce the cost of labour by lowering wages and skimping on occupational health and safety measures. As a result, Southern Rhodesian mines were probably more dangerous than those in South Africa with overwork, meagre rations, and crowded compounds producing the pneumonia and scurvy which between 1900 and 1933 cost over 30,000 miners their lives.[23] Managers were responsible for small and isolated communities and they needed to assert their authority over a male labour force that often engaged in theft or damaged plant in retaliation for beatings and low wages. In theory, mine compounds were subject to state inspection, but in 1912 there were only seven inspectors to regulate the entire industry. By 1924, there were three.[24] Compound inspectors, Native Commissioners, and police were willing to leave the matter of discipline to managers, thereby sanctioning the kinds of violence used at Battlefields. Farms were not inspected which meant that employers like Laidlaw had even greater opportunity to beat workers. Mines were largely a male universe characterized by migrant labour, male managers, and a male state inspectorate. Farms were rather different, and white women on farms were more likely to be aware of or participate in systemic violence.

Another factor encouraging such crimes was the expectations that white males brought with them to the colony. Settlers were anxious to advance their social and economic status, which for men included earning sufficient to support their children and a dependent wife. All too often their ambitions were frustrated. From 1901 to 1911, the white population of Southern Rhodesia doubled but white men outnumbered white women by more than two to one. That imbalance was particularly obvious in the age range from twenty-four to forty-four years, and competition among men for female partners was intense.[25] Wages and salaries were as much as 50 percent higher than in Durban, but the price of basic commodities was such that only those in senior positions could afford to support a family.[26] It was difficult for most

[23] van Onselen, *Chibaro*, p. 62.

[24] M. C. Steele, 'The Foundations of a Native Policy: Southern Rhodesia, 1923–1933', unpublished Ph.D. dissertation, Simon Fraser University, 1972, p. 283.

[25] See 'Census of Europeans 1911', *British South Africa Company Government Gazette* (Salisbury, 1912).

[26] 'Final Report, The Cost of Living Committee, 1913', ZNA, ZAC 4/2/3.

men to escape debt, and illness or the temporary loss of employment could mean financial ruin. Many men chose to have their wives and children remain in South Africa or Britain in the hope of being able to live more cheaply, and by 1911 as many as a third of men in Salisbury and Bulawayo were 'grass widowers'.[27] At the time of Laidlaw and Battlefields many white men were incapable of satisfying one of the most basic of masculine ambitions. In addition to 'sending away', white males faced other possibilities of failure. The most dramatic, which afflicted a small minority, was 'poor whiteism', a kind of social death for men determined to improve their standing. In Kenya it was government policy to deport indigent whites, who were seen as a threat to the prestige of the settler community.[28]

At least three structural features of Southern Rhodesia's economy encouraged assaults on workers, but were such crimes common? The archival record suggests that Laidlaw and Battlefields were part of a system of brutality that, in the period before the Second World War, permeated labour relations in parts of British Africa. Because much of the violence was 'removed behind the scenes of social life' it is difficult to determine the extent of such crimes. Apart from cases that reached court, there were others which failed to pass a magistrate's hearing or that were not pursued by police because of a lack of evidence. Many workers were migrants and even if police were dutiful in gathering evidence they often had difficulty in tracing witnesses. For those reasons the cases tried in the high courts of South Africa, Southern Rhodesia, and Kenya, probably represented only a fraction of such killings. Besides assaults which led to death there were others which did not result in serious injury. There was also the threat of assault to which, presumably, all labour was subject. Historians have conceded that assaults upon workers may have occurred before the 1920s but as colonial states became better established, they ceased.[29] The archival record suggests that such crimes continued unabated into the late 1930s.

Assaults usually took take place at work sites, which determined the ways that knowledge about violence was managed. The Battlefields miners avoided the intimacy of touching Mangesi and Sixpence, and only poorer whites like Laidlaw used their own fists or boots. There were disciplinary

[27] See Tsuneo Yoshikuni, 'Black Migrants in a White City: A Social History of African Harare, 1890–1925', unpublished Ph.D. dissertation, University of Harare, 1989, pp. 19–23.

[28] Dane Kennedy, Islands of White: Settler Society and Culture in Kenya and Southern Rhodesia, 1890–1939 (Durham, NC, 1987), p. 73.

[29] Lewis H. Gann and Peter Duigan, White Settlers in Tropical Africa (Westport, Conn., 1962).

beatings in which a single worker was brought into line, exemplary beatings
carried out as a warning to others, and torture to solicit a confession as with
Battlefields. Some assaults were motivated by revenge and occasionally beatings were carried out with a sexual intensity. There were also assaults
designed to attack imperial authority, or assaults and killings motivated by
career-building as with Ewart Grogan and the Nairobi floggings of 1907 and
Sam Lewis's murder of a newspaper seller in Bulawayo in 1911.[30] However in
most cases in which a white man was accused of maiming or killing a worker
the only witnesses were blacks, and juries were loath to accept their testimony, no matter how compelling. The quality of jurors was often poor and
judges were sometimes incompetent in their interpretation of the law.
Physicians colluded in further undermining the judicial process. In trial
after trial, courts were told by expert witnesses that death had resulted not
from a savage beating but because the deceased had a paper thin skull or a
fragile spleen which ruptured at the slightest blow.[31]

Employers and courts usually agreed that such assaults were of little
importance and historians have tended to treat the crimes as a private matter,
but the crimes were so systemic it was inevitable that they should have
exposed wider tensions between civil societies and states. For that reason
such violence leads to the question of state formations. Colonial states
sought to accumulate resources, and to legitimate their authority. Like all
states they were the bearers of gender relations, and gender dynamics were a
major factor in the construction of colonial economies and the states that
sustained them.[32] Such states were quintessentially masculine enterprises:
their administrations, legal systems, and police forces were staffed exclusively
by men. In education and medical services, women occupied subordinate
roles. Policing was the hard-edge of imperialism and often the most visible
symbol of white rule. Minority regimes, to maintain order and protect
property, relied upon an array of civilian police, armies, District Commissioners, district watchmen, 'boss boys', company security guards, forest
guards, cattle and sheep patrols, and game guards.[33] The most notorious

[30] See Leda Farrant, *The Legendary Grogan: The Only Man to Trek from Cape to Cairo, Kenya's
Controversial Pioneer* (London, 1981), and McCulloch, *Black Peril.*

[31] As a result of malaria, the spleen can swell and distend below the rib cage.

[32] See, for example, R. W. Connell, 'The State, Gender and Sexual Politics', *Theory and Society,*
XIX (1990), pp. 507–44.

[33] For a history of colonial policing, see David M. Anderson and David Killingray, eds.,
Policing the Empire: Government, Authority and Control, 1830–1940 (Manchester, 1991).

arm of the state was the tribal or Native Authority police forces, which almost everywhere had a reputation for brutality. Until the late 1930s most gazetted officers were white and police served the state rather than the communities they sought to control.

Colonial states were highly interventionist and throughout the British Empire they were major agents of capital projects. States also intervened directly in favour of white employers by driving workers on to labour markets. Paradoxically, colonial states left large areas of autonomy to employers. Ruling white minorities wanted to exercise paternal authority over labour while enjoying the benefits of tariffs, subsidies, and marketing boards designed to work in their favour. They wanted the state to provide health care for their families and schools for their children, protect them against competition from indigenous producers, and give them access to cheap and (they hoped) compliant labour. They did not want state-funded education for the subaltern classes nor state regulation of occupational health and safety, two of the hallmarks of modern societies. The colonial administrations in Kenya and Southern Rhodesia in particular had an archaic quality in which personalized forms of authority were combined with the imperatives of higher capitalism.

The age of Empire saw the gradual spread to the metropolitan working classes of what some historians have called the values and institutions of liberal civilization. That may be so, yet colonial regimes were characterized by a lack of civil and political liberties and in particular by labour practices which in Britain had become untenable by the late nineteenth century. The legal framework for the buying and selling of labour in the Empire was provided by Masters and Servants (M&S) ordinances.[34] The key element to those laws (the last of which was enacted in Britain in 1867) was that while employers could be subject to civil action for a breach of contract, workers were subject to penal sanctions. The punishments provided for offenders were a reprimand, a fine, or gaol. By the middle of the nineteenth century, M&S laws were used throughout Britain's Empire and they were particularly important in shaping labour relations in Africa.[35] The M&S ordinances were complemented by pass and locations laws designed to control the movement of labour. As the system grew so did the gulf between legislative purpose and

---

[34] The major work on this subject has been done by Hay and Cravan, 'Master and Servant'.

[35] See David M. Anderson, 'Master and Servant in Colonial Kenya, 1895–1939', *The Journal of African History*, XLI , 13 (2000), pp. 459–85.

what occurred in the labour market. Workers found endless ways of subverting the law by defacing passes, losing them, or sharing them with friends. The ordinances proved a constant irritation for District Commissioners and magistrates whose courts overflowed with offenders. Toward the end of the 1920s, pass violations were the most common criminal offences in South Africa, running at about 40,000 per annum in the Transvaal alone. By the early 1930s, fines for a single offence represented up to three or four months wages for an offender.[36] Prosecutions under the pass laws in Southern Rhodesia usually numbered more than 10,000 per annum and in 1936 there were over 16,000 convictions.[37] It is not surprising that the inability of the state to regulate labour provided fertile ground for the violence of employers.

By the time of its introduction to Africa, the M&S legislation had been rendered obsolete in Britain for a number of reasons including the rise of industrial capital and combination. The Employer's and Workmen Act of 1875 removed the sanctions of the M&S laws and recognized the rights of workers to collective representation. In 1897 the Workmen's Compensation Act gave a part of the British work-force the right to compensation for injury and, although the Act was flawed, by the mid-1930s over 450,000 cases a year were being settled.[38] The use of M&S laws in the Empire was a reversion to a mode of labour relations which best suited the political economies of the colonial world and the racist attitudes of settlers and administrators.

State violence against armed resistance was easy to rationalize, the violence of employers was not. The killing of workers drew attention to the lack of state regulation of farms and mines and clashed with the self-definition of whites in regard to their community's standards of behaviour. They also clashed with the justifications for the Empire itself. British law was central to imperial ideology, and colonial administrations in Nyasaland and Kenya, like those in Australia and New Zealand, claimed that it was the only panacea for the cruelties and injustices of pre-colonial societies.[39] Yet to the administrations of Southern Rhodesia and Kenya the difference between a disciplinary beating imposed by a magistrate and one carried out by a mine manager

[36] Chanock, *Making of the South African Legal Culture*, pp. 422–23.

[37] Letter from A. Lyton, Acting Secretary Department of Justice to Secretary of the Prime Minister, 12/4/1939, Correspondence, Office of the Prime Minister, ZNA, S482/366/39.

[38] For a history of that Act, see Peter Bartrip, 'The Rise and Decline of Workmen's Compensation,' in Paul Weindling, ed., *The Social History of Occupational Health* (London, 1985), pp. 157–77.

[39] See Martin Chanock, *Law, Custom and Social Order: The Colonial Experience in Malawi and Zambia* (Cambridge, 1985).

was trivial. White women were excused from participating in violence against workers and they were probably to some degree shielded from knowledge of such crimes. Rarely were they drawn directly into the process of coercion.

Trials for attacks upon workers that resulted in death were usually stage-managed and it took some unusual element to subvert those conventions. It was rare for a white man to be tried for murder rather than the lesser crime of culpable homicide or manslaughter. It was even rarer for a white woman to face such a charge. On 24 September 1934, Helen Selwyn and five black employees were charged with the murder of Keyen Luyamoion at Mrs Selwyn's farm in Kitale, Kenya. Geoffrey Selwyn, who was charged with his wife, became ill with malaria and died in prison while awaiting trial. The Crown's case was simple. On the morning of 8 June, the Selwyns received news that cow bells had been stolen from their cattle and as a result five or six Suk were apprehended on a neighbouring farm. When the men protested their innocence Mrs Selwyn had them beaten with a whip.[40] According to testimony from Selwyn's employees she directed the beatings with relish and demanded that a heavy, knotted whip be used.[41] The men were placed on the ground and beaten repeatedly to the back of the thighs. Dr Sermukm Singh, the assistant surgeon at Kitale, told the court that Luyamoion had received a very serious beating with a 'dirty weapon' which was certain to cause sepsis, or the death of tissue. Luyamoion died on 25 June from shock and septicaemia. Under cross-examination, Dr Singh admitted that employers frequently beat 'boys' and he had personally treated the results of beatings carried out with sticks, *sjamboks*, and canes.

Helen and Major Geoffrey Selwyn had arrived in Kenya at the end of the First World War, probably under the Oversea Settlement Committee scheme which offered free passage to ex-servicemen and their families. They lived with their two small daughters on a farm outside Kitale in the Rift Valley Province. Major Selwyn had fought in France, and as a result his left hand and leg were paralysed.[42] Consequently the day-to-day running of the farm was left to Helen Selwyn. At the beginning of the Great Depression they borrowed money to keep the farm going on the condition that Mrs Selwyn

---

[40] Transcript of Supreme Court criminal case No. 110 of 1934, Rex versus Helen Eugenie Selwyn and five native accused, 24 Sept. 1934, The Colonial Office, The Selwyn Case, KNA, CO 533/450/8, p. 21.

[41] Transcript of Selwyn, p. 125.

[42] Transcript of Selwyn, p. 162.

legally take over its management. The farm was unprofitable which meant that they could not afford night guards to prevent the constant thefts of maize, and cattle. In the preceding year they had lost six cows. The 1930s was a time of economic stress. There was growing political agitation especially among the Kikuyu. Unemployment, drought, and cattle theft from white farms were also major issues in the district. To allay administrative costs, reductions in the local police force were made in 1933.

Mrs Selwyn's defence was based on three elements. Firstly, that she had no intention of causing serious injury to the deceased, that Luyamoion did not die as a direct result of the beating, and that because of the lack of an effective police presence in the district, Mrs Selwyn was forced to take matters into her own hands. The Selwyns were too poor to provide their own security and the beatings were a desperate attempt by Mrs Selwyn to protect her property.[43] Mrs Selwyn claimed it was an 'only an ordinary beating' and she expressed annoyance that the case had been brought to trial. She also admitted that she had tortured the men to get them to confess. Her personal physician and friend, Dr Harriet Arnell, who appeared as a character witness, told the court: 'These ordinary beatings are given all over the world' (by which presumably she meant the British Empire).[44] The jury found Mrs Selwyn guilty of manslaughter with a recommendation for mercy, and she was sentenced to twelve months gaol. In passing sentence, Justice Webb, a newcomer to Kenya, expressed dismay at Mrs Selwyn's evidence, in which she treated her act as a matter of no consequence. He also observed that he would have imposed a far heavier penalty if a man had committed the offence, a remark contradicted by subsequent cases in which male offenders were given trivial sentences.

The Selwyn trial was unusual in a number of respects.[45] The charge was murder rather than culpable homicide. White males who faced trial for similar offences and were equally unremorseful were never charged with murder. Character witnesses were called for Mrs Selwyn, which was not usually done in such cases because the character of the accused was rarely questioned. At her trial, Mrs Selwyn was portrayed by the prosecution as a Lady Macbeth whose cruelty had caused Luyamoion's death. Men, who had used greater force in committing such crimes, often received a fine or

---

[43] Transcript of Selwyn, pp. 29–31.

[44] Transcript of Selwyn, p. 227.

[45] The case was viewed as so significant it was reported in the British press. See 'Flogging in Kenya', *New Statesman*, 27 Oct. 1934.

suspended sentence. The charge, like the trial and the verdict, is explained not by her crime but by her gender: Mrs Selwyn alienated the jury by managing a farm in place of her disabled husband, and treating workers in the same way as did her white male neighbours. She had in the eyes of the court behaved like a man. In that sense the Selwyn case was more complex than Laidlaw or Battlefields because it identifies a boundary between legitimate and illegitimate violence on the basis of gender.

The Kenyan administration was upset by claims made during Selwyn's trial that beatings were commonplace, and the Governor wrote in protest to the Secretary of State for the Colonies. In the following decade, the Colonial Office reviewed all criminal cases in Kenya in which a white man was charged with the murder or serious assault of a black. Despite concern at the Colonial Office, until the Second World War, such cases continued to come before the courts and the accused (who in most instances were long-term residents of the colony and therefore familiar with the conventions governing work relations) continued to offer the defence that such beatings were normal. In most cases those convicted received a trivial sentence.

During the twentieth century, violence has attracted the attention of social theorists with an interest in subjectivity and forms of power. The sociology of violence is complex and the connection between patterns of internal governance that inform the behaviour of individuals and the pacification of populations has been theorized in the work of Weber, Elias, and Foucault, among others. The central thesis in Norbert Elias's study of European manners is the connection between the growth and extension of state monopolies over the means of violence and the ever tightening self-controls over the passions of ruling classes, the very problem raised by Laidlaw, Battlefields, and Selwyn. 'The peculiar stability of the apparatus of mental self-restraint', Elias writes, 'which emerges as a decisive trait built into the habits of every civilized human being, stands in the closest relationship to the monopolization of physical force and the growing stability of the central organs of society'.[46] According to Elias, where strong centralized states emerged in Western Europe they were usually accompanied by a change in the behaviour of the nobility: the growing complexity, differentiation, and interdependence of social formations led to increased levels in the self-control expected of individuals. The process took place first among the nobility and then spread generationally to the lower strata. Where it was most advanced, self-restraint

---

[46] Norbert Elias, *The Civilizing Process: State Formation and Civilization* (Oxford, 1978), p. 235.

became habitual. The conventions Elias writes about are gendered, and violent behaviour is often sanctioned for men when it is proscribed for women. Unfortunately Elias ignores the use of violence in the imperial world, which is surprising given Germany's imperial history and the fact that in the early 1960s he had lived in Ghana.

The notion of internal governance, be it in the form of civility (Elias), work (Weber), or surveillance (Foucault), has depended upon the existence of bureaucratic states, production for exchange, universal wage labour, and incorporated populations. For Elias and Foucault, obedience involved the establishment of modern forms of subjectivity and the idea of freely rendered rather than forced compliance. While such a process may have occurred in Western Europe, it was foreign to the imperial world where the disciplines of the market-place and the authority of states was so ineffectual. Within the Empire there was no great confinement, and no widening of civil liberties to the subaltern classes. The fragility of the system is shown by the number of prosecutions under the pass and M&S laws and the attacks upon workers. Those crimes sometimes brought settlers into conflict with the imperial centre and raised the question of how white communities viewed their own behaviour. Civility was problematic for settlers in Southern Rhodesia, South Africa, and Kenya, many of whom felt some discomfort about their status. The numbers of servants in white households was a measure of settlers' preoccupation with civility. There was great emphasis upon prestige in communities in which many white families were barely middle class. Whites were expected to control their violent and sexual impulses as a means of maintaining racial and social boundaries. The models of the state used by Elias may not fit colonialism, but the ruling élites of the British Empire were habituated to the conventions about which he wrote.

The Laidlaw, Battlefields, and Selwyn crimes fell under the shadow of the M&S laws and all arose, according to the defendants, because of the intractability of labour and the failure of the state to discipline workers. The miners of Battlefields, like Laidlaw and Mrs Selwyn, rejected the right of courts to interfere in the management of the work-place. They wanted the state to drive workers on to the market, but from that point on demanded that labour relations on mines and farms be a private matter outside of the state's jurisdiction. Rhodesian courts treated Laidlaw and Battlefields as analogous to domestic violence, and in so doing they drew upon the models of patriarchal authority that underlay the M&S legislation. Those laws encouraged the use of violence by rendering it largely invisible. Those conventions

EMPIRE AND VIOLENCE, 1900–1939   237

could be subverted by special circumstances: Mrs Selwyn, for example, lost the protection of the law because of her gender. Over time the violence of employers was diluted by an expanding state which, after 1945, began to regulate the workplace far more effectively.

The Battlefields and Selwyn cases occurred in different colonies, in different periods, and fell into quite distinct political contexts. Kenya and Southern Rhodesia differed in terms of their economies, the social backgrounds of settlers, and their legal systems. Even so, the cases reveal similarities in the management of labour and the state's attitude to settler violence. In cases where there was a successful prosecution the defendants were usually unrepresented, suggesting that the men who ended up in court were poor. It also suggests that defendants did not take such charges seriously and expected support from a jury of their peers.

How did settlers reconcile their use of violence with their yearning for civility? These were not reconcilable in practice; but the question of legitimizing authority did attract the attention of white intellectuals. N. H. Wilson was a leading Rhodesian who helped found the White Rhodesia Association and contributed to debates about labour policy and segregation. Like many of his contemporaries, Wilson distrusted the social and economic changes which swept Britain after the First World War, and during the 1920s he developed a vision of social order which was to be achieved through bonds of dependence linking labour to capital.[47] In a series of articles, Wilson presents an imaginary social system in which the authority of a ruling white minority was to be based on the deference, and in the end the gratitude, not of a working class but of serfs. The design of that imaginary world, drawn from the medieval English village, neatly excised the need for violence by substituting in its place a shared understanding of subordination and superiority. The authority of white males over households was to be extended to labour while selective elements of the modern state were to be preserved for the advantage of employers. What Wilson presented in effect was an early version of apartheid.[48] Like other white intellectuals, he wanted a labour system without a proletariat.

[47] See N. H. Wilson 'The Development of Native Reserves', *Native Affairs Department Annual*, I (1923), pp. 86–93; also Wilson, 'Twin Pyramids Policy', *Rhodesian Herald*, 7 June 1929.

[48] For discussion of such anti-modern, anti-rationalist, and anti-bourgeois ideologies, see J. Barrington Moore, *Social Origins of Dictatorship and Democracy: Lord and Peasant in the Making of the Modern World* (Boston, 1967), pp. 491–96, on 'Catonism'; and E. J. Hobsbawm, *The Age of Extremes*, pp. 113–14; on 'organic statism', see also Berman and Lonsdale, *Unhappy Valley: Book Two* (London, 1992), pp. 234–38.

N. H. Wilson wished for a world resembling the patriarchalist social orders of early modern Europe, where masters held economic, judicial, and political authority over the wife, children, and workers attached to their household. They also held the right to use violence in enforcing their will. As feminists have long pointed out, the historical pacification of Western states stopped at the household door and in twentieth-century Britain for example, many forms of domestic violence remained legitimate at law. In Europe's colonial empires the racialized boundaries between public and private, civility and politics, legitimate and illegitimate violence were fiercely contested. Indigenous communities have their own histories of violence resulting from disruption and expropriation by white colonists, not just in wars but in messy, everyday contestation over land, labour, and resources. Relations between colonists and their largely male workforces remained the site of intense conflict. In Western historiography such violence has until recently been veiled behind the fiction that household authority, including that exercised over black servants, lay outside politics.

Select Bibliography

DAVID M. ANDERSON and DAVID KILLINGRAY, eds., *Policing the Empire: Government, Authority and Control, 1830–1940* (Manchester, 1991).

HANNAH ARENDT, *On Violence* (London, 1970).

BRUCE BERMAN and JOHN LONSDALE, *Unhappy Valley: Conflict in Kenya and Africa: 2 vols., Book One: State and Class* (London, 1992).

MARTIN CHANOCK, *The Making of the South African Legal Culture, 1902–1936: Fear, Favour and Prejudice* (Cambridge, 2001).

JAAP DE MOOR and H. L. WESSELING, eds., *Imperialism and War: Essays on Colonial Wars in Asia and Africa* (Leiden, 1989).

NORBERT ELIAS, *The Civilizing Process: State Formation and Civilization* (Oxford, 1978).

JONATHAN FLETCHER, *Violence and Civilization: An Introduction to the Work of Norbert Elias* (Cambridge, 1997).

E. J. HOBSBAWM, *The Age of Extremes: A History of the World, 1914–1991* (New York, 1994).

ALISTAIR HORNE, *A Savage War of Peace: Algeria 1954–1962* (New York, 1977).

DANE KENNEDY, *Islands of White: Settler Society and Culture in Kenya and Southern Rhodesia, 1890–1939* (Durham, NC, 1987).

SHULA MARKS, *Reluctant Rebellion: The 1906–8 Disturbances in Natal* (Oxford, 1970).

PAVLA MILLER, *Transformations of Patriarchy in the West, 1500–1900* (Bloomington, Ind., 1998).

IAN PHIMISTER, *An Economic and Social History of Zimbabwe, 1890–1948. Capital Accumulation and Class Struggle* (London, 1988).

CHARLES VAN ONSELEN, *Chibaro: African Mine Labour in Southern Rhodesia* (Johannesburg, 1980).

11

Childhood and Race: Growing Up in the Empire

FIONA PAISLEY

In the 1930s the Chief Protector of the Aborigines in Western Australia, A. O. Neville, began setting up a Scout and Guide troop at the Moore River Aboriginal Settlement.[1] One of several such troops operating on settlements and missions for Aborigines during these years, Australian Aboriginal children joined thousands of others, the sons and daughters of Empire who gathered periodically to salute the British flag and pay allegiance to the English Crown. Their activities consolidated new codes of manliness and womanliness spreading rapidly among not only white, but also native children in the emerging British Commonwealth.[2] This chapter considers some of the implications of this indigenous involvement in the trans-imperial child movement, and the contribution of both to our understanding of histories of gender and race in settler colonies in the early twentieth century.

As recent scholarship on gender and empire has shown, histories of childhood have been closely interconnected within imperial and colonial race politics. The dual interests of these politics were governing native races and improving the white race, both to be achieved through a focus on the rising generation. These interests merged in the case of indigenous or 'native' children, and saw governments focus increasingly on the management of childhood as a method of managing race. Where the infantilizing of native races had long been foundational to imperial race ideology, turn-of-the-century social and racial sciences found in the advancement of the individual from childhood to adulthood an evolutionary trajectory

---

[1] 'Moore River Native Settlement: Scout Troop Formation of', 1930. Perth, State Records Office of Western Australia, Box 16, AN 1/7, Acc. 933.

[2] Rosalind O'Hanlon, 'Gender in the British Empire', in Judith Brown and Wm. Roger Louis, eds., *Oxford History of the British Empire: IV The Twentieth Century* (Oxford, 1999), p. 392; and John M. Mackenzie, 'The Popular Culture of Empire in Britain', in ibid., pp. 212–31.

mirroring that of the human race progressing from its primitive origins towards civilization.[3]

In settler colonies such as Australia, taking children from their parents and communities quickly became a routine aspect of frontier life soon to be incorporated into government policy, though it is impossible to estimate the numbers of native children taken by Crown and settler colonialists as servants or indentured labourers. While Christianity had a lengthy associ-ation with the imperial civilizing project,[4] it was at the beginning of the twentieth century that the Dominion (settler colonial) states sought to replace the missionary emphasis on spiritual salvation with racial sciences of mind and body. The emerging child-subject of racially-oriented 'welfare' policies was emblematic of this change in focus.[5] By the early twentieth century, removal for employment was considered imperative to the 'civiliz-ing' of mixed-descent children and a natural responsibility of incipient welfare states. Thus children incarcerated at Moore River in Western Austra-lia in the 1930s were considered by authorities to have been saved from the damaging impact of their maternal culture and uplifted through training as domestic servants or as station hands and farm labourers.

Scientific concerns with the quality of the child for the future of the race extended beyond the management of indigenous populations to encompass white children. Following the Boer War and again after the First World War, secular authorities throughout the Empire were alarmed by low birth rates and the poor fitness of white youth. While commentators declared it was women's duty to reproduce for the nation, childhood became the primary project of middle-class social reformers aiming to promote the re-invigoration of the imperial and colonial nation.[6] This maternal project

---

[3] Anne McClintock, *Imperial Leather: Race, Gender and Sexuality in Colonial Context* (London, 1995), p. 51; Ann Laura Stoler, *Race and the Education of Desire: Foucault's History of Sexuality and the Colonial Order of Things* (Durham, NC, 1995), p. 141; Stephen Jay Gould, *Ontogeny and Phylogeny* (Cambridge, Mass., 1977).

[4] See chaps. by Patricia Grimshaw and by Catherine Hall.

[5] Russell McGregor, ' "Breed Out the Colour": Reproductive Management for White Austra-lia', *Proceedings of the History and Sociology of Eugenics Conference, University of Newcastle, 27–28 April, 2000* (Newcastle, 2000), pp. 61–70; Robert Van Krieken, *Children and the State: Social Control and the Formation of the Australian Welfare State* (Sydney, 1991); Warwick Anderson, *The Cultivation of Whiteness: Science, Health and Racial Destiny in Australia* (Melbourne, 2002), pp. 206–15; and Tony Austin, *Never Trust a Government Man: Northern Territory Aboriginal Policy 1911–1939* (Darwin, 1997), pp. 18–23.

[6] Anna Davin, 'Imperialism and Motherhood', *History Workshop*, V (1978), pp. 9–57; Seth Koven and Sonya Michel, eds., *Mothers of a New World: Maternalist Politics and the Origins of*

extended across racial as well as class lines: as mothers and civilizers of children generally, middle-class white women were enjoined to bring civilization also to the child-like lesser races.[7] From the nineteenth century, numbers of their political and philanthropic organizations in Britain and in the colonies mobilized this project as a moral duty signalling women's imperial citizenship.[8] They involved themselves in saving poor white children from city slums, or in calling for native and indigenous children to be protected from 'slavery', indenture or child betrothal, traditions that marked indigenous cultures as not only primitive but also degenerate.[9] Through various philanthropic schemes, hundreds of thousands of British working-class children were sent to the colonies, mostly to Canada from 1870 to 1925, and then to Australia, to build imperial economies and to settle and populate 'empty' lands. Many of these children were removed from their parents supposedly for their own good; sentiments and actions echoing the removal of indigenous children, especially those of mixed descent, in settler colonies such as Australia and Canada.[10]

In the years following the First World War, concern for the virility of 'the race' tightened links between the mother country and the Dominions. The imperial child-race project was of great importance to the settler colonies.[11] Immigration policies sought to exclude non-white migrants while internal

---

Welfare States (New York, 1993); Kalpana Ram and Margaret Jolly, eds., *Maternities and Modernities: Colonial and Postcolonial Experiences in Asia and the Pacific* (Cambridge, 1998); and Philippa Mein Smith, *Mothers and King Baby: Infant Survival and Welfare in an Imperial World: Australia 1880–1950* (Basingstoke, 1997).

[7] Margaret Jolly, ' "To Save the Girls for Brighter and Better Lives": Presbyterian Missions and Women from the South of Vanuatu 1848–1870', *Journal of Pacific History*, CXXVI, 1 (1991), pp. 27–48; Carol Devens, ' "If We Get the Girls, We Get the Race": Missionary Education of Native American Girls', *Journal of World History*, III, 2 (1992), pp. 219–37; Susan Pedersen, 'The Maternalist Moment in British Colonial Policy: The Controversy over "Child-Slavery" in Hong Kong 1917–1941', *Past and Present*, CLXXI (2001), pp. 161–71; and Pamela Scully, 'White Maternity and Black Infancy: The Rhetoric of Race in the South African Women's Suffrage Movement, 1895–1930', in Ian Christopher Fletcher and others, eds., *Women's Suffrage in the British Empire: Citizen, Nation, and Race* (London, 2000), pp. 68–84.

[8] Antoinette Burton, *Burdens of History: British Feminists, Indian Women, and Imperial Culture, 1865–1915* (London, 1994); Laura E. Nym Mayhall and others, 'Introduction', in Fletcher and others, eds., *Women's Suffrage in the British Empire*, p. xvi; Kumari Jayawardena, *The White Woman's Other Burden: Western Women and South Asia During British Rule* (New York, 1999).

[9] O'Hanlon, 'Gender in the British Empire', p. 390.

[10] Philip Bean and Joy Melville, *Lost Children of the Empire: The Untold Story of Britain's Child Migrants* (London, 1989), chap. 4.

[11] Martin Kitchen, *The British Empire and Commonwealth* (New York, 1996), pp. 77–78.

race policies limited the rights of indigenous aboriginal populations.[12] Under 'White Australia' following federation in 1901, for example, Aboriginal people were constituted as aliens along with 'Asians' and 'Pacific Islanders'. Ensuing state-based legislation in Australia variously aimed at the segregation of 'full-bloods' and the absorption of those of mixed descent.[13] Middle-class settler women were among an emerging 'expert' class of educators, psychologists, and anthropologists in Australia interested in child life in these years. They were among the administrators of the institutionalization of Aboriginal children. Ironically, many also employed, although without wages, native servants, often girls and young women, to work in their homes.[14]

Somewhat less virulently, white children were also targeted by burgeoning welfare states intent on race and social hygiene in the 1920s and 1930s, and middle-class children in particular were exhorted to make of themselves the citizens of tomorrow.[15] Eugenic discourse represented their 'growing up' as a difficult process with long-term significance for the race. According to child research, white children inherited savagery from their savage past, a past living on in the present through 'lesser' races such as the Australian Aborigines. The American child-study theorist G. Stanley Hall explained in 1904 that aggressiveness among boys was the natural outcome of human evolution and should not be repressed, nor should girls' instinctive motherliness.

---

[12] James Bennett, 'Maori as Honorary Members of the White Tribe', *Journal of Imperial and Commonwealth History*, XXIX, 3 (2001), pp. 33–54; W. Peter Ward, *White Canada Forever: Popular Attitudes Toward Orientals in British Columbia* (Montreal, 2nd edn., 1990); Ann Curthoys, 'Expulsion, Exodus and Exile in White Australian Historical Mythology', *Imaginary Homelands: Special Issue of Journal of Australian Studies*, LXI, (1999), pp. 1–18; Andrew Armitage, *Comparing the Policy of Aboriginal Assimilation: Australia, Canada, and New Zealand* (Vancouver, 1995); Klaus Neumann and others, eds., *Quicksands: Foundational Histories in Australia and Aotearoa New Zealand* (Sydney, 1999).

[13] Andrew Markus, *Australian Race Relations, 1788–1993* (Sydney, 1994).

[14] Jackie Huggins. ' "Firing on in the Mind": Aboriginal Women Domestic Servants in the Inter-War Years', *Hecate*, XIII, 2, (1987/8), pp. 5–23.

[15] Stephen Garton, 'Sir Charles Mackellar: Psychiatry, Eugenics, and Child Welfare in New South Wales, 1900–1914', *Australian Historical Studies* (hereafter *AHS*), XXII, 86 (1986), pp. 21–34; Garton, 'Sound Minds and Healthy Bodies: Re-Considering Eugenics in Australia, 1914–1940', *AHS*, CIII (1994), pp. 163–81. Graeme Davison, 'The City-Bred Child and Urban Reform in Melbourne 1900–1940' in Peter Williams, ed., *Social Process and the City* (Sydney, 1983), pp. 143–74; David Walker, 'Continence for a Nation: Seminal Loss and National Vigour', *Labour History*, XLVIII, (1985), pp. 1–14; Ann Curthoys, 'Eugenics, Feminism and Birth Control: The Case of Marion Piddington', *Hecate*, XV, 1 (1989), pp. 73–89.

Each was a necessary component in the development of eugenic women and men.[16]

Clubs were ideal locations for the production of eugenic child and youth subjects. Here compliance with gender and group hierarchy, and a culture of monitoring (including self-monitoring), reinforced the moral codes of racial and social hygiene. Like other girls' organizations within the Empire, middle-class standards of femininity and self-control were extolled in Australia in the 1920s through the Hearthfire Girls (a 1913 offshoot of the Campfire Girls in the United States) where girls and young women learned 'helpfulness', 'home-making', and 'happiness'.[17] Boys in the Wolf Cubs vowed that 'The cub gives in to the old wolf. The cub does not give in to himself.'[18] And the Young Men's Christian Association's 'Equilateral Man' was to civilize himself through a balanced programme of spiritual, intellectual, and physical development.[19]

Through such moral education, white imperial and settler colonial children learned responsibility for their race. Girls and young women in particular were enjoined to keep themselves in good health, and to learn domestic science because 'the health of the nation depends mainly on the women of the nation... [and] the girls of to-day are the women of to-morrow.'[20] According to the Racial Hygiene Association of New South Wales in Australia, supporters of controversial sex education, the health of the nation meant producing White Australia, 'not merely white in skin but white at heart'.[21] The informed girl and young woman could save herself from immorality and direct her reproductive capacity towards producing fit children for the nation.[22] Young indigenous women and men necessarily

[16] Gail Bederman, *Manliness and Civilization: A Cultural History of Gender and Race in the United States, 1880–1917* (Chicago, 1995), chap. 3. For Hall's influence in Australia, see Van Krieken, *Children and the State*, p. 122.

[17] Young Women's Christian Association Papers, Melbourne University Archives: Series 17, Box 6, Newscuttings, 1919–1925.

[18] 'The Cub Book for Australian Cubs', Boy Scouts Association, Sydney, 1935, Sydney, Mitchell Library: Pamphlet File 369.42 B.

[19] 'The Equilateral Man', Young Men's Christian Association, Sydney, *c.* 1930, Mitchell Library, Pamphlet File 369.42 Y.

[20] Education Department of New South Wales, *What Every Girl Should Know* (Sydney, *c.* 1930), n.p. On domestic science education, see, for example, Grant Rodwell, 'Domestic Science, Race Motherhood and Eugenics in Australian State Schools, 1900–1960', *History of Education Review*, XXIC, 2 (2000), pp. 67–83.

[21] 'Wanted—A Real White Australia', *Sunday Times*, 26 June 1927, Sydney, Mitchell Library, Racial Hygiene Association Papers, MS 3838.

[22] Clare Goslett, *Things We Must Tell Our Girls* (Melbourne, *c.* 1930), p. 28, Mitchell Library, Pamphlet File, 369.43 B.

figured within this rhetoric as dysgenic subjects. According to *The Child and Sex*, working-class city children might be susceptible to abnormality through sleeping in their parents' bedrooms, but country children who saw nature at close quarters were 'a step nearer to "savage" children...'.[23] While knowledge of racial and social hygiene was to protect the future of the white race, precocious sexual development, juvenile delinquency, and criminality were coded as dark and primitive.

One of the most successful of eugenic child movements in these years, the Scouts, began as a white middle-class organization founded to re-invigorate the manliness and virility of modern life. Boer War hero Robert Baden-Powell founded the Scouts in 1907 so that young men might put military and colonial frontier discipline to work in suburban peacetime.[24] In Melbourne on his second world tour in 1931, Baden-Powell advised: 'Scouting is in one sense a game—but a game with a deeper purpose'.[25] 'Being prepared' through organized play and physical training was to provide white boys and young men with the leadership qualities they would require in imperial national life.[26] In contrast, girls joined Baden-Powell's world community only after a shaky start. For one thing, Stanley Hall doubted whether girls ever attained the full adjustment into adult life that imperial citizenship required.[27] For another, the protection of manliness from the emasculating influences of domesticity was crucial to Baden-Powell's vision. Imagine his dismay when a troop of Girl Scouts, dressed in khaki, appeared among the boys at an international mass inspection held in London soon after the inception of the movement.[28] According to Guiding legend, he ordered the troop from the field.

[23] Lotte Fink, *The Child and Sex* (Sydney, 1945), p. 9.

[24] Allen Warren, 'Popular Manliness: Baden-Powell, Scouting, and the Development of Manly Character', in J. A. Mangan and James Walvin, eds., *Manliness and Morality: Middle-Class Masculinity in Britain and America 1800–1940* (Manchester, 1987), pp. 199–216; and on the Australian Boy Scout movement, see Martin Crotty, *Making the Australian Male: Middle Class Masculinity 1870–1920* (Melbourne, 2001), chap. 7.

[25] Gwendoline Hamer Swinburne, *Among the First People: the Baden-Powell Girl Guide Movement in Australia, 1908–1936* (Sydney, 1978), p. 68. On the importance of playing the game, see J. A. Mangan, *The Games Ethic and Imperialism: Aspects of the Diffusion of an Ideal* (New York, 1985).

[26] Robert H. MacDonald, *Sons of the Empire: the Frontier and the Boy Scout Movement, 1890–1918* (Toronto, 1993).

[27] Carol Dyhouse, *Girls Growing up in Late Victorian and Edwardian England* (London, 1981), p. 118.

[28] Australian Girl Guide Movement, *Official Souvenir Programme of the Visit to Sydney of Lord and Lady Baden-Powell, 17th to 24th March, 1931* (Sydney, 1931), p. 26.

Comparatively little attention has been paid to white girlhood and Guiding, yet the rapid growth of Guides and Brownies around the world points to a fascinating history of womanliness and civilization. Evidence of the early influence of race politics and Dominion girlhood in this history comes from New Zealand, where a Girl Peace Scouts movement was first formed in 1908 by Mrs Selina Cossgrove and her lieutenant-colonel husband who drew on 'Maori legends' for inspiration, and attracted not only white but considerable numbers of Maori girls.[29] Peace Scouting provided character-training as well as education in citizenship, while encouraging 'the youngest child in that maternal instinct, which modern society does so much to repress'.[30] Baden-Powell's girl movement largely absorbed this network in 1910 when he founded the Girl Guides. True to his imperial military theme, Baden-Powell named his girls the Guides after an Indian regiment he had trained in scouting during the Boer War.[31]

Public concerns about the spectacle of girls in military-style regiments were answered by asserting the womanly nature of Guiding.[32] Baden-Powell's sister, Agnes, claimed that the intention of the movement was to 'avoid the imitating of boys' manner and dress. We are anxious to make it a purely womanly movement ... [and] to instil into every girl ... the idea of self-improvement.'[33] In 1916, the Western Australian journal, *Western Women*, reported that local 'young womanhood' in the Girl Guides was being educated 'towards mental, moral and physical perfection ... [to] be strong worthy mothers of the unborn generation, as well as ... comrades and helpmates for their menfolk'.[34] By the 1920s, Baden-Powell's wife had assumed headship of the girl's movement, while the innately 'charming' and 'thoughtful' Princess Mary became its first royal patron.[35]

Following the First World War, the Guide and Scout movement quickly spread across the emerging British Commonwealth, claiming itself to be an international peace organization despite its military culture. The

---

[29] Lieutenant-Colonel and Mrs Cossgrove, 'The Girl Peace Scouts, 1908–1924,' Sydney. Mitchell Library: Girl Guides Association Papers, MS 88-130-01-16; Lieutenant-Colonel Cossgrove, *Nga Toro Turehu: The Fairy Scouts of New Zealand* (Wellington, 1918).

[30] Lieutenant-Col. Cossgrove, *Dominion Girl Peace Scout Association* (n.p., 1919), p. 7.

[31] MacDonald, *Sons of Empire*, p. 72.

[32] Dyhouse, *Girls Growing Up*, pp. 105–38.

[33] Agnes Baden-Powell, *How Girls Can Help Build Up the Empire* (London, 1912), quoted in Swinburne, *Among the First People*, p. 31.

[34] 'The Collie Girl Guides', *Western Women*, Jan. 1916, p. 3.

[35] 'A Message to Dominion Guides', *The Dominion Girl Guide*, I, 1 (1 Aug. 1924), p. 1.

combination was clearly attractive to many. By 1928, twenty-eight countries had joined a World Association of Scouts and Guides to promote cultural diversity, 'world co-operation', and 'harmony'. According to World Peace Scouting's internationalist egalitarianism, any boy could improve himself, regardless of creed or class, but hierarchies clearly operated within its fellowship. White children were to learn benevolence towards the 'lesser' races in their world community. In the late 1930s, for example, the Young Women's and Young Men's Christian Associations' 'Citizens Movement World Fellowship Week' studied 'how India became part of the British Empire', 'Abolition and the Negro in America', and 'the Red Indians of Canada'.[36] Such international young people's movements thus upheld Empire's claims to be inclusive while reiterating the ascendancy of 'civilization' over 'savagery'. In local context, Scouts and Guides' 'internationalism' reflected the significance of imperial legacies. In South Africa, the Baden-Powells hoped to placate white membership by rejecting frequent requests from African, Indian, and Cape Coloured troops for official affiliation. Meanwhile, in India, theosophist Annie Besant had to fight for Indian Boy Scouts, eventually leading the movement herself, though rejecting the Girl Guides as insufficiently feminine for Indian girlhood.[37]

None the less, non-white membership, whether recognized officially or not, was considerable in the world community of the Scouts and Guides. Begrudgingly, it would seem, by 1909 the movement could boast 'native' or indigenous troops in India, Canada, Australia, South Africa, New Zealand, Malaya, and Jamaica, and beyond the Empire in Chile, Argentina, Brazil, as well as among native North Americans.[38] According to the Pan-Pacific Union magazine, *The Mid-Pacific*, the Scouts offered 'a new idea in the form of discipline for young boys' of the many races in the region, and even existed in Siam (Thailand) where 'Boy Scouting is under royal protection.'[39] And although Baden-Powell continued to dissociate himself from native troops in South Africa where the indigenous population was in the

[36] 'Projects for World Fellowship Week', *The New Zealand Girl*, (1 Nov. 1938), p. 6.

[37] Tammy Proctor, ' "A Separate Path": Scouting and Guiding in Interwar South Africa', *Comparative Studies in Society and History*, XLII, 1 (2000), pp. 613; 614.

[38] Swinburne, *Among the First People*, p. 1. For an account of the subversion of Scout codes by institutionalized Native American children, see K. Tsianina Lomawaima, *They Called it Prairie Light: The Story of Chilocco Indian School* (Lincoln, Nebr., 1994), pp. 142–44.

[39] *Mid-Pacific*, XXXIX, 5 (1930), p. 564.

majority, by the 1930s he was eager to celebrate diversity in Australasia. During his 1931 visit, he celebrated the uplift of indigenous troops through his world community. 'It was particularly gratifying,' he remarked, that 'scouting has been taken up successfully and with good results among the natives.'[40]

These contrasting representations of indigenous troops (tolerance in separate organizations in South Africa, some inclusion in Canada, and promotion in New Zealand and—as we will see—belatedly so, in Australia) warrants further investigation. Different histories of early settlement and contact, and their reflection in diverse racial policies, provide some explanation, but so do early twentieth-century 'progressive' welfare policies: just as Dominion policies towards indigenous children varied considerably, so did the whiteness each sought to protect. The Maori of New Zealand have frequently been described as the least discriminated against among indigenous peoples in the British Empire, particularly in comparison with their nearest neighbours, the Aborigines of Australia. Certainly New Zealand did not pursue explicit policies of removal as in Australia.

In terms of childhood management, however, parallels can be drawn between New Zealand and Australia as well as South Africa and Canada. In each case, scientific as well as popular opinion widely pronounced the potential of indigenous children to be limited by racial difference.[41] They were separated systematically from white children in native schools and settlements in Canada and Australia, to a lesser extent in New Zealand, as well as informally from mixed state schools through white parents' objections. Segregation in South Africa was more complex, aiming to Anglicize Afrikaner children and to segregate them from African, Indian, and Coloured children, and was a cornerstone of the apartheid movement.[42] Implicit racial assumptions applied in non-segregationist policies as well, most obviously in compulsory education Acts instituted by settler colonies in the late nineteenth century. These worked to erase indigenous culture and

[40] 'Report of the Tour of Inspection of Boy Scouts and Girl Guides in New Zealand and Australia', p. 7, Mitchell Library: Girl Guide Papers, MS 88–130-3/1 (1).

[41] Bennett, 'The Maori as Honorary'. See also Andrew Sharp and Paul McHugh, *Histories of Power and Loss: Uses of the Past—A New Zealand Commentary* (Wellington, 2001).

[42] Nadine E. Dolby, *Constructing Race: Youth, Identity, and Popular Culture in South Africa* (Albany, 2001), chap. 2; David Welsh, 'Education and the Industrial Revolution', in Monica Wilson and Leonard Thompson, eds., *The Oxford History of South Africa* (London, 1971), pp. 221–26.

language (and therefore identity) through teaching English and the history of colonization as a matter of evolutionary progress.[43]

The following section considers inter-war debates about race and educational policy as applied to mixed-descent indigenous children in Australia through a closer inspection of the Western Australian case that began this chapter. It then returns to the question of indigenous troops and their relationship to imperial childhood.

In Western Australia, with one of the largest and most widely dispersed of Aboriginal populations in Australia, Chief Protector A. O. Neville began carrying out his plans for 'biological absorption' through government settlements. From the late nineteenth century, various states and federal territory governments in Australia had aimed to reduce 'half-caste' populations through the segregation of Aborigines of full descent, and the removal and eventual 'merging' of those of mixed descent.[44] By the inter-war years, these policies had been shown to be ineffectual as mixed-descent communities increased in size and number. Henceforth, their children were to be assimilated and wherever possible their institutional life was to make them white. Scouts and Guides would play a key role in this policy. Moore River remains

[43] See, for example, Colin McGeorge, 'What was "Our Nation's Story"? New Zealand Primary School History Textbooks Between the Wars', *History of Education Review*, XXVIII, 2 (1999), pp. 46–59; Clare Bradford, *Reading Race: Aboriginality in Australian Children's Literature* (Melbourne, 2001), chap. 1; Stephen Heathorn, *For Home, Country, and Race: Constructing Gender, Class, and Englishness in the Elementary School, 1880–1914* (Toronto, 1999); J. A. Mangan, *The Imperial Curriculum: Racial Images and Education in the British Colonial Experience* (London, 1993). For a comparison of indigenous conditions in New Zealand with those in Canada and Australia, see Patricia Grimshaw and others, 'The Paradox of "Ultra-Democratic" Government: Indigenous Civil Rights in Nineteenth Century New Zealand', in Diane Kirkby and Catharine Coleborne, eds., *Law, History, Colonialism: The Reach of Empire* (Manchester, 2001), pp. 78–90; Donald Denoon and others, eds., *A History of Australia, New Zealand and the Pacific* (Oxford, 2000); Paul Havemann, ed., *Indigenous Peoples' Rights in Australia, Canada, and New Zealand* (Auckland, 1999); and Duncan Ivison and others, eds., *Political Theory and the Rights of Indigenous Peoples* (Cambridge, 2000).

[44] For example, Anna Haebich, *For Their Own Good: Aborigines and Government in the South West of Western Australia 1900–1940* (Nedlands, 1988); Haebich, *Broken Circles: Fragmenting Indigenous Families 1800–2000* (Fremantle, 2000); Thom Blake, *Dumping Ground: A History of the Cherbourg Settlement* (Brisbane, 2000); Jane M. Jacobs and others, ' "Pearls from the Deep": Re-evaluating the Early History of Colebrook Home for Aboriginal Children', in Tony Swain and Deborah Bird Rose, eds., *Aboriginal Australians and Christian Missions: Ethnographic and Historical Studies* (Adelaide, 1988), pp. 140–55; Christine Choo, *Mission Girls: Aboriginal Women on Catholic Missions, in the Kimberley, Western Australia, 1900–1950* (Crawley, 2001); Daisy Ruddick, as told to Kathy Mills and Tony Austin, ' "Talking About Cruel Things": Girls' Life in the Kahlin Compound', *Hecate*, XV, 1 (1989), pp. 8–22.

among the most notorious examples of the institutionalization of
Aborigines, exposing generations of mixed-descent children to an appalling
regime of punishment, surveillance, and neglect. Denied their own language,
family, and community, even those with parents living on the settlement
were segregated in rigidly regimented dormitories under the watchful eyes of
settlement staff. Categorized in terms of colour as well as disposition (amen-
ability to biological assimilation), those defined as more 'white' in both
senses were considered to have greater potential. Boys left the settlement to
become station labourers, while girls provided domestic labour for the
settlement before being sent out to work in white homes.

   Given the perceived urgency of merging the mixed-descent population,
the potential of its children came to occupy officials and experts. Were they
capable of uplift in one generation? Did mixed-descent children inherit the
worst or the best of both races? Such questions were of importance to race
theorists internationally. Answers were to come from experts such as the
Australian educationalist, S. D. Porteus, who had headed the first school for
the feeble-minded in Australia in 1914. Porteus became the Chair in Psychology at the University of Hawaii in the late 1920s largely as a result of his
work on the intelligence of Australian Aborigines. His use of anthropometric
and mental testing in the 1920s and 1930s claimed to reveal that Aboriginal
people, once compared to 'Early Man', should now be understood as akin to
the mentally unfit.[45] His conclusions were 'confirmation' of educational and
vocational policies limiting the futures of indigenous and native children
across the Empire. In South Africa, too, the notion of the backwardness of
the 'child races' that had legitimized settlement and occupation of the
colonies was rearticulated through modern discourses of educational psychology, physical anthropology, and racial hygiene. Each proclaimed the
inferior physical, intellectual, and moral capacities of indigenous and native
children, reconstituting long-standing hierarchies of race progress into racial
hierarchies of child development.[46]

   In 1926, the New South Wales Education Department psychologist Ethel
Stoneman, who had been a student of Porteus, tested eighty-five mixed-
descent children at Moore River. She found none 'bright by white standards'

   [45] David McCallum, The Social Production of Merit: Education, Psychology, and Politics in
Australia, 1900–1950 (London and New York, 1990), p. 20; Russell McGregor, Imagined Destinies:
Aboriginal Australians and the Doomed Race Theory, 1880–1939 (Melbourne, 1997), p. 107;
Anderson, Cultivation, p. 207.
   [46] Dolby, Constructing Race, p. 20.

and concluded that their education should not 'force' them into 'competition with white children in the schools'.[47] Given the dreadful conditions at Moore River, it is painfully ironic that Stoneman should recommend training in basic domestic, health, and hygiene matters, and in 'practical lessons' such as bed-making, cooking, how to use cutlery, personal hygiene, and gardening.[48] Her inclusion of the 'use of knife and fork and spoon' and lessons in the 'disposal of waste' gives a disturbing twist to the various official and autobiographical reports of Moore River in these years. They document conditions of extreme impoverishment and neglect.[49]

Physical maturity and mental development were widely linked by experts such as Ethel Stoneman. Although growing faster than white children in their early years, she found that puberty predicted a sudden downturn in the advancement of the Moore River children.[50] This evidence that racial difference was exacerbated by sexual maturation confirmed new theories about the extended period of growing up among white children. According to Stanley Hall, unlike primitive children, civilized youth passed through 'adolescence' in order to achieve higher order moral and psychosexual development. If properly guided during these years between childhood and adulthood, white middle-class girls and boys would achieve the higher mental capacities of their race. For those children leaving childhood too abruptly, such as the unfit, delinquent, sexually precocious, or indigenous, advancement could only be limited. Hall concluded that the inherent moral and intellectual immaturity of non-white races predicted their permanent 'adolescent' status, thus endorsing white ascendancy and the moral purpose of colonial rule.[51] Nineteenth-century imperial discourses of the civilizing mission became modern pragmatism: young white women and men were to emerge as citizens, while indigenous youth were destined to remain adult-children under their direction.

Mobilizing a modern civilizing mission of his own, Neville argued that removal to institutions such as Moore River was a necessary, humanitarian response to miscegenation. He was, he claimed, 'merely thinking of the

[47] Haebich, For Their Own Good, p. 254.
[48] Susan Maushart, Sort of a Place Like Home: Remembering the Moore River Settlement (Fremantle, 1993), p. 62.
[49] Haebich, For Their Own Good, pp. 210–11.
[50] 'Investigation of Mentality of Half-Caste and Full-Blooded Aboriginal Children', Department of Public Health, State Psychological Clinic Annual Report, Western Australian Votes and Proceedings (Perth, 1929), p. 10.
[51] Bederman, Manliness and Civilization, pp. 110–17.

future life of the child'.[52] Removal would not only save the child, but would solve the 'problem' of a growing 'half-caste' community, an incubus threatening the imperial nation and a danger to itself.[53] Although the suffering of the mother might be evident, removal (particularly of girls) as preparation for their eventual marriage into the white community was essential if the whole race was to advance (that is, to disappear through inter-breeding and cultural identification with whites).[54] Girls were necessarily of particular interest to imperial and colonial authorities concerned in managing the contact between, as well as the internal constitution of, incoming and indigenous settler populations. As key figures in the emergence of racial policy during the late nineteenth and early twentieth centuries, native and indigenous girls in the Empire bore the brunt of the civilizing aims of governments, missionaries, and humanitarian campaigners alike. Through Neville's guidance, Western Australian Aboriginal girls of mixed descent were expected to become young women suitable for marriage to white men living in the isolated northern parts of Australia where white women were scarce. Still, the likelihood of inter-war white Australia accepting such marriages was never put to the test as most applications for marriage between white men and Aboriginal women were rejected.[55]

For officials like Neville, the 'serious game' of Scouting and Guiding complemented assimilation and provided an 'excellent disciplinary effect'.[56] He was supported in these views by contemporary research. In her report on the psychological potential of Moore River children, Stoneman had recommended that the Scouts and Guides would fill their leisure time productively. It was in the sewing room at Moore River that the 'girls' (including older women) made the Scout and Guide uniforms for the troop and received their usual 'payment' of one or two chocolates.[57]

One of Neville's most trenchant critics in these years was humanitarian activist, author, and teacher of the Aborigines, Mary Montgomery Bennett. She aimed not to save the child race of Australia so much as to challenge claims about its degeneration. Bennett had grown up on a Queensland

---

[52] Transcripts of Evidence, Moseley Report, 1934 (hereafter MRTE), p. 120, Perth, State Archives of Western Australia.

[53] A. O. Neville, *Australia's Coloured Minority: Its Place in the Community* (Sydney, 1947).

[54] MRTE, p. 120.

[55] Pat Jacobs, *Mister Neville: A Biography* (Fremantle, 1990), p. 195.

[56] Maushart, *Sort of a Place*, pp. 197; 223.

[57] Haebich, *For Their Own Good*, chap. 6; Maushart, *Sort of a Place*, p. 198.

pastoral property, immortalizing her father's relationship with local Aborigines in her 1927 book, *Christison of Lammermoor*. She followed this in 1930 with *The Australian Aboriginal as a Human Being*, one of the first full-length defences of Australian Aboriginal rights written in the twentieth century. Both were published in London where Bennett spent her early adult life, eventually joining other Anglo-Australian women publicizing the Aboriginal cause through the Dominion women's British Common-wealth League. After her return to Australia in the mid-1930s, she worked as a teacher and an advocate on Kunmunya and then Mt Margaret, both United Aborigines missions in Western Australia.[58]

Opposing removal but not the efficacy of mission life itself, Bennett published an account of her achievements as a classroom teacher at Mt Margaret in 1935. She proclaimed the brightness and intelligence of her pupils, and the excellent results they achieved in state school exams. Refuting poor performance in intelligence tests as evidence of incapacity, Bennett blamed instead sub-standard teaching, limited curricula, the use of pidgin instead of standard English, lack of books at home, and the long-term, inter-generational psychological trauma of removal or its threat. Above all, it was the 'colour bar' of racism that led to failure. The intellectual and emotional capacities of Aboriginal children showed that the Aboriginal race as a whole was quite capable of facilitating its own uplift within one generation.[59] Her claims for the intelligence and brightness of Aboriginal children sought to situate them alongside white Australians, as equally capable of maturity and full stature in adult life.

Rejecting the permanence of Aboriginal immaturity in the logic of empire, Mary Bennett called upon imperial youth to recognize its responsi-bility to speak for indigenous rights. 'I would ask Scouts and Guides to stand up for our oppressed natives—good scouts that they are and past masters at scoutcraft—so that in years to come our own scouts' "corob-beries" may recall, not humiliation, but obligations honoured and restitu-tion made.'[60]

---

[58] Fiona Paisley, ' "Unnecessary Crimes and Tragedies": Race, Gender and Sexuality in Australian Policies of Aboriginal Child Removal', in Antoinette Burton, ed., *Gender, Sexuality and Colonial Modernities* (London, 1999), pp. 134–47.

[59] British Commonwealth League (hereafter BCL), *Report of Conference* (London, 1934), p. 48; Mary Montgomery Bennett, *Teaching the Aborigines: Data from Mt Margaret Mission WA, 1935* (Perth, c. 1935); and R. S. Schenk, *The Educability of the Native* (Perth, c. 1940).

[60] Mary Bennett, *The Australian Aboriginal as a Human Being* (London, 1930), p. 52.

Perhaps it was for similar reasons that a white Girl Guide troop had visited Cootamundra Aboriginal Girls' Home in New South Wales in 1925. Photographs recording the event reveal white girls in broad-brimmed hats and neat uniforms holding hands with a selection of indigenous inmates in sack dresses and cropped hair.[61] It was only from the late 1930s, however, that the international Guide community (and perhaps the Scouts also) began to follow Bennett's lead and to promote the inclusion of indigenous children.[62] Many of those commenting with pleasure on indigenous troops in Australia were eager to record the enthusiasm of indigenous members, and their own concerns to be an inclusive world community. According to *Among the First Peoples*, a history of the world pioneers of the Guide Movement, by the 1920s the 'Gaps in the Map Began to Fill' and 'companies for aboriginal girls were established'.[63] The Australian entry in the 1937 Girl Guide International Exhibition Catalogue announced that: '[a] Guide badge for this subject had been instituted, and . . . several of these aboriginal companies are being run by one of themselves as trained Guiders'.[64] Unlike Bennett, however, these commentators were not inclined to ask more troubling questions about the morality of removal, the funding of institutions, or the likely futures of the Aboriginal Scouts and Guides they so admired.

More detailed reports of native troops, including the memories of participants, survive from two settlements more usually contrasted for their treatment of indigenous children: Kunmunya United Aborigines mission in northern Western Australia, and Moore River itself. Mary Bennett considered Kunmunya to exemplify the potential for progressive work among the Aborigines. In a 1934 address to the British Commonwealth League, she commended the Revd. J. R. Love and his wife for aiming to produce a self-supporting settlement that incorporated aspects of indigenous culture, and noted the troop of 'keen scouts and brownies' at the mission.[65] Chief Protector J. W. Bleakley echoed Bennett's approval of the mission in his annual report on the Aborigines in 1935. He complimented the mission teacher, Mrs MacDougall, for instilling in her pupils 'honour, willing service,

[61] Peter Kabaila, 'Cootamundra: The Aboriginal Girls' Home', Australian Institute of Aboriginal and Torres Strait Islander Studies, MS 3321; photo series P3BW-N5882.059.

[62] The US source of many of these world accounts suggests that Girl Scouts' and Campfire Girls' interest in Native American culture in that country extended to indigenous cultures elsewhere.

[63] Swinburne, *Among the First People*, p. 61.

[64] The Girl Guides Association, *International Exhibition Catalogue* (Sydney, 1937), p. 3.

[65] BCL, *Report of Conference*, p. 48.

cleanliness and many virtues' more important, he felt, than their (unlikely) educational advancement. In pursuit of these worthy aims, she led 'packs of "Cubs", "Brownies" and "Girl Guides". The children love the activities.'[66]

Writing in 1949, a past leader of the Kunmunya troop (perhaps Mrs MacDougall herself) described her experiences for an international Guides' magazine. Her memories remind us that Aboriginal Scouts and Guides might not speak English, nor were they always wearing clothes on which to sew the badges they earned. According to *Hands Around the World*, 'guiding has been adapted for the Australian aborigines and their culture'. It cited as its authority:

A Guider [who] writes of aboriginal Guiding: 'My Kunmunya Guides and Brownies were the best I ever had. There were three First-Class Guides in the company, and one of them held the only Interpreter's badge in Western Australia ... [Since starting another company at Ernabella in South Australia, I am] now working hard at Pihinjarra [sic] (local language), and my girls are slowly learning English ... it is the policy of our Board of Missions here to keep the children unclothed, so we have no uniforms, but are planning to have fair-sized calico bags on which to wear badges.

The report concluded: 'These primitive peoples have much to teach others, too, and Guiders have been interested in learning how the "bush" natives cook.'[67] Being a Scout or Guide helped to turn bushcraft into a civilizing activity, even when undertaken by natives.

Ironically, given its military origins and culture, indigenous accounts of being in Scout and Guide troops focus on the escape from uniformity they afforded. Where the impact of being institutionalized has been remembered by the 'stolen generations' as predominantly traumatic, Scouting and Guiding appears as fun.[68] Removed to Kunmunya Mission in the 1930s, Laurelle Wright worked her way up through the Brownies to become the leader of the Guide troop, a position to which 'all the girls' aspired. Just like other children, she was eager for promotion, and interested in tests and badges. Once the children had congregated:

[66] J. W. Bleakley, 'Annual Report of the Chief Protector of the Aborigines for the Year Ended 30th June, 1935', *Western Australian Parliamentary Papers* (Perth, 1936), p. 17.

[67] Girl Scouts of the United State of America, *Hands Around the World: International Friendship for Girl Scouts* (New York, 1949), pp. 72–73.

[68] Human Rights and Equal Opportunity Commission, *Bringing Them Home: A Report of the National Inquiry into the Separation of Aboriginal and Torres Strait Islander Children From their Families* (Sydney, 1997).

it was time to honour the king, raise the Australian flag, salute the leaders and participate in a range of activities from tying knots, sewing and playing games, to doing first aid. They always arrived keen and neatly dressed in uniform, complete with badges, hat and tie, but drew the line at footwear. Like most country kids they were exposed to good healthy fun and enjoyed the camaraderie more than the discipline.[69]

One of the surviving photographs of the Kunmunya Scouts and Guides provides evidence of two remarkable features. Firstly, one of the Loves' children was a member, the only evidence I have found of a mixed troop in accounts of the movement throughout the Empire. Indeed, as we have seen, Baden-Powell had considered the possibility of white and black children mixing enough to exclude native troops from the official movement in South Africa. Secondly, unlike white troops, where the segregation of girls and boys was reinforced by separate movements, indigenous troops (where boys and girls often combined) seemed to be more about the uplift of a race than the policing of prescribed gender divisions.

By the late 1930s, troops were well established at Moore River, the settlement that for Bennett represented everything that was wrong with government policy. Yet even here, Scout and Guide leaders from the Perth headquarters reported to Neville that although the 'children were naturally shy[,] ... camp-fire singing, and ... games soon overcame this and they were particularly quick to grasp what was expected of them'. According to the recollections of Sister Eileen, matron at the settlement during those years, once in uniform 'they felt they were really somebody'. Hiking thirteen kilometres to the nearest town was regularly organized 'for a change of scene' and picnics in the bush were a favourite pastime. In 1940 Moore River Scouts joined a combined Boy Scout camp south of Perth. Phyllis Narrier, a Moore River Girl Guide at the time, recalls excitement and pleasure: 'We all looked nice. We got the badges, and we thought it was great.'[70] Generally, participants remembered uniforms, games, tests and rewards, and escape from the routine and regimentation of the settlement or mission—even as the Scouts and Guides promoted routines, regimentation, and uniformities of their own. Outdoor activities no doubt attracted indigenous troop members as they did other girls and boys throughout the Empire.

---

[69] Edie Wright, *Full Circle: From Mission to Community: A Family Story* (Fremantle, 2001), p. 80.
[70] Quoted in Maushart, *Sort of a Place*, pp. 196–97.

Indeed, children across the Empire were linked by the frontier skills of bushcraft that they enacted as Scouts and Guides. Similar children's adventures were vividly described in contemporary best sellers which circulated globally, and even among settlements and missions in Australia.[71] Yet indigenous children were not the typical heroines or heroes of these tales. Australian historian Ann McGrath has remarked upon the peculiar implications of settler and indigenous Australian children playing 'Cowboys and Indians' in twentieth-century settler colonial Australia.[72] We can surmise that playing Scout and Guide required similar feats of imagination for indigenous children. After all, native trackers and police were employed widely against indigenous populations in Australia as elsewhere, including the recapture of girls and boys who escaped from Moore River.[73] No doubt tracking and stalking, among the serious pastimes of the movement, held particular evocations for indigenous and colonized peoples, their 'native' expertise routinely incorporated into colonizing practices in settler and crown colonies.

If local experience shaped being a Scout or Guide, a shared imperial loyalty was the movement's larger aim. To this end, 'playing frontier' was one among a number of temporal and spatial fantasy landscapes employed by various child movements in order to access the emotional terrain of youth and hence to inspire young people towards imperial identification. These landscapes were to provide modern children with access to their evolutionary inheritance. They offered an array of opportunities to dress up and enact larger-than-life versions of manliness and womanliness claiming to be drawn from 'primitive' culture, historical times, fairy tales, or animal society.[74] Where did Aboriginal children fit into this account of advancement through tapping the wellspring of instinct and emotion? Certainly the emotional capacity of indigenous children was considered important for their uplift in the 1930s. According to a 1931 report by South Australian medical anthropologists, H. K. Fry and R. Pulleine, it was strong emotional development rather than any intellectual capacity that provided Aboriginal children with

---

[71] Richard Phillips, *Mapping Men and Empire: A Geography of Adventure* (London, 1997).

[72] Ann McGrath, 'Playing Colonial: Cowgirls, Cowboys, and Indians in Australia and North America', *Journal of Colonialism and Colonial History*, II, 1 (2001), pp. 1–24. See also Rayna Green, 'The Tribe Called Wannabee: Playing Indian in America and Europe', *Folklore*, XCIX, 1 (1988), pp. 30–55; and Philip Deloria, *Playing Indian* (New Haven, 1998).

[73] Henry Reynolds, *With the White People* (Ringwood, 1990), chap. 2.

[74] MacDonald, *Sons of the Empire*, pp. 35–45; T. J. Jackson Lears, *No Place of Grace: Antimodernism and the Transformation of American Culture 1880–1920* (Chicago, 1994), p. 171.

abstract thought and hence their potential to advance.[75] Perhaps Aboriginal children employed a rather more sophisticated capacity than Fry and Pulleine allowed, imagining themselves within two cultures (their own, and that of the frontier constructed by Baden-Powell) as they played Scouts and Guides.

Although various forms of removal (including adoption into white families) continued into the 1970s, after the Second World War officials began to promote the idea that Aboriginal community life, and its productive relationship with the larger white community, was a necessary adjunct to effective assimilation. During the 1920s and 1930s Scouts and Guides had provided for a new kind of eugenic space for removed Aboriginal girls and boys more usually excluded as unfit. Here 'race inheritance', that great obstacle to uplift, might be valorised, suggesting, at least symbolically, that indigenous children held the capacity to succeed in settler culture without erasing their own. By the 1950s, for example in the *Dawn*, a government magazine sent to all Aboriginal homes in New South Wales, Aboriginal Scouts and Guides were featured as success stories, represented as the combined initiatives of local white and indigenous communities.[76] Unlike their predecessors, these troops comprised children living within Aboriginal communities, not extracted from them.

The quintessential imperial child movement of the 1920s and 1930s, the Scouts and Guides, provided a place for Australian Aboriginal children within its predominantly white ranks. Their presence illustrates the diverse racial taxonomies that have differently marked girls' and boys' entry into imperial adulthood in the early twentieth century, while reminding us also of their intersections. As the necessity for the Scouts and Guides makes clear, whiteness and modernity were themselves subject to the ordering and moralizing influence of Empire in the early decades of the last century. The new conditions of the British Commonwealth and its Dominions provided settler nations such as Australia with greater independence yet saw also a resurgence of Empire and concerns for the virility of the race, particularly in the child subject. Native Scouts and Guides occupied an ambivalent space in settler colonial contexts, where imperial child cultures were applied in the management of child races, and doubly so in the case of indigenous children. While the legacy of resulting removal policies continues to confront

---

[75] Anderson, *The Cultivation*, pp. 208–09.

[76] For example, *Dawn*, III, 11 (Nov. 1954), p. 20; and IV, 5 (May 1955), p. 19.

Australians in the present, indigenous recollections of 'growing up' as Scouts and Guides remind us finally of the possibilities of play and pleasure under the most unlikely of conditions and in the most unlikely of places.

Select Bibliography

ANDREW ARMITAGE, *Comparing the Policy of Aboriginal Assimilation: Australia, Canada, and New Zealand* (Vancouver, 1995).

GAIL BEDERMAN, *Manliness and Civilisation: A Cultural History of Gender and Race in the United States, 1880–1917* (Chicago, 1995).

ANNA HAEBICH, *Broken Circles: Fragmenting Indigenous Families 1800–2000* (Fremantle, 2000).

ROBERT H. MACDONALD, *Sons of the Empire: The Frontier and the Boy Scout Movement, 1890–1918* (Toronto, 1993).

RUSSELL McGREGOR, *Imagined Destinies: Aboriginal Australians and the Doomed Race Theory, 1880–1939* (Melbourne, 1997).

ROBERT VAN KRIEKEN, *Children and the State: Social Control and the Formation of Australian Child Welfare* (St Leonards, 1991).

12

Faith, Missionary Life, and the Family

PATRICIA GRIMSHAW

In the month of July 1867, Bessy Flower, a young woman of some seventeen years, disembarked with four travelling companions at the port of Melbourne, Victoria, the colony that was destined to be their new home. Mrs Anne Camfield, of the Anglican mission to Aborigines, Western Australia, had despatched Bessy, her younger sister Ada, Rhoda Toby, Nora White, and Emily Peters to take up residence at the Presbyterian mission of Ramahyuck in rural eastern Victoria. Female converts there who could marry the young male Aboriginal Christian converts were in short supply. A Moravian missionary, the Reverend Friedrich Hagenauer, had sent a call for prospective brides, to which Anne Camfield gladly responded with the first fruits of her mission school. Bessy Flower had been singled out for a special destiny. An advanced student, a talented musician, a keen chess player, Bessy was intended as a teacher for the Aboriginal school at Ramahyuck, a vacancy that mission-wife Louise Hagenauer, now with a fourth child, could not fill. Anne Camfield had faithfully educated all the girls according to a model English school curriculum as they lived in her extended household, alongside other indigenous children. Camfield once forwarded one of Bessy's letters to the *Colonial Intelligencer, or Aborigines' Friend*, journal of the British humanitarian Aborigines' Protection Society, as clear evidence of the educability of Australian Aborigines denied by malevolent settlers.

From her departure from Albany, Bessy Flower kept Anne Camfield informed by letter of her journey and first impressions of Adelaide and Melbourne. She found everything wondrous. Kindly disposed white Christians met their small party at the ports to escort them to church services that were notable for inspiring music, and to the cities' sights: the splendid Houses of Parliament, the botanic and zoological gardens. 'I cannot tell you

I thank my colleagues Peter Sherlock, Elizabeth Nelson, and Ellen Warne for assistance with this chapter.

how I love you for taking us out of the bush & making us what we are', Bessy Flower told Camfield, whom she addressed as 'dearest more than mother'; she admitted to a fear of forgetting her own poor mother. On arrival in Melbourne she confessed she found the missionary Friedrich Hagenauer quite funny-looking with his long beard, but his wife Louise was a 'dear lady' whom she longed to help. Nora and Emily met their intended grooms, were reported to be enchanted, and were married within a very short time; the other two girls were under-age as yet. Bessy herself plunged with alacrity into teaching her pupils, whom she found alert and bright, gratifyingly responsive to their new teacher.[1]

Here was an interchange of letters certain to gladden the hearts of Bessy Flower's mentors, and indeed all supporters of missions. This bright, accomplished convert was the stuff of Victorian exemplary tales of religious conversion and 'improvement', and incidentally also revealed missionaries' endeavours in a favourable light. From the hindsight of the twenty-first century, however, we read the sub-text of these letters as decidedly problematic. In the face of the appalling atrocities that settlers had visited on small hunter-gatherer bands in the Australian colonies in the process of appropriating indigenous peoples' lands, missionaries had upheld Aborigines' human and civil rights and provided them with havens from the avaricious intruders. Mission advocacy came at a high cost for indigenous survivors, however. In the Albany case, missionaries had first removed young girls from their families in their zeal to convert indigenous peoples, whom they trained intensively on mission premises; their parents had to relinquish any future control. The young women who accompanied Bessy Flower had then been despatched far from kin and traditional lands to serve another missionary goal, the founding of new Christian families. Missionaries in both colonies arranged all this without apparent self-doubt, utterly convinced of the benevolence of their intentions: they served God's purposes. The tension in

---

[1] See Elizabeth Nelson and others, eds., *Letters from Aboriginal Women of Victoria, 1867–1926* (Melbourne, 2002) for the primary sources on which the sections on the Victorian missions are based. See also Bain Attwood, *The Making of the Aborigines* (Sydney, 1989); John Harris, *One Blood: 200 Years of the Aboriginal Encounter with Christianity: A Story of Hope* (1990; Sydney, 1995); Tony Swain and Deborah Bird Rose, eds., *Aboriginal Australians and Christian Missions: Ethnographic and Historical Studies* (Bedford Park, South Australia, 1988); Patricia Grimshaw and Elizabeth Nelson, 'Empire, "the Civilising Mission" and Indigenous Christian Women in Colonial Victoria', *Australian Feminist Studies*, VI, 3 (2001) , pp. 295–309; Patricia Grimshaw, 'Colonising Motherhood: Evangelical Social Reformers and Koorie Women in Victoria, 1880s to the Early 1900s', *Women's History Review* (hereafter *WHR*), VIII, 2 (1999), pp. 311–28.

the mission project apparent between, on the one hand, concern for universal human rights that few of their contemporaries nourished, and on the other, the arrogance bred of Western cultural imperialism, underpinned mission activity across the British Empire from the late eighteenth century. Constraints on missionaries' exercise of power inevitably emerged from both the broader politics of colonizers and colonized in specific colonial situations, and where they witnessed the conversion of high numbers, from the agency of indigenous peoples in sustaining traditional values within new belief systems. Any evaluation of the ways historians might examine gender and missions cannot evade confronting this contentious dilemma.

This chapter will pursue the question of faith, mission life, and family with this crucial ambiguity to the fore. It focuses on Protestant outreach: the gendered dimensions of the significant Catholic missions in the Empire led by male and female French, German, Spanish, and Irish missionary priests, similar in many respects, lie outside the scope of this particular study.[2] Protestant missionaries, Baptists, Congregationalists, Anglicans, Methodists, Moravians, Presbyterians, and more, from Britain, the United States of America, Protestant areas of Europe, and eventually, Britain's settler colonies, covered an astonishing area of the globe, wherever successive British governments asserted economic interests. The missions created voluminous archives, and almost all have their chroniclers. The focus of much mission history on institution-building has precluded examination of the social concerns in which women were crucial actors.[3] Female missionaries' lives were usually left to the apologetic faithful. Scholars who have in recent decades conflated the specificities of missionary women within considerations of gender and colonialism have inspired revisionist studies from historians who similarly place missions at the intersection of post-colonial and feminist questions. This chapter draws on their insights, taking first the

[2] For a recent Australian study of Catholic missions, see Christine Choo, *Mission Girls: Aboriginal Women on Catholic Missions in the Kimberley, Western Australia, 1900–1950* (Perth, 2001).

[3] For general discussion of missions, see Norman Etherington, 'Missions and Empire', in Robin W. Winks , ed., *The Oxford History of the British Empire, V, Historiography* (Oxford, 1999), pp. 303–14. See also Catherine Hall, *Civilising Subjects: Metropole and Colony in the English Imagination 1830–1867* (Cambridge, 2002); Jean Comaroff and John L. Comaroff, *Of Revelation and Revolution: Christianity, Colonialism and Consciousness in South Africa* (Chicago, 1991); Antoinette Burton, *Burdens of History: British Feminists, Indian Women, and Imperial Culture, 1865–1915* (Chapel Hill, NC, 1994); Margaret Strobel, *European Women and the Second British Empire* (Bloomington, Ind., 1991).

interface of people, ideas, and events in both the metropole and the colonies that were significant for the 'civilizing mission', so influential for women's entry to overseas missions; second, it traces historical interpretations of missionaries' pursuits of their visions of gender and families once established in foreign fields.[4] Finally the chapter returns to the lives of the indigenous Western Australian women in the missions of Victoria, as a point of entry to the gender experiences of converts in the diverse Christian communities of the twentieth-century Empire.

The late eighteenth-and early nineteenth-century evangelical revivals in Britain and the United States of America inspired the intensified thrust of Protestant mission to non-Western peoples. This impulse in Britain was fuelled by the expansion of the Empire with the industrial revolution and in the United States intensified with the conviction that their new country would bring egalitarianism, republicanism, and prosperity to heathen peoples.[5] The history of gender and missions cannot be well understood without consideration of the continuing interactions between the missionary bodies and the mission-minded public of Britain and other northern countries and missionaries in the field. Metropole and colonies shared ideas on the duties of Western to non-Western peoples, as information, knowledge, and advice flowed between these locales. The direction the missions took, their recruitment of missionaries, their ideologies and key objectives on gender and family life intertwined closely with news from those abroad

---

[4] For works that engage with gender and missions, see Fiona Bowie and Deborah Kirkwood, eds., *Women and Missions: Past and Present: Anthropological and Historical Perceptions* (Oxford, 1993); Ruth Compton Brouwer, *New Women for God: Canadian Presbyterian Women and India Missions, 1876–1914* (Toronto, 1990); Diane Langmore, *Missionary Lives: Papua 1874–1914* (Honolulu, 1989); Maina Chawla Singh, *Gender, Religion, and 'Heathen Lands': American Missionary Women in South Asia (1860s–1940s)* (New York, 2000); Myra Rutherdale, *Women and the White Man's God: Gender and Race in the Canadian Mission Field* (Vancouver, 2002); Margaret Jolly and Martha Macintyre, eds., *Family and Gender in the Pacific: Domestic Contradictions and the Colonial Impact* (Melbourne, 1989); Karen Tranberg Hansen, ed., *African Encounters with Domesticity* (New Brunswick, NJ., 1992).

[5] See Hall, *Civilising Subjects*; Susan Thorne, *Congregational Missions and the Making of an Imperial Culture in Nineteenth-century England* (Stanford, Calif., 1999). For the United States, see Patricia Grimshaw, *Paths of Duty: American Missionary Wives in Nineteenth Century Hawai'i* (Honolulu, 1989); Jane Hunter, *The Gospel of Gentility: American Women Missionaries in Turn-of-the-Century China* (New Haven, 1984); Dana L. Robert, *American Women in Mission: A Social History of their Thought and Practice* (Macon, Ga., 1996); Patricia Hill, *The World Their Household: The American Women's Foreign Mission Movement and Cultural Transformation, 1870–1920* (Ann Arbor, 1985).

and its reception by evangelical Christians at the central point of mission planning.[6]

An important component of mission development was the discourse of 'the civilizing mission' wherein the benefits of Christianity, education, and Western ways of living in virtuous families came to be accepted as a key objective of imperial outreach. In Britain, evangelicals who had been instrumental in the abolition of slavery from 1834 gave impetus to this goal as they turned their attention to the fate of indigenous peoples of the Empire, especially in settler colonies. Humanitarians began to serve as a lobby group for the rights of these non-Western peoples, disturbed by news of appalling atrocities, including the virtual genocide of the Aborigines of Tasmania in just three decades of British settlement. The effect of British colonization on indigenous peoples, in widely separated parts of the world, had been disastrous unless 'attended by missionary exertions', they claimed. Where missionaries were already in place to encourage their converts to discard their 'uncivilized' ways for settled lives in European-style villages based on agriculture, great improvements were seen.[7] Rather than advocating, then, the cessation of colonization, humanitarians promoted the cause of missions to bring heathen peoples those gifts of Christianity and useful learning that alone would compensate for the disruption to their customary lives. Theirs was at heart a modernizing and assimilationist agenda, presenting as basic the adoption of those family forms—monogamous marriages, gender divisions of labour, certain ways of child-rearing—that accorded with Western understandings of goodness and propriety. As the nineteenth century proceeded, the 'civilizing mission' became at an official British government level the moral legitimation of their acquisition of an Empire of massive proportions.

The missionary societies' conviction of the virtues of Western Christian living for those outside the fold, also persuaded them of the importance of women to foreign mission endeavours. The eighteenth-century male orientation of the mission project was quickly modified. Disturbing news reached the London Missionary Society, that certain single male missionaries in the

---

[6] Andrew Porter, 'Religion, Missionary Enthusiasm, and Empire', in Andrew Porter, ed., *The Oxford History of the British Empire* (hereafter *OHBE*), III, *The Nineteenth Century* (Oxford, 1999), pp. 222–46; and Porter, 'Trusteeship, Anti-Slavery and Humanitarianism', in ibid., III pp. 198–221.

[7] Julie Evans and others, *Equal Subjects, Unequal Rights: Indigenous Peoples in British Settler Societies, 1830–1910* (Manchester, 2003).

central Pacific islands had taken 'heathen' Polynesian women as *de facto* wives, and that Church Missionary Society men were doing likewise at the Bay of Islands station in New Zealand. Mission bodies were thus swiftly alerted to the practical necessity for the presence of wives. Single men had proved themselves capable of deserting the task of spreading the gospel, to form liaisons with indigenous women and set up house in heathen communities. In 1836, the secretary of the American Board of Commissioners for Foreign Missions laid out the compelling reasons for sending wives to the mission field. A missionary's need for a wife was the same as any other man's and he lived in circumstances that strengthened that 'powerful law of nature', he wrote. Women, moreover, were potent symbols of peace and hence the strongest protection a male missionary could have against violence. A wife served as a friend and counsellor to her husband, sharing his thoughts and feelings, nursing him in sickness, securing his domestic comfort. While wives would, of course, place their household cares first, they could prove useful in the conversion of the heathen, particularly because they afforded the heathen the opportunity to observe Christian families, a matter in which example was as important as precept. And a wife could also be expected to run schools for women and children, a highly useful role, especially if she had learned modern educational practices.[8]

The model for the good mission wife emerged from new emphases in evangelical beliefs and practices. The adult married woman was increasingly prized as the good helpmeet to her husband, by no means subservient, but the conscience, the stabilizer, for the man. Chaste in youth, faithful in marriage, she was also an alert and active mother, close to her children, watchful and prudent. This was not a decorative model of femininity but a utilitarian one: women had much useful work to do.[9] Their necessary work in missions could only be rendered more urgent by news from the field that supplied the Christian public with images of non-Western women's oppression at the hands of men. Their reports affirmed accounts of explorers, traders, adventurers, and travellers who also told of the gender disorder that prevailed in exotic places. Such tales inspired social theorists to conceive of the place of women as a sensitive marker of a people's advancement from a state of 'barbarism' to civilization; Western Christian women were standing

[8] Rufus Anderson, Preface, in William Ellis, *Memoir of Mary Ellis* (Boston, 1836), cited in Grimshaw, *Paths of Duty*, pp. 6–7.

[9] Leonore Davidoff and Catherine Hall, *Family Fortunes: Men and Women of the English Middle Class, 1780–1850* (London, 1987).

at the highest peak.[10] Even more reason, then, for Christian women to assume the duty of sharing their advantages with their oppressed sisters. Women came forward who were prepared to organize and to support financially missions and encourage those of their sex who were prepared to heed the call. Other, braver, women indicated their willingness to give up home and family for the cause.[11]

The male mission bodies had a concern about commissioning women for foreign fields. Would they appear, with their tolerance of wives' active participation, to be contravening the Protestant churches' dichotomy of gender? Ironically the wives' essential work paved the way for an explicit challenge: the admission of single women to mission service in their own right. Some single women had from the first applied for mission service, even though they knew their request would appear anomalous. Where would they live, and with whom, the mission bodies asked? Would they appear to be seeking indigenous husbands? How would wives respond to women in their midst who were paid for services for which the wives themselves could expect only heavenly rewards? Despite every discouragement, keen single women had found their ways to missions, most commonly through marrying strangers, men about to depart for the field. Others married single men or widowers once they reached the field and indeed the anticipation of these marriages not uncommonly induced mission bodies' acceptance of their applications. Meanwhile mission report after mission report made plain both the pressing demands for women's services, and the onerous nature of these demands on wives' energies and health. As a group they died young.

Men in the field, slowly but surely, came to a fuller realization that to convert a people, they needed to influence not just the men but the women. Usually, however, it was culturally inappropriate for strange men to get near indigenous women. Few mission men, moreover (usually clergy), found sufficiently heroic the task of teaching restless school children. The argument for the recruitment of single women first became an urgent issue in Indian missions, where upper-class women had to be approached through home or

[10] Peter Hulme and Ludmilla Jordanova, eds., *The Enlightenment and its Shadows* (London, 1990).

[11] Judith Rowbotham, 'Soldiers of Christ?' Images of Female Missionaries in Late Nineteenth Century Britain: Issues of Heroism and Martyrdom', *Gender and History*, XII, 1 (2000), pp. 82–106; Rowbotham, ' "Hear the Indian Sister's Plea": Reporting the Work of 19th-Century British Female Missionaries', *Women's Studies International Forum* (hereafter *WSIF*), XXI, 3 (1998), pp. 247–61; Alison Twells, ' "Happy English Children": Class, Ethnicity, and the Making of Missionary Women in the Early Nineteenth Century', *WSIF*, XXI, 3 (1998), pp. 235–45.

zenana visiting. Eventually also, given the reluctance of the British government to provide schools and hospitals for large subject populations in areas of Africa and Asia, missionaries were called upon to fill the gap. It was easier to recruit idealistic single women as nurses and teachers than men, and the mission bodies did so. Eventually single women doctors joined their ranks. Male doctors anticipated a higher professional status back home.

The male leaders of the home churches appeared bent on keeping women from positions of authority and remuneration. They faced the pressure of single middle-class women's search for legitimate employment should they be destined for life-long spinsterhood. Some sought meaningful church work and, like their brothers, were attracted to the novelty of imperial ventures. Single women missionaries resembled social reformers of their countries of origin, not because the messages they transmitted presaged those of 'the new woman', but in their assumption of a position of moral authority in relation to others whom they defined as in need of 'uplift'. The demonstration of all women missionaries of the effectiveness of women's work, and in particular single women's success in carving out a notable independent career for their sex, redounded to the benefit of those in the women's movement who needed examples of female capacities for significant careers.

The strategies of Protestant missionaries in the field showed remarkable similarities despite the extraordinary differences in the cultures and previous histories of Western contact of their chosen peoples. First they had to establish a firm foothold. Initially their reception from indigenous peoples could vary from friendly hospitality to outright hostility directed at all imperial intruders. Sometimes missionaries became unwittingly embroiled in wars between indigenous groups; if they intervened in powerful rulers' handling of matters of life and death they could become specific targets for aggressive acts. Some practices that missionaries believed were occurring, they found horrifying: the burning of widows in India on their husbands' funeral pyres; the killing of twins in Nigeria; the sacrifice of women slaves in Fiji; female circumcision in Kenya and elsewhere. Health was undermined as young and old alike succumbed to exotic diseases: serious illness, sometimes leading to early death was common, especially in the early years. Some missionaries became discouraged and even deeply depressed by the burdens that they had scarcely contemplated before their departure. Homesickness and isolation from distant relatives as well as from the few Westerners outside the mission circle, whose lives and goals they frequently deplored, could overwhelm them. Everywhere they looked they could see huge obstacles. The climate, the hurricanes, floods, or droughts, the poisonous insects, and wild animals threatened their sense of identity and reality. After occasional euphoric sentiments on first arrival, few husbands and wives wrote home of their happiness or even of satisfaction in a task well done. The demands they faced often seemed overwhelming.

The wives were more deeply affected than the men, partly because of childbearing that frequently undermined their constitutions. Their insecurity was increased since they bore the chief responsibility for sustaining exemplary families and could do so only with great difficulty. It was hard to erect a decent house, and many couples lived frugally, in huts made of rushes or rough wood, situated in swamps or treeless plains, perhaps windowless, with leaking roofs, smoking fires, and crude furniture. The gracious homes they aspired to took some time coming. When such dwellings materialized they bespoke of a wealth that invited disapproval and envy, and set them apart from those they wished to convert. The wives found good mothering very difficult. Money and supplies were always short, so that bringing up children to know the 'proper' ways of eating, dressing, using furniture and utensils—which often only their parents could convey on this frontier—was a constant strain. Wives were forced to employ local servants as nannies. These helpers spoke their own language to the babies and children, often engaging the children's sympathy and affection, making problematic the children's allegiance to their white families' strict ways. If mothers struggled to care for and educate their young children by themselves, the results could appear pitifully inadequate. If parents wanted anything, it was to see their children thrive in the skills that would, in their maturity, bring girls good marriages and boys professions. For this reason, and to keep them insulated from undesirable aspects of the local culture, parents usually relinquished older children to boarding schools in their country of origin. These separations could last five years and more unless mothers returned with their children, leaving husbands, most unnaturally, to manage alone.[12] What model evangelical family in the home country sent

[12] For useful discussion, see monographs above and Padma Anagol, 'Indian Christian Women and Indigenous Feminism, c.1850–c.1920', in Clare Midgley, ed., *Gender and Imperialism* (Manchester, 1998), pp. 79–103; Hilary Carey, 'Companions in the Wilderness? Missionary Wives in Colonial Australia', *Journal of Religious History*, XIX (1995), pp. 227–48; Leslie A. Flemming, 'A New Humanity: American Missionaries' Ideals for Indian Women in North India, 1870–1930', in Nupur Chaudhuri and Margaret Strobel, eds., *Western Women and*

their children far from a mother's care for years on end, to be reared by strangers?

Sustaining the correct relationship between husband and wife—one the provider, protector, source of order and wisdom, the other the homemaker, companion, counsellor—also eluded the wives. The men might temporarily cross gender lines in emergencies, caring for children or nursing the sick when wives could not cope, but they could not fill wives' shoes in any sustained capacity. The wives conversely undertook work that constantly blurred the boundaries of the gender division of labour. True, men usually negotiated with princes and chiefs, dealt with mission administrators at home, and colonial officials in place. They took the leading part in transcribing the language, translating Bibles, preaching the sermons, presiding over church meetings, and conferring with male peers on policy. Wives were, however, teachers of indigenous children, skilled language speakers, and the instructors of the indigenous women, sometimes men, in all household crafts, from cooking to sewing. Husbands not infrequently departed for extensive periods of itinerant preaching, leaving wives to replace them in parishes and even in the pulpit. Wives quietly contributed to all such activities, interrupted though their participation might be not only by the usual domestic demands but by such crises as pregnancies, miscarriages, and nursing the sick. No matter their skills or burden, if wives were to gain official approval, however, they needed to maintain a modest self-deprecatory demeanour which translated into virtual invisibility in mission reports.

Single women's experiences very often provided a distinct contrast to those of their married sisters. Single women had been hardened by surviving the obstacles to participation: the acquisition of the necessary professional qualifications, gaining the acceptance of their families and the mission bodies. They took to their work in better heart and were more likely to sustain a spirit of hope and optimism. Those who avoided subsequent marriage in the field told far more often of satisfaction from their mission engagement. Without the physical strain of supporting husbands and worrying about children, they enjoyed appreciably higher levels of health, developed friendships with other single women, sometimes adopted indigenous babies into their homes. At a later stage of mission activity

Imperialism: Complicity and Resistance (Bloomington, Ind., 1992), pp. 191–207; Natasha Erlank, 'Jane and John Philip: Partnership, Usefulness and Sexuality in the Service of God', in John de Gruchy, ed., The London Missionary Society in Southern Africa, 1799–1999: Historical Essays in Celebration of the Bicentenary of the LMS in Southern Africa (Athens, Oh., 2000), pp. 82–98.

when facilities expanded, single women had satisfying careers for sustained periods in large established schools and hospitals. Most of their day-to-day anxieties arose from disagreements with male missionaries concerned to protect their dominance. As a group, the single women showed remarkable inventiveness and personal resilience in their determination to fulfil their ambitions. Most cheerfully evaded obstacles to their personal initiatives to pursue goals that lay outside the conventions of women's work, since the women found themselves endowed with considerable authority among the converts. Some forcefully defied convention and were able to carve out idiosyncratic careers, most notably Mary Slessor in Nigeria and Amy Carmichael in India.[13] At their 1895 annual meeting, the Women's Committee of the Church Missionary Society in London commented wryly on these conflicts over single women's activities. They recognized 'the danger lest women workers in their zeal should overstep wise and rightful limits'; but on the other hand there was 'the danger of their work through local restrictions, being confined within such limits as greatly hamper them'. In the Committee's opinion, men in the church placed greater weight on the first rather than the second consideration.[14] Though they had to fight for it, many single women attained a respected status in the church that would have been denied them at home, one that eventually male mission bodies acknowledged explicitly, if reluctantly. Single women missionaries not infrequently stayed in the field all their lives, and if repatriated against their will, pined for 'their people' who, they believed, had truly loved them.[15]

Whether demoralized by mission service or energized by it, whether embarrassed at a failure to conform to strict gender codes or blissfully unconcerned, missionaries had few qualms about asserting to non-Western peoples the virtues of their own ideal gender arrangements, with the Christian family as their crucible. Missionaries pressed non-Western peoples most heavily to reproduce the institution of Western Christian marriage and family. Excessive male dominance over women and men's sexual licence

---

[13] See William H. Taylor, *Mission to Educate: A History of the Educational Work of the Scottish Presbyterian Mission in East Nigeria, 1846–1960* (Leiden, 1996), chap. 6; Ruth A. Tucker, *Guardians of the Great Commission: The Story of Women in Modern Missions* (Grand Rapids, Mich., 1988), pp. 130–35.

[14] Ladies Consultative Committee of Church Missionary Society, 1895, cited in Elizabeth Dimock, 'Women, Mission and Church in Early Colonial Uganda, 1895–1935', *WHR* (forthcoming 2004).

[15] Nancy Rose Hunt, ' "Single Ladies in the Congo": Protestant Missionary Tensions and Voices', *WSIF*, XIII, 4 (1990), pp. 395–403. See nn. 4 and 5 above on mission women.

would be curtailed by the institution of companionate marriage, involving freely chosen partners committed to a monogamous and sexually exclusive relationship, preceded by chastity. Missionaries were convinced that incorrect marriage arrangements underlay all other anomalies of gender. India provided the example of wives shut away in unnatural exclusion from the everyday human contacts of neighbourhood and community. Many African societies embraced the custom of bride wealth, that missionaries could not perceive as a family investment in a marriage's permanency, but saw rather as the buying and selling of women. Polygamy, rife among heathen peoples, was not in missionary eyes a labour arrangement, but a mechanism for ensuring men's right to acquire successively younger wives. It was rare for women to be the recipients of multiple husbands, but in those cases it was also roundly condemned, as were the few instances—such as in Polynesian societies— where certain high-born women wielded enormous power over lesser-born men and women alike. Signs of women's physical labour such as engagement in agriculture, carrying loads of firewood, and fetching water appeared as the outward sign of male exploitation, though in most societies, women's work was seldom confined to domestic tasks. Missionaries also deprecated the opposite situation, where women were underemployed. In some Polynesian communities, wives had too much time for leisure and play, and were exhorted to invest greater energy in domestic tasks and childcare to fill their waking hours.

The family unit of parents and children, missionaries urged, should be discrete and parents in supreme control. At the root of indigenous peoples' shortcomings as parents, missionaries decided, was the strength of wives' and husbands' continuing allegiance to their families of origin. Older relatives stood in the way of progress in child-rearing by upholding traditions inimical to the civilizing project. Missionaries knew better ways, it seemed, to do just about anything; all indigenous practices were noted, remarked upon, criticized. They proclaimed prevention of pregnancy a sin, and monitored, if they could, women's conduct during pregnancy and childbirth. They promoted new management regimes for children. Wives bore too many babies or gave them away uncaringly to relatives; mothers breastfed for intervals that were too short or too long; babies were fed solid food too early or too late. Children's formal education must have priority over family needs for their labour, and girls must, like their brothers, have an education beyond household tasks. The early betrothals of children should be done away with. The young should not enter marriage until full maturity was reached, and their choices of marriage partner should be divested of kinship considerations. Conversely, young people ought not to be permitted unfettered choice. Adolescents in the Polynesian communities of the Pacific islands and New Zealand appeared to have too much liberty at far too young an age, and the tolerance of pre-marital sexuality was denounced as disgraceful.

Did heathen people need first to be touched by the power of the gospel to find the inspiration to make changes? After years of fruitless debate on whether conversion to the gospel or training in civilized arts should come first in the mission agenda, missionaries everywhere reached the same conclusion. Missionaries could expect the best results if they could isolate children from their parents and communities, for as much of the time as practicable (single-sex boarding schools were favoured) and subject them to intensive proselyzation. In this way a group of devout Christian adolescents would emerge to marry each other, with the missionaries as brokers, and found sturdy Christian families. In the places where they made headway, the missionaries did just that.

Where large populations retained their faiths, peoples of predominantly Muslim and Hindu beliefs for example, the work of Christian missionaries may seem marginal, less problematic. Conversely where Christianity became the dominant religion, in some African and Pacific countries and in the settler colonies, missionaries loomed large in the lives of individuals and communities and have been the subject of critical scrutiny. Missionaries undoubtedly cared about their protégés and established ties based on mutual affection and sometimes mutual respect. The behaviour of both mission men and women, however, was frequently ugly, despite their conviction of their own good will in everything they attempted. They sought control of indigenous adults, even converts, as though they were children in need of tutelage. They resented having their wills crossed as though an indigenous person were committing an offence against God-given ways of believing, living, and relating. The personal sacrifices that missionaries made to aid the heathen served to fuel Christian animosity towards those who thwarted their ambitions and undermined their self-belief. Destabilizing indigenous families, nurturing alternative models, alienating adults from kin, children from parents, subjecting a few children to intensive indoctrination and socialization in Western culture, were all justified by their conviction that all was God's work.

An assessment of gender and missions is incomplete without the attempt to transcend the minutiae of the mission archive to consider missionaries' influences at a wider political and social level. At this stage, it is more difficult to generalize from the sources, for while missionaries may have shared common strategies, they were certainly not the only stakeholders shaping the outcomes of their labour.

Once the initial period of proselyzation was over, the trajectories of the lives of converts and fledgling Christian communities depended on factors other than mission aims and strategies. The pathways of the colonial state, different in each site, could deter or facilitate Westerners' continuing control over local churches. Hence the capacity of converts for independence from missionary control, their ability to insist on syncretic expressions not only of Christianity but of prescribed forms of gender and family now diverged markedly. Missionaries in most colonial situations, where a few Westerners faced millions of indigenous people, had limited options to pursue their ambitions with anything other than moral suasion. Certain settler colonies, such as the colony of Victoria, lay at the other edge of the spectrum, as the settler state strengthened mission hands.

In Victoria, missionary determination to exercise control over Aborigines came to know few bounds except the resistance of Aborigines themselves. The conjunction of mission and state goals placed Christian converts in the most difficult of situations even for sustaining the integrity of the family. As new Christians in fragile churches and communities, Aborigines faced a world fraught with ambiguities and compromises. They held on to a deep sense of their Aboriginality, but found their personal lives of faith and family increasingly confined by sharp legal and material constraints. The missionaries' authoritarian tendencies came to the fore to promote their humanitarian agenda. The aim of the civilizing agenda was to 'raise up' indigenous peoples so they could be assimilated into Western society. Once Christian and literate, Victorian Aboriginal families would be urged to assimilate with the settler community, accepting a position as equals, expecting no special assistance. If resistant, they could suffer the penalties of recipients of charity everywhere: surveillance, control, and disruption of relationships.

The fate of Bessy Flower, her companions, and the mission community illustrates these trends. The outcomes of the ministrations of Protestant missionaries for those young women who arrived with high hopes in Victoria in 1867, as for their communities, were distinctly problematic. When Bessy Flower arrived at Ramahyuck station, the Victorian missions were in a state of flux as the settler legislature, having wrested local self-government from the imperial authorities, began to intervene in the conduct of missions. The first efforts of missionaries had failed as the violence of the pastoral frontier negated missionaries' efforts to protect their groups and to persuade them to locate to specific manageable sites. These early missionaries had abhorred indigenous cultural practices, discerning a dismal picture of gender arrangements: early betrothal of girls, polygamy, arduous women's labour, and infanticide.[16] While ignorant of the value of the indigenous culture which missionaries set out to suppress, mission reports, nevertheless, provided the few positive statements about Aborigines that the public heard amid virulent settler racism. From 1860, based on guilt and shame about the plight of Aborigines, the government had allocated land and modest funds to missions. Within a decade, many Aborigines on the stations accepted the Christian sacraments and attended daily religious services. By the 1870s missionaries reported that women and men alike changed for the better every day: in their conduct, cleanliness, and diligence at their learning. They formed themselves into little Christian communities which compared favourably with the villages of the old world. Any problem with educating Aborigines lay with previous ineffectual teachers, they said, not with the intellects of the people. In 1873 the Inspector of Schools reported that the Ramahyuck children had performed extraordinarily well in the annual state examination.

The missionaries oversaw Christian weddings of suitably clad couples, and nuclear families of parents and children—the relatives banished to a distance—moved into the privacy of small two-roomed cottages. Husbands and older boys were set to work on the mission farm to produce food and encouraged to supplement the mission income by taking seasonal jobs in the local area. The women of the mission taught the Aboriginal women and girls good housewifery, the care of infants, and the disciplining of older children. The missionaries were gratified when some of the women petitioned the settler government to override plans for an exhibition of men's traditional dancing to greet the incoming Governor of the colony. The Aboriginal women disapproved, they wrote, of occasions for white men to come to gaze at their husbands' near naked bodies.

[16] Patricia Grimshaw, 'Maori Horticulturalists and Aboriginal Hunter-gatherers: Women and Colonial Displacement in Nineteenth-century Aotearoa/New Zealand and Southeastern Australia', in Ruth R. Pierson and Nupur Chauduri, eds., *Nation, Empire, Colony: Historicizing Gender and Race* (Bloomington, Ind., 1998), pp. 21–40.

Missionaries, although by now able to communicate their programme in apparently privileged circumstances, were baffled at the continuing resistance to their advice. Mothers insisted on their right to control their children's lives in ways that did not accord with mission strategies. This was most obvious when parents wished to leave the stations, taking their children out of school. Missionaries found this totally discouraging. Yet all the people on the stations, with the exception of the missionaries, were desperately poor and the men needed to seek shearing and droving work, and men and women seasonal work such as fruit picking. This could take them far away. In addition, the adults often needed to fulfil obligations to sick or elderly relatives elsewhere in the colony, and this sometimes entailed prolonged absences. The Aborigines were not prepared to leave their children behind for so long a time. The missionaries, on the other hand, increasingly saw their most gratifying results in the children, many of whom were set to attain advanced skills.

The missionaries began to nurture the desire not only to discourage parents from taking the children off the mission stations, but also to prise them from their control. The missionaries sustained obligations as humanitarians towards these indigenous peoples, who were also technically British subjects. Such considerations conflicted with a competing obligation, to produce swift results in their civilizing agenda before the 'charity' of either their own sponsors' or that of the settler government ran out. This was especially difficult when the Aborigines made it clear that they viewed the meagre support the government provided as little enough exchange for the fertile lands settlers had appropriated. The Western Australians were among those who were out-of-step with the growing authoritarian mood. When Charley Foster and James Brindle, the husbands of Bessy Flower's companions, Nora and Emily, lodged a formal complaint with the Board for the Protection of Aborigines about mission treatment, the Revd Friedrich Hagenauer's amiable face changed expression. Foster was led astray by his wife Nora who, Hagenauer declared, was 'one of the worst women on the station'. As punishment, he recommended that the Fosters be dismissed from the station for six months (hence losing their provisions), and that all Emily Brindle's and Nora Foster's children over three years of age 'be taken to an orphanage or otherwise as the Board directed'.[17]

---

[17] F. Hagenauer to Secretary of Board for the Protection of Aborigines, 24 Aug. 1879, cited in Grimshaw, 'Colonising Motherhood', p. 316.

Even the model Christian woman, Bessy Flower, came into disfavour before long. Within a year of commencing her duties, she married Donald Cameron, a mission-educated man of mixed descent; a baby, the first of eight, was born the following year. Bessy and Donald Cameron were allocated rooms in a new boarding house for Aboriginal children in the mission grounds. Bessy, supposedly the principal teacher, soon found herself to her disappointment greatly occupied with housework as white people occupied her place in the classroom. The missionaries found fault with her housekeeping, her habit of reading books when there was domestic work to be done, and her independent ways. The Camerons would have liked to escape the mission's control by farming but could not make enough money to maintain themselves. Despite her numerous disputes with the missionaries, however, in 1886 Bessy was still prepared to defend them from public attack. The mission community, she wrote in a letter to a daily paper in 1886, would continue to do 'what is in our power to bring up our children to earn their own living, and be useful members of society, and ourselves to be grateful to the board and our missionaries for all their kindness and patience to us aboriginals'.[18]

Soon after this letter appeared, the Camerons and many other Aborigines living on the mission station had no choice but to leave, when the Victorian legislature passed an Act that decreed that Aborigines of mixed descent were required to find work and make their homes in the settler community. The aim of mission education, after all, was to enable Aborigines to assimilate, to live like and be accepted as white citizens with all the responsibilities and rewards that entailed. Now was the time to put the theory into practice, given there were so many trained and educated, and argumentative, Christians. A second provision of the Act was as fateful: it made legal the removal of Aboriginal children from their parents. They were to be placed in orphanages, foster homes, or industrial schools if the authorities considered the children would thus have 'better' care. Bessy Cameron and Emily Brindle, now a mother of fifteen children, moved with their families to a country town. When work for their husbands was hard to come by at a time of severe economic depression, Bessy Cameron was forced to write on behalf of her own and Emily Brindle's families' for emergency rations, but mission patience had begun to run out. The Brindles became so destitute that Emily was forced to relinquish two sons of nine and eleven years to the mercies of an

[18] *Argus*, 5 April 1886, p. 7.

industrial school. While her husband followed itinerant work opportunities, Bessy Cameron went out cleaning houses. She died in 1895, still only in her forties, fighting to keep a son from an industrial school, and her eldest daughter's infant son from an orphanage.[19]

Parents whom she had left behind on the missions—now rapidly being converted into government reserves—also struggled to keep their children, who were sent some distances to work for white families when they reached the age of twelve. Parents who exemplified the strong family commitment that the missionaries had upheld fought to keep their families together, mostly in vain. In 1912, Jemima Dunolly, the mother of six children and a model church member, sought the Board's assistance to obtain fifty acres of land and three years' rations. she wrote:

I have daughters rising into womanhood now & these I would like to be a little more under my control for... when they go out to service it is the last control of mothers lost, for as you know that they are rarely allowed back again even for a holiday. For the sake of my girls I would like a home of my own.[20]

The Board told Jemima Dunolly sharply that she could rent or buy land like anyone else, at her own expense. It was not long before she reported, with regret, that she could not afford anything. One of her daughters who was out to service, she noted sadly, she had not seen for seven years.[21] And so it was for so many others.

Those who remained on the missions found that new managers were preferred, often ex-military men. They continued to monitor all aspects of the people's lives, including their expressions of religion. When some people held charismatic prayer meetings on the stations, they were sharply pulled into line. In 1916 a woman was reprimanded for instigating services of 'a very exciting nature'; screams and wails were audible even from a great distance and when people were under that spell, nothing could be done to silence them.[22] Similarly, Lizzie and Mary McRae were refused permission to hold their own religious meetings when they found renewed Christian faith

---

[19] Patricia Grimshaw, 'Indigenous Women's Voices in Colonial Reform Narratives–Victoria and Aotearoa/New Zealand', in Solvi Sogner and Gro Hagemann, eds., *Women's Politics and Women in Politics: In Honour of Ida Blom* (Bergen, 2000), pp. 173–96.

[20] Jemima Dunolly to Secretary of BPA, Jan. 1912, in Nelson and others, eds., *Letters from Aboriginal Women*, p. 136.

[21] Mr and Mrs Dunolly to Secretary of BPA, 4 March 1912, in ibid., *Letters from Aboriginal Women*, p. 136.

[22] Mr Robarts to Secretary of BPA, 17 July, 1916, in ibid., *Letters from Aboriginal Women*, p. 230.

through Sister Isabella Hetherington, an Irish missionary who had established her own small mission at Bunyip in Gippsland. In 1921 Lizzie McRae
defiantly informed the Board that 'through Miss Hetherington we have seen
and been taught more about Jesus, than ever any Manager and his wife on the
Aboriginal Reserves in this State or any other could teach us'.[23] All dissidents
were ordered to attend the regular church services run by white clergy, or
leave. Aboriginal resistance to such domination persisted.

The fortunes of missionaries and their converts in Victoria represent just
one particular story of the outcomes of missions for the gender and family
arrangements of a subject people. In Victoria, and eventually throughout the
country, missionaries colluded with a settler government unrestrained, after
the initial phase, either by fears of indigenous numbers or aggression.
Throughout the twentieth century, Australian Aborigines faced appalling
disruption to their family lives, although conversely the period also saw the
commencement of indigenous campaigns in the public arena to win back
control over their own lives. That dual edge to Christian humanitarianism,
its concern for rights and its conviction that assimilation would bring
rewards, showed its face again. As some Australians from the 1930s mounted
campaigns to offer restitution for the losses Aborigines had suffered in the
first century and a half of contact, certain missionaries were among the small
group of people of settler descent who took up the Aborigines' cause as a
pressing human and civil rights issue. Among the Aborigines who came
forward in that decade to organize welfare and rights lobby groups, mission-
educated people were to the fore, but hereon the story of the missions
becomes Australian rather than imperial history.

There were echoes of the situation in Victoria elsewhere, but the long-term
outcomes of missionary labours, of mission policies on gender and families,
are specific to individual peoples and places.[24] From the first missionary
outreach, the missions' fortunes were dependent on new Christians whose

[23] Elizabeth and Henry McRae to Mr Heathershaw, Chief Commissioner of Police,
Melbourne, 6 Sept. 1921, in ibid., *Letters from Aboriginal Women*, p. 238.

[24] For studies of Christian converts and new churches, see works cited above and Antoinette
Burton, *At the Heart of Empire: Indians and the Colonial Encounter in Late-Victorian Britain*
(Berkeley, 1998); Deborah Gaitskell, ' "Praying and Preaching": The Distinctive Spirituality of
African Women's Organisations', in Henry Bredekamp and Robert Ross, eds., *Missions and
Christianity in South African History* (Johannesburg, 1995), pp. 211–32; Anne Dickson-Waiko,
'Women, Individual Human Rights, Community Rights: Tensions within the Papua New
Guinea State', in Patricia Grimshaw and others, eds., *Women's Rights and Human Rights:
International Historical Perspectives* (London, 2001), pp. 49–70.

special knowledges of their peoples, as well as courage and loyalty, were critical for the spreading of the word. Converts found their labour gendered in mission-appropriate ways. The men who showed commitment and talent were frequently drawn from an élite whom the missionaries had groomed, and held the key posts to which converts could aspire. Women's chances were compromised, as the denial of female talent endemic in the metropolitan churches was duplicated in mission treatment of new members. The women had to take their part in the raising of Christian families, and in the parishes taught children and ran the women's groups, when they were not cleaning the churches and sewing vestments. The missionaries' education of girls along with boys did offer a few of both sexes who chose to enter Western systems of work and association the means to negotiate within a fast-changing world.

From the 1920s and 1930s the missionaries' grip on the direction of the new churches began to loosen, and the decades of decolonization that followed the Second World War hastened this disengagement. In terms of new churches, policies and practices that missionaries initiated swiftly became intertwined with secular aspects of the modernity that the missionaries presaged but ultimately could not control. In most African, Asian, and Pacific nations, and in indigenous minority churches in First World countries, churchmen and women emerged in the leadership of churches with the agency to pursue their own paths. These encompassed the gender order in the church and family as well as public life. Most of the indigenous people in the erstwhile colonies who entered the professions, politics, or advocacy for the rights of their own peoples, did so from the initial basis of a mission education. Increasingly often, historians from these new nations will share with Western historians the challenge of creating these crucial narratives.

Select Bibliography

FIONA BOWIE and DEBORAH KIRKWOOD, eds., *Women and Missions: Past and Present: Anthropological and Historical Perceptions* (Oxford, 1993).

RUTH COMPTON BROUWER, *New Women for God: Canadian Presbyterian Women and India Missions, 1876–1914* (Toronto, 1990).

JEAN COMAROFF and JOHN L. COMAROFF, *Of Revelation and Revolution: Christianity, Colonialism and Consciousness in South Africa* (Chicago, 1991).

NORMAN ETHERINGTON, 'Missions and Empire', in Robin W. Winks, ed., *The Oxford History of the British Empire, Vol. V, Historiography* (Oxford, 1999).

PATRICIA GRIMSHAW, *Paths of Duty: American Missionary Wives in Nineteenth-Century Hawai'i* (Honolulu, 1989).

CATHERINE HALL, *Civilising Subjects: Metropole and Colony in the English Imagination 1830–1867* (Chicago, 2002).

KAREN TRANBERG HANSEN, ed., *African Encounters with Domesticity* (New Brunswick, NJ, 1992).

MARGARET JOLLY and MARTHA MACINTYRE, eds., *Family and Gender in the Pacific: Domestic Contradictions and the Colonial Impact* (Melbourne, 1989).

DIANE LANGMORE, *Missionary Lives: Papua 1874–1914* (Honolulu, 1989).

MYRA RUTHERDALE, *Women and the White Man's God: Gender and Race in the Canadian Mission Field* (Vancouver, 2002).

MAINA CHAWLA SINGH, *Gender, Religion, and 'Heathen Lands': American Missionary Women in South Asia, 1860s–1940s* (New York, 2000).

SUSAN THORNE, *Congregational Missions and the Making of an Imperial Culture in Nineteenth-century England* (Stanford, Calif., 1999).

13

Archive Stories: Gender in the Making of Imperial and Colonial Histories

ANTOINETTE BURTON

Historians who visit the Oriental and India Office Collections (OIOC) for the first time are often surprised by how powerfully the archival space itself evokes the Raj. Recently re-located in the new British Library in central London, the India Office produces the same promontory effect that Mary Louise Pratt argues was characteristic of modern European imperialism.[1] Portraits of 'oriental despots' who were courted and then displaced by the East India Company—painted mainly by European artists—grace the walls of the Reading Room, giving one the sense not just of being watched by figures from the past, but of being surveyed by the old colonial state and its minions as well.[2] These spoils of rule give the place a residual clubland feel: they are a powerful reminder that the social worlds of imperial power, like those of Imperial history, have been male-dominated for a very long time. If the Olympian perspective established by these images dominates visually, it does not necessarily shape the total archive experience. For despite the atmosphere of sepulchral hush which the Company paintings try to guarantee, conversations among patrons can reach such a whispered pitch that the Reading Room resembles 'an Indian bazaar,' especially as the hour of

---

[1] Mary Louise Pratt, *Imperial Eyes: Travel Writing and Transculturation* (New York, 1992).

[2] These portraits are: the Coat of Arms of the East India Company from the Directors' meeting room; Lord Clive receiving the grant for the pension fund, commissioned by the EIC, by Edward Penny (1772); Naqd Ali Beg, commissioned by the EIC, by Richard Greenbury; Hasan Reza Khan, minister to the nawab of Oudh, by Zoffany; General Sir Jang Bahadur Rana, 1817–77, commander of Nepal, by Bhajuman Citrakar, gift in 1850 (after Nepal had been 'pacified'); Asaf-ud-daula, nawab of Oudh, by Zoffany; Fath Ali, Shah of Persia, 1797–1834, by Mirza Babu, presented by Wellesley (1826); Nadir Shah, Shah of Persia who sacked Delhi in 1739, unknown painter; presented by N. Vansittart (1822); Mirza Abu'l Hasan Khan, ambassador from Persia to George III, commissioned by the EIC (1810), by William Beechey. I am grateful to Douglas Peers and Durba Ghosh for confirming these details.

elevenses approaches, or so I have been told by more than one India Office *wallah.*

The genteel orientalism of such a remark is matched only, perhaps, by the indelible imprint which imperial culture, both metropolitan and colonial, continues to leave on the production of imperial histories well into the twenty-first century. To be sure, the ornamentalism of the India Office is in many respects *sui generis,* derivative of the peculiar place which India held in the British imperial imagination. Not all imperial archives are as conspicuously marked by the trappings of colonial rule and its comprador élites. And even when they are, they are still likely to have been the collaborative product, as the Indian Office collections themselves are, of 'native' agency and state-sponsored information-collection. They are hybrids rather than hegemons. What most if not all imperial archives surely contain, however, is the memory of imperial power in all its complexity and instability. And just as the decor of the India Office enacts a certain Company drama, so too do imperial archives stage—both organizationally and aesthetically—a variety of imperial stories which shape how historians of Empire confront the 'archival' evidence they find there.

By drawing attention to the lived experience of imperial archives, I want to address a dimension of imperial history rarely talked about: the role of such places in shaping the imaginations of historians who rely upon them for the stories they tell, the (counter)narratives they craft, and the political interventions they make. And I want to argue that archives, no less than any other public spaces, affect people differently—though not necessarily predictably—depending on their gender, nationality, class, race, age, and sexuality. Historians of Empire have tended to understand archives as a delineated physical space from which to reconstruct an equally delimited imperial past. Colonial and imperial archives are also museological sites, whispering galleries, land mines, and crime scenes, to name only a few of the metaphors available for signifying the kind of work that goes on in these repositories of historical knowledge.[3] As such they set up boundaries, guard against intruders, recognize only some forms of expertise, and privilege some credentials over others. As sites of transnational labour relations (by which I mean, as places where 'locals' and 'foreigners' work, one typically in the service of

---

[3] See Barbara Harlow, 'Sappers in the Stacks: Colonial Archives, Land Mines and Truth Commissions', in Paul Bové, ed., *Edward Said and the Work of the Critic: Speaking Truth to Power* (Durham NC, 2000), pp. 165–86.

the other), they are implicated in a matrix of global power relations and—in light of corporate research funding—in international capitalism as well. Because such archives are important 'contact zones' with the imperial past, it is not too much to say that they produce a variety of colonial encounters which are thoroughly, if not exclusively, gendered. Like the historical experience of colonialism itself, research in imperial archives is, then, as much an embodied experience as it is a political project. Understanding how and why this is so is arguably crucial for appreciating the achievements and the limits of women's and gender history in the imperial context, and for identifying new archival horizons for future feminist research on the British Empire.

Evidence gathered in 2002 through a multi-page questionnaire suggests that confronting the logics and the logistics of the imperial archive has posed particular challenges to scholars of women and gender.[4] Though a number of historians can recall positive experiences with archivists, some working in the 1970s faced hostile or indifferent librarians. One historian of Africa remembered:

the sheer effort and energy I (and everyone else) put into finding references to 'women' in the files of the medical department, the public works dept., and whatever else made me exceptionally alert to what I was reading. Long before anyone talked of reading against, or with, the grain anybody who spent the late 1970s and early 1980s looking for hints that women were recorded in the documents they were reading learned to read carefully and problematise as they went. You had to think about what was there and what wasn't there at the same time. All the time.

The spectre of card catalogues and their categories recurred across generations among the historians who shared their experiences with me. Another respondent remarked on the fact that: 'the "woman" and "women" entries, say, in the B[ritish] L[ibrary] [catalogue] proved [an] extraordinarily useful point of entry in my early searches... It always struck me how these classifications and entries were being used in an altogether different way than intended.' For those doing their research in the 1990s, the absence of women *per se* in catalogues or collections necessitated a 'conceptual shift' from

---

[4] I circulated a questionnaire to about sixty scholars of gender and empire via e-mail, under the heading 'Archive Stories: Gender in the Making of Imperial and Colonial Histories.' Thirty-seven responded. Eight were men; 29, women; 26 were white, 11 non-white; 4 had earned Ph.D.s prior to 1980; 5 between 1980–1989; and 27 in the 1990s. One did not have a Ph.D. All but 4 were historians by training. Twelve out of 37 live outside North America. Each responded on condition of anonymity.

women to gender in their work, itself a response to a changing secondary literature, but also to the availability of sources. Significantly, scholars who have been working in archives since the 1970s commented on the ways in which many collections had been rationalized over the years, especially through computer technology.[5] Even with technological advances, however, the need to read *against* the classificatory systems that remain in place was a persistent theme. One historian of aboriginal peoples and female reform culture insisted that 'lateral thinking is required':

Looking under education, health, welfare, motherhood, girls' clubs, women's organizations is useful. Sometimes individual white women held government positions, or were of wealthy families and left personal papers. 'Native' women are the subject of government programs or inquiries re health, sexuality, motherhood etc. Their evidence occasionally appears, but they are usually only glimpsed through the accounts of white women.

Whether such lateral thinking was also required to work out more practical issues remains an open question, as the memory of 'being the only woman in the archives of an order of priests . . . [was] a bit of a hoot, once you find out where you can go to the toilet' testifies.

Memories of the solitude and isolation of archival work were intense in some cases, but not distinctive for their gender difference. Though a number of scholars recalled frustration, no one admitted to panic in his or her encounter with the archive, as Nicholas Dirks has recently done.[6] The relationship between femaleness, legitimacy, and professional embodiment was a persistent theme among the women surveyed. The men who responded registered no such connection; one even commented that despite arriving at the House of Lords Record Office with a shaved head, a nose ring, and Doc Martens, he was subject to no more scrutiny than any other patron. The contrast for women—and especially for women of colour—is striking. One respondent spoke frankly of the impact of being an African-American woman working on women and slavery:

The fact that I was looking for enslaved women seemed to reflect directly on my person. When I think back on it, it seems quite obvious that the lack of attention

---

[5] For longer histories of archive rationalization, see Philippa Levine, 'History in the Archives: The Public Record Office and its Staff, 1838–1886', *English Historical Review*, CI (1986), pp. 20–41 and Alan Sekula, 'The Body and the Archive', *October*, XXXIX, 3 (1986), pp. 3–64.

[6] Nicholas B. Dirks, 'Annals of the Archive', in Brian Keith Axel, ed., *From the Margins: Historical Anthropology and its Futures* (Durham, NC, 2002), p. 48.

from most archivists was not simply about their ignorance of available source material, but it was also about the fact that somehow my historical work was personalized. You can't be a real historian if you share the characterizations of your historical subjects, now can you?

To a person, the women of colour among the respondents commented on the ways in which their 'respectability' was an issue in archival spaces. One recounted being required to show her passport on demand in an archive in Britain: just one example of what she called 'the insolence of petty functionaries . . . who could so materially interfere, if they took a dislike to [you]'. Another recalled being subject to unwanted overtures from a senior male historian, again in a British archive, leading her to remark that 'the archives remain a kind of untamed jungle when it comes to gender harassment'.

Being the object of archival predators was not limited to women of colour, or even to archives in the West. Nor was nationality irrelevant in the archival experiences of those surveyed. Several recalled anti-American feeling among archive staff in Britain, and more generally anti-Western sentiment in some South Asian archives, an effect of what one respondent called the asymmetrical 'economies of the post-colonial world'. A young Australian researcher remembered being made to feel like a 'colonial' in both London and Oxford in the 1990s, thereby echoing the peculiar reverberations of white settler colonialism in the metropole.[7] By no means all who responded to my inquiry wished to attribute their archival experiences to gender alone, or to gender at all (even the person who made the toilet remark). One commented that 'being white, and middle class (at once young . . . and female) means I am acceptable in certain ways that I would have difficulty even quantifying'. Youth was a factor for many as graduate students, in whom sufficient 'gravitas' was deemed lacking; and status played a role for both junior and untenured faculty, whether men or women. One respondent explained as follows:

When I was a graduate student researcher, there were certainly occasions when I felt I wasn't taken seriously. I think it had as much to do with my age as my gender . . . In Britain, I really don't have a sense of how race or national identity shaped my gendered/aged experiences . . . but when I first began to be a presence in the Ghanaian archives, I am sure that being a white American in many ways

[7] Angela Woollacott, *To Try Her Fortune in London: Australian Women, Colonialism, and Modernity* (Oxford, 2001).

mitigated gender and age experiences. I don't think that a young [African] woman would have been given the same respect or attention.

Another senior historian of India concurred: 'as my status has risen and I have become [a] full professor, received awards, etc., I am treated very well and in many cases get what I want. And this is far and above what a young Indian male student could get'. These observations raise questions for imperial history that are very similar to those which currently beset post-colonial studies: namely, who researches and writes the histories of colonized women so sought after in the Western academy? And how do questions of uneven development and even more uneven resources shape the political claims which undergird the production of these new histories? Equally pressing (and not unrelated) are the uneven power relations at work in archives between patrons and workers, 'the legion of "fetchers" ' whose class/status resentment was understood by some, less so by others. The extent to which these 'structures and relations of access' are embedded in larger frameworks of transnational capitalism upon which historians rely for their livelihoods was not addressed by respondents as frequently as it could, and perhaps should, have been. Nor were the ways in which the 'archive hound' model—with its presumptive freedom and mobility—remains a white, male, middle-class ideal in a context of women academics trying to balance professional labour and production with 'domestic' labour and reproduction.

Tellingly, perhaps, the basic task of locating women in the archives remained the preoccupying challenge for those who responded to my questions. Most agreed that the ease of turning up evidence by or about women depends on the particular archive. As one historian of Africa observed:

I've found that in the case of government archives it is particularly difficult to 'locate' women... unless they are the focus of some sort of an official inquiry. Otherwise, you just have to use your intuition and dig through mounds of files that are likely repositories... Most of the mission societies whose papers I've worked with began to focus on 'women' in the 1920s, so it is extremely easy to locate women after the First World War. Before that time... well, it's pretty much like the government archives—hunt and peck... For social history topics, therefore, I end up thumbing through medical records, customary law records, government diaries, sanitation reports, etc.—you name it.

There was general agreement on the comparative accessibility of mission archives, though at least one respondent commented that 'when I first started using the microform records of the Society for the Propagation Gospel (Series E, marketed in the 1980s as the 'complete' archives), the records of the Committee on Women's Work were simply not filmed'.[8] There was an overwhelming consensus, however, on the relative invisibility of indigenous women compared to white British women. Another Africanist commented that:

It is often hard to find even the mediated voices of African women in the colonial archives, because Colonial and Foreign Office representatives generally did not interview African women and seldom reproduced their translated testimonies in correspondence, let alone reports. British officials privileged the opinions of male representatives of African communities, and, more broadly, they privileged property ownership on a colonialist model.

Whether this was a question of 'collection priorities', the 'pell-mell' method of archival acquisition, or the insouciance of some archivists about material on natives and women, was a matter of some debate across the questionnaires I gathered. Several respondents insisted that the imbalance was as much an effect of class as of race, reasoning that white women of the past were more likely to be literate and to recognize the market value of the written word. In turn, their 'imprint' on the historical record was more highly prized. Indeed, the problem of elite voices was, if not a universal concern, then certainly a consistent one among those surveyed. One scholar recalled that:

I spent quite some time at Wellcome/GLRO [Wellcome Institute, London; Greater London Record Office] reading [Florence] Nightingale on Indian women, Aboriginal women in Australia, need for women practitioners etc. In that archive, there simply was no utterance from indigenous women. The expert and philanthropic women were very loud! The local archive—e.g. Mitchell [Library] in Sydney, Queensland—offered much more by indigenous women—although still fragments. I think the 'colonial' public record offices (in the colonies) offer much more in the way of native voices [than metropolitan ones].

The pressures of contemporary political developments could be felt especially by historians interested in indigenous populations in both the Antipodes and Canada. As a feminist historian of Australia remarked, 'while I support the protocols governing this sensitive material, the bureaucracy surrounding access to Aboriginal material has become rather obstructive'.

---

[8] He later discovered them at Rhodes House, Oxford.

All manner of impediments produced originally by the protocols of colonial government continue to structure the research experience. As one male historian observed, 'non-European women are harder to locate in colonial archives because they've been erased from the official records, often not named at all, or only named in partial or anglicized ways that make it difficult to determine their personal identity and social status'.[9] A South Asianist put it more bluntly: 'only a few Indian women have been deemed worthy of archivization'. Native women's words were elusive in any number of archival sources, as this account testifies:

I found no women's voices within the colonial files I looked at in Lucknow. There were a few Indian women's voices... in the Sarda reports in Delhi. In the private papers of western men and women in London and in the US, there were certainly more western women's voices than Indian women's voices. If there were any utterances by Indian women, these were elite voices for the most part. For instance Pillay, one of the Indian male advocates, mentions using women as models for different contraceptive technologies, but he provides no information about these women models and of course their voices are totally silent in the traditional archives—colonial and national.

This latter point is well worth underscoring, since one of the major contributions of recent work on gender and Empire has been to draw lines of connection between the operations of patriarchal colonialism and those of patriarchal nationalism and, increasingly, to read the archives of élite colonized women's participation in nationalist struggles, at least, through that doubly critical lens.[10]

Despite the lingering presumption in some circles that historians of women and gender have neglected archival sources in their scholarship, the majority of respondents professed their attachment to archival research, however critical they were of it as a relatively under-theorized example of colonial power still at work. One respondent called herself an 'archive junkie', while another remarked that the archive was both her 'favourite place to be' and a 'millstone' around her neck because of the ways in which it was often

---

[9] He went on to say that 'all is not hopeless, as Durba Ghosh has shown in her brilliant dissertation, "Colonial Companions: Bibis, Begums, and Concubines of the British in North India, 1760–1830"' (Berkeley, 2000).

[10] See, for example, Susan Geiger, Tanu Women: Gender and Culture in the Making of Tanganyikan Nationalism, 1955–1965 (Portsmouth, NH, 1997); and Mrinalini Sinha, 'Refashioning Mother India: Feminism and Nationalism in Late-Colonial India', Feminist Studies, XXVIII, 3 (2000), pp. 623–44.

used in the profession as an arbiter of truth, rather than simply as one investigative tool among many. Still another acknowledged that 'certainly there is the thrill of the archival "paydirt" moment'. Not surprisingly, however, nearly two-thirds of the respondents either had or developed an elastic view of what counts as an archive, drawing on alternative sources such as private diaries held in personal or family hands (as opposed to being housed in official repositories) and creating new archives through oral histories. One historian cast this as a question of necessity but also of methodological conviction:

Archive used to mean the PRO, the National Archives in Ghana and other such official government repositories. They always have played an important part in my work, but were never the very centerpiece. The further the 'official' archive from the seat of colonial power, the more valuable I have found it to be and more central to my work. So, for example, Manhyia Record Office in Kumasi (sort of the private archive of the Asante king) is chock full of customary court cases from about 1908 to after independence. It is a gold mine of material. In my experience, as I move closer to the center of archival power (Britain), the archive becomes less valuable to me. That said, I am increasingly interested ... in extending our notions of archive. It started for me when older folks started sharing their personal papers. But then what do you do with the old woman, non-literate, who (after you ask her about early missionaries in the area) ... sends her granddaughter inside to bring out her women's fellowship card, her bible and several doilies that she crocheted? Is that a personal archive? I think that the term is really up for grabs now—and that is a very good thing.

'Official archives' are often, of course, the fillip for the creation of alternative archives. As Susan Geiger recounts, she was led to Bibi Titi Mohamed (a Tanzanian nationalist) and her oral life-history by an off-hand comment about her in the papers of a District Officer in Rhodes House, who described her 'as a "great mountain of a woman, and a reputed bitch"!'[11]

One respondent to the survey commented on the scepticism with which all archival sources—even and especially oral histories—must be treated, in part because individuals and families were wary of narratives that might be humiliating. Indeed, contrary to what some critics have said about the status of oral testimony as evidence, the majority of those who reported developing alternative archives of whatever kind (textual or material)

[11] Susan Geiger, *Life Histories of Women in Nationalist Struggle in Tanzania: Lessons Learned* (Dar-es-Salaam, 1996), p. 8.

displayed tremendous sensitivity about the benefits and dangers of such evidence.[12] Such manœuvres often result in creative disciplinary borrowings and methodological mixings. So, for example, in *A Colonial Lexicon*, Nancy Rose Hunt reads missionary narratives as 'inscribed forms of oral tradition' and 'postcolonial routines as historical evidence'—in part to track the ways in which colonialism was negotiated, in part to understand what she calls 'the hygienic modality of colonial power'.[13] Lest there be any doubt, what we learn about women and gender resonates well beyond the confines of the domestic and the private, manifestly demonstrating the capacity of feminist history to shed light on the political, the social, the economic, all domains where imperial historians as recently as fifteen years ago did not think women existed, let alone exercised power as historical subjects.

In the search for women and for evidence of gendered experiences under colonialism, analytical and methodological rigour has not, in other words, been sacrificed. To the contrary: work on women and gender in the British Empire has raised challenges to the discipline which continue to be grounds for animated debate.[14] By insisting that the traces of women and other 'others', however ghostly, testify to their capacity to stand as subjects of History, feminist historians of Empire have thrown the burden of proof of their presence (back) on to History itself, thereby making women's historicity a question of recognition rather than of certain standards of empirical depth. And yet as must be clear, the problem of evidence, who has access to it, and with what consequences, emerged as the dominant theme among the scholars from whom I heard. Although a number of people commented on the protectiveness of archivists over their collections, three historians of quite different parts of the British Empire recounted occasions on which librarians allowed them or someone they knew to remove archival material on women from the archive and xerox it themselves. Yet another recalled an incident in which a similar flexibility was accorded her inside the space of the archive itself:

One year when I was . . . [doing research] with my entire family, the kids had to be at school quite early, but the archive didn't open until an hour or two

---

[12] For a discussion of these critiques, see Antoinette Burton, *Dwelling in the Archive: Women Writing House, Home and History in Late-Colonial India* (Oxford, 2003).

[13] Nancy Rose Hunt, *A Colonial Lexicon of Birth Ritual, Medicalization, and Mobility in the Congo* (Durham, NC, 1999).

[14] See, for example, Robin Winks, ed., *The Oxford History of the British Empire, V. Historiography* (Oxford, 1999).

later. I mentioned this to someone one day, and he volunteered to walk over and open the place up at 7:30 a.m., so that I could get a good start each morning after I dropped the kids at school! At this particular archive, there was no archivist on staff for the year I worked there. However, I was allowed into the repository and just set up shop in there. The files were in a complete shambles when I first arrived and I spent two months of my time just putting things into order and making a class list so that I could actually begin looking at documents in some kind of a systematic way. I also worked with several local scholars to get funding from the Danish embassy to pay for an air conditioner and pesticides to kill the silverfish and rats.

If this is a long way from the genteel ornamentalism of the India Office Library, it is also evidence of the enduring asymmetries of colonial power and of their persistent re-inscription in post-colonial archival spaces as well. Imperial historians would do well to remain vigilant about the ways in which the official archive 'reflects the forms and formations of historical knowledge that have been so markedly shaped by their implication in the history of the state whose past it is meant to enshrine', materially as well as symbolically.[15]

Clearly all historians, regardless of what they work on, have archive stories. Most if not all of us read against the grain; we all stumble around in unfamiliar surroundings to find the facilities; and we all invent creative strategies so that we can excavate the material we need to answer the questions we have and produce new ones in the process. Strategic antagonism toward sources is, or should be, the hallmark of all historians interested in a critical engagement with the past, rather than in its reproduction. I do not wish to suggest that historians of women and gender work harder, longer, or under worse conditions than other historians of empire, not only because they do not, but because such a claim would replicate both the moral superiority argument which undergirded the Victorian imperial gender system *and* the logic of archive–as–boot–camp which has been invoked as the dominant disciplinary regime in debates about the old versus the new imperial history. More significantly perhaps for the future of British imperial history, the archive stories which feminist historians have to tell interrogate the presumptive objectivity of traditional history, surely one of the discipline's more cherished foundations. By laying bare the conditions of production, we can more fully appreciate the logics of archival spaces as well as their irrationalities; the serendipity of 'discovery' as well as its careful

[15] Dirks, 'Annals', p. 58.

management by representatives of the national and post-colonial state; the predictability of some absences as well as the often totally unlooked-for presences. Imperial archives are not, and never have been, sites of pure knowledge, bearing as they do the still-legible traces of imperial power and colonial rule. Though this is not a uniquely feminist insight, the search for women in imperial archives dramatizes it in irrefutable ways. The more deliberately we acknowledge the impact of our archival experiences on our research and our teaching, the better we are able to historicize the British empire, its strategies of containment, its disciplinary mechanisms, and its visible and invisible forms of rule.

If feminist work of the last quarter century has taught us anything, it is to be creative about what counts as an archive and to learn to recognize that history resides in any number of locations: some of which resemble the India Office Library, some of which may be scarcely embodied at all. Indeed, the new frontier of imperial history, whether focused on women and gender or not, is arguably the virtual archive: that breathless corridor of cyberspace where you find your way to evidence not through card catalogues but via search engines, often from the comfort of your own home. Collections such as those in the process of being mounted on-line by Adam Matthew Publications are vast: they range from India to Africa to Ireland to Australia and New Zealand, and they reproduce everything from travel writing to anti-slavery archives to personal papers to diaries to entire runs of missionary print journals.[16] Clearly such archives have their own aesthetics and architectures; nor are they necessarily any more accessible than repositories in Britain, India, or Africa, given the high cost of technological access and the uneven distribution of technological resources world-wide. In fact, the web creates the possibilities for new 'virtual empires' available for discovery by browsers tellingly called 'Navigator' and 'Explorer'. These are financed not by the state, but by multinational corporations who, in turn, derive revenue from the virtual tourism that such sites provide.[17] As feminist historians know from experience, there is no place outside power when it comes to archives, imperial or otherwise. Rather than representing the end of history, this is the very condition from which future feminist histories of Empire can and must proceed.

---

[16] See 'Empire On-Line': www.adam-matthew-publications.co.uk.

[17] Debbie Lee and Tom Fulford, 'Virtual Empires', *Cultural Critique*, XLIV (2000), pp. 3–28. This is a manifestation of the phenomenon Michael Hardt and Antonio Negri describe in their book *Empire* (Cambridge, Mass., 2000).

Select Bibliography

ANTOINETTE BURTON, *Dwelling in the Archive: Women Writing House, Home and History in Late-Colonial India* (Oxford, 2003).

NICHOLAS B. DIRKS, 'Annals of the Archive', in Brian Keith Axel, ed., *From the Margins: Historical Anthropology and its Futures* (Durham, NC, 2002).

SUSAN GEIGER, *Life Histories of Women in Nationalist Struggle in Tanzania: Lessons Learned* (Dar es Salaam, 1996).

—— *Tanu Women: Gender and Culture in the Making of Tanganyikan Nationalism, 1955–1965* (Portsmouth, NH, 1997).

MICHAEL HARDT and ANTONIO NEGRI, *Empire* (Cambridge, Mass., 2000).

BARBARA HARLOW, 'Sappers in the Stacks: Colonial Archives, Land Mines and Truth Commissions', in Paul Bové, ed., *Edward Said and the Work of the Critic: Speaking Truth to Power* (Durham, NC, 2000).

NANCY ROSE HUNT, *A Colonial Lexicon of Birth Ritual, Medicalization, and Mobility in the Congo* (Durham, NC, 1999).

DEBBIE LEE and TOM FULFORD, 'Virtual Empires', *Cultural Critique*, XLIV (Winter 2000).

PHILIPPA LEVINE, 'History in the Archives: The Public Record Office and its Staff, 1838–1886,' *English Historical Review*, CI (1986).

MARY LOUISE PRATT, *Imperial Eyes: Travel Writing and Transculturation* (London, 1992).

ALAN SEKULA, 'The Body and the Archive', *October*, XXXIX, 3 (1986).

MRINALINI SINHA, 'Refashioning Mother India: Feminism and Nationalism in Late-Colonial India,' *Feminist Studies*, XXVIII, 3 (2000).

ROBIN WINKS, ed., *The Oxford History of the British Empire. V. Historiography* (Oxford, 1999).

ANGELA WOOLLACOTT, *To Try Her Fortune in London: Australian Women, Colonialism, and Modernity* (Oxford, 2001).

INDEX